abstracts
of the

Collected Works
of
C. G. Jung

abstracts
of the
Collected Works
of
C. G. Jung

edited by

Carrie Lee Rothgeb,
Chief

Siegfried M. Clemens,
Technical Information Specialist

NATIONAL CLEARINGHOUSE FOR MENTAL HEALTH INFORMATION

with an Introduction by
Andrew Samuels

Karnac Books
London
1992

This printing by
H. Karnac (Books) Ltd.
58 Gloucester Road
London SW7 4QY

British Library Cataloguing in Publication Data.
A catalogue record for this book is available from the British Library.

ISBN 1 85575 035 X

Printed in Great Britain by BPCC Wheatons Ltd, Exeter

CONTENTS

CONTENTS

INTRODUCTION

Andrew Samuels

When Cesare Sacerdoti, Managing Director of Karnac Books, asked me to write an Introduction to the re-publication of the *Abstracts of the Collected Works of C. G. Jung*, I must confess that my heart sank. As a good 'Jungian', I experienced a feeling of dismay, almost of revulsion, at the very idea of there being *Abstracts* of Jung's texts, fearing that compression would ruin the subtlety of Jung's writing and that a spurious clarity would render his thought meaningless. I have to say that I muttered, 'Let them eat cake'—meaning that people wanting to know Jung's ideas should read Jung's books. At the same time—and this is also part of the self-critical heritage of being a Jungian analyst—I have been aware for many years of the enormous difficulties many people experience on reading Jung. The difficulties are with the voluptuousness of his style (at least as this comes over in the English translations of R. F. C. Hull), with his tendencies to generalize and to contradict himself, and with the unavoidable vagueness that attaches itself to the communication of concepts that often began life as personal experiences of Jung's, stemming from dreams, visions, and relationships.

I was surprised and relieved to find that these *Abstracts* really do work. I use "work" deliberately because *Abstracts* are nothing if not tools. (Of what trade they are the tools, I shall discuss shortly.) The abstracters have been given sufficient space for each summary to enable a degree of differentiated expression. In particular, it seems to me to be perfectly possible to use the *Abstracts* in conjunction with a reading of one section of a longer text of Jung's. The reader is therefore enabled to place a passage of Jung's that he or she may have been studying in its correct textual setting. I tested this proposition for myself by consulting the *Abstracts* to see, first, how well the abstract of the *Two Essays on Analytical Psychology* (Volume 7) had been done, and, second, to see whether, had I been studying the first part of *The Relations between the Ego and the Unconscious*, I would have found the abstract of the second part helpful. In my view, the abstract is accurate, and it is indeed possible to use the relevant part of the abstract to flesh out a reading of the full text of another part. Moreover, numerous rather arcane points have been noted by the abstracters; for example, in connection with the *Two Essays* the abstracters have realized the importance of the series of prefaces that Jung wrote to the various editions of his books.

Having praised and commended the overall level of the *Abstracts*, I want to do more with this short Introduction. The cultural, intellectual, and clinical locations of Jung's analytical psychology have changed so rapidly that a few lines on these phenomena are surely in order.

For many who are interested in depth psychology, Jung has often been regarded as a marginal and somewhat unreliable figure. His work has been castigated as mystical, characterized by an avoidance of the instinctual dimension, élitist to the point of being fascist, and, in general terms, as an intellectual and clinical *cul-de-sac*. No doubt there are serious criticisms to be made of the corpus of analytical psychology. But, as must be the case with any field of endeavour, these criticisms do not come from neutral sources. The penumbra of the shattering break with Freud is still with us. Moreover, in a personalizing age, Jung's anti-semitic writings of the 1930s, and certain aspects of his clinical behaviour that strike the modern observer as unethical, have not helped his cause.

But, as I said, the situation is changing.

From the clinical standpoint, analytical psychology has not remained static since Jung's death in 1961. I have chronicled post-Jungian productivity elsewhere (Samuels, 1985). Even those analysts who consider themselves members of the classical school, who try to work in ways congruent with Jung's own core philosophies, have evolved their clinical practice. Those analysts who are members of the developmental school have integrated clinical concepts from contemporary psychoanalysis to such a degree that a hybrid is often claimed to have come into being. There are now over 1500 Jungian analysts world-wide and, I would judge, approximately the same number of practitioners whose appellation could be said to be "Jungian analytical psychotherapist". This hugely expanding clinical project gives lie to any idea that analytical psychology is some kind of new-age phenomenon (which is not to deny the influence of Jungian thinking on new-age ideas, or on humanistic psychology).

Increasingly, the pioneering contributions to depth psychology of Jung and the post-Jungians are being recognized. In many respects, developments within psychoanalysis have been anticipated by analytical psychology, often by decades, even if the degree of detailed working out has sometimes not been present.

From academic and intellectual standpoints, a new field of Jungian Studies is beginning to open up. Central to this field is a historically based re-evaluation of the origins of Jung's ideas and practices and of the break with Freud. Literary and art criticism, often based (it must be said) on somewhat mechanistic and out-of-date applications of Jungian theory, are beginning to flourish. Anthropological, social, and political studies that tend to rest on Jung's intuitions about directions to explore rather than on his conclusions are also being developed. Jung's influence on religious studies has existed for a long time.

It seems inevitable that the *Abstracts*, necessary tools of the trade for students and perhaps even for scholars, would come into being. So it is a bit of a shock to discover the prescience of the National Institute of Mental Health, which first published this work in 1978. In fact, the *Abstracts* would have been issued earlier, had it not been for a delay caused by waiting for the publication of Volume 18 of the *Collected Works*. (For obvious reasons, the abstracts do not cover the supplementary volumes or the seminar volumes of the *Collected Works*, nor do they make use of the General Index. All of these were published later.) The *Abstracts* were not sold but were given free to those who requested them. About 10,000 copies were distributed by this method. The figure can be compared with the Freud *Abstracts*, also published by the NIMH, of which about 20,000 were distributed. The *Abstracts* were written by professional abstracters and then reviewed by a Jungian analyst.

It is undoubtedly significant that the Jung *Abstracts* followed the Freud *Abstracts*! The two great divisions of depth psychology exist in a competitive, complementary, mimetic love–hate relationship. Psychoanalytic Studies, as an academic discipline, is much more established than Jungian Studies, which is really just getting of the ground. There are advantages to being a generation behind in that it might be possible—and I would stress the word "might"—for analytical psychology to avoid the huge ravines that have tended to separate clinicians and the various kinds of academics within psychoanalysis.

If this separation—surely an unhealthy phenomenon—is to be avoided in Jungian studies, then both the academic and the clinical camps will have to give ground. In psychological language, they will have to withdraw projections from the other group—take back shadow elements that they would rather disown. Clinicians will have to become more aware of the theoretical and cultural assumptions that permeate everything they do. Although this will run counter to the idealization of analytical practice as an intuitive activity sensitive mostly to the individual psychology of the patient, it has to be admitted that clinical practice is a heavily theorized thing. Academics, in their turn—and, in a way, following Jung—will have to question their privileging of Enlightenment-style rationalism and scientism. *Much will have to change in our conceptions of care and of pedagogy.* Perhaps it is a question of realizing the potential for intellect and affect to flourish side-by-side within a fully psychological attitude. Academics need not be "schizoid"; clinicians need not be "woolly". Nor is a struggle between competing groups to appropriate analytical psychology so as to acquire legitimation necessarily inevitable.

Abstracts like these may help us to fashion desirable and necessary bridges between the established clinical project of analytical psychology and its growing academic projects. And, who knows—there may even be a possible function for the *Abstracts* as bridge-building between analytical psychology and psychoanalysis.

Reference

Samuels, A. (1985). *Jung and the Post-Jungians*. London and Boston, MA: Routledge and Kegan Paul.

FOREWORD

> And yet each of us can carry the torch of knowledge but a part
> of the way, until another takes it from him.
>
> *Carl Gustav Jung*

From its beginning, the National Institute of Mental Health has envisioned the dissemination of knowledge to be an important part of its service to the mental health of the Nation, broadening the dimensions of the new research, treatment, and prevention efforts which the Institute encourages. Behavioral scientists, researchers, and those entrusted with the training of new workers in the field thrive on sharing their theories and discoveries and on receiving new concepts, balanced and evaluated in turn with the products of other theoretical convictions and practice.

The Institute makes the fruits of theory, research, and treatment from diverse therapeutic efforts available and easily useful for further study through the computerized information retrieval service of its National Clearinghouse for Mental Health Information. To mark the 25th anniversary year of the Mental Health Act, and to furnish a broader perspective of past contributions toward the understanding of the mind and behavior, in 1971 the Clearinghouse published the *Abstracts of the Standard Edition of Freud*, in a comprehensive compilation of abstracts, keyed to all the psychoanalytic concepts found in the *Standard Edition of the Complete Psychological Works of Sigmund Freud*, edited by James Strachey.

The *Abstracts of the Collected Works of C. G. Jung* is a fitting and welcome sequel, furthering the Institute's goal of encouraging wider scientific investigation of varied philosophies. Like the predecessor, this publication is a comprehensive compilation of abstracts. These abstracts are keyed to the papers and essays of Jung as they appear in the Bollingen Series XX, translated by R. F. C. Hull, edited by Sir Herbert Read, Michael Fordham, M.D., and Gerhard Adler, Ph.D., and published by the Princeton University Press.

Vis-à-vis the Freud *Abstracts*, the *Abstracts* of Jung will be of great historical value to those interested in the range of psychotherapies. The publication will be gratifying to disciples of Jung, agreeably provocative to followers of other theoretical persuasions, and useful to all graduate psychoanalysts as a general reference tool. Indeed, it will be helpful to all who work in the behavioral sciences—psychiatrists, psychiatric residents, psychologists, psychiatric social workers, and the many college, graduate, and medical students who wish to broaden their knowledge and understanding of analytical psychology. Pastoral counselors and art therapists as well will discover in greater depth Jung's theories of the scope and potential of their disciplines. And those who may agree with Jung that "the very number of present-day 'psychologies' amounts to a confession of perplexity" should find clarification and guidance, whatever their own theories and practice may be.

The revival of interest in the thought of Carl Gustav Jung which has occurred in recent years will stimulate the appreciation of this timely publication by lay persons as well as by professionals in the mental health field. His theory of the archetype within the unconscious of each individual and his belief in the Self—in fact, the title of one of his essay collections, "Modern Man in Search of a Soul"—speak to our seeking age in which, according to many social scientists, great numbers are suffering, as Jung said many of his patients were, "from the senselessness and emptiness of their lives."

A little more than a century after his birth, the publication of this compendium of Jung's prolific essays and lectures is an appropriate salute to the man and to all who are committed to solving mental and emotional ills and to promoting mental and emotional health.

Francis N. Waldrop, M.D.
Acting Director
NATIONAL INSTITUTE OF MENTAL HEALTH

EDITORS' PREFACE

The mission of the National Clearinghouse for Mental Health Information is to provide effective dissemination of mental health information by all appropriate means and to all appropriate people. In carrying out its mission, the Clearinghouse attempts to remain eclectic, and thus presents information from various schools of philosophy in order to inform its audience of the diversity of thought in the mental health field.

The *Abstracts of the Collected Works of C. G. Jung*, therefore, becomes a suitable companion for the earlier volume, *Abstracts of the Standard Edition of Freud*.

It should be stated that no abstract can replace a careful reading of the original document. These abstracts serve as guides for the users to enable them to select those chapters or articles to be read in-depth.

These abstracts were initially written under contract; however, it was necessary for the editors to rewrite many abstracts extensively. As the abstracts were written, they were immediately added to one of the Clearinghouse computer files and were searchable by computer since late 1975. However, due to the delayed publication by Princeton University Press of Volume 18 of the *Collected Works*, the Clearinghouse publication of its abstract volume was postponed. The Clearinghouse neither endorsed nor assisted in any other version of the publication of the abstracts from its computer files.

The Key-Word-Out-of-Context (KWOC) subject index,* based upon the title of each article abstracted, was selected as we understand that a comprehensive index is in preparation by Princeton University Press.

---

*[The Index has been omitted from this volume, since the Index to the *Collected Works* has been published in the meantime.]

The abstracts are numbered sequentially. In the index this sequential number is followed by four digits. The first two zeros refer only to this abstract volume; the next two digits refer to the volume number of the *Collected Works*. Since Volume 9 has two parts, "91" refers to Volume 9, part I, and "92" refers to Volume 9, part II. Abstracts are arranged sequentially by volume.

Carrie Lee Rothgeb,
Chief
Siegfried M. Clemens
Technical Information Specialist
NATIONAL CLEARINGHOUSE FOR MENTAL HEALTH INFORMATION

abstracts
of the

Collected Works
of
C. G. Jung

ABSTRACTS

01 PSYCHIATRIC STUDIES

000001 On the psychology and pathology of so-called occult phenomena: 1. Introduction. In: Jung, C., Collected Works of C. G. Jung, Vol. 1. 2nd ed., Princeton University Press, 1970. 260 p. (p. 3-17).

Certain conditions of psychopathic inferiority and altered states of consciousness, previously thought to be occult phenomena, are discussed to classify them and to resolve previous disagreement about them among scientific authorities. These include narcolepsy, lethargy, ambulatory automatism, periodic amnesia, somnambulism, and pathological lying, which are sometimes attributed to epilepsy, hysteria, or neurasthenia and sometimes described as diseases in themselves. The exceptional difficulty in defining these states is outlined and a case of somnambulism is presented to illustrate the problems of classification. A 40-year-old unmarried female, an accountant and bookkeeper in a large firm, had been in a highly nervous state for some time and took a vacation. While walking in a cemetery, she began to tear up flowers and scratch at the graves, remembering nothing of this later. In an asylum in Zurich she reported that she saw dead people in her room and her bed and heard voices calling from the cemetery. The conclusion was that the patient suffered from a psychopathic inferiority with a tendency to hysteria. In her state of nervous exhaustion, she had spells of epileptoid stupor. As a result of an unusually large dose of alcohol, the attacks developed into somnambulism with hallucinations, which attached themselves to fortuitous external perceptions in the same way as dreams. When she recovered from her nervous state, the hysteriform symptoms disappeared. Other cases of somnambulism and the findings of other researchers are briefly discussed. 17 references.

000002 On the psychology and pathology of so-called occult phenomena: 2. A case of somnambulism in a girl with poor inheritance (spiritualistic medium). Anamnesis. Somnambulistic states. Records of seances. In: Jung, C., Collected Works of C. G. Jung, Vol. 1. 2nd. ed., Princeton University Press, 1970. 260 p. (p. 17-30).

Detailed records of a case of somnambulism in a 15-year-old girl, with powers of a spiritualistic medium, are presented, whose family had exhibited symptoms of eccentricity and personality disorders. Records of family members reveal waking hallucinations, eccentric and bizarre behavior, personality aberrations, extended trance states, and varying degrees of neurotic and psychopathic behavior. Her own behavior was reserved, though she was susceptible to sudden mood changes. Intellectually she was undistinguished, and poorly educated. Her mother was a tyrannical and inconsistent disciplinarian, and her father had died during S's early adolescence. Her proficiency as a spiritualistic medium emerged when she attempted table turning for amusement. It improved rapidly and dramatically, until she could communicate with deceased relatives and acquaintances and mimic people whom she knew only by hearsay. Gradually, gestures accompanied words, until she acted out whole dramatic scenes, depicting a full range of emotions and using standard literary German fluently -- though she spoke only the rural dialect in a waking state. At first, trances occurred spontaneously, beginning as somnambulistic attacks she was able to predict; then later she could induce them at will. In the gradual awakening, an ecstasy state was usually followed by catalepsy with flexibilitas cerea. S exhibited two different personalities side by side or in succession, each striving for mastery. Highlights from the recorded dialogs in the seances are presented, in which a variety of psychic and occult phenomena occurred (automatism, clairvoyance, premonitions, forebodings, and descriptions of visions). Some became manifest through psychographics, and some through the voices of many different persons, mostly S's deceased relatives -- her grandfather in particular. 1 reference.

000003 On the psychology and pathology of so-called occult phenomena: 2. A case of somnambulism in a girl with poor inheritance (spiritualistic medium). Development of the somnambulistic personalities. The romances. Mystic science. In: Jung, C., Collected Works of C. G. Jung, Vol. 1. 2nd. ed., Princeton University Press, 1970. 260 p. (p. 30-43).

A discussion of a case of a 15-year-old girl details phenomena that occurred during somnambulistic episodes. At the request of spiritualists attending S's seances, the names of well-known dead persons and sometimes unknown names appeared. The control spirit was S's grandfather, who produced Biblical maxims, edifying observations, and song book verses he had presumably composed himself, which was not in accord with the character of the real grandfather. A subsequent personality, who spoke with a different accent, was frivolous and superficial. When he began to dominate the seances, the serious character of the meetings could not be sustained, and the sittings were suspended for periods. All of these personalities had access to the whole of the medium's memory, including the unconscious. In these trances, S's consciousness displayed an extraordinarily rich fantasy. She was almost totally amnesic about the automatic phenomena during ecstasy, but had a clear memory of other ego connected phenomena such as glossolalia. After each ecstatic trance she suffered amnesia, which was replaced gradually by fragmentary memories. In later seances, S described some of her experiences in the spirit world, where she had a special name, Ivenes. As such, she understood and spoke the language of the spirits. She talked of star dwellers and the Martian canal system, and the beings that live on Mars. Ivenes, who spoke as a serious, mature person, in contrast to some of the other personalities, directly controlled S's semi-somnambulistic state. She had embodied herself numerous times over the centuries, and described some of her states and romantic adventures. Later still, S developed a complete mystic system of the cosmos, received from the spirits, which was explained in a diagram. The interesting and significant seances then ended. After Jung ceased to attend them, S was caught cheating at a seance. She subsequently ceased to take part in seances, and became employed in a business where she was apparently successful. Her character also improved and she became quieter, steadier, and more agreeable, with no further abnormalities. 2 references.

000004 On the psychology and pathology of so-called occult phenomena: 3. Discussion of the case. The waking state. Semi-somnambulism. Automatisms. In: Jung, C., Collected Works of C. G. Jung, Vol. 1. 2nd. ed., Princeton University Press, 1970. 260 p. (p. 44-61).

Various aspects of somnambulism are discussed in studying the case of a 15-year-old girl. She was absentminded, displayed a variety of moods, was reasonably intelligent but narrow-minded. Her memory was good, but impaired by distractibility. Her frequent misreading demonstrated hysterical distractibility, and she exhibited a pathological dream state; its genesis was spontaneous, and usually regarded as hysterical. In her case, the misreading, psychologically typical of the mechanism of somnambulistic dreams, was a prodromal symptom of later events. For some time before and after somnambulistic attacks she was in a preoccupied state. In this semi-somnambulistic state, she was grave and dignified, in contrast to her usual personality. She gave the impression of acting, with considerable dramatic talent, the role of a mature woman. Her conversation was about equally divided between answers to real questions and to hallucinatory ones. The phenomena of automatic movements of the table, psychography, and other automatisms were observed. The table turning occurred in its most pronounced form in the waking state, which then usually developed into semi-somnambulism, with the onset announced by hallucinations. In psychography, another phenomenon that occurs under partial hypnosis, a primary suggestion is directed to the conscious mind when sensibility is retained, and to the unconscious when it is extinct. In the second seance, the coincidence of the descent of darkness and the deceased grandfather's brusque interruption seems to have caused a rapid deepening of hypnosis, which favored the hallucinations. An entirely new personality (Jung's grandfather) appeared. This was probably a dissociation from the already existing personality, which seized the nearest available material for its expression. 32 references.

000005 On the psychology and pathology of so-called occult phenomena: 3. Discussion of the case. The change in character. Nature of the somnambulistic attacks. Origin of the unconscious personalities. In: Jung, C., Collected Works of C. G. Jung, Vol. 1. 2nd. ed., Princeton University Press, 1970. 260 p. (p. 61-78).

The development of alternate personalities in somnambulism is discussed in studying the case of a young girl. A review of several cases in the literature indicates that the second state is usually separated from the first by an amnesic split, with a break in the continuity of consciousness and a change in character. In S's case there was no amnesic disturbance. The transition was gradual, and the continuity of consciousness was preserved. Considering S's age, 15, the supposition is that there was a connection between the disturbances and the physiological changes of character at puberty, which becomes clearer on examination of her second personality, Ivenes. Ivenes was the continuation of S's ego, and comprised its whole conscious content. Ivenes' calm composure, her modesty and reserve, her more uniform intelligence and confidence were an improvement on S's character. But Ivenes gives the impression of being an artificial product, suggesting the protype of the Clairvoyante of Prevorst. Ivenes was what S wished to be in 20 years, an assured, influential, wise, gracious, pious lady. S differed from other pathological dreamers discussed in that it could not be proved that her reveries had been the objects of her daily interests. Her ''romances'' showed the subjective roots of her dreams. There were open and secret love affairs, with illegitimate births and other sexual innuendos. S's reincarnation theory, in which she was the ancestral mother of thousands, was a fantasy that is characteristic of puberty. The main cause of this clinical picture was the patient's budding sexuality, a dream of sexual wish fulfillment. In the second seance, S had a fainting fit from which she awoke with memory of some hallucinations, but she said she had not lost consciousness. Etiologically, two elements should be considered: the influence of hypnosis and psychic excitation. The characteristic feature of hysterical splits of consciousness is that that they are surface disturbances, none

of them going so deep as to attack the firmly knit basis of the ego complex. Somewhere, often extremely well concealed, is the bridge. The various personalities were grouped around S's grandfather and Ulrich von Gerbenstein. 44 references.

000006 On the psychology and pathology of so-called occult phenomena: 3. Discussion of the case. Course of the disorder. Heightened unconscious performance. Conclusion. In: Jung, C., Collected Works of C. G. Jung, Vol. 1. 2nd. ed., Princeton University Press, 1970. 260 p. (p. 78-88).

In the presentation of a case of somnambulism in a young girl, the exceptional course of the disorder is discussed. The entire case began and reached its climax within 4 to 8 weeks; then a decline was noticed. The characters manifest during her somnambulistic attacks, who had been well differentiated, became mixed. The attacks decreased in frequency and intensity and a change from somnambulism to lying emerged. Following the episodes, S's character became pleasanter and more stable, reminiscent of other cases in which the patient's second character replaced the first. Somnambulistic symptoms are particularly common in puberty, and many well-known cases occurring at this age are cited. Heightened unconscious performance is defined as that automatic process whose results are not available for the conscious psychic activity of the individual. Thought reading by means of table movement and cryptomnesia (the coming into consciousness of a memory image that is not recognized as memory) are included. The cryptomnesic image can be brought into consciousness in three ways: a) without the mediation of the senses, as a sudden idea whose origin is hidden; b) by mediation of the senses, as in hallucinations; or c) by motor automatism. In this case, the mystical system that S devised can be regarded as an example of heightened unconscious performance that transcended her normal intelligence. 17 references.

000007 On hysterical misreading. In: Jung, C., Collected Works of C. G. Jung, Vol. 1. 2nd. ed., Princeton University Press, 1970. 260 p. (p. 89-92).

In reply to the review of an earlier paper, accepted views on hysterical misreading are reiterated, and the theories are supported by interpretations from a clinical case. A patient misread frequently at school, always substituting a Swiss dialect word for the word in the text. Since the words were synonymous, proving that the meaning was understood, there was no reason for a healthy person to reproduce the word incorrectly. This kind of misreading was considered an indicator of hysteria. S read mechanically, so the psychic processes set in motion were feeble. In S's case, as in all hysterical misreading, the formal connection broke down but the sense was preserved. This is explained by the hypothesis of a split consciousness: in addition to the ego complex, which follows its own thoughts, another conscious complex is functioning. S's ego complex was displaced from the act of reading by other ideas, but the act continued automatically and formed a little conscious complex of its own, which also understood correctly but reproduced in a modified form. Hysterical misreading is significant in that it demonstrates the splitting off of psychic functions from the ego complex, which is characteristic of hysteria; it also demonstrates the strong tendency of the psychic elements towards autonomy.

000008 Cryptomnesia. In: Jung, C., Collected Works of C. G. Jung, Vol. 1. 2nd. ed., Princeton University Press, 1970. 260 p. (p. 95-106).

A theoretical discussion is presented on cryptomnesia (hidden memory) and the distinction between direct and indirect memory, which have the common quality of being individually known, though it is possible to recognize an association as a remembered image. The combined images lack the quality of being known. The word "combined" is used because originality lies only in the combination of psychic elements and not in the material. This association can occur with no assistance from the conscious. Drastic examples of this are provided by hysteria, which is a caricature of normal psychological mechanisms. In hysterics, a feeling toned memory complex, though not present in consciousness at the moment, motivates certain actions from its seat in the unconscious just as if it were present in the conscious. The unconscious can perceive and associate autonomously. All new ideas and combinations of ideas are premeditated by the unconscious. When the conscious approaches the unconscious with a wish, it was the unconscious that gave it this wish. Cryptomnesia, a technical term from French scientific literature, is defined as the psychic process in which an automatic creative force causes lost memories to reappear in sizeable fragments and with absolute clarity. The reappearance of long forgotten impressions can be explained by the physiology of the brain, which never forgets any impression, no matter how slight. Under special conditions, old memory traces reemerge with photographic fidelity. The work of genius consists of building these traces into new and meaningful structures. A state of mental abnormality to some degree is considered by many a necessary adjunct to genius, as is illustrated by a passage from Nietzsche's Zarathustra. 5 references.

000009 On manic mood disorder. In: Jung, C., Collected Works of C. G. Jung, Vol. 1. 2nd. ed., Princeton University Press, 1970. 260 p. (p. 109-134).

Several cases of chronic hypomanic behavior are described under the term "manic mood disorders" in an attempt to derive a proper definition and classifcation of the disorder. Occasional elation, exaggerated self-confidence, mental productivity, and conflicts with the law are not sufficient to warrant a diagnosis of chronic mania, the cardinal symptoms of which are: emotional lability with predominantly elated mood, flight of ideas, distractability, overactivity, restlessness, and -- dependent on these symptoms -- exaggerated self-importance, megalomanic ideas, alcoholism, and other moral defects. The term "chronic mania" seems too strong, for these are cases of a hypomanic state that cannot be regarded as psychotic. The relatively mild manic symptoms are not partial manifestations of a periodic mania and are seldom found in isolation, but are frequently mixed with other psychopathic symptoms. In the relationship between the intellect and the will, the role played by the intellect is mostly a subsidiary one, since it imparts to the already existing characterological motive the appearance of a logically compelling sequence of ideas, and often allows the individual to construct intellectual motivations after the act. The prime motivation for any abnormal action should be sought in the realm of the affect. In the literature on morally defective persons, emotional excitability and lability are frequent entries. It is concluded that manic mood disorder is a clinical condition belonging to the field of psychopathic inferiority characterized by a stable, hypomanic complex of symptoms generally dating back to youth; that exacerbations of uncertain periodicity can be observed; and that alcoholism, criminality, moral insanity, and social instability or incapacity are, in these cases, symptoms dependent on the hypomanic state. 11 references.

000010 A case of hysterical stupor in a prisoner in detention. In: Jung, C., Collected Works of C. G. Jung, Vol. 1. 2nd. ed., Princeton University Press, 1970. 260 p. (p. 137-156).

The clinical picture of a 48-year-old female offender is presented to study the psychopathology of hysteria and prison psychosis. The patient was arrested on a charge of theft and imprisoned. The next morning she was found standing rigid by the cell door and became furious with the jailers, demanding that they return the money they had stolen from her. By evening she was totally disoriented, with an almost complete lack of memory, easily provoked changes of mood, megalomanic ideas, stumbling speech, complete insensibility to deep pinpricks, strong tremors of the hands and head, and shaky and broken writing. She thought she was in a luxury hotel, and the jailers were hotel guests. She was excitable, and at times shouted and screamed gibberish. She was taken to an asylum for medical evaluation. Her alternating state of consciousness, with defects of memory, along with other hysterical symptoms, provided the diagnostic basis for hysterical twilight state. An accompanying phenomenon of stuporous behavior was noted. In the loneliness of her solitary confinement S became intensely preoccupied with her sudden misfortune. She was worried about her daughter -- arrested with her -- who was in the last stages of pregnancy, and about the charge of theft (which later turned out to be false). Her "not knowing" the answers to questions about her life is a primary phenomenon in the genesis of hysterical symptoms which Breuer and Freud have called hysterical conversion. In this case, the determining factor seems to have been the idea of forgetting. Her not knowing is partly an unconscious and partly a half conscious not wanting to know. This form of hysterical illness -- disregarding the prison complex of hallucinations and delusions -- may be described as "prison psychosis" since, with few exceptions, such cases have been observed only in prisoners. 13 references.

000011 On simulated insanity. In: Jung, C., Collected Works of C. G. Jung, Vol. 1. 2nd. ed., Princeton University Press, 1970. 260 p. (p. 159-187).

A discussion of the detection of simulated insanity in diagnostic psychiatric interviews is presented. Successful simulation demands shamming, self-control, and psychic toughness. This cannot be achieved by mere lying, for the deception must be kept up with consistency and unshakeable willpower for weeks and even months, which requires an extraordinary amount of energy. Cases in which simulation changes into a real twilight state begin with a feeling toned idea that develops through suggestibility into an automatism. A large number of malingerers are hysterical and therefore provide favorable soil for autosuggestion and disturbances of consciousness. A confession of simulation at the end of a disturbance should be received with caution, for in persons of a hysterical disposition, defects of memory that are unknown to the subject himself can be discovered only by an accurate catamnesis. Several cases are cited demonstrating shadings of simulation by patients accused of crime. The case of a 17-year-old girl who passed herself off as a saint, refusing food, driving nails through her feet, etc.,can hardly be described as a simulation, for the means employed bore no relation to the desired end (she wished to stay with a relative, a priest) but were merely symptoms of a known mental disorder. When a criminal simulates insanity, it is to get transferred to an asylum. But when a hysterical girl tortures herself in order to appear interesting, both means and end are the outcome of morbid mental activity. It is concluded that: 1) there are people in whom the aftereffect of violent emotion shows itself in the form of a lasting confusion, which could be described as "emotional stupidity"; 2) by acting specifically upon the attention, affects favor the appearance of psychic automatisms in the widest sense; 3) some cases of simulation are probably due to the aftereffect of violent emotions and their automatization (or to autohypnosis) and must therefore be regarded as pathological. 4) Ganser's complex in prisoners can probably be explained in the same way and must be regarded as an automatized symptom closely related to simulation. 32 references.

000012 A medical opinion on a case of simulated insanity. In: Jung, C., Collected Works of C. G. Jung, Vol. 1. 2nd. ed., Princeton University Press, 1970. 260 p. (p. 188-205).

Simulation of insanity is presented and illustrated in a detailed report of a prisoner who showed psychopathic inferiority with half conscious simulation. S had led a vagrant existence, had been married twice, and had committed a number of thefts. Personality deviations that were considered signs of degeneracy included: hypalgesia, Daltonism, reduced attention, poor comprehension of things seen and heard, retardation, and lack of accuracy, all of which more nearly resembled congenital degeneracy than any known mental illness. His chief symptoms, instability of character and forgetfulness, play a particularly prominent role in hysteria. An earlier attempt at suicide was definitely hysterical in character. He had no clear idea of what he wanted to gain by simulation. The prisoner acted the part of a madman so well that some of his actions were difficult to explain as pure simulation. A pathological factor in his background enabled him to play his role successfully. His intention to simulate insanity became a powerful autosuggestion that blurred his consciousness and influenced his actions regardless of his conscious will. This development of simulation was accompanied by strong affects. The psychological mechanism of his simulation suggests that the initial psychic weakness was the final cause of the idea of simulation. In answer to specific questions posed by legal authorities, the asylum decided that the respondent was not at the moment mentally ill; the condition, which had existed presumably since birth, did not preclude responsibility for theft, but was assumed partially responsible for the simulation.

000013 A third and final opinion on two contradictory psychiatric diagnoses. In: Jung, C., Collected Works of C. G. Jung, Vol. 1. 2nd. ed., Princeton University Press, 1970. 260 p. (p. 209-218).

The inadequacy of expert opinion as to a defendant's mental competence is illustrated in the case of a woman accused of fraud after obtaining money to pay for a nonexistent winning ticket in the Hungarian lottery. Interesting aspects of the case are that the opinions are based only on reports about the defendant, rather than on personal interviews with her, and that a principle concerning the relation of moral defect to hysteria is involved. A final opinion was formed after an interview with the defendant, in addition to a study of the documents. In the first opinion, the most important finding was the presence of hysteria. The opinion held that lying and fraud cannot be judged the same way in constitutionally hysterical persons as in normal people but found the defendant partially responsible. The second opinion also concluded that the defendant suffered from hysteria. Her unlawful aberrations were regarded as symptoms of her hysterical aberration. She was, therefore, held totally irresponsible and was considered incurable. This second opinion established that there was a total lack of moral feelings, but a criticism of it contends that such a defect is not a hysterical symptom and does not belong to the hysterical character. Moral defect and hysteria are considered different conditions that occur independently. A final opinion, which, in answer to the examining magistrate's questions, agrees with opinion A in charging partial responsibility but considers the

material adequate only in opinion B, states that hysteria does not cause a moral defect, although it can mask or exaggerate one. Neither of the opinions proved that the defendant was acting under the compulsion of a pathological persuasion, a delusional idea, or a pathological and irresistible instinct. The standpoint of opinion B means, in practice, the abandonment of the scientific concept of moral defect, which could exclude moral defectives from the legal concept of insanity and overfill mental institutions with criminals.

000014 On the psychological diagnosis of facts. In: Jung, C., Collected Works of C. G. Jung, Vol. 1. 2nd. ed., Princeton University Press, 1970. 260 p. (p. 219-221).

In an effort to set straight the record as to the origin of the concept "psychological diagnosis of facts," a number of articles in various journals are cited in which that subject was discussed. In his and Riklin's work, "The Associations of Normal Subjects," the concept of the feeling toned complex and its effects on the associations is outlined. The psychological diagnosis may be applied to disclosing a complex of ideas related to crime by presenting the subject with a series of word associations. Jung assigns credit for the discovery of this method to Galton or Wundt, but claims the origin of feeling toned complexes for himself and his work at the clinic in Zurich. A brief case report is appended, in which the existence of a theft complex was brought to light by the application of a series of association questions, after which the subject broke down and confessed his guilt.

02 EXPERIMENTAL RESEARCHES

000015 The associations of normal subjects. General experimental procedure. Classification. In: Jung, C., Collected Works of C. G. Jung, Vol. 2. Princeton University Press, 1973. 649 p. (p. 3-39).

In an effort to determine standard reactions of normal people to association stimuli and, in turn, to establish a basis of comparison between normal and mentally disturbed subjects, diagnostic word association studies were conducted with known normal subjects. A total of 38 normal Ss were studied to determine their association patterns and to investigate the effects of attention on the associations. Ss were 9 educated men, 14 educated women, 7 uneducated men, and 8 uneducated women, between the ages of 20 and 50, all judged to be normal. The study was limited to associations produced by calling out stimulus words. The 400 stimulus words, 231 nouns, 69 adjectives, 82 verbs, and 18 adverbs and numerals, were taken from everyday life. The number of syllables was not taken into account. Care was taken to eliminate any discrepancy between standard German speaking subjects and Swiss German speaking subjects. The research design also attempted to control the differences in education. The study was broken into three segments: 1) measurement of reaction time in the first 200 reactions and description of psychic state; 2) 100 reactions recorded under the condition of internal distraction; and 3) a series, sometimes not carried out until the second day, which observed the effects of external distraction in 100 reactions. Some 300-400 word assocations were obtained from each S and classified, resulting in about 12,400 associations. Using a schema developed by Aschaffenburg, the results were divided into four main categories, internal associations, external associations, sound reactions, and a miscellaneous classification including indirect associations, meaningless reactions, failures, and repetition of the stimulus word. Also noted were the phenomena of perseveration, the egocentric reaction, repetition of the reaction, and linguistic connection. Tables and breakdown patterns of various associations are appended. 13 references.

000016 The associations of normal subjects. General experimental procedure. Results obtained from individual subjects. Educated women. In: Jung, C., Collected Works of C. G. Jung, Vol. 2. Princeton University Press, 1973. 649 p. (p. 40-70).

In a study of word associations and attention in 38 normal subjects, 14 educated women comprised one homogeneous study group of known normal subjects. The level of education in the group of educated women was in general very high and most were well read. Their colloquial language was predominantly the Swiss-German dialect. Although the material gathered from 4046 reactions in this group was quantitatively uneven and the results, which are presented individually, differed from subject to subject, certain patterns were observed. Of the six subjects over 30 years old, three showed an average predominance of internal over external association. Of the eight subjects under 30 years old, however, only one showed a predominance of internal association. Of the ten women undergoing distraction experimentation, five were subjected to both internal and external distraction, two to internal distraction only, and three to external distraction only. In four cases, external distraction was successful, and internal distraction in three cases. One case of internal distraction and one case of external distraction were partially successful. Distraction failed in four cases, of which three were of the predicative type, a type that showed an overall resistance to distraction as compared to the other subjects. 5 references.

000017 The associations of normal subjects. General experimental procedure. Results obtained from individual subjects. Educated men. In: Jung, C., Collected Works of C. G. Jung, Vol. 2. Princeton University Press, 1973. 649 p. (p. 70-101).

In a study of word associations and attention in 38 normal subjects, a group of nine educated men comprised one homogeneous study group of known normal subjects. The group spoke mainly the Swiss German dialect, ranged from 23 to 47 years of age, and produced 3793 associations. Five Ss were subjected to both internal and external distraction, one underwent internal distraction only, one underwent external distraction only, and two were not subjected to any distraction experiments. Five Ss were also treated for association during fatigue and one was tested for association during a state of drowsiness. Only one S was of the predicative type; a distraction experiment could not be carried out on him. External distraction was successful in two cases and moderately successful in two others. In one case, no definite effect was noted. Internal distraction was successful in four cases; the most characteristic feature was a sharp increase in sound reactions. In one other case, there was no definite result. In three of five cases, the associations obtained in fatigue gave a result similar to that of distraction. The association experiment in drowsiness also yielded results similar to those of a distraction experiment. Under normal conditions, four of the subjects exhibited extensive complex phenomena. It also appeared that a lengthening reaction time indicates that the particular stimulus word has touched upon a feeling toned complex. 2 references.

000018 The associations of normal subjects. General experimental procedure. Results obtained from individual subjects. Uneducated women. In: Jung, C., Collected Works of C. G. Jung, Vol. 2. Princeton University Press, 1973. 649 p. (p. 101-128).

A group of eight uneducated women comprised one homogeneous group of Ss in a study of association and attention of 38 normal Ss. All were fairly intelligent, ranged in age from 18 to 21, and more than half had attended secondary schools. They produced a total of 2400 associations. Each completed 200 associations under normal conditions and 100 associations under external distraction. The uneducated Ss were not tested under internal distraction conditions. Two Ss were of the predicative type and the distraction experiment failed. One S demonstrated predicate type behavior by not following instructions all the time and another doubled her efforts, making the distraction phase only partially successful. Four Ss showed positive results during the distraction experiment, although this experiment required a much greater effort of them than the same experiment under normal conditions. The uneducated women as a whole showed the least ability to divide their attention. The results show measurable differences between these subjects and both educated women and educated men, the most notable being that sound associations have a lesser role as distraction phenomena in uneducated women than in the educated groups of either sex. There are usually relatively more internal reactions and fewer linguistic motor forms in uneducated than in educated subjects. 1 reference.

000019 The associations of normal subjects. General experimental procedure. Results obtained from individual subjects. Uneducated men. In: Jung, C., Collected Works of C. G. Jung, Vol. 2. Princeton University Press, 1973. 649 p. (p. 129-137).

Seven uneducated men, comprising one homogeneous group of 38 Ss who took part in a study of associations and attention, were all fairly intelligent, but five of them had had only elementary education. Five of them spoke the Swiss-German dialect. The group produced 2086 associations. As in experiments with uneducated women, only external distraction was used. Five of the Ss were affected by external distraction. Of the two who were predicative types, one was not affected and one showed some reaction to external distraction. In all these Ss, as in the group of uneducated women, sound associations as signs of distraction occurred less than in the educated groups. Two Ss who produced many groupings, few predicates, and many reactions with the same grammatical form also showed a paucity of egocentric reactions and constellations. Two of the uneducated women had shown the same features. The group as a whole was distinguished by the fact that there were few complex constellations. Subjectivity and feelings were less prominent in the uneducated men than in the uneducated women. This difference between the sexes was not demonstrated in the educated Ss. Also noted was the high incidence of erotic complexes among the complexes that were uncovered. Although significant in all Ss, erotic complexes were highest among the uneducated men.

000020 The associations of normal subjects. General experimental procedure. Results obtained from individual subjects. Calculations of averages. In: Jung, C., Collected Works of C. G. Jung, Vol. 2. Princeton University Press, 1973. 649 p. (p. 137-196).

The interrelations of various reactions in a study of associations and attention in four different groups of 38 normal subjects are presented. A number of tables illustrate: 1) results of the experiment under normall conditions; 2) sex differences in the experiment under normal conditions; 3) averages of the distraction experiments; 4) averages of the predicative type under normal conditions and under distraction; and 5) influence of the stimulus word on the reaction. Graphs present the arithmetical means of internaal associations, external associations, sound reactions and miscellaneous reactions in different groups under varying conditions. Results of the experiment show normal variation under the influence of attention, education, and individual characteristics of the subject. Decrease of attention owing to internal or external factors causes a blunting of the reaction type. Distraction of attention causes additionally an increase of indirect associations. Educated subjects generally showed a blunter reaction type than uneducated subjects, which can be explained by a difference in interpretation of stimulus words, but there was no noticeable difference between educated and uneducated subjects in the degree of division of attention. The most dramatic variations in associations were due to individual differences. No differences between sexes emerged except that in the distraction experiment female subjects appeared less able to divide attention than male subjects. The results also show that the blunting of reaction type in fatigue, alcoholic intoxication, and mania may be attributed to a disturbance of attention. 13 references.

000021 An analysis of the associations of an epileptic. In: Jung, C., Collected Works of C. G. Jung, Vol. 2. Princeton University Press, 1973. 649 p. (p. 197-220).

The word association reactions of a typical case of epilepsy are analyzed as part of a larger investigation attempting to separate what is specific for epileptic associations from the various types of the normal and from congenital mental deficiency. The case was drawn from studies of 158 patients at the Swiss Asylum for Epileptics in Zurich and the Burgholzli psychiatric clinic, limited to subjects who were not congenitally mentally defective and had not shown signs of epilepsy in early youth. Ss were carefully prepared for the experiments and presented with 200 stimulus words, 75 denoting concrete ideas, 25 denoting abstract ideas, 50 adjectives, and 50 verbs, all drawn from everyday life. One male S had appeared normal until his wife developed a psychosis and died when S was 30. He then began wandering all over Europe, was frequently apprehended for drinking and theft, had been hospitalized for violent manic episodes and delirium, and had fractured his skull nine years before the study took place. The results of the experiment showed some similarities to associations of normal persons, some similarities to associations of imbeciles, and some unique peculiarities. S adapted himself to the meaning of the stimulus word in the same way as normal uneducated subjects, with no superficial word associations. In common with the associations of imbeciles there were associations in sentence form, or the stimulus word was frequently repeated. There was an intense adaptation to the meaning of the stimulus word so that a great number of the associations were explanations, and the reaction times were considerably longer than in normal subjects. They showed the greatest variation only after the critical reaction, which indicates the influence of perseverating emotional charges rather than of particularly difficult words. This case suggests that feeling tone probably sets in later and lasts longer in the epileptic than in normal Ss. 12 references.

000022 The reaction-time ratio in the association experiment. In: Jung, C., Collected Works of C. G. Jung, Vol. 2. Princeton University Press, 1973. 649 p. (p. 221-271).

The reaction time ratio was analyzed in 26 of 38 normal subjects, male and female, educated and uneducated, participating in a word association experiment. Reaction times that exceeded the probable mean for the S concerned were examined particularly closely. The average reaction time, measured with a stop watch, came out to 1.8 seconds for both educated and uneducated Ss. Males averaged 1.6 seconds, compared to

2.9 seconds for females, and educated Ss averaged 1.5 seconds, compared to 2.0 seconds in the uneducated group. The quality of the stimulus word seemed to exert an influence on reaction time. The average shortest times followed concrete nouns, and the longest times followed abstract nouns and verbs. Educated men were the exception to this rule in that their longest average times followed concrete nouns. The quality of the reaction also seemed to influence reaction time. The longest times occurred with abstract nouns (1.98 seconds) and the shortest times with adjectives and verbs (1.65 seconds). Again, educated men were an exception; their longest time occurring with concrete nouns. The quality of the association also exerted influence. Internal associations required a longer reaction time than external ones. Sound reaction, usually caused by inner distractions, also showed a relatively long reaction time. Long reaction times were usually caused by intense emotions and may have been used to uncover conscious and unconscious complexes, which could be important in hysteria. Sometimes the feeling tone can extend to subsequent reactions. The majority (83%) of prolonged reaction times tended to follow certain stimulus words that have affective value, while only 17% of prolonged reaction times were due to the difficulty of the word. 21 references.

000023 Experimental observations on the faculty of memory. In: Jung, C., Collected Works of C. G. Jung, Vol. 2. Princeton University Press, 1973. 649 p. (p. 272-287).

A new technique, the reproduction method, was used to identify associations attributable to complexes to determine whether failures of memory are accidental or whether there is a pattern to them. After the completion of an association test the experiment was repeated to find out whether the S remembered how he reacted to individual stimulus words. In two Ss, both male, one aged 32 and undergoing psychoanalytic treatment and one aged 22, an excitable and sensitive person, it was found that the incorrect reproductions of answers to the repeated stimulus words were those that were directly constellated by a feeling toned complex or those that immediately followed a critical one. These disturbances of memory are cases of a general tendency to repress and forget an unpleasant impression. In the case of a 23-year-old hysterical woman, the amnestic blockages extended over many subsequent reactions, and were considered hysterical amnesia. The reproduction method could be very useful in cases where analysis is difficult and in criminology. 7 references.

000024 Psychoanalysis and association experiments. In: Jung, C., Collected Works of C. G. Jung, Vol. 2. Princeton University Press, 1973. 649 p. (p. 288-317).

The usefulness of the association experiment in psychoanalysis is illustrated in a case of obsessional neurosis. The patient, female, single, 37 years old, an educated, intelligent teacher, wanted to try hypnosis for insomnia. She was extremely nervous and restless, had a tic, and admitted to having obsessional ideas. She felt that a woman neighbor who had died recently had, on S's account, died without the last sacrament and, before that, had been haunted for several years by the fear that a boy whom she, as a governess, had brought up had died because she had occasionally beaten him. When she could not be hypnotized, the association experiment and the reproduction test were used. The mean reaction time of 2.4 seconds, very high for an educated person, indicated a strong emotionality. The associations showed that the woman had an erotic complex, which she denied. Gradually, however, she revealed a repressed obsession with sexual fantasies, which was traced back to a childhood sexual trauma.

Repressing her sexual obsessions had led to obsessions in other areas in her life. Although S still suffered from insomnia after three weeks of Freudian analysis, she announced several months after treatment that all obsessional ideas had disappeared, and she could now sleep. It is concluded that word associations can be a valuable aid in recognizing the nature of the complex that is the cause of the illness, facilitating and shortening Freudian psychoanalysis. Once the split-off contents of the mind are released from a repression, they can be destroyed through an effort of the will. The associations also supply scientific insight into the origin and structure of psychogenic neuroses. 7 references.

000025 The psychological diagnosis of evidence. In: Jung, C., Collected Works of C. G. Jung, Vol. 2. Princeton University Press, 1973. 649 p. (p. 318-352).

Diagnosing criminal cases by studying the psychological makeup of the witness through the word association method is discussed. The historical development of the method is outlined, and the association experiment is described. When stimulus words are called out, a subject's reaction is determined by the individual content of his ideas. A large number of component ideas charged with a feeling tone constitute a complex, which can be identified by reaction content, lengthened reaction time, and memory lapses during the reproduction method, in which the experiment is repeated. The practical application of the association method in criminal cases is illustrated by its use in a case of a young man suspected of theft. Thirty seven critical stimulus words distributed among 63 irrelevant ones produced such suspicious reactions, reaction times, and memory lapses in the reproduction phase that the investigator accused the young man, and S finally confessed. Since it was considered possible that S reacted more strongly than a hardened criminal would have, a control experiment was conducted with an informed subject and an uninformed one. The disappointing results, with symptoms of a complex observed at critical points in both subjects, reveal a fundamental weakness in the experiment: the multiplicity of meanings that the stimulus words can have. Many more than 100 stimulus words should be used. The young man's reactions did, however, show more symptoms of a complex than the controls'. Although the association method should be used only by experts and, until it is further refined, cautiously, it has many possibilities. 9 references.

000026 Association, dream, and hysterical symptom. In: Jung, C., Collected Works of C. G. Jung, Vol. 2. Princeton University Press, 1973. 649 p. (p. 353-407).

The anomalies of word association in hysteria are illustrated by the case of a 24-year-old girl who was extremely restless, feared madness, and complained of unbearable heat sensations in the head. The symptoms dated from her first menstruation at 15 and superseded chorea that had developed at age 7. S, physically healthy and fairly intelligent, was the youngest child of five. Her mother was completely crippled by osteomalacia. The association experiment was marked by an enormous number of failures, abnormally long reaction times, and other complex constellations showing that she was dominated by a number of complexes, particularly an illness complex, a sexual complex, and a school complex. Since the psychoanalysis was proceeding with difficulty, the patient's dreams were also studied. The dream analysis confirmed the sexual complex, and accompanying blockages revealed by the association test suggested a possible childhood sexual trauma. This erotic complex included some romantic attachment to the therapist, accompanied by a feeling of rejection and denial. The childhood

chorea was diagnosed as a hysterical symptom devised to avoid writing lessons and going to school, and the heat sensations were symptomatic of the sexual complex, intensified in S's case by her fear of osteomalacia in pregnancy. Although the patient showed some improvement in treatment, her condition deteriorated after discharge. Effective treatment of hysteria should strengthen what remains of the normal ego, and is best achieved by introducing a new complex to liberate the ego. 5 references.

000027 The psychopathological significance of the association experiment. In: Jung, C., Collected Works of C. G. Jung, Vol. 2. Princeton University Press, 1973. 649 p. (p. 408-425).

The value to psychopathology of the association experiment, in which the subject says what is immediately called to mind when a stimulus word is called out, lies in the fact that association is a necessary sequence following certain laws. In spite of objections based on the principles of chance and free will, the work of Kraepelin, Aschaffenburg, and others has empirically established certain patterns and rules. The associations have been divided into internal associations, in which the meaning of the words is the connecting link, and external associations, in which the connecting link is an external contingency. In sound associations the response is a word that sounds like the stimulus word. It has been discovered that the more the attention of the subject decreases, the more the external and sound associations increase. This law is potentially important to understanding psychopathological states, in which the ability to concentrate is often disturbed. The associations are determined by the whole personality and background. Long reaction times indicate feeling toned complexes, found in all normal subjects and very pronounced in psychopathology. In hysterical patients the times of critical reactions are much longer, and the barriers to recollection much stronger than in normal subjects. Two simple examples of the symptomatology of hysteria show that the hysterical patient suffers from a disorder of the affect he has been unable to conquer, and which his conscious mind finds unbearable. The same mechanism is demonstrated in dementia praecox, although other elements are also found in this disease. 13 references.

000028 Disturbances of reproduction in the association experiment. In: Jung, C., Collected Works of C. G. Jung, Vol. 2. Princeton University Press, 1973. 649 p. (p. 426-438).

Statistics are given to support an earlier, unfinished paper ("Experimental Observations on the Faculty of Memory") introducing the reproduction method, which was repeatedly criticized. The earlier paper maintained that most of a subject's memory failures in attempting to reproduce the original answers given on an association test can be traced to complexes. Although this memory failure had been observed in many cases, it was investigated in only two cases, in which it was particularly pronounced. The material presented from 28 cases is heterogeneous, since only three subjects were normal and the rest were widely varying neurotics and psychotics. The results are similar to those of the first study. A relation is established between incorrect reproduction and prolonged reaction time on the original association. The disturbance is usually correlated directly with a prolonged reaction time, but in some cases it follows a prolonged reaction time. The association that is incorrectly reproduced has, on the average, twice as many complex signs as the correctly reproduced one, including such characteristics as reaction by two or more words if this is not typical for the subject; repetition or misunderstanding of the the stimulus word; slips of the tongue; and use of a foreign word. The complex characteristics tend to be grouped around certain specific associations. 3 references.

000029 The association method. In: Jung, C., Collected Works of C. G. Jung, Vol. 2. Princeton University Press, 1973. 649 p. (p. 439-465).

The association method is described and some of its practical applications are discussed. In the association experiment, the subject gives his immediate response to each of 100 preselected stimulus words. The listed stimulus words represent a mixture of different parts of speech, and are chosen to touch on the complexes that commonly occur. Emotionally charged reactions are revealed by such disturbances as prolonged reaction times, failure to respond, responding with additions, repetition of the stimulus words, and perseveration. The four principal types of associations are: 1) the objective type, with undisturbed reactions; 2) the complex type, showing many disturbances caused by constellations of complexes; 3) the definition type, found chiefly among stupid people; and 4) the predicate type, which usually betrays a deficiency of feeling. In the reproduction test, the stimulus words are repeated and the subject is asked to recall his earlier reactions. Memory lapses are often caused by stimulus words that touch on a feeling toned complex, or that immediately follow critical words. Practical aspects of the association method are illustrated in a case where it was used to detect the real culprit among three nurses suspected of theft. In the interview of the guilty nurse, the critical stimulus words relating to the theft produced the longest reaction times, the most complex characteristics, and the most incorrect reproductions.

000030 The family constellation. In: Jung, C., Collected Works of C. G. Jung, Vol. 2. Princeton University Press, 1973. 649 p. (p. 466-479).

To investigate theories on the family, the association experiment was applied to 24 families, consisting of 100 subjects, who produced 22,000 associations. The associations were processed according to logical linguistic criteria, and it was found that: 1) relatives tend to show an agreement in reaction type; 2) reaction types of children are closer to those of the mother than those of the father; and 3) marriage seems to change the association type more in women than in men. The similarity of associations of related subjects is often remarkable, as is illustrated in the case of a mother and daughter that demonstrates how unhealthy emotions, understandable and no longer dangerous in a parent, can be transmitted to a child, in whom they can be dangerous. The strongest influences on a child are the unconscious personal affective states of his parents and teachers. Other cases show how lives and marriages that are founded on too strong an attachment to the parents can be crippled through neuroses, so that the child remains imprisoned in infantile relationships. One of the most important aims of education should be to free the growing child from his unconscious attachment to the influences of his early environment so that he may keep what is valuable and reject what is not. The need for additional research into children's emotional processes, about which not enough is known, is stressed.

000031 On the psychophysical relations of the association experiment. In: Jung, C., Collected Works of C. G. Jung, Vol. 2. Princeton University Press, 1973. 649 p. (p. 483-491).

The galvanic phenomenon, reported by Dr. Veraguth of Zurich, which he called the "galvanopsychophysical reflex", and its use in validating the results of the association experiment are discussed. A galvanometer was introduced into the circuit of a 2 volt current passed through the human body. It was found that a stimulus applied to the subject would cause an increase in the current. The increase was related not to the strength of the stimulus, but to the intensity of the resulting feeling tone, and appeared not at the moment the stimulus was perceived, but after a latent period of 1-6 seconds. Veraguth concluded that in this experiment feelings were objectively represented. A specially designed apparatus can record long curves to represent feeling tones aroused by the association experiment. An example shows how strong feeling tones that accompany an association cause characteristic and regular disturbances in the association processes, but the method of interpreting the disturbances is still not scientifically developed. The "galvanopsychophysical reflex" may be a means to help define the complex and its feeling tone. Graphic representations of galvanic oscillations during two association experiments produced distinct curves that showed strong feeling tones corresponding to disturbances in association reactions. 2 references.

000032 Psychophysical investigations with the galvanometer and pneumograph in normal and insane individuals. In: Jung, C., Collected Works of C. G. Jung, Vol. 2. Princeton University Press, 1973. 649 p. (p. 492-553).

Galvanometric and pneumographic curves recorded simultaneously on the kymograph under the influence of various sensory and psychical stimuli were studied to evaluate the "psychophysical galvanic reflex" and the respiratory innervation curve as records of psychical changes; to determine their normal and pathological variations; and to compare these curves. In word associations the reaction time was also recorded. Forty series of curves were recorded in eight normal subjects, and 30 in 11 cases of dementia praecox of different types. In normal subjects it was found that every stimulus accompanied by an emotion caused a rise in the electric curve directly proportional to the intensity and actuality of the emotion. The information gathered from the pneumograph curves in both normal and pathological cases was inconclusive, but it appeared that there was very little relationship between the galvanometric and pneumographic curves, other than an inverse one. Inhibitions in breathing were caused by expectation and tension rather than by the unconscious emotions that register strongly on the galvanometer. The galvanometer curves in the dementia praecox patients included some that were very labile and some that were similar to curves in normal subjects. Some catatonic patients hardly registered at all and their period of latency was markedly protracted. Word associations in normal subjects, carried out with only four subjects, showed that there was a relationship between length of reaction time and height of the galvanometer curve, and between altered reproductions and height of the galvanometer curve. These relationships support the hypothesis that long reaction times and altered reproductions are affective phenomena. Only two of the dementia praecox patients could be tested with associations. There was nothing unusual in their galvanometer curves during the association experiment, but they both showed abnormal associations, lengthened reaction times, numerous complex constellations, and an abnormal number of altered reproductions. It is concluded that the thought mechanisms in dementia praecox are probably not pathological, but that the abnormality is in the patient's reaction to his complexes. 16 references.

000033 Further investigations on the galvanic phenomenon and respiration in normal and insane individuals. In: Jung, C., Collected Works of C. G. Jung, Vol. 2. Princeton University Press, 1973. 649 p. (p. 554-580).

A series of simple physical and mental stimuli was administered to 15 normal subjects and 61 patients suffering from various mental diseases to determine effects on the galvanic phenomenon and on respiration. The galvanometric changes were recorded by a galvanometer introduced into the circuit of a low volt current passed through the body; the respiration was recorded by pneumograph. In many of the abnormal Ss, however, the pneumograph could not be used. These experiments indicate the following: the galvanic reaction depends on attention to the stimulus and the ability to associate it with previous occurrences; this association may be conscious, but is usually unconscious. Galvanic reactions show great individual variation and, within some limits, are independent of the original bodily resistance. In these experiments physical stimuli caused greater galvanic fluctuations than psychological ones, which may have been due to the fact that the physical stimuli occurred earlier in the experiment. Early stimuli usually cause stronger reactions than later ones because of the elements of tension and expectation. Normal reactions vary widely, but are nearly always stronger than pathological ones. Galvanic reactions are low in depression and stupor because of poor attention and inhibition of associations, and are virutally nonexistent in dementia because of lack of associations. Reactions are high in alcoholism and in the euphoric stage of general paralysis. From the pneumographic measurements, it was concluded that the inspiratory rate varies from individual to individual. There is usually a decrease in the amplitude of the inspirations during the rise of the galvanic curve. This decrease varies according to the subject, however, and has no relation to the height of the galvanic curve. In cases of dementia in which there is no galvanic reaction, there are respiratory changes, but they are very slight. 1 reference.

000034 Statistical details of enlistment. In: Jung, C., Collected Works of C. G. Jung, Vol. 2. Princeton University Press, 1973. 649 p. (p. 583-585).

Observation of an enlistment of Swiss military recruits revealed a high percentage of them who were mentally or emotionally handicapped or otherwise medically unfit for military service; in fact, fewer than half were considered fit. Of 506 men examined, 47 (9.2%), most of whom were from rural areas, were patently imbecile. Many alcoholics were found among the even higher number of recruits who were physically unfit. Of 78 men between the ages of 20 and 30, 10 (12.9%) were discharged for chronic alcoholism, although such cases are usually classified under various medical euphemisms. A comparison of homes of record revealed a preponderance of mental and emotional deficients, alcoholics, and recruits with a variety of personality disorders came from rural rather than urban localities.

000035 New aspects of criminal psychology: contribution to the method used for psychological diagnosis of evidence. In: Jung, C., Collected Works of C. G. Jung, Vol. 2. Princeton University Press, 1973. 649 p. (p. 586-596).

The applicability of the association experiment to the psychological diagnosis of a crime is examined. A hypothetical case shows how a culprit can be identified from a number of suspects by elements in his reactions to critical stimulus words that reveal the influence of a feeling toned complex. These characteristics include: prolonged reaction time in the critical reaction or in the one immediately following; reaction with two or more words, if this is not usual for the subject; repetition of the stimulus word; failure to react; lapsus linguae, etc. Measuring oscillations of body resistance to galvanic current has lent experimental support to identifying these deviations as complex characteristics. The experiment will not provide proof of guilt, but may point the way to future investigative procedure. An analysis of a case in which three nurses were suspected of theft demonstrates the successful use of the association experiment in identifying the guilty nurse by her reactions to critical stimulus words: prolonged reactions, numerous complex characteristics, and incorrect reproductions. 4 references.

000036 The psychological methods of investigation used in the psychiatric clinic of the University of Zurich. In: Jung, C., Collected Works of C. G. Jung, Vol. 2. Princeton University Press, 1973. 649 p. (p. 597).

Diagnostic tests used in the psychiatric clinic of the University of Zurich, noted in outline form, consist of the following: 1) Rapidity of apperception: short exposure of simple pictures; 2) working through psychological material and fidelity of reproduction: retelling three fables, the first containing two simple similar situations that differ in one important nuance, the second similar, but more complicated, and the third similar, but containing a whole series of similar situations; 3) fatigability of the will: Kraepelin's method of reckoning; 4) emotionally charged contents ("complexes"): Jung's association method; and 5) psychogenic mechanism and symptom determination: Frued's psychoanalytic method.

000037 On the doctrine of complexes. In: Jung, C., Collected Works of C. G. Jung, Vol. 2. Princeton University Press, 1973. 649 p. (p. 598-604).

Theoretical views on the neuroses and dementia praecox, founded on results of the association experiment, are summarized. When a subject gives an answer to each of a series of stimulus words, occasional delayed reactions and other disturbances such as slips of the tongue, repetition of the stimulus word, etc. occur that indicate emotional excitement. These disturbances often refer to a distressing personal matter called a complex. A pathogenic complex, usually psychosexual, is the basis of neuroses. The association experiment and the reproduction method, in which memory lapses often occur where the complexes interfered originally, are useful in diagnosis. Complex associations are either obsessionally stable or disappear from the memory altogether. The psychogenic complex is autonomous and can temporarily replace the ego, possessing all the characteristics of a separate personality, and acting in opposition to the individual's conscious will. Symptoms of hysteria originate from these conflicts. In spite of objections from some quarters, dementia praecox is also defined as a complex disease. In hysteria there is usually a continuous accommodation to the surroundings, but in dementia praecox the complexes are fixed. Thought processes do not cease in dementia, but continue in fantasy form. Previous works on these subjects are cited.

000038 On the psychological diagnosis of evidence: the evidence-experiment in the Naf trial. In: Jung, C., Collected Works of C. G. Jung, Vol. 2. Princeton University Press, 1973. 649 p. (p. 605-614).

An evidence examination was carried out on a subject accused of a crime to detect a possible guilt or innocence complex. In an association experiment lasting more than three hours, S was given 407 stimulus words, 271 neutral, 96 referring to the evidence, and 40 personal and emotional words selected to determine his emotional makeup. Stimulus words referring to emotionally charged contents evoke disturbances such as delayed reaction time, repetition of the stimulus word, failure to respond, slips of the tongue, perseveration, defective reproduction, etc. In this case, stimulus words taken from the evidence produced prolonged reaction times, disturbing influence on the memory, and four times as many complex characteristics as the neutral stimuli. When the evidence is well known to a subject, it is natural for him to react to critical stimulus words, but an innocent person will not react particularly strongly to words referring to concrete details. In this case, S reacted more strongly to words referring to distinctive details of the evidence than to the more general evidence stimulus words. In the opinion of the expert, the subject's reactions were not those of an innocent person, but the assessment of his signs as revealing a guilty conscience was left to the judge.

03 THE PSYCHOGENESIS OF MENTAL DISEASE

000039 The psychology of dementia praecox. 1. Critical survey of theoretical views on the psychology of dementia praecox. In: Jung, C., Collected Works of C. G. Jung, Vol. 3. Princeton University Press, 1972. 303 p. (p. 1-37).

A critical survey of the theoretical views on the psychology of dementia praecox includes discussions and comparisons of the works of Freud, Gross, Jiling, and a number of others. An overview of the literature on the subject shows that the research, although fragmentary and apparently uncoordinated, agrees that the symptoms commonly include a central disturbance -- a lowering of attention or apperceptive deterioration. This is typically manifest in superficiality of associations, symbolism, stereotypies, perseverations, command automatisms, apathy, aboulia, disturbance of reproduction, and negativism. Rene Masselon's exhaustive study on catatonic psychology emphasizes the characteristic reduction of attention. He feels the patient suffers a perpetual distraction in which perception of external objects, awareness of his own personality, judgment, the feeling of rapport, belief, and certainty all fade or disappear when power of attention disappears. Freud was the first to demonstrate the "principle of conversion" in a case of paranoid dementia praecox. In explaining the emotional impoverishment characteristic of dementia praecox, Neisser observed that the mobility of symptoms in hysteria is due to the mobility of affects, while paranoia is characterized by a fixation of affects. It is hypothesized that in dementia praecox there is a specific concomitant of the affect that causes the final fixation of the precipitating complex, impeding the further development of the personality. The possibility that in some cases the primary factor may be a change in the metabolism is postulated. Such ideas and their detailed psychological processes are outlined for a large selection of the leading authors on dementia praecox near the turn of the century. 58 references.

000040 The psychology of dementia praecox. 2. The feeling-toned complex and its general effects on the psyche. In: Jung, C., Collected Works of C. G. Jung, Vol. 3. Princeton University Press, 1972. 303 p. (p. 38-51).

Observations based on experimental work are made on the feeling toned complex and its acute and chronic effects on the psyche. The feeling toned complex is defined as the whole fabric of ideas surrounding the feeling tone, an affective state accompanied by somatic effects. The attempt is made to define the essential basis of personality, which is held to be affectivity. Virtually every individual association is deemed to relate to some complex, as well as to the ego complex, the whole mass of ideas pertaining to the ego -- in a normal person the strongest complex. Egocentric ideas are commonly interrupted by affects leading to new complexes that inhibit other ideas. The acute effects and the chronic effects of the com-

plex are defined and compared. Disturbances caused by complexes have been demonstrated in association experiments by prolonged reaction times, abnormal reactions, and forgetting critical or postcritical reactions. The effect of a strong complex on a normal psyche is illustrated in the classical state of being in love. Other forms of the sexual complex and other complexes are sometimes influenced by various types of displacement, including disguising the complex by superimposing a contrasting mood. 11 references.

000041 The psychology of dementia praecox. 3. The influence of the feeling-toned complex on the valency of associations. In: Jung, C., Collected Works of C. G. Jung, Vol. 3. Princeton University Press, 1972. 303 p. (p. 52-69).

The diminution of the valency of associations caused by the feeling toned complex is discussed and general remarks on the complexes are made, based on word association tests and illustrated with examples from cases. It was shown that a sudden striking increase in superficial associations during the association experiment without any artificial distraction indicates a reduction in attention, caused by a feeling toned complex. If the complex is repressed, the subject may not be conscious of it. Other examples of disturbances of attention are found in slips of the tongue, slips of the pen, misreading, melodic automatisms (in which whistling or humming contain the complex in metaphorical form), and puns. Dreams, symbolic expressions of the repressed complex, are excellent examples of expression by similarity of imagery. A detailed analysis of a dream emphasizes the ambiguity of dream images, comparable to the superficial associations seen in a state of reduced attention in distraction experiments. The complexes have a tendency to cause contrasting associations, seen as emotional and verbal contrasts in hysteria and as verbal contrasts in dementia praecox. It is concluded that every affective event becomes a complex. Most complexes are held to be sexual, as are most dreams and most of the hysterias, especially in women. Time usually frees the normal individual from obsessive complexes, but sometimes he needs artificial aid, and it has been found that displacement can help. If the complex is successfully repressed, the S will be complex sensitive for a long time. If the complex remains entirely unchanged, which happens only after severe damage to the ego complex, dementia praecox can develop. It is conjectured that toxic effects may be involved in this degeneration. 20 references.

000042 The psychology of dementia praecox. 4. Dementia praecox and hysteria. In: Jung, C., Collected Works of C. G. Jung, Vol. 3. Princeton University Press, 1972. 303 p. (p. 70-98).

A review of the psychological similarities of dementia praecox and hysteria compares emotional disturbances, character abnormalities, intellectual disturbances, and stereotypy in the two diseases. The emotional indifference in cases of acute dementia praecox is similar to the inadequate responses of the hysteric whose complex is under special inhibition. Explosive excitements may be brought about in dementia praecox in the same way as the explosive affects in hysteria. Typical symptoms of dementia praecox include lack of self-control and lack of emotional rapport, both of which are sometimes found in hysteria as well. Character disturbances common to the two illnesses include affectation, especially when patients are out of their social element, lack of consideration, narrow-mindedness, inaccessibility to persuasion, and stupid behavior, although in dementia praecox the mechanisms go much deeper. Intellectual impairments found in both dementia praecox and hysteria include shades of clouding of lucidity of consciousness, ranging from perfect clarity to deepest confusion, disturbance of attention, disorientation, delusions, hallucinations, compulsive thinking, negativism, and sleep disturbances. Stereotypy, a characteristic symptom of dementia praecox, is also seen in hysteria and, in the form of automatization, is a common phenomenon in normal development. It is concluded that in hysteria the psyche is disabled because it cannot rid itself of a complex, but many hysterics can regain their equilibrium by partially overcoming the complex and avoiding new traumas. In dementia praecox, one or more complexes have become permanently fixed and cannot be overcome, but it is not clear whether the complex caused or precipitated the illness, or whether at the onset of the illness a definite complex was present which then determined the symptoms. 25 references.

000043 The psychology of dementia praecox. 5. Analysis of a case of paranoid dementia as a paradigm. In: Jung, C., Collected Works of C. G. Jung, Vol. 3. Princeton University Press, 1972. 303 p. (p. 99-151).

The analysis of a case of paranoid dementia in a middle-aged unmarried dressmaker suffering from delusions and auditory hallucinations is discussed as a typical paradigm of psychoanalysis. It is shown how the patient in her psychosis creates a complicated and utterly confused and senseless fantasy structure. She describes the hopes and disappointments of her life in her symptoms. The nearest analogy to her thinking is the normal dream, which employs the same or similar psychological mechanisms. Word associations revealed a series of complex constellations including the complex of personal grandeur (exaggerated according to the patient's morbidly intensified self-esteem), the complex of injury, and an erotic complex. The first part of the analysis (conducted in the manner of dream analysis) describes her sufferings and their symbols; the second, her wishes and their fulfillment in symbolic images and episodes; and the third deals with her intimate erotic wishes and the solution of the problem through the transfer of her power and sufferings to "her children". 10 references.

000044 The content of the psychoses. In: Jung, C., Collected Works of C. G. Jung, Vol. 3. Princeton University Press, 1972. 303 p. (p. 153-178).

Case studies are presented in which an argument is presented for the present position regarding the content of the psychoses. It is contended that the difference between his theory and E. Bleuler's is whether psychological disturbance should be regarded as primary or secondary in relation to the physiological basis, and that resolution depends on whether the prevailing dogma -- that mental diseases are diseases of the brain -- represents a final truth or not. It is pointed out that 45% of the patients admitted to Burgholzhi Mental Hospital over a period of 4 years suffered from dementia praecox, usually with some disturbance of feeling and often with delusions and hallucinations. However, even in the most severe cases, lasting for a period of years, an intact brain was frequently found post-mortem, which is proof that the purely anatomical approach leads only indirectly to an understanding of psychic disturbance. Following the lead of older clinicians, it was found that mental illness often occurred at a moment of some great emotional episode that had arisen in a more or less normal manner, and that there were a number of symptoms in the ensuing disturbances that could not be understood from a purely anatomical standpoint but became comprehensible when considered from the standpoint of the individual's previous history. Freud's study of the psychology of hysteria and

dreams is cited as the greatest stimulus and aid in this work. These insights may have general or limited validity but nonetheless there is no symptom in dementia praecox that can be described as psychologically meaningless. 3 references.

000045 On psychological understanding. In: Jung, C., Collected Works of C. G. Jung, Vol. 3. Princeton University Press, 1972. 303 p. (p. 179-193).

A constructive method of approaching the workings of the mind in the diagnosis of dementia praecox, based on prospective understanding, is advanced in preference to Freud's analytical, reductive method, based on a causality or retrospective understanding, which seems better suited to understanding hysteria. Principal criticism of the analytic method is that it does not engage the wealth and variety of symbolism of the psychotic. The futility of understanding symbolism by the causative, analytic methods applied in science is illustrated in attempts to understand the symbolism in Faust II, which requires the subjective conditioning of knowledge to be fully appreciated. Similarly, any understanding of the human psyche, of man's dreams, or of anything psychological must be tempered by the evaluator's subjective attitude toward it. Mental development results from active speculation based on experience, not from experience alone. The psyche, therefore, creates it own future as it lives; therefore, any causative evaluation of it in retrospect can be only partially true; its dynamic quality as a creative entity eludes us. A patient, therefore, should be asked what his goals are, not only what he has felt and thought. Extraversion and introversion are explained in detail and, to simplify pathological typing, the hysterics are assigned to the former, and the psychasthenics and schizophrenics to the latter. 14 references.

000046 A criticism of Bleuler's theory of schizoph.enic negativism. In: Jung, C., Collected Works of C. G. Jung, Vol. 3. Princeton University Press, 1972. 303 p. (p. 197-202).

E. Bleuler's theory of schizophrenic negativism, examined in the light of the complex theory, is criticized because it gives the impression that the ideas or tendencies of the schizophrenic are always accompanied by their opposites. Bleuler presents the new and interesting concept of ambivalence, which hypothesizes that every tendency is balanced by a contrary one. It is noted that all feeling tones are balanced by their opposites, giving the feeling tone an ambivalent character. But a strict sequence of psychological causes conditions the negative reaction. The characteristic of the diseased mind is not the ambitendency, ambivalence, or schiozphrenic splitting of the psyche cited by Bleuler, but resistance, which is set up by the pathological thought complex. The "splitting of the psyche" is not a predisposing cause but a manifestation of inner conflict. Bleuler's list of causes of negativism (autistic withdrawal, a "life wound", hostile relationship with the environment, sexuality, etc.)is examined and each is found to be directly related to the complex. Bleuler does not put much emphasis on the role of sexuality, which is suprising since psychoanalysis has shown that the source of negativism is resistance, which in schizophrenia as in the neuroses arises from the sexual complex. 5 references.

000047 On the importance of the unconscious in psychopathology. In: Jung, C., Collected Works of C. G. Jung, Vol. 3. Princeton University Press, 1972. 303 p. (p. 203-210).

The function of the unconscious in mental disturbances as a compensation of the conscious psychic content is discussed. The unconscious is defined as the sum of all those psychic events that are not intense enough to enter into consciousness.

In normal people the unconscious effects a compensaton of all conscious tendencies through a counter impulse and produces a balance. This agency expresses itself in unconscious, apparently inconsistent and uncharacteristic activities, which Freud calls symptomatic actions. Dreams are examples of the compensating functions of the unconscious. In psychopathology the working of the unconscious, seen most clearly in such disturbances as hysteria and obsessional neurosis, is also seen clearly in the delusions and hallucinations of the psychoses, but is not so easily recognized. The mentally unbalanced person, suffering from a real imbalance between the conscious and the unconscious, struggles against his own unconscious, as in the case of the eccentric inventor, the paranoid alcoholic, or the fanatical religious convert. Because of the characteristic onesidedness of conscious striving in such cases, the normal functioning of the unconscious breaks through in an abnormal form, which upsets the mental balance and disturbs the person's adaptation to his environment. 1 reference.

000048 On the problem of psychogenesis in mental disease. In: Jung, C., Collected Works of C. G. Jung, Vol. 3. Princeton University Press, 1972. 303 p. (p. 211-225).

Psychogenesis in mental diseases is discussed, with arguments presented for their physiological and psychological origins. The materialistic dogma in psychiatry is attributed to the fact that medicine is a natural science and the psychiatrist, as a physician, is a natural scientist. The psychological and emotional experiences, however, have been proved to play a decisive role in the courses of neuroses and in mental diseases. Although there are some cases of dementia praecox in which there is change in the brain cells, these changes are not usually present, and there are striking differences between the usual symptoms of dementia praecox and those occurring in organic brain disease. Cases of dementia praecox frequently improve or deteriorate in response to psychological or environmental conditions, demonstrating that this disease should not be considered only organic. Several cases are described in which the onset of the disease, or a new outbreak of it, took place under special emotional conditions. One comparatively simple case of a sudden outbreak of dementia praecox in a young girl stresses the importance of examining the psychological factors in the etiology and course of psychoses. Psychosis considered from the psychological viewpoint is primarily a mental condition in which unconscious elements replace reality in the mind of the patient; therefore, this area is recommended to psychiatrists as a wide unexplored field for psychological research.

000049 Mental disease and the psyche. In: Jung, C., Collected Works of C. G. Jung, Vol. 3. Princeton University Press, 1972. 303 p. (p. 226-230).

The question of psychogenesis in mental diseases other than the neuroses, which are now generally considered psychic in origin, is discussed, and the psychic etiology of schizophrenia is affirmed. Mental processes are products of the psyche, and that same psyche produces delusions and hallucinations when it is out of balance. In turn, schizophrenia is considered as having a psychology of its own. But whereas the healthy person's ego is the subject of his experiences, the schizophrenic's ego is only one of the subjects. In schizophrenia, the normal subject has split into a plurality of autonomous complexes, at odds with one another and with reality, bringing about a disintegration of the personality. The simplest form of schizophrenia is paranoia, a simple doubling of the personality. The idea of being a persecuted victim gains the upper hand, becomes autonomous, and forms a second subject that at

times replaces the healthy ego. The healthy ego, unable to counter the affectivity of the second subject, becomes paralyzed. This is the beginning of schizophrenic apathy. An example shows how the individual, perhaps predisposed toward schizophrenia, becomes ill because of an emotional shock and is overwhelmed by the pathological idea of persecution at a given psychological moment. A study of the psychogenesis of schizophrenia explains why some milder cases can be cured by psychotherapy. Such cures are rare, however, as the nature of the disease, involving the destruction of the personality, rules against the possibility of psychic influence. The microscopic lesions of the brain often found in schizophrenia are regarded as secondary symptoms of degeneration.

000050 On the psychogenesis of schizophrenia. In: Jung, C., Collected Works of C. G. Jung, Vol. 3. Princeton University Press, 1972. 303 p. (p. 233-249).

In a discussion on the psychogenesis of schizophrenia an attempt is made to gain insight into the nature of its origin -- whether psychic or organic -- by comparing certain of its primary symptoms with those of hysteria and other neuroses. Tracing the development of expert opinion on the etiology of mental disorders, a swing from a belief in organic to psychic primary causes is evident. In the neuroses, as in schizophrenias, the normal associations are disturbed by the spontaneous intervention of complex contents, typical of an "abaissement" (A decline in conscious mental strength). Its effect on the personality and a variety of conditions that may produce it are outlined in detail. Most are evident in the neuroses and the psychoses. In the neuroses, however, the unity of the personality is potentially preserved, whereas in the schizophrenias it is almost always irreparably damaged. The dissociation of thought, present in both types of diseases, is more permanent and more severe in the schizophrenias. In its extreme form, an abaissement reduces the mental level to a point where the ego lacks the power to overcome the more powerful unconscious, whether this be in the form of dreams or hallucinations. No reliable evidence is reported for organic causes of schizophrenia; on the other hand, the psychogenic conditions are at best indicators of symptoms that favor the disease, and not proved causes of its origin. A thorough understanding of psychology and aberrant mentality by clinicians who practice psychotherapy is advocated.

000051 Recent thoughts on schizophrenia. In: Jung, C., Collected Works of C. G. Jung, Vol. 3. Princeton University Press, 1972. 303 p. (p. 250-255).

The need for extensive research in psychology and psychopathology, particularly in the area of schizophrenia, is emphasized in a paper prepared for a symposium on "the frontiers of knowledge and humanity's hopes for the future" in December 1956. A thorough description of the schizophrenic mental process dominates the paper, in which its complexity is highlighted by comparisons with the neuroses. The hypothesis is advanced that certain systemic toxins may be the cause of psychotic dissociation in schizophrenia. The profound understanding of psychology and the human mind, including the mystic, mythological and cultural ramifications, is deemed necessary, since the psychotic dreams are generally numinous and highly impressive, and their imagery often contains motifs analogous or identical to those of religion or mythology. The principal ailment is considered mental or psychic, in which the normal thought processes are weakened (abaissement), concentration and attention are relaxed, and the value of associations decreases and becomes relaxed. As a result, thoughts and fractions or flashes of ideas become manifest in the conscious (weakened) mind, interrupting thematic continuity, and producing illogical images. This process and the source of its images requires thorough study and understanding.

000052 Schizophrenia. In: Jung, C., Collected Works of C. G. Jung, Vol. 3. Princeton University Press, 1972. 303 p. (p. 256-271).

Comments on 50 years' experience in observing schizophrenia contain impressions from experimental investigations of the distintegration of ideas prevalent in the disease. Similarity to dreams and dream content is observed, in that ideas and images appear in random, abrupt, absurd, grotesque, and fragmentary confusion. Latent and potential psychoses among neurotics are estimated to run as high as 10:1. Obsessional impulses typical of neuroses are converted to auditory and visual hallucinations common to psychoses. In such cases, the psychosis still has not undermined the compensating activity of consciousness. Therapeutic intervention aims at restoring conscious awareness by changes in methods, by inducing concentration on reality, and by engaging the patient in activities that lure him away from the unconscious. This may be accomplished by having him draw or paint his visions, a process by which the terrifying images become commonplace to him, and the applied colors draw his feelings into the picture, causing the chaotic situation to be visualized and objectified and thus depriving it of its power to terrify. Rather than applying numerous therapeutic methods, the therapist's personal devotion to the patient and his problems are more effective. However, excessive personal involvement, unless adequately controlled, may produce an induced psychosis in the therapist. In a summary statement outlining the nature and mental mechanics of schizophrenia, it is admitted that no true etiology for the disease has so far been discovered. A shift of an older opinion now holds that an entire psychogenic complex dominates schizophrenia, and that the weakening of the ego personality, formerly thought to be causal and primary, is but a secondary manifestation of the feeling toned complex; furthermore, a psychogenic causation is considered more probable than toxic causes previously hypothesized as important.

000053 Letter to the chairman, symposium on chemical concepts of psychosis. In: Jung, C., Collected Works of C. G. Jung, Vol. 3. Princeton University Press, 1972. 303 p. (p. 272).

In a letter to the chairman of the Symposium on Chemical Concepts of Psychosis, held at the second International Congress for Psychiatry in Zurich, September 1957, the etiology of schizophrenia is considered to be both chemical and psychological. It is hypothesized that the emotions that are the initial cause of metabolic changes are accompanied by chemical processes that cause temporary or chronic mental disturbances.

04 FREUD AND PSYCHOANALYSIS

000054 Freud's theory of hysteria: A reply to Aschaffenburg. In: Jung, C., Collected Works of C. G. Jung, Vol. 4. Princeton University Press, 1970. 368 p. (p. 3-9).

Freud's theory of hysteria is defended against Aschaffenburg's criticism of the role assigned to sexuality in the formation of the psychoneuroses. This criticism is directed specifically at Freud's psychology of sexuality, the determinants of hysterical symptoms, and the early methods of his psychoanalysis. Aschaffenburg accepts the view, now generally supported, that hysteria is a psychogenic illness; that surely an essential component of the psyche is sexuality. Aschaffenburg's claims that there are entirely traumatic hysterias prove only that not all cases of hysteria have sexual roots. His point is not valid unless it is demonstrated by the psychoanalytic method. He asserts that this method is autosuggestion on the part of both doctor and patient, but again there is no proof. The association experiments, which uphold the results of psychoanalysis, have nothing to do with autosuggestion, and can be repeated by anyone. Aschaffenburg considers exploration of the patient for sexual ideas immoral in many cases. The decision on the use of sexual enlightenment in treatment can be made only on the basis of whether it harms or helps the individual, not on the basis of "higher" considerations. It is concluded that Freud's theory of hysteria has not yet been proved erroneous; that such proof could be supplied only by psychoanalysis; that psychoanalysis has not produced results other than Freud's; and that psychoanalysis itself has not been discredited.

000055 The Freudian theory of hysteria. In: Jung, C., Collected Works of C. G. Jung, Vol. 4. Princeton University Press, 1970. 368 p. (p. 10-24).

The development of Freud's theoretical formulations on hysteria is traced. They are defined as working hypotheses that agree with his experience, rather than a formal theory. By 1895 Freud and Breuer had concluded that psychogenic symptoms arise from feeling toned complexes of ideas that have a traumatic effect by conversion into abnormal somatic innervations (classical hysteria) or by displacement to a less significant complex (obsessional neurosis). The traumatic affect is not abreacted as in a normal person because it is incompatible with the consciousness and is repressed. The following year, the results of 13 analyses led Freud to announce that the etiology of hysteria is found in sexual traumas of early childhood. After extensive research into general sexual psychology and dream psychology, and refinement of his psychoanalytic techniques, his present views have been formulated: a. Certain perverse infantile sexual activities, which do not lead at first to symptoms of hysteria, are retained. b. At puberty, the fantasies tend in the direction of the infantile sexual activity, leading to complexes of ideas that are incompatible with the consciousness and are repressed. c. With the transfer of the libido to a love object, the struggle of the libido against the repression causes the outbreak of actual illness. It is not known whether Freud's schema can be applied to all forms of hysteria, but his findings are true of a large number of cases. Further investigation is recommended. 3 references.

000056 The analysis of dreams. In: Jung, C., Collected Works of C. G. Jung, Vol. 4. Princeton University Press, 1970. 368 p. (p. 25-34).

In a discussion of Freud's work on the analysis of dreams, the dream is defined as a product of psychic activity susceptible to analysis. It is far from meaningless or a result of somatic sensation. Freud calls the confused images typical of dreams the manifest content; behind this is the essential latent content. In analyzing a dream, he asks why this particular person dreams this particular thing, since the dream is individual an in agreement with the psychological disposition of the subject. Gretchen's song in "Faust," telling of a faithful king, clearly reflects her concern with Faust's fidelity. Freud says every dream represents the fulfillment of a repressed wish. In Gretchen's song, the pain of dwelling on the real characters -- herself and Faust -- is too strong to be openly admitted. Similarly, wishes that form the dream thought are desires repressed because of their painful character. The mechanism that prevents the repressed thought from showing itself clearly is called the censor. Direct questioning is not useful in getting beyond the manifest content. A full association exercise may be used, or the subject may be questioned about associations attaching to the striking portions of the dream. It is difficult to get the subject to associate freely without arousing resistances. The method of overcoming resistance gradually, by finding small associations, one at a time, is illustrated by analyzing a young bachelor's dream of a dinner in company with the Pope and several attractive young ladies, in which the dreamer was constantly obliged to leave the party because of a need to urinate. The analyst asked about the dinner, the seating arrangements, the dream characters' features, etc. and the subject associated to each of these until analysis of more major elements could proceed. Study of the psychoanalytic method is recommended not only for psychiatrists and neurologists but also for psychologists.

000057 A contribution to the psychology of rumour. In: Jung, C., Collected Works of C. G. Jung, Vol. 4. Princeton University Press, 1970. 368 p. (p. 35-47).

The case of a 13-year-old girl who had been expelled from school for starting an ugly rumor about her male teacher sheds light on the psychology of rumor and shows how rumor figured in the interpretation of a dream. The youngster had simply reported a dream to her classmates. In the dream she and a sister changed into bathing suits in the presence of boys, because of lack of room; then went swimming with their teacher; rode on a steamer; took part in a wedding; went on a journey "like a honeymoon"; spent the night in a barn, again for lack of room; and the dream ended with the teacher's becoming the godfather of a woman's child. The versions of the classmates, as they identified with S in her repressed desire for sexual relations with the teacher, function as interpretations of the dream. Some are more explicit than others. Some of the versions have S riding on the teacher's back while swimming, rather than riding on a steamer; others introduce two unknown fat men (the teacher was plump) for the swim. Many other versions, reported by S's classmates who had heard her tell it, refer to "indecent" parts of the dream that the children refused to describe. S had been troublesome to the teacher, of whom she had originally been fond. After the teacher had given her a bad report, S's dream operated first as an expression of her repressed wish for sexual union with him, compensating for the hate consciously felt; and then, in the retelling, as a means of getting back at him.

000058 On the significance of number dreams. In: Jung, C., Collected Works of C. G. Jung, Vol. 4. Princeton University Press, 1970. 368 p. (p. 48-55).

Examples show that number dreams reveal the unconscious roots of number symbolism, rather than conscious speculations on the symbolic relations between numbers. One example is that of a middle-aged man engaged in an extramarital love affair, whose dream involved a large number, analyzed to represent the total of important dates and ages for his family. Severe conflicts were apparent due to the patient's attachment to his family and love for his mistress. Another dream involving a number showed the patient's repressed tendency to reckon the costs of his affair. In his waking life the patient gave free rein to number fantasies, for instance celebrating, when he was 35, their hundredth birthday with his 65-year-old mother. He played with the numbers appearing in his dreams, and by association, related them to expressions of envy and wish fulfillment. Another example is given by the dream of the patient's wife. Her entire dream was: Luke 137, alluding, in

various chapter/verse combinations, to passages from that book. The number has a dual representation, expressing how many children she would have had if all (including miscarriages) were living, and a repressed fantasy desiring the death of her husband. Although the patient herself was quite unfamiliar with the Bible, the content of the material found in Luke 1:37, in Luke 13:7, and in Luke 7:13, can be interpreted as expressing wishes for more children, rejection of her husband, resentment of his impotence, and the wish for him to be cured of his impotence.

000059 Morton Prince, "The mechanism and interpretation of dreams": a critical review. In: Jung, C., Collected Works of C. G. Jung, Vol. 4. Princeton University Press, 1970. 368 p. (p. 56-73).

Morton Prince's article on an analysis of six dreams of a patient is criticized as being unscientific, although Prince is commended for his interest in the controversial subject of dream analysis. Prince agrees with Freud that dreams have a meaning, that the meaning is hidden in symbols, and that memory material is needed to find the meaning. He disagrees, however, with Freud's view that every dream represents a wish fulfillment, finding that some dreams represent fear or anxiety. These dreams clearly illustrate transference to the analyst on the part of the patient, a middle aged woman suffering from hysterial dissociation, but Prince does not interpret them that way. Dream 1 has not been sufficiently analyzed, as Prince ignores the significance of a man in a dressing gown, bringing firewood. Dream 2, which Prince interprets as the patient's fear that she will become ill again, can be seen as the desire to fall ill again to retain the analyst's attention. Prince sees the third dream, in which the doctor pounds the patient with a stone to hammer it into her head that he cannot be bothered with her, as nonfulfillment of her wish for his attention, but it actually represents an erotic wish. The fourth dream has been censored by Prince, unscientifically deleting "intimacy." In the fifth dream, which Prince has made no attempt to analyze, offering instead a general impression, the patient is forced to walk through cats without making a sound. Although S had a cat phobia, the dream cats represent love, and the aphonia that persisted after the dream was a symptom with which to interest the analyst. Prince does not see any repressed wish or conflict in the sixth dream, but it concerns vengeful tortures that the patient probably desires for the analyst who is abandoning her. These dreams are insufficiently analyzed or misinterpreted because some elements are ignored and the meaning is too often taken literally instead of symbolically. It is concluded that Prince has no basis for a serious criticism of Freud's dream theory when his own methods are so lacking in scientific thoroughness. 1 reference.

000060 On the criticism of psychoanalysis. In: Jung, C., Collected Works of C. G. Jung, Vol. 4. Princeton University Press, 1970. 368 p. (p.74-77).

A discussion of criticism of psychoanalysis notes that the strongest antagonism comes from physicians and psychologists. Most laymen understand the truths of psychoanalysis and realize that a psychological proof must be different from a physical one. The violent resistance of professionals usually arises from scientific prejudices based on a different way of thinking. These critics attack the psychoanalytic method as if it rested on a priori principles, whereas it is actually purely empirical. Occasionally, however, the critic's scientific attitude is warped by his personal feeling. A sarcastic review by Kurt Mendel, presented in entirety, expresses repugnance at the latest work on anal eroticism, the sexuality of children, and the exposure of the vulgar aspects of sex in general. Mendel believes that Freudian teaching has opened up many new and valuable perspectives, but finds it filled with exaggeration and fantasy and questions the concept of the universality of sexual feelings. It is felt that such criticism has scientific value and deserves reading. 2 references.

000061 Concerning psychoanalysis. In: Jung, C., Collected Works of C. G. Jung, Vol. 4. Princeton University Press, 1970. 368 p. (p. 78-81).

A letter to an editor defends psychoanalysis against some of the charges brought against it. No reply is offered to critics who say the theory is wrong because they think the method is morally dangerous, or to those who claim that the facts unearthed by Freudians do not exist, as no one can assert a priori that certain facts do not exist. The sexual indelicacies that appear in psychoanalytic literature are not to be blamed on psychoanalysis itself. Medical work merely brings the fantasies to light; blame for their existence lies with our sexual morality. Psychoanalytic education covers not only sex, but every facet of life, and its goal is not to deliver man to his passions but to help him attain self-control. The concept of libido is taken in a general sense, like the instinct of preservation of the species; it does not mean "localized sexual excitation." No one should blame psychoanalysis itself because there are some clumsy and irresponsible people who misuse it for their own purposes. 1 reference.

000062 The theory of psychoanalysis. Foreword. In: Jung, C., Collected Works of C. G. Jung, Vol. 4. Princeton University Press, 1970. 368 p. (p. 83-87).

A series of lectures on the theory of psychoanalysis is introduced in an attempt to outline the prevailing attitude to the guiding principles evolved by Freud from long experience. In spite of heavy and often premature criticism, psychoanalysis has continued to flourish in Europe and America. As a scientific discipline, psychoanalysis needs to take stock of itself; this attitude has been wrongly interpreted as a "split" in the psychoanalytic movement. Although present experience does not approach Freud's extraordinary experience and insight, some more modern formulations are felt to express the observed facts better than Freud's version. This moderate criticism is intended to promote continued growth of the psychoanalytic movement. 1 reference.

000063 The theory of psychoanalysis. 1. A review of the early hypotheses. In: Jung, C., Collected Works of C. G. Jung, Vol. 4. Princeton University Press, 1970. 368 p. (p. 88-101).

A review of the early psychoanalytic hypotheses shows how some of these concepts have changed over the years. The trauma theory developed by Breuer and Freud held that neuroses were derived from a trauma in early childhood. Normally the excitation was abreacted, but was retained in hysteria. The task of therapy was to release the accumulated excitation. This "cathartic" method was bound up closely with the symptoms, in contrast to psychoanalytic techniques in use today. The concept of repression, the mechanism by which conscious content is displaced into the unconscious, is based on observation of the neurotic capacity for forgetting significant events. The concept of repression is somewhat in contradiction to the trauma theory, as it suggests an etiological theory of environment, while the trauma concept is a theory of predisposition. Pursuit of the solution to this riddle led to the theory that the childhood trauma was sexual. Freud abandoned the idea that all childhood sexual traumas had actually occurred, and it is now assumed that many of these traumas

are childhood fantasies. The sexual element in a trauma is, according to Freud, chiefly responsible for its pathological effect. Precocious manifestations of sexual fantasy and their traumatic effect now seemed to be the source of the neurosis, an opinion that has met opposition and indignation. The decision as to what is the truth must be left to observation and research. 3 references.

000064 The theory of psychoanalysis. 2. The theory of infantile sexuality. In: Jung, C., Collected Works of C. G. Jung, Vol. 4. Princeton University Press, 1970. 368 p. (p. 102-110).

Freud's theory of infantile sexuality is discussed, and the more modern divergence from some of these views is noted. The discovery of precocious sexual fantasies led Freud to assume the existence of a richly developed infantile sexuality. A biological conception of sexuality includes such phenomena as pregnancy, birth, natural selection, and a series of psychological and physiological functions. Sexuality may be identified with the instinct for preservation of the species, in some contrast to the instinct for self-preservation. Some of Freud's conclusions are considered untenable. Freud is inclined to see even in the infant's sucking at the mother's breast a kind of sexual act. This assumes that sexuality -- preservation of the species -- exists apart from the nutritive function -- self-preservation -- as in adults, but it is not possible to separate the two modes of the life instinct at this stage. Both intrauterine and extrauterine periods of infancy belong to an asexual stage of nutrition and growth. Acts such as sucking the fingers, while evidently pleasurable, belong more to the sphere of nutrition. These acts can lead into distinctly sexual acts, as the child derives pleasure from his own body. Freud's belief that the child's sexuality, centered on his own body, is perverse because of analogies with subsequent perversions. He then hypothesized that sexuality is divided into a plurality of several drives, giving rise to the concept of "erogenous zones" such as mouth, skin, anus, etc. The later "monomorphic" sexuality is thus conceived as consisting of several components. Perversions exist at the expense of normal sexuality; increased application of one form of sexuality follows a decrease in the application of another form. The example of a young man who was homosexual in his teens and heterosexual in his twenties, returning to homosexuality after being jilted, illustrates the mobility of the sexual components. The theory thus far does not explain how such transformations come about. Freud's conception of components was modified, to be replaced by the libido conception of energy.

000065 The theory of psychoanalysis. 3. The concept of libido. In: Jung, C., Collected Works of C. G. Jung, Vol. 4. Princeton University Press, 1970. 368 p. (p. 111-128).

An extensive discussion of the concept of libido elucidates Freud's accepted definition (a basic sexual need -- hunger -- desire) and formulates a total libido theory to include modern research and concepts. Regarded as a dynamic unity, the libido is discussed in context of the energic theory, whereby it is compared with the laws of energy conservation. The unconscious fantasy systems are held to be objects of the libido only in neuroses. Conservation of the libido involves the nature of infantile libido and the theory that abnormalities and perversions exist in childhood in latent form. Manifestations and distinctions of the libido in three phases of life -- presexual, prepubertal and mature -- are briefly contrasted. Thoughts on sexual terminology point out the difficulty of applying them to prepubertal children, in whom intensity of the libido is not any less than in adults, though the localization of it may be different. Discussion of the libido problem in dementia praecox brings out how the patient's lack of adaptation to reality is compensated by a progressive increase in the creation of fantasies. A genetic conception perceives libido as a type of psychic energy, that manifests itself in the life process and is subjectively perceived as conation and desire. The infantile perversions as a libidinal concept round out the theory on infantile sexuality which, in turn, is important to the theory of neuroses. The nutritive function of the libido (sucking) is one of the child's transitional phases, which develops into normal sexuality at maturity. 2 references.

000066 The theory of psychoanalysis. 4. Neurosis and aetiological factors in childhood. In: Jung, C., Collected Works of C. G. Jung, Vol. 4. Princeton University Press, 1970. 368 p. (p. 129-138).

To clarify those events of childhood that lay the foundation for later neuroses, the roles of sexual predisposition, the parental complex, and general parental influences are discussed. The sexual predisposition toward neurosis is conceived as a retardation in the freeing of the libido from activities of the presexual stage. Maturity points up the retardation, leading to dissociation of the personality. The inadequacy of the trauma theory is illustrated by the case of a patient who reacted hysterically to bolting horses. A peculiar early fantasy system, rather than traumatic childhood events, is responsible for uncontrolled affect in the patient's later life. This involvement of libido in fantasy activity, rather than in real life, demonstrates partial introversion. The parental complex, in which emotions still cling to the parents' effigies, contributes to this retardation of the libido. The imitativeness of primitives and children, often to the point of inner identification with parents, explains the strength of parental influences. Many neurotics, spoiled as children and expecting the same tenderness from the outside world that they received from their families, realize the difference between the past and the present, but are unable to adapt because of the lag of emotions behind intellect. 1 reference.

000067 The theory of psychoanalysis. 5. The fantasies of the unconscious. In: Jung, C., Collected Works of C. G. Jung, Vol. 4. Princeton University Press, 1970. 368 p. (p. 139-150).

The concept of the unconscious, the functions of the dream, dream analysis, and the association experiment in reaching the unconscious are discussed. The unconscious, with its infantile fantasies, is considered the key to the etiology of neurosis. Remarkable parallels are evident between the fantasy products of the unconscious and ideas from mythology, though the patient may be uninformed on mythology. The dream is an effect of the unconscious, expressed in terms of conscious symbolism. Dream analysis seeks associations to images in the dream, showing their origin in the recent past. Dream material consists of elucidated memories of these experiences combined with meaningful associations and connections. The association experiment is a basically simple test by which the influence of the unconscious may be explored and certain complex indicators identified. These, in turn, point to potential disturbances. When such phenomena are cumulative, they constitute a neurosis, the effect of an unconscious constellation.

000068 The theory of psychoanalysis. 6. The Oedipus complex. In: Jung, C., Collected Works of C. G. Jung, Vol.4. Princeton University Press, 1970. 368 p. (p. 151-156).

The most frequently occurring childhood fantasy, the Oedipus complex, is described and its development is explained. The complex, which can be viewed simply as the demand for parental love, can have a very intense affect in chil-

dren, though less sexual than an adult's emotion. Since the child's first love is directed toward the mother, a girl may also have an Oedipus complex. The complex may involve the child's unconscious wish to kill the father and have the mother to himself. The element of eroticism gains strength with the years, so that the complex assumes the classic form in maturity. If the child cannot free himself from his infantile milieu in the postpubertal period, the complex will precipitate a conflict, with possible neurotic disturbances. The now sexually developed libido shapes into the Oedipal "mold," raising fantasies that show the existence of the complex, which until now has been unconscious. Intense resistances to these "immoral" impulses may manifest themselves either in direct violent resistance against the father and affection toward the mother, or by compensation in marked submissiveness to the father and antagonism toward the mother. Sometimes these attitudes alternate. Normally the libido moves outside the family for objects, aided by religion, which leads it away from the infantile objects toward symbolic representations of the past. According to Freud, the Oedipus complex is pushed into the unconscious by a moral repression called the "incest barrier."

000069 The theory of psychoanalysis. 7. The aetiology of neurosis. In: Jung, C., Collected Works of C. G. Jung, Vol. 4. Princeton University Press, 1970. 368 p. (p. 157-180).

A discussion of the development of neurosis investigates the etiological significance of unconscious determination, conflicts of the present moment, regression of the libido, and the relative weighting of traumatic events and innate characteristics. Unconscious determination is illustrated by the case of the young woman with a hysterical reaction to bolting horses. Freud's theory of infantile sexuality is considered an inadequate explanation of adult neuroses. It is refuted in the doctrine of the "period of sexual latency." This period is really the beginning of sexuality, and everything that precedes it is considered a preliminary stage with no real sexual character. There is little etiological significance assigned to infantile development; the cause of the pathogenic conflict is found more often in the present. Childhood experiences have a significance for neurosis only when they are made significant by a regression of libido, in which the reminiscences determine the form while the present supplies the dynamic element. This reversion to the infantile level is illustrated in the case of two sisters who reacted differently to conflicts presented by approaching marriage. It is concluded that the sole cause of neurosis is neither a traumatic event nor a predisposition, but that both function to produce the condition. Regressive fantasies serve not only as a neurotic substitute for action, but for both normal and neurotic persons as groping attempts to find new ways of adapting to reality.

000070 The theory of psychoanalysis. 8. Therapeutic principles of psychoanalysis. In: Jung, C., Collected Works of C. G. Jung, Vol. 4. Princeton University Press, 1970. 368 p. (p. 181-204).

Some therapeutic techniques are discussed, with emphasis on the dangers and advantages of the use of transference as an instrument in treating neurosis. The analyst's entry into the patient's fantasies serves to bring up these fantasies from the unconscious, and to free the attached libido. This often results in the patient's attaching to the analyst fantasies formerly attached to parent images. Although this transference can be a bridge to reality, the hazard is that it can become too comfortable for the patient. A parallel is drawn between psychoanalysis and religious confession, but the guiding role is rejected for the analyst, as his goal is to educate his patients to become independent. Analysis of the transference must then take place to free the libido completely from fantasy and to overcome the patient's infantile equating of love with demands for attention. The analyst must have gone through psychoanalysis himself, so that his own infantile demands do not identify with those of the patient. The technique of analyzing the transference is the same as in the first stage of the analysis, with dreams now utilized not only to understand the involvement of libido in fantasy, but as a guide to the use of the freed libido. Dreams may be considered subliminal combinations of future events; these future tendencies are elaborated, freeing the patient from the semi-infantile transference and ending treatment. A brief discussion of future uses of psychoanalysis predicts that psychoanalysis will never be polyclinical, and refers to parallels found between the symbols of individual modern people and those found in the history of the human race.

000071 The theory of psychoanalysis. 9. A case of neurosis in a child. In: Jung, C., Collected Works of C. G. Jung, Vol. 4. Princeton University Press, 1970. 368 p. (p. 204-226).

An analysis of an 11-year-old girl is presented as an example of the actual process of psychoanalytic treatment, and a demonstration of regressed libido. The child had a clinical history of nausea and headache that kept her from school, and had also been blackmailed by a little boy who had heard her call her teacher a name. In 10 interviews, the pleasures of staying home from school, the girl's liking for the teacher, and her unhappiness at losing the teacher's esteem were brought out. Also discovered were her concerns with the mysteries of pregnancy and childbirth, fear of her father, experiences with masturbation, and the desire to have a baby herself. An account is given of how the material was drawn from the child, how her dreams were used both in eliciting material and in aiding her self-understanding, and of how the analyst explained the material and its interpretation to the child. In addition, there are extensive comments on the symbolism found in the child's dreams and on philosophical aspects of the analysis that were never mentioned to the patient. Parallels are drawn between mythology and the fantasies of the modern individual. It is suggested that much of this child's difficulty could have been prevented by receiving clear sexual information at home.

000072 General aspects of psychoanalysis. In: Jung, C., Collected Works of C. G. Jung, Vol. 4. Princeton University Press, 1970. 368 p. (p. 229-242).

A discussion of the principles of psychoanalysis suggests that it is now a science, which could be called analytical psychology, that has grown from psychoanalytic techniques. Working through the unconscious rather than the conscious, psychoanalysis attempts to overcome neurotic disorders by relying on clues furnished by the patient. The analysis starts with an examination of the conscious content supplied by the anamnesis. The association experiment is applied in studying the patient's current conscious activity. Examples from the interview of such an experiment are included. The analysis of dreams is considered a valuable instrument of psychoanalysis, but in the early stages of treatment most patients cannot recall enough detail for complete, successful analysis. Patients who do not dream, or who cannot recall their dreams, are usually holding back conscious material. Dream images are interpreted both sexually and as symbols of other areas, and an overtly sexual dream may have other connotations. Freud's concept of the dream as a disguise for repressed wishes is discarded in favor of the idea that the dream is a subliminal picture of the actual psychological situation of the individual in his waking state. The volitional content of the dream, which Freud calls

the repressed wish, is considered essentially a means of expression. Practical limits to the analyst on his attitude toward the patient and general philosophical aspects of psychoanalysis are included.

000073 Psychoanalysis and neurosis. In: Jung, C., Collected Works of C. G. Jung, Vol. 4. Princeton University Press, 1970. 368 p. (p. 243-251).

Freud's theory of neurosis is reviewed, some aspects of it are questioned, and an energic concept is substituted for the purely sexual point of view. Freud's etiological progress from the early childhood sexual trauma to infantile sexual activity has led to his latest view that the neurotic is fixated to a certain early period and that the main task of treatment is to resolve this infantile fixation. This point of view seems doubtful, however, since in many cases there is no sign of neurosis until the moment of breakdown. It appears, rather, that the neurotic has a congenital sensitiveness causing early resistance to adaptation and that the outbreak of neurosis occurs when a new psychological adjustment is required. When the libido meets an obstacle that seems insurmountable and the individual abandons the task of overcoming it, the stored up libido regresses to an abnormal adaptation. It is still considered important to investigate the infantile sexual fantasies, but they are regarded as symptoms, not causes. The treatment goal is to free the libido from them and to bring it under control of the will.

000074 Some crucial points in psychoanalysis: A correspondence between Dr. Jung and Dr. Loy. In: Jung, C., Collected Works of C. G. Jung, Vol. 4. Princeton University Press, 1970. 368 p. (p. 252-289).

Questions arising during the analysis of Dr. Loy, undertaken to assist Loy in his practice of psychoanalysis, are discussed in correspondence. The topics include the reasons for giving up the cathartic method and suggestion therapy through hypnosis, the relation of these methods to the phenomenon of transference, and ethical questions comparing the conflicts of researcher and physician when one man is both. Psychoanalysis is regarded as a more scientific treatment, but in practice, the method the physician feels will work best with the patient, whether it be hypnosis or full analysis, is the preferred modality. Questions from Loy concerning the role of the psychoanalyst in society, suggesting that he is an educator, are postponed until "a later stage in the analysis," and more study of the literature is recommended. Dr. Loy brings up possible differences in aim for the patient, the patient's need to understand the psychoanalytic method, and the limit of responsibility of the analyst for the patient's future. In commenting on these points, the nature and function of transference are explained, criticizing any interference on the analyst's part with the patient's progress. The positive value of transference is reasserted, relating it to his conception of "biological duties," and the moral question of helping patients to adapt to both their own internal demands and the external requirements of society is discussed.

000075 Prefaces to "Collected papers on analytical psychology." In: Jung, C., Collected Works of C. G. Jung, Vol. 4. Princeton University Press, 1970. 368 p. (p. 290-297).

Prefaces to the first and second editions of "Collected Papers on Analytical Psychology" concentrate on the attitudinal differences between the Viennese and the Zurich schools of psychoanalytic thought. The Viennese school takes an exclusively sexualistic stand and interprets the psychological symbol semiotically, as a sign of primitive psychosexual processes. Its method is analytical and causal. The Zurich point of view is symbolistic, adding a positive, prospective value to the symbol. Its methods are synthetic and prospective. Freud's principle of hedonism and Adler's theory of the power principle are not necessarily unfounded, as both principles operate in everyone, but they are considered incomplete. Finality, in addition to causality, is presented as a psychological principle, and it is pointed out that life will not allow uncontrolled expression of either childish pleasure seeking or childish power seeking. Freud's (Vienna) causality is mechanistic; Jung's (Zurich) finality is teleological and functional. Both views are necessary to understanding psychological functioning, and they are not antagonistic if regarded as regulative principles of thought rather than constituent principles of the process of nature itself. 2 references.

000076 The significance of the father in the destiny of the individual. In: Jung, C., Collected Works of C. G. Jung, Vol. 4. Princeton University Press, 1970. 368 p. (p. 301-323).

Four case histories illustrate the influence of the "imago" of the father on the lives of the children. As the father's personality is overwhelming in each of these cases, it is postulated that the power derives not from the individual human being, but from the representation in him of a preexistent instinctual model or pattern of behavior, an archetype. This is the imago charged with dynamism that cannot be attributed to an individual human being. The first case, a woman who married a man much like her father and on being widowed remained so for years, provides an example of living out a copy of one's youth. The second case is a man whose life repeats his masochistic homosexual relationship with his father. The third presents a woman who sacrifices all present happiness on the altar of being dutiful to a now dead father. The last case concerns an 8-year-old boy who used bed wetting to separation mother from father. These cases show that the parental influence, even though repressed into the unconscious, directs the maturing mind. The role of the father imago is an ambiguous one, characteristic of the archetype, whose potentialities exceed human capacity in the unconscious. 4 references.

000077 Introduction to Kranefeldt's "secret ways of the mind." In: Jung, C., Collected Works of C. G. Jung, Vol. 4. Princeton University Press, 1970. 368 p. (p. 324-332).

The historical, social, and philosophical ramifications of psychoanalysis are discussed in an introduction to Kranefeldt's work on psychology. Positive aspects of the development of psychoanalysis include a worldwide interest in psychology, seen in medicine and criminal law, and one negative effect is the decline in religion. Adler's "individual psychology," which has developed into a system of social education, has grown away from Freud's psychoanalysis. Jung's point of view is pluralistic, in contrast to their monistic psychologies. A more positive value assigned to the unconscious leads to a different interpretation of dreams and fantasies, which are seen as creative seeds of the future. The unconscious is the basis of vitality and must be united with the conscious, but Freud's approach, which does not emphasize the unconscious, is not mistaken in cases where consciousness is not firmly established, as in young people. Different stages of psychological development, the concept of extraversion and introversion, and differentiated functions demonstrate the complexity of the psyche.

000078 Freud and Jung: Contrasts. In: Jung, C., Collected Works of C. G. Jung, Vol. 4. Princeton University Press, 1970. 368 p. (p. 333-340).

The differences between Jung's views and those of Freud are attributed to differences in their basic assumptions. Jung believes that Freud erred in turning his back on philosophy, whereas Jung takes a positive view of religion, as well as biology and natural science, and is able to incorporate other views within his own. Jung subsumes all forces and drives under the concept of energy, in contrast to Freud's reluctance to admit to any other psychic drive besides sexuality. Freud's preoccupation with biological events is contrasted to Jung's consideration of the life of the spirit, for which he has been accused of mysticism. Freud's superego can be seen, as a matter of fact, as Jehovah dressed in psychological terms. Since the history of man includes the developing of religious functions, the study of religion belongs in the study of man's psyche; for thousands of years of rites of initiation have been teaching a rebirth from the spirit.

05 SYMBOLS OF TRANSFORMATION

000079 Symbols of transformation. Part I. Introduction. In: Jung, C., Collected Works of C. G. Jung, Vol. 5. 2nd ed., Princeton University Press, 1967. 557 p. (p. 3-6).

Freud's exposition of the incest fantasy, which he derived from the Oedipus legend, is proposed as an example of classical legends which express basic psychological concepts, and which can be more fully understood and appreciated through the exploration of these concepts. The works of Riklin, Rank, Abraham, Maeder, Jones, Silberer, and Pfister are mentioned as contributing clues in historical research that furnish insights into the unconscious of modern man. As the study of the activity of the unconscious in modern man can expand the understanding of the psychology of historical problems and symbolism, so the reverse procedure, a comparative study of historical material, would shed light on individual psychological problems of today. It is in this perspective of gaining new insight into the foundations of psychology that the study of historical material is proposed.

000080 Two kinds of thinking. In: Jung, C., Collected Works of C. G. Jung, Vol. 5. 2nd ed., Princeton University Press, 1967. 557 p. (p. 7-33).

The concept of ontogenetic recapitulation of phylogenetic psychology is explained by showing the relation between man's unconscious, or nondirected thought, and mythology or legend. Two types of human thought are described: a directed thinking, of which the highest form is science and which is based on speech; and a nonverbal, undirected, associative thinking, commonly called dreaming. These two modes of thought deal with two activities of man: adapting to outer reality, and reflecting on subjective concerns. Undirected thought is seen as characteristic of ancient cultures, of primitive man, and of children. The parallels that are drawn between the mythological thinking of the ancients and that of children and primitives, or that found in dreams, lead to the supposition that there is a correspondence between ontogenesis, or individual development, and phylogenesis, or the racial development of man, in psychology. An examination of certain fairy tales and myths illustrates the concept that what is in modern man an unexpressed fantasy was once an accepted custom or belief: the source of fantasy in the individual is described as an attempt at compensation, exemplified by the adolescent who dreams of belonging to wealthy, important parents, a fantasy found in myths and legends such as Romulus and Remus, or in the story of Moses. Through the fantasies, directed thinking comes into contact with the product of the unconscious, although not with its motivation. For example in Anatole France's story, Abbe Oegger's unconscious motivation to become a "judas" led to his study of the Judas legend and formulation of the concept of a merciful God, which motivated him to leave the Catholic Church. It is concluded that fantasies experienced in adult life reflect not only individual conflicts, but archaic patterns as well, and that any interpretation of fantasy should be based upon both aspects of the fantasy mechanism. 33 references.

000081 The Miller fantasies: anamnesis. In: Jung, C., Collected Works of C. G. Jung, Vol. 5. 2nd ed., Princeton University Press, 1967. 557 p. (p. 34-38).

Flournoy's publication of the recorded fantasies of a Miss Miller illustrates the autosuggestibility and suggestive influence of this young woman. Of the complicated fantasy system she presents, a few detailed examples illustrate how her fantasies expressed her own immediate conflicts. These conflicts, plus the psychic energy provided by her detachment from reality, are considered the source of her suggestibility and her tendency to experience certain impressions with unusual intensity. 2 references.

000082 The hymn of creation. In: Jung, C., Collected Works of C. G. Jung, Vol. 5. 2nd ed., Princeton University Press, 1967. 557 p. (p. 39-78).

An analysis of the unconscious conflict which produced Miss Miller's dream poem, "The Hymn of Creation", and an inquiry into the purpose this dream served for her leads to an investigation of the place of God and religion in man's psychic adaptation. The "Hymn of Creation", written down by Miss Miller after waking, represents a projection of her repressed conflicts over her erotic attraction to a sailor she had just met, while her own explanation of the content of her dream shows her identification with Job in protesting innocence and attributing all "evil" to outside sources. The role of God as a projected archetype of the father and the repository of man's problems is discussed relative to religion's requirements for confession of sins; the latter activity is seen as keeping conflicts conscious -- a requirement of psychotherapy. Love as a characteristic of God, and the difficulties of distinguishing human from spiritual love, are analyzed. The priest as a representative of the archetype is suggested. Christianity as an inevitable reaction to barbarism, and its functioning for moral subjugation of the baser instincts by alienation from reality and encouragement of abstraction, is contrasted with the Mithraic nature worship. The role of Christianity in freeing man's energy for civilization is reviewed, with the later, scientific attitude toward nature (which Christianity had made possible by its creed of the sovereignty of the idea) and the resultant questioning of the realities of Christian subjective concepts, such as "soul", are analyzed. 40 references.

000083 The song of the moth. In: Jung, C., Collected Works of C. G. Jung, Vol. 5. 2nd ed., Princeton University Press, 1967. 557 p. (p. 79-117).

The symbolism underlying Miss Miller's poem "The Song of the Moth" is explored in detail, and an attempt is made to describe Miss Miller's psychological state on the basis of this symbolism and her explanations of the poem's content. Like the "Hymn of Creation", this is a dream poem, and the same complex is being worked out. As Miss Miller herself interprets the longing of the moth for the sun as representing the longing of man for God, so research on the symbolism of the sun repeats this theme. The poem is seen to serve the psychological purpose of transforming her desire for the man, her love objective (a singer), into a desire for God. Psychic energy (the

libido) creates the God image using archetypal patterns, leading to the psychic force itself being worshiped as divine; this enables man to feel divinity within himself, giving him an increased feeling of importance and power. Numerous texts and references support the symbolism of sun, light and fire as representations of the Divine. These recurrent concepts are considered to exemplify an archetype -- not an inherited idea, but a disposition of man to produce similar ideas. By tracing the historical precedents of the symbols "moth" and "sun", it is the sun hero for whom Miss Miller's soul moth burns. Miss Miller's death fantasies are seen as representative of the ambivalence of the worshiper toward his passion, whose power is both beneficent and destructive. 32 references.

000084 Symbols of transformation. Part II. Introduction. In: Jung, C., Collected Works of C. G. Jung, Vol. 5. 2nd ed., Princeton University Press, 1967. 557 p. (p. 121-131).

Classic references of the symbolism referred to in the dream poem "The Song of the Moth" and the symbolism of the phallus in legends are discussed in relation to the psychological concept of libido. References to the sun as an image of God, the sun representing the creative power of the soul (libido) are quoted. The rationality of sun worship, considering man's physical dependence on the sun, is pointed out. Quotations from the Shvetashvatara Upanishad and the Kasha Upanishad present phallic symbols such as Tom Thumbs and dwarfs as well as the sun as divinities, similar in potency to the key presented Faust by Mephistopheles. All of these symbols are seen as representing the power of the libido, the phallus particularly representing creative divinity. These examples serve to illustrate that the "libido" introduced by Freud is not exclusively sexual, although sexuality is one component of its force. Cicero's definition of libido as "unbridled desire" in contrast to "will" and St. Augustine's broad definition of libido are quoted to support a wider use of the term. 19 references.

000085 The concept of libido. In: Jung, C., Collected Works of C. G. Jung, Vol. 5. 2nd ed., Princeton University Press, 1967. 557 p. (p. 132-141).

Freud's original definition of libido is discussed, and the reasons for modification of the definition are presented. Although Freud considered at one time equating libido with interest in general, he ultimately returned to his original definition of libido as sexual energy which overflows into the other instincts, and felt that paranoia could be explained by a loss of libidinal interest. There is more lacking in the schizophrenic than mere erotic interest -- what is lost is the whole relation to reality, and consequently the libido is identified with what is termed psychic energy, appetite in its natural state. Differentiation in the human psyche of elemental needs and drives deriving from the reproductive instinct has created complex psychic functions which are now independent of sexuality. This broader, energic conception of libido is considered to explain the observed fact that one instinct can be depotentiated in favor of another; disturbances found in the sexual sphere, in neurosis, are thus secondary, not primary phenomena. The loss of reality in schizophrenia, then, is not caused by an uncontrolled libido, but stems from the investment of psychic energy in archaic fantasy. Reality in neurosis is seen as falsified rather than lost, and the fantasy is of individual rather than archaic origin. A value to man of this investment off psychic energy into analogy making is felt to exist in the general development of the human mind from prehistory to the present. 14 references.

000086 The transformation of libido. In: Jung, C., Collected Works of C. G. Jung, Vol. 5. 2nd ed., Princeton University Press, 1967. 557 p. (p. 142-170).

The patterns of regressive reactivation of the presexual stage in a schizophrenic patient are examined and compared with the transformation of libido associated with fire making and rhythmic movement in earlier stages of human development. The case history demonstrates a regression to early rhythmic movements, such as are found in the rhythmic sucking of infants when libido is still primarily invested in the nutritional zone. With the transformation of libido in the developing child, this model of rhythmic movement is transferred to the zones of other functions, with sexuality as its ultimate goal. The period from birth to the first clearly sexual actions, however, is labeled as the "presexual stage." Literature and legend provide instances of the relation between the rhythmic, boring activity seen in the patient's regression and fire making. Examples from different periods of history and different peoples are provided to support the existence of a widespread similarity between fire making rituals and sexuality. As sexuality is the psychic component with the strongest affective tone, regressions as well as primitive rituals will show analogies to it while they are actually derived from a presexual libidinal stage. The transformation of libido is seen as presexual as well. While fear is undoubtedly involved, the suppression of libido is based on external and internal factors rather than on the incest taboo proposed by Freud. The strength for such suppression comes from primordial images, archetypes with characteristically numinous effects. Indian literature on fire making; the legends of fire coming from the mouth; references to fire from the mouth in the Bible; and Goethe's poetry fusing sound, light, speech and fire are given as examples of the conversion of libido focusing on the nutritive zone, rather than the sexual, as a point of origin. Fire symbolism is further discussed in references to the book of Daniel, the Bhagavad Gita, and Plato, as well as incendiarism and ceremonial fire making. Fire ceremonies are discussed in terms of a paradigm for canalizing psychic energy into progressive activity. 32 references.

000087 The origin of the hero. In: Jung, C., Collected Works of C. G. Jung, Vol. 5. 2nd ed., Princeton University Press, 1967. 557 p. (p. 171-206).

The hero, called the "finest symbol of the libido" is discussed as he appears in mythology, legend and the dramatic dream of one patient, Miss Miller. A passive introversion which rejects an external object of love and a concentration of the libido on an internal substitute created by the unconscious is considered the source of Miss Miller's vision. For mankind in general, this internalization of libidinal attention is seen in the cult of the hero, who symbolizes archaic psychic power suppressed to conform to society. This human need is recognized by the Catholic Church by providing Jesus as a visible hero, a sought after superman who symbolizes the idea, the forms, and the forces of the soul. Ramifications of the meaning of the Sphinx which appeared in Miss Miller's dream are explored, and it is concluded that it means for her what it did for Oedipus, the incest danger. A masculine figure, an Aztec, emerging from the Sphinx, supports this interpretation, and symbolic meanings of the figure's dress and appearance are discussed. The processes of repression and regression which lead to such archetypal figures appearing from the unconscious, are explained. Since these products of the unconscious are made of repressed infantile material, the psychology of the child's interest in excremental and anal concerns, his confusion between creation and defecation, and other symbolic

meanings, are examined. The creation of personality by the unconscious is explored through the legend of the Wandering Jew, another figure in Miss Miller's dream. Related legend and tradition from Christian, Islamic, and Mithraic history are reviewed, returning to the symbols of the sun, and finding the fish as a symbol of renewal and rebirth. Heroes in these references are seen to be simultaneously mortal and immortal. Regularly the psychic life force, the libido, symbolizes itself in the sun or personifies itself in figures of heroes with solar attributes, again a sign of mortality and immortality. Unconscious motivations such as the incest problem and desires striving for consciousness are briefly discussed. 28 references.

000088 Symbols of the mother and of rebirth. In: Jung, C., Collected Works of C. G. Jung, Vol. 5. 2nd ed., Princeton University Press, 1967. 557 p. (p. 207-273).

Through exploration of the symbols for mother and rebirth, Miss Miller's vision of communication with a god/hero is interpreted, and the cultural importance of canalization of libido through the use of symbols is demonstrated. In Miss Miller's vision the city is a maternal symbol as it is in the myth of Ogyges, in Hindu mythology, and in the Bible. In these myths and in others referring to sea journeys, (also found in Miss Miller's vision), an expression of the longing to return to the womb and to become immortal through rebirth is found. This symbol creating process analyzes the libido and allows it to be progressive again at a higher level of consciousness. Other symbols of the mother imago, such as water, wood of life and tree of life, are examined and studied. From these examples, support is found for the contention that the object of desire is rebirth not incestuous cohabitation. The incest taboo provides an obstacle, forcing canalization upon the libido, and spiritualizing it. Religion aids in systematizing the canalization. Symbolism and symbol formation are viewed as civilizing and natural, with the symbol representing a psychological truth, though not an external one. In many maternal symbols the motifs of devouring and entwining recur, as in the symbol of the tree entwined by a snake. This symbol, as it appears there and in many other myths, is interpreted as an example of the archetypal father opposing pure instinctuality. It is concluded that incest is a narrow and crude explanation for symbol formation, and that the law which expresses itself as the "incest prohibition" should be interpreted as the impulse to domestication, with religious systems seen as institutions which organize the instinctual forces of man's nature and make them available for higher purposes. 65 references.

000089 The battle for deliverance from the mother. In: Jung, C., Collected Works of C. G. Jung, Vol. 5. 2nd ed., Princeton University Press, 1967. 557 p. (p. 274-305).

In examining Miss Miller's vision of her hero on horseback, threatened by an Indian arrow, the symbolic meanings of the fantasy are explored and the vision is shown to be an expression of Miss Miller's impending need to discard infantile dependence on her mother. The hero of the vision expresses his author's infantile demands and even behaves in a feminine way, reflecting Miss Miller's continuing infantilism and identification with her parent. The analysis is expanded by reviewing the symbolism of the horse and the arrow as they appear in mythology, drama and poetry. Wounding of the hero is seen as a symbolic piercing of self in which the libido turns inward to replenish itself, as if returning into the mother. This internalizing is characterized as occurring whenever man faces a difficult phase in his struggle for personal independence (from the mother and from the entire atmosphere of infancy). The mother image and the maternal archetypes are discussed, with the distinction made between the attitudes held toward them during the first and second half of life. In Miss Miller's vision, the arrow does not fell the hero, which indicates that Miss Miller is not yet ready to give up the connection with her mother. 29 references.

000090 The dual mother. In: Jung, C., Collected Works of C. G. Jung, Vol. 5. 2nd ed., Princeton University Press, 1967. 557 p. (p. 306-393).

Miss Miller's vision of the hero Chiwantopel, and the associations she herself suggests with the legends of Hiawatha, Siegfried, and other heros from religion and mythology, are discussed in an expansion of the theory of the hero figure. Chiwantopel, seeking a beloved "She who understands", is an archetype of the unconscious itself, governed by the mother image. Since Miss Miller's battle is for independence, the hero enters as a savior figure who does all she cannot do. Detailed analyses of Hiawatha and Siegfried support the theory of hero as symbolic of self. The extraordinary circumstances of the hero's birth are due to being born of a mother wife; this dual mother motif results in a dual birth: one mortal, the other quasi divine. In the struggle, death and rebirth of the hero, one sees the symbol of the struggle of the self against the attraction of returning to the unconscious (mother). While religion and society condemn and attempt to block this regressive return, it is strongly recommended that therapy support it, for it is not an incestuous return to the mother but a regression to the presexual wholeness of the unconscious. This conflict between the ego conscious and the unconscious is observed to be at the source of the typical representation of the hero as carrying on an unending struggle against hazardous and evil forces. That the hero and his adversary often resemble each other is seen as a symbol of their relationship as two parts of the same whole. Similarly, the treasure which is the goal of many legendary heros is seen as life itself, the resolution of the struggle between conscious and unconscious; through introversion, the entering of the cave, the treasure/self is regained/reborn. A similar interpretation of dreams is suggested, since the hero myth as an unconscious drama is in fact a kind of dream.

000091 The sacrifice. In: Jung, C., Collected Works of C. G. Jung, Vol. 5. 2nd ed., Princeton University Press, 1967. 557 p. (p. 394-440).

By comparing Miss Miller's mental attitude with that of the poet Holderlin and with many religious, legendary and mythological sources, the meaning of the death of the hero Chiwantopel is derived. Miss Miller's conscious mind is seen as threatened by an invasion from the unconscious; were the invasion completed, the conscious mind would be freed to break inertia and move forward. A similar situation is detailed in the poetry of Holderlin, particularly in his increasing estrangement from reality. This material is used to discuss regression as involuntary introversion, of which depression is an unconscious compensation. Holderlin's poems are further used to illustrate regression as a link with primal material, which must be assimilated by the conscious mind, lest it keep its chaotic form, producing schizophrenia. References to the sacrificial death and resurrection of Christ illustrate the poet's similarity in thought to mythological ideas of death or a hero's self-sacrifice as leading to immortality. Miss Miller's sacrifice of Chiwantopel is interpreted as the urging from the unconscious to renounce her longing for regression to the maternal depths. More than just a study in individual psychology, Miss Miller's problem is seen as reflecting that of humanity in general. The symbols employed in her visions are mythological

figures born to the unconscious; it was not the incest taboo that forced mankind forward but the evolutionary instinct from which this and other taboos came. Indian philosophy, as a sort of refined mythology dealing with sacrifice is reviewed with other legendary and mythological sacrifice symbolism, and a comparison is made of the differences between Mithraic and Christian sacrifice. Based on this difference, Miss Miller's fantasy, which kills both horse and hero, is interpreted as the unconscious urge to renounce not only the biological drives represented by the horse, but her egohood, which is represented by the hero. The drama enacted through Chiwantopel and the horse will now have to be acted out in life by Miss Miller herself. 31 references.

000092 Symbols of transformation. Epilogue. In: Jung, C., Collected Works of C. G. Jung, Vol. 5. 2nd ed., Princeton University Press, 1967. 557 p. (p. 441-444).

The conception of the role of psychotherapy in cases such as Miss Miller's is detailed. It is felt that, at the conclusion of Miss Miller's visions, the threat to her from the unconscious was apparent, but that she was unable to deal with it and assimilate her hero to her conscious personality, because she had no understanding of the meaning of the symbols present in her fantasies. Fantasy production is described as psychic energy not under conscious control and is seen as a precursor of psychic disturbance. The role of the psychotherapist is to help the patient assimilate part of the unconscious and abolish dissociation by integration of unconscious tendencies with the conscious mind. Miss Miller's individual case is considered an example of the unconscious manifestations which precede psychic disorder, which led to this survey of problems of greater proportions; thus fantasies, dreams, and delusions as an expression of the patient's psychic situation are the material with which a scientist augments human knowlege.

000093 Symbols of transformation. Appendix: the Miller fantasies. In: Jung, C., Collected Works of C. G. Jung, Vol. 5. 2nd ed., Princeton University Press, 1967. 557 p. (p. 445-462).

The Miller fantasies, forming the foundation material for "Symbols of Transformation", are reproduced as written by Miss Frank Miller. They include remarks on suggestion, two dream poems and the hypnagogic vision of the story of Chiwantopel. Brief background information on what she was doing or thinking just before the poems and the story vision occurred to her is given. Miss Miller assumes that all persons of a sympathetic nature experience suggestion or autosuggestion as she does. She explains the dream poems as combinations of impressions from literature, plays and philosophy. The vision of Chiwantopel, experienced in what Miss Miller describes as an anticipatory mood before sleep, is detailed. It includes the appearance of the Aztec, the horses, battle, a dream city, a change of scene to a wood where Chiwantopel defies the threat by an Indian arrow, his search for a soul mate, his despair, the appearance of a viper and the ensuing death of his horse and himself. Miss Miller calls Chiwantopel, hero of the story, her "spirit guide", and analyzes the vision by finding the everyday sources of its contents (such as the hero's name and the appearance of the volcano) in Shakespeare, Hiawatha, other literature, philosophy, and experiences of her own. She also feels that her search for an original idea, continuing over several days preceding the vision, may have played a role in precipitating the hypnagogic fantasy. She considers her visions generally in a literary and superficial light, without questioning whether any deeper psychic forces have contributed to them.

06 PSYCHOLOGICAL TYPES

000094 Psychological types. Introduction. In: Jung, C., Collected Works of C. G. Jung, Vol. 6. 2nd ed., Princeton University Press, 1971. 608 p. (p. 3-7).

Through insights gained from the clinical study of patients, two broad personality types are distinguished: the introverted and the extraverted. In the introduction to "Psychological Types," the theory is stated; the method to be followed to understand them is described; and the definition, characteristics and effects of these two personality types are summarized. For the introverted personality, subjective and psychological processes are the center of interest: all life-giving energy seeks the subject himself; the object has a lower value than the subject. The extraverted personality, on the other hand, is drawn to the object as the center of interest: ultimate value rests in the object and the subject subordinates his own subjective processes to the object. The psychological result of these two standpoints is two totally different orientations: one sees everything in terms of the objective event (extraverted); the other sees everything in terms of his own situation (introverted). This broad classification does not exclude the existence of a second set of psychological types determined by the four basic psychological functions: thinking, feeling, sensation, and intuition, found within both introverted and extraverted personalities. This work, then, will discuss both sets of types: one determined by the predominant center of interest; the other determined by the predominance of one of the four basic psychological functions. 1 reference.

000095 The problem of types in the history of classical and medieval thought. 1. Psychology in the classical age: the Gnostics, Tertullian, Origen. In: Jung, C., Collected Works of C. G. Jung, Vol. 6. 2nd ed., Princeton University Press, 1971. 608 p. (p. 8-20).

The psychological types postulated by Gnostic philosophy, the types represented by Tertullian and Origen, and the relationship of Christianity to later thought and knowledge are discussed. In early history, one finds a collective attitude rather than a concept of the individual. Gnostic philosophy postulated three types, corresponding to three basic psychological functions: the pneumatikoi, related to the thinking function; the psychikoi, related to feeling; and the hylikoi, related to sensation. In Gnosticism, feeling was devalued in favor of thought; in Christianity the reverse was true. Tertullian, the fanatic who created Church Latin is described as a classic example of introversion, sacrificing intellect to the inner soul. Origen, another Christian scholar, is classified as a classic extravert. By his self-castration he sacrificed feeling and sensation to intellect or objective fact. 3 references.

000096 The problem of types in the history of classical and medieval thought. 2. The theological disputes of the ancient church. In: Jung, C., Collected Works of C. G. Jung, Vol. 6. 2nd ed., Princeton University Press, 1971. 608 p. (p. 20-23).

The early religious schisms resulting from attempts to define the nature of Christ are examined as examples of the opposition between extraverted and introverted psychological types. The Ebionite/Docetist opposition, the homoousia/homoiousia debate of Arianism, and the Monophysite/Diophysite struggle all reveal a great psychological schism beneath the theological disputes. One set of positions placed an extreme value on the sensually visible; the other valued the abstract and extrahuman. This type conflict reappeared in the Pelagian/Augustinian controversy of the fifth century: Pelagius and Celestius defended the rightness of the feeling of human value against Augustine's pessimistic view of man and his exaltation of the Church as idea. Nestorius and Cyril, in their respective definitions of Mary as Christ bearer and God bearer, are also considered as typifying the opposition of the attraction of the sensual versus that of the abstract.

000097 The problem of types in the history of classical and medieval thought. 3. The problem of transubstantiation. In: Jung, C., Collected Works of C. G. Jung, Vol. 6. 2nd ed., Princeton University Press, 1971. 608 p. (p. 23-26).

Continuing the progression through history in search of other examples of the appearance of the two basic psychological types, Radbertus' doctrine of Communion (transubstantiation) is contrasted with that of Scotus Erigena (commemoration) as examples of the opposition between extraverted and introverted thinking. Abbot Paschasius Radbertus concretized the symbols of bread and wine by maintaining that the wine and bread of Communion were transformed into the body and blood of Christ. Scotus Erigena, praised by Hales in his History of the Christian Church as one of the most advanced thinkers of his day, maintained that Communion was nothing more than a commemoration of the last supper of Christ with his apostles. No conclusions are drawn about the individual psychology of the two protagonists, but a brief description of their lives and their fates is given. The effect of the belief in miracles analyzed; extraverted thinking is qualified as "rational," introverted as "programmatic." The fact that Radbertus' extraverted thinking was accepted as doctrinal and Scotus' introverted thinking rejected as lifeless, is considered to indicate that the age itself longed for the reality of religious miracles and that Radbertus' thought was perceived as life giving because it concretized the desire of the age.

000098 The problem of types in the history of classical and medieval thought. 4. Nominalism and realism. a. The problem of universals in antiquity. In: Jung, C., Collected Works of C. G. Jung, Vol. 6. 2nd ed., Princeton University Press, 1971. 608 p. (p. 26-38).

The definition, historical roots, characteristics and significance of Nominalism and Realism are examined. The Nominalists held that universals such as beauty, goodness, animal, man, etc.,are nothing but names or words; the realists maintained that universals exist in themselves, before the thing, (ante-rem). The roots of the opposition between these two philosophies are traced to the Platonic and Megarian schools. Gromperz is credited with perceiving the fundamental opposition in terms of inherence and predication. Using the progression from our perception of warm to our recognition of the existence of energy as an example, the development of the thing-likeness of the purely conceptual is demonstrated. This "thing-likeness" was apparent in primitive man's perception of the imago as a sensory colored memory image or hallucination. Since modern man desensitizes the psychic image and thinks abstractly, this process can only be recaptured in dreams or mystical vision. Both these examples support the theory that the reality of the predicate is given a priori, since it has always existed in the human mind. 6 references.

000099 The problem of types in the history of classical and medieval thought. 4. Nominalism and realism. b. The problem of Universals in Scholasticism. In: Jung, C., The Collected Works of C. G. Jung, Vol. 6. 2nd ed., Princeton University Press, 1971. 608 p. (p. 38-46).

The problem of defining the nature of universals and the relationship between these definitions and God concepts is reviewed. Porphyry defined the problem as the opposition between the belief that universals are substantial, corporeal and existing in corporeal things and the belief that they are intellectual, incorporeal and separate things. Between the Platonic view of reality in which the universal idea was considered to exist before the thing and the Nominalist attitude that generic concepts were mere words, stood Aristotle's realistic view that form and matter coexist. In the Middle Ages, this controversy became the quintessence of Scholasticism. Roscellinus represented the Nominalist view; Anselm and Abelard, the realistic. Anselm's ontological proof of the existence of God -- that the idea of God proves his existence -- is considered psychologically important: it is a demonstration of the reality of the world of ideas. Psychology must recognize the difference between these two approaches, since they now influence current oppositions between idealism and realism, spiritualism and materialism. Other champions of the opposing arguments are discussed and Kant's position is summarized. Kant's mediatory position is accepted as being as definitive and conclusive. The God concept is explained in terms of analytical psychology. The God concept coincides with a particular ideational complex, which, in accordance with its definition, concentrates in itself the maximum amount of libido or psychological energy. 5 references.

000100 The problem of type in the history of classical and medieval thought. 4. Nominalism and realism. c. Abelard's attempt at conciliation. In: Jung, C., Collected Works of C. G. Jung, Vol. 6. 2nd ed., Princeton University Press, 1971. 608 p. (p. 46-64).

The analysis of Abelard's conceptualism as an intermediary position between Nominalism and Realism leads to the discussion of the role of psychology and fantasy in establishing a point of conciliation between the idea and the object and concludes with an examination of the theories of Freud and Adler. From Nominalism Abelard took the idea that universals are words, in that they are intellectual conventions expressed by language. From realism he borrowed the theory that genera and species are combinations of individual facts and things by reason of similarity. His position, conceptualism, maintained that individual objects are perceived and classified into genera and species by reason of similarities, thus reducing the absolute multiplicity of the Nominalists into a relative unity. Abstraction and empathy are discussed as the underlying methods of the conceptualist. Had psychology existed in Abelard's age, his position would have been that of esse in anima (reality in the self). However, his conciliation was unsatisfactory and confusing because he attempted to resolve the differences on the level of a logical/intellectual formulation, whereas the problem is a psychological one requiring the recognition of concrete reality. Psychology, on the other hand, in so far as it recognizes that the unity of the idea and the thing occurs within the human psyche, arrives at a true conciliation. The process of conciliation and the role of fantasy in this process are described. Fantasy is defined as the clearest expression of the psyche, the creative activity from which all answers come, the sole mechanism which unites introversion and extraversion. Some of the difficulties that prevent the recognition of the role of fantasy are examined. The influence of Christianity in suppressing the unconscious in the individual, thus paralyzing the activity of fantasy, is analyzed, as is the role of the sciences. Psychology, as an abstract science, does not escape the tendency to condemn fantasy. It is only in practical psychology that the conciliation in its totality is treated. Freud viewed fantasy as a causal, elementary process; he explained the problems of the psyche as resulting from the repression of

incompatible wish tendencies. Adler's psychology is dominated by the belief in ego superiority that never allows man to be subject to the object. It is concluded that the theory of Freud was extraverted; that of Adler introverted. Fantasy is seen as the key to the synthesis of the opposing mechanisms. 5 references.

000101 The problem of types in the history of classical and medieval thought. 5. The Holy Communion controversy between Luther and Zwingli. In: Jung, C., Collected Works of C. G. Jung, Vol. 6. 2nd ed., Princeton University Press, 1971. 608 p. (p. 64-66).

The difference between the subject oriented and the object oriented types (introverts and extraverts) is illustrated with an example drawn from a religious controversy: the differing beliefs of Luther and Zwingli regarding Holy Communion. Luther, the object oriented type, believed in the doctrine of transubstantiation, not because he was unable to let go of tradition, but because the actual sense contact with the bread and wine and the feeling value resulting therefrom determined his belief. Zwingli, in his belief that Communion was a symbol, was faithful to the new evangelism and the dictates of reason. He ignored the sense impression and the feeling value derived from the contact with the object and thought only of the principle or ideal beneath the object. Their views were mutually exclusive and irreconcilable since they sprang from the extraverted (Luther) and introverted (Zwingli) conceptions of things.

000102 Schiller's ideas on type problem. 1. Letters on the aesthetic education of man. a. The superior and inferior functions. In: Jung, C., Collected Works of C. G. Jung, Vol. 6. 2nd ed., Princeton University Press, 1971. 608 p. (p. 67-96).

Friedrich Schiller's conscious differentiation of typical attitudes into superior and inferior functions serves as the basis for the analysis of the typical conflict present in the introverted thinking type. Schiller's letters on the esthetic education of man, "Uber die asthetische Erziehung des Menschen" (1795), are used as the source of the analysis. Schiller's perception of culture as cause of the separation is examined; the ancient world's emphasis on the development of the few is contrasted with Christianity's collective culture; the present situation of individual development is analyzed in relation to collective functions. Schiller's recognition that certain functions have been repressed (inferior functions) and his fear of the conflict that would ensue within the individual once he was liberated is the basis for an analysis of the effects of an imperfectly developed function, operating unconsciously and autonomously, on the conscious mind. Schiller overcame his fear of confronting the conflict by relating his personal struggle to the larger contemporary scene as did Rousseau. Both sought the solution in earlier historical periods. The disadvantages of the retrospective orientation is exposed and it is proposed that the beginning of a solution resides in the acceptance of the inferior functions and the creation of a gradient that will allow them to come into play. A detailed description of the way in which the inferior functions rise to the surface is provided. Schiller's perception of the problem is that of the introvert; Goethe's that of the extrovert. This judgement is substantiated by examples drawn from Schiller's definition of God and by a quotation from Schiller that expresses the conscious attitude of the introvert: "Externalize all within and shape everything without." 12 references.

000103 Schiller's ideas on the type problem. 1. Letters on the aesthetic education of man. b. Concerning the basic instincts. In:

Jung, C., Collected Works of C. G. Jung, Vol. 6. 2nd ed., Princeton University Press, 1971. 608 p. (p. 96-129).

Schiller's identification of two basic functions: feeling/sensation and thinking, his awareness of their opposition and the need for a third function (play instinct), to mediate this opposition are discussed. Schiller's ideas are examined in the light of the theory on the role of fantasy and the symbol in resolving the conflict between the two instincts. Schiller's theories are colored by his own introverted thinking and personality type. Nevertheless, it is demonstrated that Schiller was aware of several psychological realities: the two basic functions can replace each other; identification with one differentiated function can occur; both sensuality and spirituality have a right to exist; and symbols arise from the living out of both instincts at the same time. Schiller is also credited with the discovery of an individual nucleus in which both instincts exist but which is not identified with either. These discoveries of Schiller are the springboard for descriptions of the transcendent function of the symbol, the collaboration of the unconscious in fantasy and the methods by which the basic instincts can be defused. Schiller's "esthetic condition" is compared to the state produced by certain Indian practices: yoga, tapas, brahmanism, rta and the like. Schiller's solution is criticized and his limitations are analyzed as reflecting his own unconscious ideal. Schiller is praised for his intuitive grasp of the things he observed and for recognizing that the mediatory position produces "something positive," namely the symbol. The conclusion emphasizes the importance of the symbol: it unites antithetical elements within its nature -- conscious and unconscious, real and unreal, psychic and physical, real and apparent.

000104 Schiller's ideas on the type problem. 2. A discussion of naive and sentimental poetry. a. The naive attitude. In: Jung, C., Collected Works of C. G. Jung, Vol. 6. 2nd ed., Princeton University Press, 1971. 608 p. (p. 130-132).

Schiller's definition of the naive poet as he who "follows nature and sensation and who confines himself to the mere copying of reality" is examined. The characteristics of the naive poet, as described by Schiller, are listed and analyzed as an example of a typical mechanism. Insofar as the naive poet's relation to the object expresses an introjection of the object or an a priori identification based on an analogy between the object and the unconscious of the poet, the naive poet is conditioned by the object. The poet, in turn, lends his expressive function to the object as it represents itself to him. It is concluded that the poet, described by Schiller as naive, is extraverted to the extent that this process gives the object supremacy over the subject.

000105 Schiller's ideas on the type problem. 2. A discussion on naive and sentimental poetry. b. The sentimental attitude. In: Jung, C., Collected Works of C. G. Jung, Vol. 6. 2nd ed., Princeton University Press, 1971. 608 p. (p. 132-133).

Schiller's commentary on the naive and sentimental poets is continued; the characteristics of the sentimental poet are examined and are shown to be expressive of the introverted attitude. Additional consideration is given to the functions of sensation and intuition in order to further specify the introverted and extraverted attitudes. Schiller's description of the sentimental poet indicates that an a priori separation from the object is the foundation of the sentimental poet's attitude. The work that results is a product of reflection and abstraction. The dualism of the sentimental poet is discussed as stemming from the twofold source of his creativity: the object itself and the poet's perception of it. In that the sentimental

poet stands above the object and bestows value or quality on it, his attitude is that of introversion. The introverted and extraverted attitudes do not exhaust the understanding of the two types of poetry, however. Sensation and intuition are considered in their relation to the introverted and extraverted attitudes: a preponderance of sensation characterizing the naive poet; a preponderance of intuition characterizing the "sentimental" poet. 1 reference.

000106 Schiller's ideas on the type problem. 2. A discussion on naive and sentimental poetry. c. The idealist and the realist. In: Jung, C., Collected Works of C. G. Jung, Vol. 6. 2nd ed., Princeton University Press, 1971. 608 p. (p. 133-135).

The division of the poets into naive and sentimental types leads Schiller to the recognition of two fundamental psychological types whose significance in Schiller's scheme of things corresponds to the introverted and extraverted types. By subtracting the creative genius from both mechanisms, Schiller arrived at the isolation of two reciprocal psychological types: the realist and the idealist. The former, the naive poet, depends on the testimony of his senses and is attached to the object which maintains an autonomy in the subject; the latter, the sentimental poet, remains detached from the object, depends on his speculative powers and uses the object to arrive at the absolute. Schiller's observations are abandoned at this point since they relate exclusively to the faimilar phenomena of the realist and idealist attitudes. 1 reference.

000107 The Apollianian and the Dionysian. In: Jung, C., Collected Works of C. G. Jung, Vol. 6. 2nd ed., Princeton University Press, 1971. 608 p. (p. 136-146).

The analysis of Nietzsche's Apollinian and Dionysian types, as defined in his "The Birth of Tragedy," leads to a discussion of intuitive and sensation psychological types. The Apollinian type based on an inner perception of beauty and producing a psychological state that Nietzsche called dreaming, is analogous to the mechanism of introversion. The Dionysian type is based on a streaming outwards, akin to Goethe's diastole or Schiller's world embracing. It produces a psychological state that Nietzsche termed intoxication; this "streaming outwards" is analogous to the extraverted mechanism. The reconciliation of the two types was perceived by Nietzsche to be an esthetic solution apparent in Greek tragedy. This explanation is rejected and religion is posited as the source of the reconciliation. The esthetic solution, however, leads to the identification of sensation and intuitive types. These two types are defined, and a distinction is made between them and the rational thinking, feeling types. The intuitive type raises the unconscious perception of the world to the level of a differentiated function; the sensation type relies exclusively on sense impression and is psychologically oriented toward instinct. Nietzsche himself is classified as an intuitive leaning toward introversion and reasons are given for this classification. 4 references.

000108 The type problem in human character. 1. General remarks on Jordan's types. In: Jung, C., Collected Works of C. G. Jung, Vol. 6. 2nd ed., Princeton University Press, 1971. 608 p. (p. 147-152).

The two characterological types proposed by Furneaux Jordan in "Character as Seen in Body and Parentage" are examined and compared to function types. Jordan's typology reveals his intuitive grasp of the introverted and extraverted types. Although his analysis of function types is confused by the introduction of the activity factor, ascribing a more impassioned but less active nature to the introvert and a less impassioned but more active nature to the extravert, Jordan is praised for his characterization of the types in terms of affectivity. The reflective, contemplative nature of the introvert is compensated by the archaic unconscious instinct and sensation; the busy, outward seeking nature of the extravert is compensated by unconscious archaic thinking and feeling. Thus the introvert is more influenced by his passions and the extravert by his inner psychic life. Jordan's intuitive analysis is compared to rational analysis, showing that both arrive at the same conclusions. Jordan's intermediate group is recognized as analogous to sensation and intuitive types. 1 reference.

000109 The type problem in human character. 2. Special description and criticism of Jordan's types. a. The introverted woman. In: Jung, C., Collected Works of C. G. Jung, Vol. 6. 2nd ed., Princeton University Press, 1971. 608 p. (p. 152-156).

A psychological portrait of the introverted woman is drawn from Jordan's analysis of her affectivity and the description of her conscious inner life and its relation to affectivity. Jordan's view is seen as relying too heavily on the introverted woman's capacity for deep hatred, love, sympathy, jealousy, intensity and capacity for intimacy. This limitation is counterbalanced by the analysis of her contemplative, analytical, logical powers. Her well ordered intellectual life is perceived as a defense against an elemental, confused and ungovernable affective life; this view leads to the conclusion that the mind of the introverted woman is more to be relied upon than her untamed affectivity.

000110 The type problem in human character. 2. Special description and criticism of Jordan's types. b. The extraverted woman. In: Jung, C., Collected Works of C. G. Jung, Vol. 6. 2nd ed., Princeton University Press, 1971. 608 p. (p. 156-160).

Jordan's description of the extraverted or less impassioned woman is given, with comments on the manner in which thought and affect appear in this type. Jordan describes the extraverted woman as "idealess, restless, emotionless and spotless." It is agreed that the tendency toward incoherent and inconsequential criticism that Jordan ascribes to this type reveals an absence of independent reflection. However, it is felt that Jordan undervalues affect in the extraverted woman. In contrast, the value of the differentiation of affectivity is emphasized: although shallow, it is socially oriented, thus promoting the life of the community and the welfare of society. It is maintained that neither the introverted nor extraverted type is the more valuable; both are necessary to the individual and to society. 1 reference.

000111 The type problem in human character. 2. Special description and criticism of Jordan's types. c. The extraverted man. In: Jung, C., Collected Works of C. G. Jung, Vol. 6. 2nd ed., Princeton University Press, 1971. 608 p. (p. 160-163).

Jordan's description of the extraverted or less impassioned man is given along with the criticism that Jordan's intellectual approach is an inadequate method for evaluating the extraverted man. Jordan's description of the extravert is felt to be a caricature of the concrete man. The difficulty that a reflective man like Jordan encounters in attempting to grasp the value of the lived reciprocal relationship of the extravert to the object is explained. The reflective man or introvert sees the shadow cast by the unconscious of the positive man. Although the judgment of the unconscious is correct, it neglects the conscious man. A warning is given to psychologists: they must differentiate the conscious man from the unconscious in order to arrive at true understanding and avoid reducing the man to his unconscious background. 1 reference.

000112 The type problem in human character. 2. Special description and criticism of Jordan's types. d. The introverted man. In: Jung, C., Collected Works of C. G. Jung, Vol. 6. 2nd ed., Princeton University Press, 1971. 608 p. (p. 163-165).

Jordan's brief description of the introverted or more impassioned man is given with an explanation for the cause of its inadequacy. It is observed that the brevity of Jordan's description and the total absence of a description of the passion attributed to this type can be explained by positing that Jordan himself was an introvert and was therefore incapable of perceiving and explaining his own unconscious. This leads to the conclusion that neither the extravert nor the introvert is capable of giving an adequate description of his own unconscious nor can one adequately explain the concrete in the other. Jordan's observation on the introvert's genuine love of pleasure is considered important, however, since it provides a valuable insight into the nature of introverted feeling. Jordan's analyses are abandoned at this point because of the fallacies derived from the introduction of the activity factor, although Jordan is credited with having given an appropriate character sketch of the emotional types. 1 reference.

000113 The type problem in poetry. Carl Spitteler: Prometheus and Epimetheus. 1. Introductory remarks on Spitteler's typology. In: Jung, C., Collected Works of C. G. Jung, Vol. 6. 2nd ed., Princeton University Press, 1971. 608 p. (p. 166-173).

Using the poetic work of Carl Spitteler, Prometheus and Epimetheus, the struggle waged for the possession of the ego by the introverted and extraverted lines of development in one individual is illustrated. Prometheus, an example of the introverted side, surrenders himself to his inner psychic function. He perceives the soul as an object separate from the individual ego, rejects the tendency to adapt to the real, and hence experiences great suffering. This surrender reveals the demonic nature of the soul; that is, it allows a glimpse of all the engrams or traces of the functions of the human psyche as they appear in the unconscious from time immemorial. Epimetheus, on the other hand, the extraverted side of man, abandons his soul, is caught up in the desires and expectations of the world and, with his conscience as a shield against surrendering totally to the object, conforms to society. He fulfills the wishes of all with self-righteousness and self-assurance, thus achieving success. The confrontation between Prometheus and Epimetheus makes visible the conflict in the man who is outwardly Epimethean and inwardly Promethean. 3 references.

000114 The type problem in poetry. Carl Spitteler: Prometheus and Epimetheus. 2. A comparison of Spitteler's with Goethe's Prometheus. In: Jung, C., Collected Works of C. G. Jung, Vol. 6. 2nd ed., Princeton University Press, 1971. 608 p. (p. 173-188).

The struggle between differentiated and undifferentiated functions, whether introverted or extraverted, is presented by means of a comparison between Goethe's Prometheus and that of Spitteler. The attempts at a solution, as evident in Schiller, Spitteler and Goethe, are examined, with Goethe's Faust offering the best grasp of the necessary steps for reconciliation. Spitteler's Prometheus, the introvert, in his withdrawal into the soul's depths, represents the psychological principle of compensation. The Pandora interlude describes in full the compensatory process; her jewel becomes a symbol of the redeeming work of Prometheus. Epimetheus, the rational attitude, cannot comprehend the jewel, the work of the unconscious, and thus it is lost. In Spitteler's work, this marks the beginning of Epimetheus' downfall: the collective undifferentiated attitude stifles man's highest values, forcing Promethetus to place himself at the service of the unconscious. Goethe's Prometheus is a creative artist who works outwards toward the world, the extraverted side, whereas his Epimetheus is the brooding introvert. It is Prometheus who represents the collective function while Epimetheus is the undifferentiated function of thinking and feeling. The soul, Pandora, is coupled with the undifferentiated function, producing a pathological egocentricity. Goethe's solution is the marriage of Phileros, the unconscious erotic compulsion of Prometheus, with Epimetheus' daughter, Care. Thus the two are reconciled in the recognition that Prometheus' industriousness is nothing but unadmitted eroticism and Epiemtheus' brooding, a rational misgiving that would have checked the uncontrolled productivity of Prometheus. The myths are seen as illustrations of the conflict that arises whenever an individual or an historical change of attitude takes place: a difficult task is encountered; libidio withdraws (regression) and a primitive analogue of the conscious situation emerges. The choice of a classical image is considered to be a reaction on the part of the 18th century classicists to the Christian division of man into two halves: one valuable, the other degraded. It is pointed out that this regressive renaissance of paganism was stillborn; Geothe's Faust, in taking into account the Christian heritage of the age, is viewed as providing a better solution to the conflict. 6 references.

000115 The type problem in poetry. Carl Spitteler: Prometheus and Epimetheus. 3. The significance of the uniting symbol. a. The Brahmanic conception of the problem of opposites. In: Jung, C., Collected Works of C. G. Jung, Vol. 6. 2nd ed., Princeton University Press, 1971. 608 p. (p. 189-199).

The significance of the religious symbolism used in Spitteler's solution to the conflict between opposite psychological types is discussed and related to the Brahman solution. The religious solutions of Spitteler, Nietzsche, Schopenhauer, and Goethe are analyzed as voicing the workings of the collective unconscious: the god image is the symbol of the unconscious while the symbol of god renewal is intimately connected with the opposition of types and functions. The renewal of god is a primordial, universal image of a transformation in attitude. The psychological point of departure for this symbol is the splitting of the libido (Prometheus and Epimetheus); the unconscious, a middle way between the two, is projected as a mediating god or messiah. In Western religions, this new life bearer is perceived as God or Savior who ends the division in his time and according to his will. Several quotations from Sanskit texts reveal that, in the Eastern religions, this redemptive middle ground is attainable by a conscious attitude. The Brahmanic solution and its meaning are explained: the external, emotional and ideational opposites are denied participation in the psyche in order to liberate the self for the new life in Brahman. Brahman is then both the state of the irrational union of opposites and the process by which one arrives at this state. This irrational union is expressed in the Upanishads as libido symbols. 19 references.

000116 The type problem in poetry. Carl Spitteler: Prometheus and Epimetheus. 3. The significance of the uniting symbol. b. The Brahmanic concept of the uniting symbol. In: Jung, C., Collected Works of C. G. Jung, Vol. 6. 2nd ed., Princeton University Press, 1971. 608 p. (p. 199-208).

Examples of Brahmanic symbols provide the basis for a discussion of the role of libido in the creation of symbols, the psychological phenomenon of personification and the effects of one-sided introversion or extraversion. The symbols of Brahman, usually pairs of opposites, reveal the Eastern concept of Brahman as both a divine entity and a redemptive psychological state. These symbols of dynamic or creative power are related to the concept of libido and the yogi's method of prayer is explained as producing a concentration of libido by withdrawing it from both extraverted and introverted functions. From the Rig Veda and Shatapatha Brahmana, symbols representing the paring of opposites are selected; these symbols are interpreted as principles of the psychological functions of extraversion and introversion. The speech/mind opposition (vac-Manas), takes the form of devouring monsters, and indication of the dissociation that results when the conscious ego, with a selected function (extraversion or introversion), splits away from the other components of the personality. This form of dissociation is common in people who are too deeply immersed in one of their psychic functions, such as we find in Goethe's Faust. In conclusion, the demonic nature of libido in those persons who are unconsciously caught in a one-sided extraverted or introverted attitude is demonstrated. 18 references.

000117 The type problem in poetry. Carl Spitteler: Prometheus and Epimetheus. 3. The significance of the uniting symbol. c. The uniting symbol as the principles of dynamic regulation. In: Jung, C., Collected Works of C. G. Jung, Vol. 6. 2nd ed., Princeton University Press, 1971. 608 p. (p. 208-213).

The uniting symbol of Brahman philosophy and its relation to the concept of libido are discussed as basic principles for arriving at true morality. Rta represents the source of libido in Brahman philosophy, although it is a less concretistic symbol than sun, wind and rain. It can be likened to the Stoic concept of heimarmene, a predetermined regular process or an established order. Libido, the energy of the life process, follows the same laws as all vital energy: it passes through many transformations, keeping to a definite path in order to allow for the optimal discharge of energy. Libido, then, is the law of our being. This understanding of libido is basic to the understanding of morality. It is stated that there can be no higher moral principle than harmony with natural laws that guide the libido in the direction of life's optimum. It is not surrender to instinct but a difficult path to be attained, as is evident in the philosophy of the Upanishads. It requires freedom which modern man fears because of the barbarism lurking beneath the veneer of modern culture. It is concluded however, that it is only in experiencing the conflict of opposites that an individual will recognize moral principles as constituents of his own nature and not as external restriction. 8 references.

000118 The type problem in poetry. Carl Spitteler: Prometheus and Epimetheus. 3. The significance of the uniting symbol. d. The uniting symbol in Chinese philosophy. In: Jung, C., Collected Works of C. G. Jung, Vol. 6. 2nd ed., Princeton University Press, 1971. 608 p. (p. 214-221).

The unifying of opposites as it appears in Tao is described and related to Brahman philosophy, the philiosophy of the Japanese Toju, Wagner's Parsifal and the role of analytical psychology. The two mutually antagonistic tendencies, expressed as yeng/yin and shen/kwei in Chinese philosophy, are perceived as striving to bring man into extreme attitudes. Tao is the middle way, the irrational counterweight which enables man to live in harmony with the opposites and to find deliverance from cosmic tensions. This same perception of two opposing forces and a mediating third way is evident in Brahman, in the ri/ki/ryochi formulation of the Japanese philosopher Toju, and in the Kundry/Amfortas/Parsifal creations of Wagner. The constant recurrence of this perception is explained by showing that it is part of the collective unconscious of all ages, an exteriorization of the lived conflict which involves the domestication of libido. The role of analytical psychology is to raise the conflict to the level of consciousness and, through self-awareness, to enable man to reflect on what he experiences rather than living it blindly. 3 references.

000119 The type problem in poetry. Carl Spitteler: Prometheus and Epimetheus. 4. The relativity of the symbol. a. The worship of woman and the worship of the soul. In: Jung, C., Collected Works of C. G. Jung, Vol. 6. 2nd ed., Princeton University Press, 1971. 608 p. (p. 221-240).

The importance, purpose and method of symbol formation is presented by tracing the image of woman as it appears in several religious works: litanies, The Song of Songs, The Divine Comedy, Faust and The Shepherd. The union of opposites in the works of Spitteler and Goethe took the form of worship of woman, a symbol for worship of the soul. This transition from woman to soul is illustrated by selections from "The Shepherd" of Hermas. Through analysis of the visions and revelations of Hermas, it becomes evident that the libido, originally attracted to the woman in an erotic fashion, is detached from the real object, concentrates on a symbol, the tower standing for the Church, and is canalized into a symbolic function -- the consolidation of the Christian view of the world. The importance of symbol formation is derived from the fact that it prevents absolute relation of subject to object or absolute identity of subject with object. For, should the latter occur, all cognition would be impossible and a dangerous inferiority in affectivity would result. The purpose of the symbol is stated: to free the subject for the possibility of choice. This is accomplished by drawing the libido away from the object, devaluing the object and bestowing surplus libido on the subject, which libido works on the unconscious, placing the subject between an inner and outer determinant. The symbols emerge at the stage of withdrawal of libido into the unconscious where certain archaic engrams are found. These engrams correspond to inherited ways of functioning which owe their existence to the differentiation of instinct. The vessel symbol is analyzed as an illustration of how symbols are derived from archaic conceptions and, in the case of the Christian Church, are turned toward a figurative object. 14 references.

000120 The type problem in poetry. Carl Spitteler: Prometheus and Epimetheus. 4. The relativity of the symbol. b. The relativity of the God-concept in Meister Eckhart. In: Jung, C., Collected Works of C. G. Jung, Vol. 6. 2nd ed., Princeton University Press, 1971. 608 p. (p. 241-258).

The concept of the relativity of God, as it appeared in the writings of the medieval thinker Meister Eckhart, is defined and related to the historical development of the individual, a concept that reached a point of culmination in the Reformation. This discovery of the relativity of God is considered a major landmark for a psychological understanding of religious phenomena. This concept of relativity implies a reciprocal relation between God and man wherein man is a function of God and God, a psychological function of man. The psychological explanation of this concept is given. If God is outside the soul, as in the absolutist view, he is projected into objects, giving them overpowering influence over the soul. The subject must detach and internalize the surplus of libido from the object, turning it into an inner possession. The blissfulness which results is an indication of a dynamic relation between unconscious and conscious in which the former

predominates. In order to understand this concept of God, it is necessary to understand the term "soul." Therefore, the soul is defined; the historical evolution of the concept of soul is traced; and the capacity to mediate between the subject and the unconscious is attributed to it. In this meeting place, God -- the unconscious -- is apprehended and the creative function of the soul gives birth to symbols. This "birth of God" is described as a continual process, a psychologically recognized vital rhythm that goes on unconsciously. In his description of his concept, Meister Eckhart uses symbols that reflect those of the primitive world. He, like the poet Angelus Silesius whose work is cited, were the voices of the collective psyche of their age, an age in which the individual psyche was claiming more attention. It is concluded that the unconscious contents of this collective psyche rose to the surface in the Reformation. 4 references.

000121 The type problem in poetry. Carl Spitteler: Prometheus and Epimetheus. 5. The nature of the uniting symbol in Spitteler. In: Jung, C., Collected Works of C. G. Jung, Vol. 6. 2nd ed., Princeton University Press, 1971. 608 p. (p. 258-273).

The description of the nature and condition of the jewel symbol in Spitteler's work is compared to the Biblical prophecies and circumstances surrounding the Savior. Both these examples illuminate the psychological process of uniting introversion and extraversion in the individual. In the interpretation of the jewel symbol, several parallels to the human psyche are drawn. The appearance of the jewel is accompanied by a sense of danger, just as the emergence of the repressed libido is perceived as threatening to the rational universe; its appearance is irrational; i.e., salvation comes from the least valued function. The jewel is compared to a great catastrophe as is the afflux of energy accompanying the release of the repressed libido. The rational functions, represented by king, priest, academician, and police reject the jewel as contemporary man rejects the glimpse of the still present, barbaric side of his nature. Because of this rejection the jewel falls into the hands of the Wandering Jew, a symbol of the unredeemed state of unchecked libido, and destruction begins in the kingdom of Epimetheus or rationality. Only the appearance of Prometheus, who saves Messias and makes him heir to the throne, saves men. Epimetheus and Prometheus (extraversion and introversion) retire, and Messias, the symbol of the new attitude, the union of opposites, reigns. Extraversion and introversion cease to dominate as exclusive principles. 16 references.

000122 The type problem in psychopathology. In: Jung, C., Collected Works of C. G. Jung, Vol. 6. 2nd ed., Princeton University Press, 1971. 608 p. (p. 273-288).

The two psychological types introduced by Otto Gross in 1902 are described and critiqued. These types are compared to Jordan's "less impassioned, more impassioned" types and to extraverted and introverted types. Although Gross' analysis was originally applied to pathological types, it can also be applied to normal individuals. A review of Gross' theories show that he believed that there were two kinds of cerebral brain action: chemical or energic. The performance of the cell in such activities as thinking was considered to be the primary function of the cell; the secondary function consisted in the recovery or rebuilding of the cell through assimilation. Gross maintained that the speed of the secondary function determined the type: rapid recovery or rebuilding would allow for the frequent operation of the primary function, therefore, a distractible psychological type with superficial affectivity would result. This description resembles Jordan's less impassioned type and the extravert. According to Gross, the opposite type was characterized by a prolonged secondary function resulting in a type with fewer ideas, more abstractions and intense affectivity -- the introvert. The secondary function as a type determinant is rejected, and it is maintained that attitude and the primary function determine type. The development of these tendencies into psychopathologies is discussed; their characteristics are described and analyzed; and Jung's theory is summarized. 7 references.

000123 The type problem in aesthetics. In: Jung, C., Collected Works of C. G. Jung, Vol. 6. 2nd ed., Princeton University Press, 1971. 608 p. (p. 289-299).

The basic, antithetical attitudes of abstraction and empathy as described by Worringer, Lipps, and Jodl are analyzed and related to the attitudes of introversion and extraversion. Worringer's definition of the esthetic experience of empathy is cited as the predominant Western attitude to art since classical antiquity. The counterpole of it, abstraction, is also defined and recognized as basic to Oriental art forms and religions. The definitions of empathy and abstraction are given: empathy consists in going out to the object, imbuing it with life and displaying trust in it; abstraction, presuming the object to be alive and acting, withdraws from it. Worringer's abstraction is found to correspond to the Jungian definition of introversion, and empathy to extraversion. The role of the unconscious influencing these two responses is examined. It is proposed that the abstracting individual has unconsciously projected his own negative feelings into the object and that it is from these that he consciously withdraws. The empathetic observer has first unconsciously neutralized the object in order to make it a suitable receptable for his own subjective contents. Introversion and extraversion, empathy and abstraction are explained as mechanisms of defense. In this function, they can protect man from external dangers. When carried to extremes, however, they can produce "self-alienation." Worringer sees this self-alienation as basic to both esthetic attitudes; Jung, on the other hand, shows how it can lead to dissociation of personality. 8 references.

000124 The type problem in modern philosophy. 1. William James' types. In: Jung, C., Collected Works of C. G. Jung, Vol. 6. 2nd ed., Princeton University Press, 1971. 608 p. (p. 300-307).

The two philosophical types, the rationalist and the empiricist, presented by William James are described and their thought processes analyzed. The relationship to the categories of introversion and extraversion is shown. A list of characteristics for each type is given. The rationalist, devotee of abstract and eternal principles, is prone to intellectualism; he is idealistic, monistic, feeling, dogmatic and tender-minded. The empiricist, lover of facts and prone to sensationalism, is materialistic, pluralistic, hard-headed, fatalistic, sceptical and tough-minded. These opposing characteristics become the topics of the subsequent sections in this chapter. The analysis of the thought processes of these two types reveals that they are determined either by objects (empiricist), or by primordial images existing in the subject (rationalist), and parallel extraverted and introverted types. The empiricists' theory that the mind is a tabula rasa to be informed by experiences is criticized. Instead, the existence of certain functional dispositions that are the deposit of phylogenetic experiences is posited. The characteristics of abstract thinking are contrasted with those of empirical thinking and the contemporary popularity of the latter is noted. 2 references.

000125 The type problem is modern philosophy. 2. The characteristic pairs of opposites in James' types. a. Rationalism versus empiricism. In: Jung, C., Collected Works of C. G. Jung, Vol. 6. 2nd ed., Princeton University Press, 1971. 608 p. (p. 307-311).

The term "ideologism" to describe abstract thinking is proposed as an alternative to James' term "rationalism" in order to avoid the error of exclusively associating reason with abstract thought. Using quotations from Lipps, Baldwin, Herbart and Schopenhauer, it is shown that the attitude or capacity to be reasonable is common to both empiricism and ideologism. Their opposition stems from the source of their objective values: the empiricist derives his objective values from experience; the ideologist from the positive act of evaluation. This is evident in the views of reason held by Kant and Wundt, introverted and extraverted views respectively. Empirical or extraverted thinking is described as reductive; ideological or introverted thinking as synthetic. The opposition of the two types becomes especially clear in the conclusion: the introvert shapes psychic data using his unconscious and arrives at experience; the extravert is guided by sensory material that in fact reflects his unconscious projections and thus comes to the idea. It is maintained that this opposition is at the base of many futile scientific discussions. 6 references.

000126 The type problem in modern philosophy. 2. The characteristic pairs of opposites in James' types. b. Intellectualism versus sensationalism. In: Jung, C., Collected Works of C. G. Jung, Vol. 6. 2nd ed., Princeton University Press, 1971. 608 p. (p. 311-312).

William James' statement that the qualities of intellectualism and sensationalism are opposites is questioned; ideologism as a more accurate antithesis of sensationalism is proposed. It is maintained that sensationalism is a reliance on sense experience as the sole source of knowledge. Rational analysis, or intellectualism, is considered to be compatible with sensationalism when the object of thought is a concrete concept derived from sense experience. Thus intellectualism and sensationalism are not necessarily opposing qualities.

000127 The type problem is modern philosophy. 2. The characteristic pairs of opposites in James' types. c. Idealism versus materialism. In: Jung, C., Collected Works of C. G. Jung, Vol. 6. 2nd ed., Princeton University Press, 1971. 608 p. (p. 312-313).

The meaning intended by William James in his use of the term "sensationalism" in philosophical thinking is explored. The alternative interpretations of sensationalism as a reflexive response to sense excitations or the extreme empiricism which is only sense oriented intellectualism are described. The observation that James commonly associated sensationalism with materalism leads to the conclusion that he meant both in the philosophical sense. James' philosophical idealism as the antithesis of materialism represents an introverted ideologism.

000128 The type problem in modern philosophy. 2. The characteristic pairs of opposites in James' types. d. Optimism versus pessimism. In: Jung, C., Collected Works of C. G. Jung, Vol. 6. 2nd ed., Princeton University Press, 1971. 608 p. (p. 313-314).

The qualities of optimism and pessimism that William James associated with his idealistic and materialistic types respectively, are ascribed to inaccuracies of description into which James fell because of his own point of view. To the idealist, the materialist's empirical view may seem cheerless and therefore pessimistic; the fact that James labels it as such indicates that James himself is an idealist, a view supported by a passage from James' Pragmatism, in which the mutual aversion of the two types is expounded.

000129 The type problem in modern philosophy. 2. The characteristic pairs of opposites in James' types. e. Religiousness versus irreligiousness. In: Jung, C., Collected Works of C. G. Jung, Vol. 6. 2nd ed., Princeton University Press, 1971. 608 p. (p. 314-315).

William James' description of the idealist as religious and the empiricist as irreligious depends on his defintion of religiousness. If religious is taken to mean an attitude in which religious ideas (rather than feelings) are dominant, then James' empiricist type can be called irreligious. However, a religious attitude can also represent feeling; moreover, psychological (uncritical) devotion to either the idea of God or the idea of matter can exist, although this attitude can be called ''religious'' only when it is absolute. Thus the empiricist can be religious. It is concluded that, in developing these terms, James was led astray by his own emotions.

000130 The type problem in modern philosophy. 2. The characteristic pairs of opposites in James' types. f. Indeterminism versus determinism. In: Jung, C., Collected Works of C. G. Jung, Vol. 6. 2nd ed., Princeton Unversity Press, 1971. 608 p. (p. 316-318).

The attitudes of determinism and indeterminism are shown to be intrinsically related to the extraverted and introverted types, respectively. Due to this orientation toward the object, the empiricist (an extravert) is impressed with the necessity of effect following cause; thus determinism is inevitable in true empiricism. The idealist (introvert), divorced from the object and drawing on primordial images over external facts, has a distinct feeling of power over and independence from objective facts; this leads him naturally to a belief in free will.

000131 The type problem in modern philosophy. 2. The characteristic pairs of opposites in James' types. g. Monism versus pluralism. h. Dogmatism versus scepticism. In: Jung, C., Collected Works of C. G. Jung, Vol. 6. 2nd ed., Princeton University Press, 1971. 608 p. (p. 318-319).

James' qualities of monism versus pluralism, and dogmatism versus skepticism, attributed to his two philosophical types, are described as essentially similar to Jungian typology. Monism is seen as natural to the idea oriented attitude, in which the idea always has a hierarchical character. The object oriented attitude necessarily tends toward a plurality of principles because the multiplicity of objects demands a plurality of concepts. Monism is typical of introversion; pluralism of extraversion. Dogmatism represents a clinging to ideas, which is characteristic of the introvert. The object oriented empiricist (extravert), on the other hand, is skeptical of all ideas, letting each experience speak for itself.

000132 The type problem in modern philosophy. 3. General criticism of James' typology. In: Jung, C., Collected Works of C. G. Jung, Vol. 6. 2nd ed., Princeton University Press, 1971. 608 p. (p. 319-321).

A critical examination of James' philosophical typology shows the limits of pragmatism as a means of reconciling the philosophical antagonism between empiricism and ideologism while recognizing the contributions of James' typology to understanding the role of temperament in philosophical differences. James' typology is a useful but not an absolute construct, valid only as long as no other factors are operative in the formation of philosophical concepts. Although James was the first to draw attention to the importance of temperament in coloring philosophical thought, he focused primarily on thought and gave no attention to the role of intuition. The introduction of intuition, and its use in solving the conflicts of opposites, is seen in the works of Bergson, Nietzsche, Schopenhauer, and Hegel. Further pragmatism is considered to obstruct creativeness, seen as the only possible source of final resoluton of the typological conflict; Nietzsche is felt to be alone in having transcended, through an act of artistic creation, the limits of both intuition and intellect. 1 reference.

000133 The type problem in biography. In: Jung, C., Collected Works of C. G. Jung, Vol. 6. 2nd ed., Princeton University Press, 1971. 608 p. (p. 322-329).

The psychological pair of opposite types formulated by Wilhelm Ostwald on the basis of his study of the biographies of scientists is presented and compared with Jung's typology. Ostwald stated that classic romantic types of scientists differed largely in their speed of reaction, the classic being slower to develop lines of thought and to produce, while the romantic is rapid and more varied in his production. Ostwald also compared his two types to the four classical temperaments: sanguine and choleric (romantic) and melancholic and phlegmatic (classic). It is felt that Otswald's conclusions depend on appearances rather than on underlying differences in affectivity. Examples from the lives of Helmholtz, Robert Meyer, Gauss, Liebig, Humphrey Davy, and Faraday illustrate the contrasts between the romantic and classic types in terms of their ability to communicate their thoughts rather than in the speed of reaction. The observed slowness of the classic thinker is due to a tendency to react inwardly and elaborate his reactions before expressing them. Although Ostwald's distinction between the types, based solely on the speed of reaction is considered inadequate the resemblance of the romantic to the extravert, and the classic to the introvert is quite clear. 1 reference.

000134 General description of the types. 1. Introduction. In: Jung, C., Collected Works of C. G. Jung, Vol. 6. 2nd ed., Princeton University Press, 1971. 608 p. (p. 330-333).

The attitude types of introversion and extraversion are described as inborn and having a biological foundation, distinguishable by their different attitudes toward the object. The introvert's attitude is one of abstraction, withdrawing libido from the object; the extravert's attitude constantly relates to and is oriented by the object. As these types are randomly distributed among cultures, levels of society, and within families, difference in attitude is thought to have a biological foundation. Since the biological relation between subject and object is considered to be one of adaptation, the two psychological attitudes can be compared with two natural modes of adaptation. One mode (extraversion) has a high rate of fertility, with few defensive powers; the other (introversion) combines a lower rate of fertility with greater means of self-preservation. It is thought likely that most persons are born with a greater capacity to adapt in one way rather than the other, and that an early falsification of type is a source of neurosis in later life.

000135 General description of the types. 2. The extraverted type. a. The general attitude of consciousness. In: Jung, C., Collected Works of C. G. Jung, Vol. 6. 2nd ed., Princeton University Press, 1971. 608 p. (p. 333-337).

The conscious behavior and attitudes of the extraverted type, the implications of his adjustment to the object, and the psychological dangers for this type are discussed. The extraverted attitude is described as one in which decisions and actions are based on objective conditions. The extravert does not expect to find absolute factors in his inner life. He tends to adjust to the moral laws of his society, changing when they change; but adjustment is not true adaptation, and the extravert risks all the crises of his society in whatever ways the society is not adaptive. Dangers are observed to arise from an extravert's tendency to ignore the subjective state of his own body until symptoms are so severe as to force themselves upon him. Hysteria is considered the most frequent neurosis developed by the extravert, growing out of his tendencies to lose himself in objects, his constant adjustment to his immediate surroundings, and his extreme suggestibility.

000136 General description of the types. 2. The extraverted type. b. The attitude of the unconscious. In: Jung, C., Collected Works of C. G. Jung, Vol. 6. 2nd ed., Princeton University Press, 1971. 608 p. (p. 337-341).

The nature of the unconscious in the extravert, its expression, primitive character, and the danger it can present to the personality are discussed. The attitude of the unconscious is compensatory to that of the conscious; in the extravert the unconscious is subjective and egocentric. The demands of the unconscious, for the extravert, have an infantile, archaic character, and the more they are repressed, the more regressive they become. When conscious extraversion is extreme, the unconscious more openly opposes it, causing difficulties to the personality either through ridiculous exaggeration of conscious aims, or by nervous breakdown from a split in the personality. The point at which unconscious attitudes cease to be compensatory occurs when, continually deprived of conscious acceptance, they become destructive as they reach a regressive level totally incompatible with the conscious attitude. The functional differentiation that can occur between objective and subjective factors in normal extraverts is described in terms of its obvious manifestations.

000137 General description of the types. 2. The extraverted type. c. The peculiarities of the basic psychological functions in the extraverted attitude. Thinking. The extraverted thinking type. In: Jung, C., Collected Works of C. G. Jung, Vol. 6. 2nd ed., Princeton University Press, 1971. 608 p. (p. 342-354).

The particular function of thought in the extraverted thinking type and its manifestations as a predominant or subordinate function are discussed. Extraverted thinking is described, not necessarily as concretized thinking, but as thought of which both the source and the aim are situated outside the subject. In this type, activity is considered dependent on intellectual conclusions oriented by objective data, and the extravert makes these conclusions into a formula for his whole environment. Depending upon the broadness or rigidity of the formula, the extravert can play a useful role in society or an oppressive one. As all the other functions are secondary, esthetic activities, friends, passion tend to be repressed; feeling is most likely to be forced into the unconscious and distorted. The more strongly the secondary functions are forced into the unconscious, the more strongly they will oppose the control of intellect, leading to the undermining of conscious goals. Ultimately these repressed doubts may lead to the overcompensation of fanaticism. Extraverted thinking is characterized as generally predicative, synthetic, and progressive, but if other functions predominate, thinking in the extravert becomes uncreative or negativistic.

000138 General description of the types. 2. The extraverted type. c. The peculiarities of the basic psychological functions in the extraverted attitude. Feeling. The extraverted feeling type. In: Jung, C., Collected Works of C. G. Jung, Vol. 6. 2nd ed., Princeton University Press, 1971. 608 p. (p. 354-359).

The feeling function in the extraverted type is discussed. For the extravert, feeling is oriented to external factors, observed reality and accepted standards. Women are considered to predominate among this type. All thinking that might disturb feeling is suppressed. It is considered possible for objects to become so important that constantly changing feeling states result in accordance with the changes in surroundings. The basic ego remains the same and is constantly at odds with these changing states, giving an appearance of mood changes. The thinking function, primarily unconscious in the extraverted feeling type, is infantile, archaic, and negative; when contradictory feeling states occur, the most negative thoughts released from the unconscious are directed toward the most valued objects of feeling. Hysteria is considered the principal form of neurosis for this type.

000139 General description of the types. 2. The extraverted type. c. The peculiarities of the basic psychological functions in the extraverted type. Summary of the extraverted rational types. In: Jung, C., Collected Works of C. G. Jung, Vol. 6. 2nd ed., Princeton University Press, 1971. 608 p. (p. 359-361).

The extraverted thinking type and the extraverted feeling type are presented as examples of rational or judging types. This classification, based on the conscious rather than the unconscious psychology of the individual, reflects the emphasis this type places in the reasoning and judging functions, to the exclusion of the irrational or accidental. The functions of perception (sensation and intuition) are repressed. In the extravert, the rationality of both the thinking and feeling types is object oriented. Subjective reason is suppressed with the risk of too heavy a repression leading to a disruption of the personality by the unconscious.

000140 General description of the types. 2. The extraverted type. c. The peculiarities of the basic psychological functions in the extraverted attitude. Sensation. The extraverted sensation type. In: Jung, C., Collected Works of C. G. Jung, Vol. 6. 2nd ed., Princeton University Press, 1971. 608 p. (p. 362-366).

The characteristics and potential difficulties of the extraverted individual in whom the function of sensation predominates is described. Although the sensation function is dependent on both subject and object, in the extraverted type the subjective aspect is repressed. Those objects that excite the strongest sensations are decisive in orienting the individual's psychology, and they are always concrete objects. Intuition is considered to be the secondary function most repressed. Usually observed in men, this type appears easy going, rational, and if normal, well adjusted to reality; the type may vary from esthete to voluptuary. If sensory bondage to the object is extreme, the unconscious intuitive function is forced out of its compensatory role and into open opposition. The repressed intuitive factor appears as projections; phobias and compulsion systems emerge from other repressed inferior functions. The resulting neurosis is considered hard to treat rationally, because reason is undifferentiated for the extraverted sensation type.

000141 General description of the types. 2. The extraverted type. c. The peculiarities of the basic psychological functions in the extraverted attitude. Intuition. The extraverted intuitive type. In: Jung, C., Collected Works of C. G. Jung, Vol. 6. 2nd ed., Princeton University Press, 1971. 608 p. (p. 366-370).

The characteristics of and hazards for the extraverted type whose primary function is intuition, are presented. On the conscious level, intuition is an attitude of expectancy and vision; however, intuition is mainly an unconscious process transmitting perceptions of relations between things that could not be seen in any other way. Sensation, as the greatest hindrance to insight, is largely suppressed. Extraverted intuition tries to see the widest range of possiblities in an objective situation. Stable conditions suffocate the intuitive extravert, and his concern for the welfare of others is weak. Both thinking and feeling are inferior functions for him, unable as he is to modify his vision with judgment. When the intuitive dimension dominates, the undifferentiated repressed functions of thinking and feeling break out in projections and compulsions somewhat like those of the sensation type. Hypochondriacal ideas and inexplicable bodily sensations may result.

000142 General description of the types. 2. The extraverted type. c. The peculiarities of the basic psychological functions in the extraverted attitude. Summary of the extraverted irrational types. In: Jung, C., Collected Works of C. G. Jung, Vol. 6. 2nd ed., Princeton University Press, 1971. 608 p. (p. 370-373).

The two irrational types of extravert (those who overemphasize either sensation or intuition) are described, and the psychic relationship between the rational and irrational types is discussed. Both the sensation and intuitive types depend on perception rather than rational judgment and are considered in the highest sense "empirical." The rational judging functions are present, but largely unconscious, appearing in the form of sophistries, cold criticism, and calculating choices. The impressions, generally unfavorable, that each type (rational and irrational) is apt to form of the other are described. It is found that a psychic relationship or rapport between the rational and irrational types does occur, in spite of enormous differences in viewpoint when the one type assumes the other to be of the same opinion as himself, while the other sees an objective community of interest. This kind of rapport rests on mutual projections and, as is the rule in the extravert, is governed by external determinants.

000143 General description of the types. 3. The introverted type. a. The general attitude of consciousness. In: Jung, C., Collected Works of C. G. Jung, Vol. 6. 2nd ed., Princeton University Press, 1971. 608 p. (p. 373-378).

The nature of introverted consciousness is discussed relative to the difference between self and ego, orienting archetype, and the role of the collective unconscious. The introvert is governed by subjective factors; although aware of external conditions, he selects subjective determinants as decisive. When the subjective function dominates, psychological action merges with the perception of the object and gives rise to new psychic material. The introverted attitude develops from a hereditary psychic structure, anterior to ego development, which includes consciousness and unconsciousness. The psychic structure of the introvert is described as identical to the collective unconscious, and it functions when conscious ideas are not present or are inhibited. It is the source of the introvert's subjective views. Complete identity of the self with the ego in the introvert is felt to result in neurosis characterized by a power complex and consuming egocentricity. 2 references.

000144 General description of the types. 3. The introverted type. b. The attitude of the unconscious. In: Jung, C., Collected Works of C. G. Jung, Vol. 6. 2nd ed., Princeton University Press, 1971. 608 p. (p. 378-380).

The unconscious attitude in the introvert, particularly when too much importance is attached to the ego, is discussed. When the ego usurps the claims of the subject and attempts to dominate the object, an unconscious compensation for the influence of the object takes place. Because this attempted domination of the object by the ego is nonadaptive, the unconscious takes charge of object relations, and the ego is forced to develop a system of defenses. The typical neurosis for the introvert is seen as psychasthenia characterized by extreme sensitivity and chronic exhauastion.

000145 General description of the types. 3. The introverted type. c. The peculiarities of the basic psychological functions in the introverted attitude. Thinking. The introverted thinking type. In: Jung, C., Collected Works of C. G. Jung, Vol. 6. 2nd ed., Princeton University Press, 1971. 608 p. (p. 380-387).

Characteristics of the introverted thinking type are described. Oriented to the subjective factor is experience which guides and determines judgment, the introverted thinker is observed to be more interested in producing new views than new facts. With a tendency to force facts into the shape of his private images, the introvert can fall prey to mystical thinking. Kant is offered as an example of the normal introverted thinking type, strongly influenced by ideas having a subjective foundation. This type is found to be often impractical not only neglecting the object, but defending against it unnecessarily. However lucid the inner structure of his thought, the introvert does not clearly understand how to communicate it to the world of reality. In personal relations he is described as taciturn, domineering and inconsiderate, appreciated only by his intimates. With more intense members of this type, convictions become more rigid, and they shut off outside influences completely. Up to a point, their thinking is positive and synthetic, producing ideas that reflect the primordial images; but when totally divorced from objective experience, the ideas become mythological and unintelligible to others. 1 reference.

000146 General description of the types. 3. The introverted type. c. The peculiarities of the basic psychological functions in the introverted attitude. Feeling. The introverted feeling type. In: Jung, C., Collected Works of C. G. Jung, Vol. 6. 2nd ed., Princeton University Press, 1971. 608 p. (p. 387-391).

The characteristics of the introverted feeling type are described. Principally guided by subjective factors, introverted feeling can be inferred only indirectly, as it seldom appears on the surface. It aims to subordinate the object in order to realize underlying images. It is found that the introverted feeling type is usually a woman, silent, inaccessible and giving an impression of pleasing repose unless the object is too strong. In such cases the obvious turning of her feeling away from it would make her appear indifferent and cold. Intemperate passion is taboo for her, although her feelings are intensive rather than extensive. Her passions may flow into her children, but are generally secretive. A tendency to coerce others with her secret feeling rarely disturbs the normal introvert, but a trace of domineering is evident. When the unconscious subject is identified with the ego, the individual becomes a despot and ultimately neurotic. In this type, unconscious thinking takes the form of archaic consciousness that helps compensate for the exaltation of the ego; however, if the ego assumes the subject, projection occurs; the power of the object is felt; and elaborate counterplots are produced by the ego as defenses. The neurosis is usually found to be neurasthenic, with severe physical complications.

000147 General description of the types. 3. The introverted type. c. The peculiarities of the basic psychological functions in the introverted attitude. Summary of the introverted rational types. In: Jung, C., Collected Works of C. G. Jung, Vol. 6. 2nd ed., Princeton University Press, 1971. 608 p. (p. 391-393).

The difficulties of the introverted rational types are described as based on the natural difference in outlook between the extravert and the introvert. The rationality of the introvert is seen to have a bias toward the subjective, not in the logic of the thought itself, but in the premise upon which it is based. The principal difficulty of the introvert is considered to be that the prevailing mode of Western thought is extraverted. The subjective mode is devalued in Western culture, and the introvert comes to devalue it in himself, to feel inferior, and to become more egotistical, thus ultimately deserving his general censure.

000148 General description of the types. 3. The introverted type. c. The peculiarities of the basic psychological functions in the introverted attitude. Sensation. The introverted sensation type. In: Jung, C., Collected Works of C. G. Jung, Vol. 6. 2nd ed., Princeton University Press, 1971. 608 p. (p. 393-398).

The nature of sensation in the introvert and the characteristic normal and neurotic behavior of the introvert sensation type are discussed. Such types dwell predominantly on the subjective aspects of perception so that the object becomes secondary to the excitation produced by it. A subjective perception is defined by the meaning associated with it rather than by the mere image of the object represented; this meaning is not consciously developed, but springs from a primordial psychic organization. Therefore, no proportional relation exists between object and sensation for the introverted sensation type, and such an individual may seem unpredictable and arbitrary. This subjective content to perception intervenes and intercepts the effects of the object, and in more serious cases a protective defense obscures its influence; in pathological cases the type is no longer able to distinguish between the real object and the subjective perception. The intervention of the unconscious is seen to cause even a normal introverted sensation type to act according to an unconscious model and not the real environment; further, his lack of comparative judgment leaves him unaware of his alienation from reality. When extreme detachment for the object occurs, intuition is repressed into the unconscious and has an extraverted and archaic quality, producing compulsive ideas of the most perverse kind, and usually resulting in a compulsion neurosis.

000149 General description of the types. 3. The introverted type. c. The peculiarities of the basic psychological functions in the introverted attitude. Intuition. The introverted intuitive type. In: Jung, C., Collected Works of C. G. Jung, Vol. 6. 2nd ed., Princeton University Press, 1971. 608 p. (p. 398-403).

Introverted intuition is described as directed to the inner object, to the archaic contents of the unconscious. It excludes sensation and perceives the world by filtering sensory information through the background processes of consciousness, which consist of primordial archetypal images; these images take on the reality of things for the intuitive introvert. The artist is described as a typical representative of this type. Ordinarily there is little inclination to extrapolate these images to the world, but when there is, a different type of individual is produced, one who attempts to relate himself to his visions and find meaning in them while remaining unadapted to everyday reality. The psychological danger of this type is considered to lie in the extreme suppression of sensation, which gives rise to a compensatory extraverted sensation function of

archaic character. Normally this serves to compensate the conscious introverted attitude; but if it cannot, the unconscious becomes excessively dependent on the object, causing a compulsion neurosis with hypochondriacal symptoms.

000150 General description of the types. 3. The introverted type. c. The peculiarities of the basic psychological functions in the introverted attitude. Summary of the introverted irrational types. In: Jung, C., Collected Works of C. G. Jung, Vol. 6. 2nd ed., Princeton University Press, 1971. 608 p. (p. 403-405).

The characteristics of the introverted irrational types are described in terms of their inability to communicate and in terms of their contribution to society. Outwardly visible traits of these types are seen as a general secretiveness, lack of sympathy, and uncertainty. They are mostly misunderstood and, lacking in judgment, do not understand themselves. It is thus doubly difficult for them to communicate intelligibly the richness of the subjective events they experience. From a rationalistic, extraverted viewpoint, they are useless to society; yet they are, in a way, educators and promoters of culture through the example of their life rather than by their production of ideas. Their lives are considered to illustrate the possibility of a rich and fulfilling interior life, an ideal lacking in Western civilization.

000151 General descriptions of the types. 3. The introverted type. d. The principal and auxiliary functions. In: Jung, C., Collected Works of C. G. Jung, Vol. 6. 2nd ed., Princeton University Press, 1971. 608 p. (p. 405-407).

The interrelationships of the functions of thinking, feeling, sensation and intuition at the conscious and unconscious levels are discussed. The consciousness of any function is taken to mean that control of the will that decisively orients consciousness. Only one function can have principal orienting power, unless there is no differentiation of any function, as in the case of primitive mentality. A second function can operate as an auxiliary or complementary one, if its nature is different from but not opposed to the dominant function; thus a rational principal function (thinking) can have either of the irrational functions (sensation or intuition) as an auxiliary, because they are functions of perception, not of judging. This auxiliary function proves useful only inasmuch as it serves the primary function. In addition to the primary conscious function, auxiliary, unconscious functions are observed to exist which group themselves in patterns correlated with and, at times, opposed to the conscious ones and exist in an archaic, animal state. Implications of these functions for psychoanalytic treatment are discussed.

000152 Psychological types. Definitions. In: Jung, C., Collected Works of C. G. Jung, Vol. 6. 2nd ed., Princeton University Press, 1971. 608 p. (p. 408-486).

In order to clarify the use of terms, and to establish the precise sense in which concepts that have widely divergent meanings in psychology as a whole are used, explanations of the principal psychological concepts are presented. Attitude, fantasy, feeling, idea, image, sensation, soul (as anima and as persona), symbol, and unconscious are explained at length. Reference to other psychological theorists is made when the meaning of their original concepts has been modified. Among the concepts defined are: traditional terms pertaining to psychic structure, such as ego and libido; descriptive terms such as introjection and participation mystique; and general terms that take on a specific meaning, such as thinking, collective, and constructive. 58 references.

000153 Psychological types. Epilogue. In: Jung, C., Collected Works of C. G. Jung, Vol. 6. 2nd ed., Princeton University Press, 1971. 608 p. (p. 487-495).

The paradoxical problem of explaining or understanding human psychology by means of human psychology is raised. The heterogeneity of men is such that no one perfect world could be devised for all; hence the concept of typical attitudes is intended to reflect the heterogeneity of man, and is seen as a necessary antidote to theories that account for the uniformity of man. Explanations of man's uniformity can be discovered in the foundations of the consciousness; his individual differentiation can be found in a psychology of types. Based on the observation that the psychic process is not merely the object of psychology, but also its subject, it is deemed inevitable that each psychological theory will reflect its author; thus it is concluded that an intellectual examination of the human psyche must necessarily incorporate elements of paradox and relativity. 2 references.

000154 Appendix: Four papers on psychological typology. 1. A contribution to the study of psychological types. In: Jung, C., Collected Works of C. G. Jung, Vol. 6. 2nd ed., Princeton University Press, 1971. 608 p. (p. 497-509).

The contrast between hysteria and schizophrenia suggests the existence of a similar contrast in psychological types in normal individuals. Hysteria, with its high activity level, fantasies explicable by personal history, and realistic simulation of physical illness, illustrates a centrifugal movement of libido. Schizophrenic apathy and fantasy related to dream material of an archaic quality illustrate the centripetal movement of libido. These movements of libido are termed extraverted and introverted, respectively. Although both movements are observed to operate alternately in the same person, the existence of the pathological extremes suggests that types can be distinguished in normal individuals by the predominance of one mechanism or the other. Jungian types are compared to those of various other theorists, including: William James's tender-minded and rough-minded types; Wilhelm Worringer's abstraction and empathy; Schiller's naive and sentimental types; Nietzsche's Apollinian and Dionysian; and Franz Finck's linguistic distinction between transitive and intransitive verb structure. In the field of psychiatry itself, Otto Gross's proposal that there are two types of inferiority, characterized by the weakness or the intense activity of a second function which resembles affectivity, is examined. Freud's reductive, pluraltistic, causal and sensualistic psychology is seen as exemplifying a centrifugal movement of libido, or the extraverted attitude, while Adler's intellectualistic, monistic and finalistic psychology is regarded as a demonstration of the centripetal movement of libido, or the introverted attitude. 9 references.

000155 Appendix: Four papers on psychological typology. 2. Psychological types. In: Jung, C., Collected Works of C. G. Jung, Vol. 6. 2nd ed., Princeton University Press, 1971. 608 p. (p. 510-523).

The psychological types are reviewed and their basis in the subdivision of attitudes and of functions, crediting Galen with the first attempt to classify humans based on affectivity is described. Beyond affectivity, most persons can be grouped in terms of one of two attitudes: either they are primarily motivated by external impersonal factors, or by internal subjective factors. As the two attitudinal types perceive everything differently, they are usually incompatible. In addition to these two attitudes, the conscious psyche is seen as an apparatus for adaptation that consists of four basic psychic

functions: sensation (perceptions by means of the sense organs); thinking (drawing conclusions in terms of subjective valuation); feeling (a function of subjective valuation); and intuition (perception by means of the unconscious). Although these would ideally balance one another perfectly in the individual psyche, in reality one function usually occupies the foreground, while the others remain as background. Each of these four functions is linked in some way with the extraverted or introverted attitude, so that no man is simply introverted or extraverted, except in terms of one dominant function. The unconscious stands in a compensatory relation to the conscious, and accommodates the repressed functions, which remain undeveloped, archaic, and are of the opposite attitude from the conscious one. Conflict is considered to occur if a conscious attitude becomes too one-sided. At least eight distinguishable types are found, but it is acknowledged that more could be established, each with greater subtlety of description. 2 references.

000156 Appendix: Four papers on psychological typology. 3. A psychological theory of types. In: Jung, C., Collected Works of C. G. Jung, Vol. 6. 2nd ed., Princeton University Press, 1971. 608 p. (p. 524-541).

The history and logic of the development of a psychology of types is presented as growing from the study of psychogenic symptoms, and from the realization that the complexes were important in that they contained conflicts. Between the demand for adaptation and the individual's constitutional ability to respond to that demand, the complex alone, although it is most basic and occurs earliest, is inadequate to explain individual differences in neurotic reactions. These differences, apparently innate, showed certain fundamental peculiarities that invited grouping. An active/passive grouping proved unsatisfactory, as did a reflective/unreflective grouping, although the latter more nearly approximated the observations. The classification of a negative versus a positive reaction to an object was undertaken, with the negative called introversion, and the positive, extraversion. This definition still did not account for observed differences between individuals, and a further exploration into the psychic functions was needed to explain, for example, why one introvert hesitates in a certain way, and another in a different way. Concepts of thinking and feeling were taken from general speech to represent the rational approaches, and those of sensation and intuition to represent perceptions, which are not evaluative or rational but irrational. Each of the irrational functions (sensation and intuition) is considered incompatible with the other. The effect of one function's domination over the others is observed to be the repression of the subordinate functions into the unconscious.

000157 Appendix: Four papers on psychological typology. 4. Psychological typology. In: Jung, C., Collected Works of C. G. Jung, Vol. 6. 2nd ed., Princeton University Press, 1971. 608 p. (p. 542-555).

A discussion of the psychological typology that takes into account individual differences is preceded by a brief history of attempts at psychological classification. Included are descriptions of Galen's melancholic, sanguine, choleric and phlegmatic temperaments as forerunners of studies relating hormones to temperament, and the theories of Flournoy, James and Freud, which view the psyche as a totality. Through extensive clinical contact with people from many classes and nations, a theory of the attributes certain groups had in common was developed; it became clear that there were two basic psychological types, which are called extravert and introvert. Extraversion is characterized by interest in the external object, responsiveness, and a ready acceptance of external happenings; the extravert as a subjective entity is seen as hidden from himself, and his psychic life is enacted outside himself, in accordance with the environment. The introvert is directed not to the object, but the subject; he is aloof from external happenings, and finds his inner life his foremost pleasure. His psychic life is played out wholly within. These two attitudes are described as opposing modes, for which the numinal accent (the essential orientation of the type) decides between subject and object and selects the conscious function of which the individual makes most use. Four basic psychological functions are postulated: thinking, feeling, sensation and intuition, of which the first two are rational or judging, and the last two irrational or perceiving. As sensation and intuition rule each other out, so that only one can become a conscious function, so do thinking and feeling. These four types of psychological functions correlate and combine with either the introverted or the extraverted attitude, making for eight demonstrable types. 5 references.

07 TWO ESSAYS ON ANALYTICAL PSYCHOLOGY

000158 On the psychology of the unconscious. Prefaces. In: Jung, C., Collected Works of C. G. Jung, Vol. 7. 2nd ed., Princeton University Press, 1966. 349 p. (p. 1-8).

The five prefaces introducing this volume indicate that the original work, "The Psychology of the Unconscious Process," has been revised and refined many times. The purpose of the work, mentioned in the 1917 and 1918 editions, is to provide a broad survey on the nature and the psychology of the unconscious. The growing concern with the human psyche and the interest in man's chaotic unconscious is seen as a result of the First World War. This concern, motivating self-reflection is seen as a favorable trend since the psychology of nations and that of individuals are interrelated. The hope is expressed that the individual's return to his own deepest being will result in a cure for the illnesses of the times. It is frequently noted that this work attempts to popularize a highly complicated science still in the process of development. The essay is not intended to be comprehensive. Its purpose is to supply background information to be used as an introduction to the unconscious. Because this study is virtually virgin territory, the essay may contain inadequacies and errors. The preface to the fifth edition, the edition that applies to this volume, indicates that the previous versions had been thoroughly revised and that the material on psychological types has been included in a separate volume, title "Psychological Types."

000159 On the psychology of the unconscious. I. Psychoanalysis In: Jung, C., Collected Works of C. G. Jung, Vol. 7. 2nd ed., Princeton University Press, 1966. 349 p. (p. 9-18).

A brief overview of the theories which led from experimental psychology to a psychotherapy of neuroses is presented along with an analysis of a case study illustrating the role of the unconscious in the development of neuroses. Charcot, Janet, Bernheim, Liebault and Freud are compared, and Breuer's work is singled out at the starting point for this new psychology. Breuer's classic case of Anna, an hysterical neurotic, is used to illustrate the so-called trauma theory. Numerous other hysterical neuroses are presented. Freud is credited with carrying Breuer's work forward and posing the problem in terms of predisposition, a term used to signify the role of an early unconscious trauma in neurosis. The hysterical disorder of a young female patient is explored in detail, revealing the role of a disturbance in the erotic sphere, as well as the presence of a trauma, as a factor in creating the neurosis.

000160 On the psychology of the unconscious. II. The Eros theory. In: Jung, C., Collected Works of C. G. Jung, Vol. 7. 2nd ed., Princeton University Press, 1966. 349 p. (p. 19-29).

A general discussion of the role of the erotic conflict and its place in neurosis precedes the discussion of the techniques of psychoanalysis and therapy. The historial role of sexual conflict in the development of psychoanalysis is discussed. Methods of analyzing the unconscious include hypnotism, association, and dream analysis. Dream analysis, the most important method, is described. A hypothetical dream is presented and evaluated in terms of the theory of wish fulfillment. The purpose of Freudian psychoanalysis is explained as an attempt to make the animal instincts conscious in order to incorporate them into a purposeful whole. Freud's theory of repression of sexuality as the foundation of neurosis is evaluated and it is concluded that, although it is grounded on a true and factual principle, it is, nevertheless, one-sided and exclusive. A broader understanding of Eros as energy is suggested as the key to arriving at a harmony between spirit and instinct, the goal of psychoanalysis.

000161 On the psychology of the unconscious. III. The other point of view: the will to power. In: Jung, C., Collected Works of C. G. Jung, Vol. 7. 2nd ed., Princeton University Press, 1966. 349 p. (p. 30-40).

Freud's theory of neurosis, based on Eros and Adler's theory which stems from the will to power, are compared and contrasted. The instinct of self-preservation and its relation to the will to power are examined in the light of Nietzsche's teachings. An analysis of the dangers lurking in an "identification with the shadow," i.e.,with just one of the instincts, explains Nietzsche's neurotic one-sidedness. The importance of both Eros and the will to power, manifested in a drive for the preservation of the species and self-preservation, are stressed. Wagner is mentioned briefly as an advocate of the former, and Nietzsche as his polar opposite. A clinical case is studied in detail from two perspectives: Freud's belief that a neurosis arises from antecedent circumstances (causality) and Adler's contention that teleological causes are paramount. The Freudian analysis concentrates on Eros, the Adlerian approach emphasizes the power instinct, and they contradict one another. 1 reference.

000162 On the psychology of the unconscious. IV. The problem of attitude-type. In: Jung, C., Collected Works of C. G. Jung, Vol. 7. 2nd ed., Princeton University Press, 1966. 349 p. (p. 41-63).

The attitudes of introversion/extraversion are introduced to explain the opposition of the Freudian and Adlerian viewpoints. Theories are seen as reflecting an author's peculiarities and, consequently, they are often narrow in scope. The two very different theories of neurosis, the first emphasizing the object and the second emphasizing the subject, are viewed as manifestations of a type antagonism. The introversion personality type focuses on the subject; the extraversion type focuses on the object. However, these types are seldom observed in a pure state. The dynamics of a relationship between individuals who possess opposite personality types is examined. In contrast with the views of Freud and Adler, neuroses are described as sometimes serving useful adjustive functions. Freud and Adler are criticized for refusing to recognize the inexorable role of irrational fate in the development of both humanity and the individual. Psychic energy, defined as "libido," is the focus of much of the discussion. Examples are used to demonstrate that the psychic energy released during treatment follows an unpredictable path known only to the unconscious. This energy has its source in the tension of opposites and can only be used when the proper gradient is found. Several type theories, all based on opposites, are cited. It is felt that in order to advance in treatment, i.e.,to achieve a balance in the psyche, one must recognize the principle of opposition. 8 references.

000163 On the psychology of the unconscious. V. The personal and the collective (or transpersonal) unconscious. In: Jung, C., Collected Works of C. G. Jung, Vol. 7. 2nd ed., Princeton University Press, 1966. 349 p. (p. 64-79).

The idea of the collective unconscious is introduced and its role in the process of transference in psychotherapy is discussed. Guidance for the existence of the collective unconscious is found in ancient myths and primitive religions. Robert Mayer's discovery of the conservation of energy is presented as evidence of the workings of the transpersonal unconscious, and of the manner in which the archetypes or primordial images may contribute, at times, to our intellectual advancement. On the other hand, the harmful effects of introjection and projection are also pointed out. The transition between the two stages of life, instinctual and cultural, is examined in terms of Heraclitus' psychological law of enantiodromia or the force of opposites. 12 references.

000164 On the psychology of the unconscious. VI. The synthetic or constructive method. In: Jung, C., Collected Works of C. G. Jung, Vol. 7. 2nd ed., Princeton University Press, 1966. 349 p. (80-89).

It is suggested that the traditional method of dream analysis reduction must be followed by synthesis when the symbols originate in the collective unconscious. The value of this approach is supported by a detailed dream analysis utilizing both the redirective and synthetic modes of interpretation. The process of reconciling the conscious with the unconscious, or dealing with both the real and imaginary, is termed the transcendent function. A dream reported by a female patient is interpreted in two ways and used to support the use of the synthetic mode. This constructive (subjective) process refers the dream images back to the patient, while the Freudian analytical (objective) method equates dream images with objects in the real world. It is recommended that the therapist should search for archetypal motifs when an analytical dream interpretation no longer elicits new information. If these are found, the interpretive procedure should be altered accordingly. 2 references.

000165 On the psychology of the unconscious. VII. The archetypes of the collective unconscious. In: Jung, C., Collected Works of C. G. Jung, Vol. 7. 2nd ed., Princeton University Press, 1966. 349 p. (p. 90-113).

Lengthy analyses of the dreams of two patients (one female, one male) are presented as examples of the importance of the archetype in revealing the contents of the unconscious. The examination of the dreams demonstrates that material from the collective unconscious is often projected onto persons in the immediate environment. Attention is given to the "magic demon," a commonly projected archetype, and several references to this and other symbols from literature, religion, and history are cited as examples. The purpose of dreams is stated: dreams act as a compensation, aid in maintaining psychic equilibrium and serve as a mental corrective. The analysis of the dreams of the male patient demonstrates that the symbols and metaphors of the dream are a preparation for effective therapy. One of the basic themes revealed in dream analysis is that of the "individuation process," defined as the

goal of the transcendent function; i.e.,to uncover and facilitate the original potential wholeness of the individual. The whole discussion emphasizes how important it is for the therapist to gain a complete understanding of dreams and the various manifestations of the unconscious. Such an understanding enables the therapist to prevent the formation of unconscious oppositions and to utilize the healing factor of compensation. 3 references.

000166 On the psychology of the unconscious. VIII. General remarks on the therapeutic approach to the unconscious. In: Jung, C., Collected Works of C. G. Jung, Vol. 7. 2nd ed., Princeton University Press, 1966. 349 p. (p. 114-118).

The risks and the benefits of gaining an understanding of the unconscious are described and reference is made to the contributions of Freud, Adler and Nietzsche to this understanding. The dangers inherent in the unconscious are demonstrated by allusions to latent psychoses, controlled by artificial normalcy, and to overt manifestations which often take the form of accident proneness. However, the favorable side of the unconscious is also presented: one who has the capacity and urge for higher differentiation can gain access to its therapeutic potential. Only by means of this transcendent function can harmony be achieved. The therapist is advised to meet the needs of the individual since no formula can indicate how and when a cure will be effected. Concluding remarks concern the differing views of practitioners in medical psychology, something which compounds the difficulty for the reader new to the subject. All investigators compose theories from their existing cognitive frameworks and unique life experiences. These views are contrasted with those of Freud.

000167 On the psychology of the unconscious. Conclusion. In: Jung, C., Collected Works of C. G. Jung, Vol. 7. 2nd ed., Princeton University Press, 1966. 349 p. (p. 119).

The worth of the preceding pages is left to the judgment of the future. Apologies for the difficulty of the material are presented, and all who venture into a new area are urged to proceed, but with caution. For progress to occur in the field of human behavior, the psychology of tomorrow must have a broad foundation that encompasses human emotions and the contents of the psyche as well as the intellect.

000168 The relations between the ego and the unconscious. Prefaces. In: Jung, C., Collected Works of C. G. Jung, Vol. 7. 2nd ed., Princeton University Press, 1966. 349 p. (p. 123-125).

In prefaces to the second (1935) and third (1938) editions, the purpose of the work, "the relation between the ego and the unconscious," is cited: to give a summation of 28 years of psychological and psychiatric experience, in order to form an intellectual conception of the unconscious. The idea that the development of the unconscious is an independent process, a view which distinguishes these theories from Freud's, is traced back to a study of somnambulism made in 1902. The present book describes the relation between the conscious and the unconscious, although it does not claim to offer the final answers to the nature and essence of the unconscious. It is mentioned that Oriental philosophy has been interested in similar problems for centuries and thus is valuable as comparative material. 2 references.

000169 The relations between the ego and the unconscious. Part 1. The effects of the unconscious upon consciousness. I. The personal and the collective unconscious. In: Jung, C., Collected Works of C. G. Jung, Vol. 7. 2nd ed., Princeton University Press, 1966. 349 p. (p. 127-138).

The personal and the collective unconscious are defined, and Freud's view of the personal unconscious, the storehouse of repressed material, is expanded to include deenergized conscious material as well as subliminal sense perceptions. The unconscious is seen as acting in a compensatory fashion, creating the seeds of future conscious thoughts. These unconscious processes and all the unconscious material acquired during the individual's lifetime are defined as the personal unconscious. A case study is presented that reveals the presence of certain unconscious material beyond the scope of the individual's life experiences. The presence of this material is explained by postulating the existence of a collective unconscious. To illustrate this theory, the case of a female patient who has reached the upper limit of the therapeutic benefits of transference is presented. In order to discover a more permanent basis for her recovery, her dreams, thought to be indicators of hidden psychic processes and desires, are analysed. In one of her dreams, the analyst assumed superhuman proportions akin to those of a gigantic primordial father. This dream also contained an image of God as the wind which was interpreted as the patient's longing for absolute faith. This image is not personal since the woman, an agnostic, thought of God as an abstract life force and was unaware that the phrase "God is spirit" is a free translation of the original Greek of the New Testament that reads "God is wind." Thus an historic image of world wide distribution is shown to have come into existence again through a natural psychic function. It is concluded, then, that the unconscious contains not only personal, but also impersonal and collective components in the form of inherited thought categories or archetypes. Furthermore, it is shown that these archetypes can be restored to consciousness by the primitive analogical mode of thinking peculiar to dreams. 4 references.

000170 The relations between the ego and the unconscious. Part 1. The effects of the unconscious upon consciousness. II. Phenomena resulting from the assimilation of the unconscious. In: Jung, C., Collected Works of C. G. Jung, Vol. 7. 2nd ed., Princeton University Press, 1966. 349 p. (p. 139-155).

The salutary effects of the assimilation of the unconscious and consciousness are studied and the dangers inherent in uncovering the collective unconscious are examined. Typically, the individual feels either unduly elated or depressed upon discovering the contents of his personal unconscious. Both are reactions to the obliteration of former conscious psychic boundaries that the uncovering of the unconscious inevitably produces. When the opposites of the conscious and the unconscious are brought together the analysand feels either cursed by the evil in him that went previously unperceived or vindicated by the unperceived good. The cure is seen as stemming from the individual's ability to recognize that the two, taken together, comprise his reality. If, however, portions of the collective unconscious are dredged up with the personal unconscious, the results can be catastrophic. The transpersonal contents of the unconscious are living entities and the individual's discovery of their existence within his own psyche can lead to personality disintegration. The development of personality demands strict differentiation of the individual from the collective psyche. A partial or blurred differentiation can lead to the melting away of the individual into the collective. The annexation of the deeper layers of the unconscious can, on the other hand, lead to an enlargement or inflation of the personality. This inflation can be harmful or beneficial depending on the individual's ability to assimilate the new knowledge. It is important, therefore, in practical treatment, to keep the integrity of the personality constantly in mind and avoid over-

loading the patient with too much knowledge of his unconscious. 7 references.

000171 The relations between the ego and the unconscious. Part l. The effects of the unconscious upon consciousness. III. The persona as segment of the collective psyche. In: Jung, C., Collected Works of C. G. Jung, Vol. 7. 2nd ed., Princeton University Press, 1966. 349 p. (p. 156-162).

The distinction between personal and collective unconscious is reiterated and persona is defined in relation to the collective psyche. The persona consists of the sum of psychic facts that are felt to be personal. It is, however, only a mask for the collective psyche. One's real individuality lies in the unconscious self which, despite the ego consciousness' feeling of exclusive identity with the persona, makes itself felt directly and indirectly in the choice and delineation of the persona. Through the analysis of the personal unconscious, the conscious mind becomes suffused with collective material which brings with it the elements of individuality. The case of the philosophy student presented in chapter one is reviewed as an example of the manner in which individuality and aspects of the collective psyche begin to emerge in a coalescent state once personal repressions are listed. In an almost magical way the collective psyche begins to determine the individual's fate. It is often beneficial in analysis to induce artifically a predominance of unconscious influences; this breaks down the persona and undermines the authority of the conscious mind thereby leading a patient past a difficulty that might block further development. As long as the conscious mind is capable of assimilating the products of the unconscious, the latter's instinctive inclination to correct the balance of the conscious mind will be benefical. However, if the unconscious simply rides roughshod over the conscious mind, a psychotic condition will develop. 1 reference.

000172 The relations between the ego and the unconscious. Part 1. The effects of the unconscious upon consciousness. IV. Negative attempts to free the individuality from the collective psyche. a. Regressive restoration of the persona. In: Jung, C., Collected Works of C. G. Jung, Vol. 7. 2nd ed., Princeton University Press, 1966. 349 p. (p. 163-168).

Regressive restoration of the persona is described as an unsatisfactory attempt by the patient to extricate himself from the collective psyche. The contact of the unconscious psyche and the collective psyche results in a collapse of the conscious persona, a traumatic event for the patient. To escape it, some people climb to new heights while others dive into the abyss below. Those people who categorically reject and repress the contents of the collective psyche are cited as examples of the second form of escape which inevitably leads to the reestablishment of a now diminished persona. This is likened to Faust's rejection of freedom and yearning for a simple life. Since one's earlier state of naive consciousness cannot be recovered, the person who chooses this road often leads a life of resignation self-embitterment and chronic neurotic sickliness. 6 references.

000173 The relations between the ego and the unconscious. Part 1. The effects of the unconscious upon consciousness. IV. Negative attempts to free the individuality from the collective psyche. b. Identification with the collective psyche. In: Jung, C., Collected Works of C. G. Jung, Vol. 7. 2nd ed., Princeton University Press, 1966. 349 p. (p. 169-171).

The effect of identification with the collective psyche as a means of escaping the trauma resulting from the collapse of the conscious persona is described. To free himself from the embrace of the collective psyche, instead of denying it, as in regressive restoration of the persona, the afflicted individual accepts it so totally that he is devoured by it, becomes lost in it, and thus is no longer capable of perceiving it as a separate entity. Such people often feel that they possess a great truth. There are powerful psychological inducements for holding onto this identification with the collective psyche: it enhances one's life feelings, promises a rich harvest of knowledge, and makes one feel as though life has suddenly acquired a new direction. But the final effects of identification are considered harmful in that one does not reap the benefits of the collective psyche but merely becomes one with them (inflation). Despite the seeming rewards and gratifications accompanying inflation, it is shown that the ability for effective self-criticism vanishes.

000174 The relations between the ego and the unconscious. Part 2. Individuation. I. The function of the unconscious. In: Jung, C., Collected Works of C. G. Jung, Vol. 7. 2nd ed., Princeton University Press, 1966. 349 p. (p. 173-187).

Individuation, as an alternative and more desirable form of development than those forms wherein the collective psyche has the upper hand is discussed. The aim of individuation, to divest the self of the false wrappings of the persona and the suggestive powers of primordial images, is presented. Although the persona is easily understood by all, since everyone can consciously experience it, the workings of the unconscious processes are seen to be more difficult to understand since they are more subtle. Analyses of those unconscious factors can be effected in part by examples from mental illness, creative inspiration and religious conversion. The unconscious is seen as standing in a compensatory relation to the conscious mind. Several examples from case histories are presented to illustrate the specific ways in which the unconscious performs its compensatory function. In general, it works by producing images, usually revealed in dreams, that respond to a conscious situation. In so doing the unconscious does not "think" but rather acts automatically. Since man's consciousness is circumscribed, this compensatory function of the unconscious supplies psychic contents which, if properly recognized, extend the range of consciousness. The result of this process is evaluated: the increase in self-knowledge diminishes the layer of the personal unconscious that is superimposed over the collective unconscious. 3 references.

000175 The relations between the ego and the unconscious. Part 2. Individuation. II. Anima and animus. In: Jung, C., Collected Works of C. G. Jung, Vol. 7. 2nd ed., Princeton University Press, 1966. 349 p. (p. 188-211).

The anima/animus concepts are presented and defined in relation to the process of individuation. For the purposes of psychological inquiry, the soul is defined as a semiconscious psychic complex that has partial autonomy. The feminine part of a man's soul is called the anima. The soul's femininity derives from three sources: man's life experiences with women, the inherited collective image of woman that exists in man's unconscious, and an innate psychic structure that allows man to experience in the subject manner of woman. Fundamental differences in the psyches of man and woman are said to exist. Man is described as more objective and rational, woman as more subjective and emotional. Man represses his feminine qualities in order to develop his persona; hence, the relation between the anima and the persona is compensatory. Since complete identification with the persona leads to neurosis, the compensatory function of the anima is salutary. In order for individuation to take place, however, man must free himself from both the persona and the anima and realize that

the interplay between the inner and the outer forces represents the energetics of the life process, the polar tension necessary for self-regulation. Because the anima is an inner process and harder to recognize it is more difficult to deal with than is the persona. As a method for perceiving the anima it is suggested that it be objectified; i.e.,granted the status of a separate, concrete entity, and allowed to speak. By making the anima conscious the individual builds a bridge to his unconscious. Since the animus is the corresponding entity in women, it plays its role in the development of a woman's personality. 4 references.

000176 The relations between the ego and the unconscious. Part 2. Individuation. III. The technique of differentiation between the ego and the figure of the unconscious. In: Jung, C., Collected Works of C. G. Jung, Vol. 7. 2nd ed., Princeton University Press, 1966. 349 p. (p. 212-226).

The aim of differentiation and techniques for facilitating it are examined. Individuation, the attainment of a personality at mid-point between the ego consciousness and the unconscious, is seen as the result of differentiation. In order to facilitate differentiation in neurotics, it is suggested that the production of fantasies be encouraged. The theory behind this technique is explained: if the unconscious has gained an ascendancy over the conscious, the strength of the former can be sapped by funneling its energy into the production of fantasies. This continual conscious realization of unconscious fantasies extends conscious horizons by the inclusion of unconscious contents and gradually diminishes the dominant influence of the unconscious. Only by dissolving autonomous complexes such as the anima can the individual come to terms with his unconscious. Two case studies are presented to document the therapeutic effects of fantasy production. It is stressed that the patient must take his fantasies literally, participate in them actively, and thereby derive the maximum therapeutic benefit. The analyst, however, is cautioned to ignore the literal content of the fantasies and to probe beneath them in order to discover the underlying operative processes.

000177 The relations between the ego and the unconscious. Part 2. Individuation. IV. The mana personality. In: Jung, C., Collected Works of C. G. Jung, Vol. 7. 2nd ed., Princeton University Press, 1966. 349 p. (p. 227-241).

The formation and characteristics of the mana personality, a stage of development that follows the transformation and dissolution of the anima as an autonomous complex, are described. The power (mana) that infused the anima is often usurped by the ego. As a consequence the individual feels, mistakenly, that he has vanquished the unconscious and that his new knowledge of it will give him power. Hence, he perceives himself as a wise and powerful man. This self-concept, termed the mana personality, is a flat, collective figure, as are all archetype dominated personalities; consequently, it restricts the individual's growth. In order to continue to develop, the individual must go through the process of differentiating the ego from the mana personality. This involves bringing those contents of the unconscious specific to the mana personality to consciousness. The danger of identifying or concretizing the contents of the mana personality into a god are pointed out with Goethe's Faust and Nietzsche's Zarathustra cited as attempts to master the contents of the mana personality. Since these approaches are obviously not suited to the man who lives in the real world, the assimilation of the contents of the mana personality into the conscious mind is seen as the best solution. The results will be the formation of the concept of self, a psychological construct akin to the religious concept of the "god within us." 3 references.

000178 Appendices: I. New paths in psychology. In: Jung, C., Collected Works of C. G. Jung, Vol. 7. 2nd ed., Princeton University Press, 1966. 349 p. (p. 245-268).

An overview of the history of psychology is outlined with analytic psychology heralded as the present state of the art. Prior to analytic psychology there was a great gulf between what was demanded of psychology and what it could deliver. Sigmund Freud is cited as the father of analytic psychology and credited with fashioning its most valuable tool -- dream analysis. A detailed case history involving a neurotic disorder in a young woman is used to demonstrate the concept that neurosis originates in a disturbance in the psyche. The explication of the roots of the woman's neurosis illustrates how the trauma theory of neurosis came to be replaced by the erotic conflict theory. The recognition of repressed sexual impulses and the resultant tension between the conscious and the unconscious as the most frequent cause of neurosis is held to be an important breakthrough for psychological theory. Likewise, dream analysis is seen as an advance over hypnotism and free association in the area of analytic technique. Dreams are seen as windows into the interior workings of the unconscious. It is pointed out that the general resistance to these new psychological theories and practices is, in accordance with psychoanalytic principles, a sure indicator that something significant is being brought to light. 4 references.

000179 Appendices: II. The structure of the unconscious. 1. The distinction between the personal and the impersonal unconscious. In: Jung, C., Collected Works of C. G. Jung, Vol. 7. 2nd ed., Princeton University Press, 1966. 349 p. (p. 269-273).

The difference between Jungian and Freudian theories of the unconscious are analayzed showing that the development of Jung's theory was aided by his split from the Viennese school of psychology. An argument against Freud's conception of the unconscious as a mere receptacle for repressed incompatible sexual impulses is presented. According to Freud, by means of analysis, the repressions would be lifted rendering conscious the contents of the unconscious; as a result Freud believed the unconscious would wither and disappear. But since this never occurs, the unconscious must contain more material than previously thought and perform more than a repressive function. It is suggested that the unconscious contains all the psychic materials that have fallen below the threshold of consciousness, the subliminal sense perceptions and material that has not yet reached consciousness. These last are the seeds of future conscious contents. It is held that the unconscious is never quiescent but always producing unconscious fantasies that stand in a compensatory relation to conscious thoughts. The personal unconscious is defined as that layer of the unconscious that contains the unconscious material and processes that were acquired in the course of the individual's life. A case history of a youth who develops a psychosis as a result of glimpsing a portion of the collective unconscious is presented to illustrate the fundamental difference between the personal and the collective unconscious. It is observed that anyone who desires self-realization must make conscious and assimilate the contents of his personal unconscious. 1 reference.

000180 Appendices: II. The structure of the unconscious. 2. Phenomena resulting from the assimilation of the unconscious. In: Jung, C., Collected Works of C. G. Jung, Vol. 7. 2nd ed., Princeton University Press, 1966. 349 p. (p. 273-280).

Different reactions to the process of assimilation are discussed, along with the role of the collective psyche in primitive and modern societies. The process of assimilation

gives rise to some remarkable phenomena: some patients display an increase of self-confidence, while others become markedly depressed. Analysis of these two reactions reveals that they are but masks for a feeling of helplessness and the will to power respectively. The feeling of "godlikeness" seen in some patients is further dissected to discover its source. The feeling derives from a certain psychic function of a collective nature that is superordinate to the individual. The collective psyche is the orginal basis for the individual psyche. Modern man, as opposed to primitive man, has been able to differentiate his individual psyche from the collective. If, however, during analysis parts of the collective unconscious are annexed to the conscious mind the personality will inevitably begin to dissolve into its paired opposites. The collective psyche contains good and evil in undifferentiated form. Only with the development of the individual modern mind does a distinction between the two and the resultant repression of evil occur. Repression of the collective psyche was necessary for the development of the civilized personality. The danger is that during analysis the collective unconscious may become dominant. For this reason analysts are cautioned to remember that the goal of analysis is the development of personality, which requires that a clear distinction between the contents of the personal and the collective unconscious must always be maintained. 1 reference.

000181 Appendices: II. The structure of the unconscious. 3. The persona as a segment of the collective psyche. In: Jung, C., Collected Works of C. G. Jung, Vol. 7. 2nd ed., Princeton University Press, 1966. 349 p. (p. 280-283).

A distinction is made between persona and the conscious mind, and the difference between schizophrenic investment in the unconscious and analytic release of the collective psyche is explained. Analytic experience reveals that the conscious mind is only an arbitrary segment of the collective psyche. It exists because it is ignorant of the universal characteristics of humanity. In addition, it has repressed more or less arbitrarily psychic elements awareness of which might be useful. This arbitrary segment of consciousness is termed the persona and, though it feigns individuality, it really is no more than a mask worn by the collective psyche. During analysis this mask is stripped off and the individual is seen to be, at bottom, collective. The analysand's perception of his collectiveness gives rise to the feeling of "godlikeness." This feeling is characterized by dreams of flying and growth, disorientation in regard to one's identity, and the release of unconscious fantasies. This state borders on and is analagous to schizophrenia. In schizophrenia the unconscious usurps the reality function: unconscious thoughts are heard as though they were voices, and fantasies are seen as though they were real objects. During analysis, however, the patient is aware that he is calling up the unconscious and does not invest its contents with an objective reality.

000182 Appendices: II. The structure of the unconscious. 4. Attempts to free the individuality from the collective psyche. In: Jung, C., Collected Works of C. G. Jung, Vol. 7. 2nd ed., Princeton University Press, 1966. 349 p. (p. 283-286).

Two common reactions to the initial awareness of identification with the collective psyche are discussed. The feeling that results from awareness of the condition of "godlikeness" drives the patient to seek relief. Two common escape mechanisms are: regressive restoration of the persona and identification with the collective psyche. The first solution results in the reestablishment of the previous persona and is thus regressive. Here the unconscious is mastered by a reductionist analysis of its contents, allowing them to be rejected categorically as mere infantile sexuality or will to power. This solution retards growth and does nothing to diminish the influence of the unconscious on the conscious. The second solution entails accepting the "godlikeness" so totally that it becomes a part of the self and thus is no longer threatening. Such identification is always a retrograde step; the patient forfeits his chance to use the treasures of the collective psyche by becoming identified with them. 1 reference.

000183 Appendices: II. The structure of the unconscious. 5. Fundamental principles in the treatment of collective identity. In: Jung, C., Collected Works of C. G. Jung, Vol. 7. 2nd ed., Princeton University Press, 1966. 349 p. (p. 288-300).

An overview of the facts involved in the individuation process is provided. It is shown that since both the collective and the individual psyche are valuable, harm results from identifying with one to the exclusion of the other. This tendency in man to seek a unique solution is reinforced by his rationalism, the essence of which is the categorical denial of all that is not already known or understood. The human psyche, however, is both individual and collective. To attempt to divide the two is pointless and impossible. What the analyst must ask himself is: What is it, at this moment and in this patient, that represents the natural urges of life? The answer can only come from observing those psychological germs of life that are born from the natural collaboration of the conscious and the unconscious on the one hand, and of the individul and the collective on the other. Creative fantasies, not dreams, perform this unifying function. Understood hermeneutically, creative fantasies are the signposts to a harmonious life; when coupled with the patient's desire to rid himself of neuroses, they can effect a cure. The addendum to this chapter briefly sketches the process of individuation. It also defines consciousness, the collective unconscious, the collective psyche, individuality, the persona, and the anima. The relationship of these concepts to each other is briefly reviewed.

000184 Appendices: II. The structure of the unconscious. 6. Summary. In: Jung, C., Collected Works of C. G. Jung, Vol. 7. 2nd ed., Princeton University Press, 1966. 349 p. (p. 300-304).

A summary of two versions of an outline that arranges and defines the key constructs of human psychology is provided. The six major headings are: the division of psychological material into conscious and unconscious contents, the composition of the persona, the composition of the collective psyche, individuality, collective and individual unconscious, and the anima. Each major theme is further divided into its constitutent parts. These are defined and related to the development of the whole schema. The result is a concise picture of the logical processes used for assembling the material.

08 THE STRUCTURE AND DYNAMICS OF THE PSYCHE

000185 On psychic energy. I. General remarks on the energic point of view in psychology. a. Introduction. In: Jung, C., Collected Works of C. G. Jung, Vol. 8. 2nd ed., Princeton University Press, 1972. 588 p. (p. 3-6).

The introduction to a reexamination of the author's concept of libido is presented. It is generally recognized that physical events can be looked at from a mechanistic or from an energic standpoint. The mechanistic view is purely causal and is concerned with the moving substance itself; the energic view, on the other hand, is final; it is not founded on the substances themselves but on the relations of the movement of substances. A third conception, which is a compromise of mechanistic and energic, gives rise to many theoretical hybrids

but yields a relatively faithful picture of reality. It is mentioned in closing that all explanatory principles are only points of view depending less upon the objective behavior of things than upon the psychological attitude of the investigator and thinker.

000186 On the nature of the psyche. 1. The unconscious in historical perspective. In: Jung, C., Collected Works of C. G. Jung, Vol. 8. 2nd ed., Princeton University Press, 1972. 588 p. (p. 159-167).

The existence of the unconscious is reviewed in the writings of several authors starting in the 17th century. Prior to that time, the history of psychology consisted mainly in the enumeration of doctrines concerning the soul. This study was entirely subjective and philosophical. It was not until the seventeenth century that Christian von Wolf put forth the idea of impirical or experimental psychology. Psychology then became a natural science. But it did not enjoy the status of the older and more recognized sciences. At the turn of the 20th century, the unconscious as a hypothetical concept was being generally rejected by such writers as Wilhelm Wundt; but Fechner, Lipps, and Herbart foretold its present significance. Lipps' remarks form the theoretical basis for the psychology of the unconscious in general. Nevertheless resistance to the hypothesis of the unconscious persisted for a long time afterwards.

000187 On the nature of the psyche. 2. The significance of the unconscious in psychology. In: Jung, C., Collected Works of C. G. Jung, Vol. 8. 2nd ed., Princeton University Press, 1972. 588 p. (p. 167-173).

The importance of the unconscious as a psychological concept and the impact of its formulation on European intellectual history are examined. The unconscious, tentatively described as a "subliminal consciousness," was first posited by Fredric Meyers in 1886. This discovery is considered to have revolutionized psychology as much as the discovery of radioactivity has changed physics. It was resisted at first, however, by both psychologists and philosophers. Wundt's objections to the theory of the unconscious are reviewed and rebutted, and its momentous impact on the theory of knowledge is documented. Once the hypothesis of the unconscious is accepted, then it follows that all our knowledge must be incomplete since the repository of knowlege, the psyche, is only partially accessible to consciousness. Thus, the validity of conscious knowledge was threatened much more seriously than it ever had been by critical epistemology. The trend in German philosophy, since Hegel's "victory" over Kant, had been to rebuke Kant's critique of reason and to reinstate the godlike sovereignty of the human spirit. This movement culminated in the hubris of reason that was Nietzsche's superman and led to the catastrophe of Nazi Germany. It is pointed out that all philosophical statements that transgress the bounds of reason are anthropomorphic and have no validity other than as unintentional psychology.

000188 On the nature of the psyche. 3. The dissociability of the psyche. In: Jung, C., Collected Works of C. G. Jung, Vol. 8. 2nd ed., Princeton University Press, 1972. 588 p. (p. 173-178).

The phenomenon of the psyche's dissociability is explored as an explanation of the capacity of the unconscious for volition. Wundt had objected to the theory of the unconscious on the grounds that the ability to perceive, feel, and act presupposes an experiencing subject. This subject could not be logically posited in the unconscious. It is pointed out that clinical experience verifies the dissociability of the psyche, that unconscious processes are independent of the conscious mind, and that conscious processes display a discreteness. Psychiatric experience indicates that the unity of consciousness can easily be shattered. This dissociability accounts for the existence of a secondary consciousness that is subliminal. It represents a personality component that is separated from ego consciousness, either because it was repressed or because it was never conscious in the first place. This second category represents those contents of the unconscious that are the seeds of future conscious contents but as yet are not understood by the conscious mind and hence remain unconscious. Consciousness is compared to the sense modalities in terms of having a threshold for perception. This concept of threshold is extended to the psyche, and the term "psychoid" is discussed as a designation for those psychic processes that fall at each end of the psychic scale. It is concluded that the hypothesis of the unconscious can be verified only if the contents of the unconscious can be brought into consciousness. 3 references.

000189 On the nature of the psyche. 4. Instinct and will. In: Jung, C., Collected Works of C. G. Jung, Vol. 8. 2nd ed., Princeton University Press, 1972. 588 p. (p. 178-184).

The place of instinct and will in the superstructure of the psyche is examined. The pioneering work of Freud and Janet in the field of the unconscious is briefly reviewed as an introduction to the problem of how to delineate the psyche from the physiological. The link between the repressed contents of the unconscious and instinct was established by Freud. As instincts are bound up in physiology the problem of separation was made more difficult. Janet's division of the psyche into the partie inferieure, which is ruled by instinct, and the partie superieure, which is under the influence of the will, provided a tentative solution. The intrinsic energy of function is no longer oriented by instinct once it passes from the lower to the upper realm. Moreover, just as instinct is the lower limit of the will, so is spirit its upper limit. Thus the psyche is conceived as an emancipation of function from instinctual form. The psyche proper is said to consist of all functions that can be brought under the influence of the will. But, as will resides only in consciousness, this discussion of will and instinct is seen to lead a full circle to the axiom that the psyche is identical with consciousness, a point of disagreement with Janet. 3 references.

000190 On the nature of the psyche. 5. Conscious and unconscious. In: Jung, C., Collected Works of C. G. Jung, Vol. 8. 2nd ed., Princeton University Press, 1972. 588 p. (p. 184-190).

The nature of the unconscious is explored vis-a-vis the conscious in an attempt to refute the axiom that the psyche is equivalent to consciousness. The unconscious is said to be composed of all that has been forgotten, repressed, and perceived by the senses but not recognized by the conscious mind, all the future contents of the conscious that are germinating in the unconscious, and the contents of the psychoid system. The state of these contents when they are not related to the conscious ego is surmised to be much the same as when they are. There is perception, feeling, thinking, volition and intention just as if the unconscious were a "subconscious." One difference, however, is in the area of feeling-toned complexes. In the unconscious these complexes are not subject to correction as they are in the conscious mind and are capable of developing an automatic or compulsive character. The unconscious processes are seen to stretch across a broad spectrum of behaviors ranging from the conscious to the instinctual. It is the near conscious area that holds the answer to whether or not the psyche is equivalent to consciousness. An examination

of this border area reveals that consciousness is relative, that the light of consciousness has many degrees of brightness, and that the ego complex has many gradations of emphasis. It is concluded that the ego consciousness is surrounded by a multitude of little luminosities. 1 reference.

000191 On the nature of the psyche. 6. The unconscious as a multiple consciousness. In: Jung, C., Collected Works of C. G. Jung, Vol. 8. 2nd ed., Princeton University Press, 1972. 588 p. (p. 190-199).

The hypothesis that ego consciousness is surrounded by a multitude of luminosities rests partly on the quasi conscious state of the unconscious and partly on the high incidence of light imagery in descriptions of consciousness. Various alchemic, Hindu, and Christian writings are examined for their use of light imagery in describing the nature of consciousness, man, and their metaphysics. The alchemists Khunrath, Dorn, and Paracelsus wrote of a lumen naturae that illuminates consciousness, and of scintillae, sparks, that are the germinal luminosities shining forth from the darkness of the unconscious. Ignatius Loyola wrote of a recurrent vision he had of a bright light that took the shape of a multieyed serpent. Multiple eyes also characterize Purusha, the Hindu cosmic man. These metaphysical systems and visions are interpreted as introspective intuitions that capture the nature of the unconscious. Since consciousness has always been described in terms derived from the behavior of light, it is concluded that these multiple luminosities correspond to tiny conscious phenomena, many of which reside in the unconscious.

000192 On the nature of the psyche. 7. Patterns of behavior and archetypes. In: Jung, C., Collected Works of C. G. Jung, Vol. 8. 2nd ed., Princeton University Press, 1972. 588 p. (p. 200-216).

The relationship between instinct and archetypes is explored and their effects on the psyche is discussed. Though they are polar opposites, instinct and the archetype meet in the biological conception of patterns of behavior. The problem of discovering these patterns of behavior is solved through an analysis of the dreams, fantasies, and art work of mental patients. The chaotic assortment of images found therein fell into well defined themes and categories that corresponded to the universal motifs of mythology. From this remarkable finding it is deduced that impulses from the unconscious, i.e.,archetypes, are the spiritus rector of the human intellect. Opposed to the spiritual aspect of the psyche is the instinctual. Instincts are seen to be grounded in physiology and to provide the driving energy of the psyche. It is just such an instinctual drive that forces the archetypal contents of the collective unconscious into consciousness. The psyche is compared to the light spectrum to illustrate how it gradually passes from the physiology of instinct to the spirituality of archetypes. Only the representations of archetypes are mediated by the unconscious to the conscious mind as the archetypes themselves are at the ultraviolet end of the spectrum and are thus unknowable. It is concluded that both matter and spirit appear in the psychic realm as distinctive qualities of conscious contents. The ultimate nature of both is transcendental since the psyche and its contents are the only reality that is given to us without a medium. 3 references.

000193 On the nature of the psyche. 8. General considerations and prospects. In: Jung, C., Collected Works of C. G. Jung, Vol. 8. 2nd ed., Princeton University Press, 1972. 588 p. (p. 216-226).

The importance of psychology for man's continued existence is discussed. Psychology is unique among the sciences in that its object of study is the experiencing subject of the other sciences. Therefore an alteration of the psychic factor, be it an alteration of principle, is of the utmost significance for knowledge of the world and our world view. The integration of unconscious contents into consciousness is such an alteration, and one that is held to be essential for man's survival. Modern man identifies too closely with the contents of the collective conscious and represses the contents of the collective unconscious. This leads to a one-sidedness that allows modern man to fall easy prey to various "isms." The catastrophe of Nazi Germany underlines the seriousness of this mistake. Medieval man was protected by his religious faith which, in terms of effectiveness, corresponds to the attitude induced in the ego by the integration of the contents of the collective unconscious. With the decline of religious faith in the West, the "isms" rose up as sophisticated substitutes for man's lost link with psychic reality. Since religious ideas have their origin in archetypes, man can reestablish his psychic balance by assimilating the contents of the collective unconscious into the conscious mind. This process, termed individuation, is held to be the goal of psychology. Its accomplishment requires special conditions and it carries with it the possibility of taking a pathological turn, with disastrous consequences.

000194 On the nature of the psyche. Supplement. In: Jung, C., Collected Works of C. G. Jung, Vol. 8. 2nd ed., Princeton University Press, 1972. 588 p. (p. 226-234).

The investigative problems and procedures of psychology are compared to those of physics in order to elucidate the conceptual foundations of the psyche. The objection that the psychology of the unconscious is a philosophy designed to explain mythologems is answered by demonstrating that the theory of archetypes evolved as an explanatory construct for the observed effects of the unconscious. It is admitted, however, that a true knowledge of the states and processes of the unconscious is not attainable since these phenomena are not directly observable. the psychology of the unconscious is compared to atomic physics in that both draw inferences about the nature of unobservable events from their observable effects. It is also pointed out that both sciences have to deal with the methodological problem that is raised when the observing subject has an effect on the observed object. In psychology the observing consciousness produces a reactive effect in the unconscious and thus limits the objective character of the latter's reality. Since the unconscious has a reciprocal influence on the conscious mind, it follows that the nature of the archetype cannot, with certainty, be designated as psychic. Grounds for this conjecture are found in the phenomenon of telepathy, which is perfectly explicalbe on the assumption of a psychically relative space/time continuum. It is hypothesized that perhaps the psyche touches matter at some point and, conversely, that matter contains a latent psyche.

000195 General aspects of dream psychology. In: Jung, C., Collected Works of C. G. Jung, Vol. 8. 2nd ed., Princeton University Press, 1972. 588 p. (p. 237-280).

A summary of the established facts of dream psychology together with an outline of Jung's dream theory vis-a-vis Freud's theory are presented. It is accepted that the origin, structure, and content of dreams are discontinuous with waking consciousness. It is further recognized that there is a hidden meaning to dreams beyond their manifest content. The method for discovering this hidden meaning is illustrated through the analysis of a psychiatric patient's dream. It is

pointed out that the explanation of a psychological fact will be determined by the point of view of the explainer. Therefore the dream is explained in regards to causality, the Freudian point of view, and finality, the Jungian point of view. The former attempts to find the cause of the dream, while the latter seeks its purpose. The symbolism of the dream is interpreted accordingly; the one discovers symbolism that conceals, the other symbolism that guides. This theory of dreams also differs from Freud's in regard to the proposed function of dreams. Freud posits a wish fulfilment function to dreams, while Jung assigns them a compensatory function. According to the latter theory, dreams should be interpreted on a subjective level; i.e.,all figures in the dream are interpreted as personified features of the dreamer's personality, rather than reflections of external reality. The classification of dreams is held to have little practical or theoretical value, but the recognition of typical motifs is seen as an invaluable insight in that it points out the correspondence between dream motifs and mythological motifs. Thus the figurative language of dreams can be interpreted as a surviving remnant of the archaic mode of thought. The charge that these psychological views are metaphysical are refuted by pointing out that religious concepts are useful in explaining psychological facts, since they themselves are psychological facts. 6 references.

000196 On the nature of dreams. In: Jung, C., Collected Works of C. G. Jung, Vol. 8. 2nd ed., Princeton University Press, 1972. 588 p. (p. 281-297).

The fundamental aspects of dream psychology and interpretation are explained for edification of the layman. Dreams are defined as irrational fragments of involuntary psychic activity. A procedure for interpreting dreams presented consists of eliciting from the dreamer every shade of meaning which each salient feature of the dream has for him. Though dreams refer to a definite conscious situation, their roots lie buried in the unconscious. Since the meaning of most dreams is not in accord with the tendencies of the conscious mind, it is assumed that they serve an unconscious function. The unconscious is seen to have a compensatory function in relation to the conscious mind; i.e.,it acts to balance any one-sidedness that may occur in the conscious sphere. Thus the analysis of dreams is an invaluable aid in treating a neurosis which results from a psychic imbalance. Another function of dreams, which expresses itself in the symbolism of a long dream series, is to aid in the individuation process. Such dreams spring from the collective unconscious, which is replete with mythological motifs that guide the individuation process. Though the form of dreams has great flexibility, many dreams fall into a definite structure. This structure is analayzed and shown to be essentially dramatic and to consist of four phases. In conclusion it is pointed out that no generally satisfying theory of dreams, that would enable one to deal with the far reaching philosophical and religious problems encountered when studying them has yet been formulated. 4 references.

000197 The psychological foundation of belief in spirits. In: Jung, C., Collected Works of C. G. Jung, Vol. 8. 2nd ed., Princeton University Press, 1972. 588 p. (p. 301-318).

A psychological interpretation of the problem of spirits is sketched from the standpoint of the present knowledge of unconscious processes. Only the psychological side of the problem is examined. The question of whether spirits exist in themselves is left to a two paragraph epilogue that refers the reader to other authors. Although the past history of man reveals a universal belief in the existence of spirits, among

Western peoples this belief has been counteracted by rationalism. For the primitive, the phenomenon of spirits is direct evidence of a spiritual world, and for them, a belief in the human soul is a necessary premise for belief in spirits. The three main sources that put the belief in spirits on a solid foundation are: dreams, visions, and psychic disturbances. These three phenomena are analyzed and their common denominator is found to be the psychological fact that the psyche is a divisible entity. Among the separate parts of the psyche are certain fragments that never become associated with the ego. These are termed "autonomous complexes." Spirits, viewed from a psychological angle, are unconscious autonomous complexes which appear as projections because they have no direct association with the ego. Parallels are drawn between the belief of primitive peoples in souls and spirits, and psychology's formulation of the personal and collective unconscious: souls correspond to the autonomous complexes of the personal unconscious; spirits to those of the collective unconscious. The association experiment is discussed as a means for demonstrating the existence of these complexes. It is noted that, when excited by an external stimulus, these complexes can produce sudden confusion or violent effects, or they may express themselves as hallucinations. Spirits, then, are autonomous complexes of the collective unconscious that appear when the individual loses his adaptation to reality.

000198 Spirit and life. In: Jung, C., Collected Works of C. G. Jung, Vol. 8. 2nd ed., Princeton University Press, 1972. 588 p. (p. 319-337).

The connection between spirit and life is the theme of a lecture delivered to the literary society of Augsburg. The basic ambiguity of the term "spirit," which causes many to confuse it with "mind," noted, and an empirical definition of the term is sought. The psyche and the conscious mind are examined and, though their natures are seen to be ultimately unknowable, it is concluded that anything psychic will take on the quality of consciousness if it comes into contact with the ego. Since ego consciousness, however, is not seen as embracing the entire psyche, one is cautioned that what lies beyond it may be far different from what is imagined. A review of epistemology and a survey of the various usages of the word "spirit" reveal that "spirit" denotes a psychic experience which can neither be grasped from a rationalistic standpoint, nor proven to exist in the external world. A concept of "spirit" is advanced that goes beyond the animistic framwork and holds "spirit" to be a suprapersonal guiding force. It is hypothesized that it is this "spirit" that lies beyond the scope of ego consciousness. The intent of this unconscious force is held to be superior to the intent of consciousness. Life is seen as the touchstone for the truth of the spirit. Man finds himself between these two powers: consciousness and unconsciousness, with the spirit giving meaning to life, and life giving expression to the spirit.

000199 Basic postulates of analytical psychology. In: Jung, C., Collected Works of C. G. Jung, Vol. 8. 2nd ed., Princeton University Press, 1972. 588 p. (p. 338-357).

The prevailing materialistic outlook of the age is seen to be opposed to the basic postualtes of analytic psychology. Materialism is criticized as a philosophical system and characterized as an overreaction to the excessively spiritual outlook of the Gothic age. Materialism, with its view that the psyche is nothing but a product of biochemical processes, is rejected in favor of analytic psychology, "a psychology with a psyche" that postulates the existence of an autonomous spiritual princi-

ple. A survey of primitive man's view of the soul and the psyche reveals a remarkable resemblance between these primitive beliefs and the postulates of analytic psychology. Both recognize that the soul is the life of the body, that ego consciousness is an expression of the soul, and that ego consciousness grows out of the unconscious. Analytic psychology further holds that the unconscious psyche is a system of inherited psychic functions that predates the development of ego consciousness and that it is a source of knowledge. The conflict between nature and spirit, so obvious in the world today is seen to be a reflection of the paradoxical nature of the psyche. It is concluded that psychic reality still exists in its original oneness and awaits man's advance to that level of consciousness, where he will no longer believe exclusively in one side of its dual nature and repress the other.

000200 Analytic psychology and Weltanschauung. In: Jung, C., Collected Works of C. G Jung, Vol. 8. 2nd ed., Princeton University Press, 1972. 588 p. (p. 358-381).

The contribution of analytic psychology to the formation of a new Weltanschauung is discussed. The personality is seen to be essentially related to Weltanschauung, since consciousness detetermines man's world view, and that, conversely, man orients himself and adapts to reality in accordance with his world view. The basic tenets of psychoanalysis are examined and judged to produce a Weltanschauung of rationalistic materialism; this perspective is considered inadequate in that it ignores the vast irrational production of the psyche. Analytic psychology, on the other hand, is considered to contribute to a more complete Weltanschauung by its recognition of the existence of certain unconscious contents which cannot be rationalized but with which the conscious mind must come to terms. The contents of the collective unconscious, the result of the psychic functioning of man's whole ancestry, are seen to represent the matrix of experience from which all future ideas will come. However, the contents of the unconscious do not themselves constitute a world view, but must be translated into the language of the present. It is felt that if this process is successfully completed, the world will be perceived as having reunited with the primordial experience of mankind; it is toward this ideal world view that analytic psychology attempts to break down the confining walls of rationalism by unearthing the irrational fantasy material of the unconscious. 1 reference.

000201 The real and the surreal. In: Jung, C., Collected Works of C. G. Jung, Vol. 8. 2nd ed., Princeton University Press, 1972. 588 p. (p. 382-384).

The Western view of what constitutes reality is compared to the Eastern view. According to the Western view everything is "real" which comes, or seems to come, from the world as revealed by the senses. This restriction of reality to the material, although seemingly comprehensive, is but a fragment of reality as a whole. This narrow perspective is alien to the Eastern view of the world which grants everything the status of reality. Therefore the East, unlike the West, does not need to formulate a concept of "superreality" to account for the nature of the psyche. Previously Western man had granted the psyche only an indirect reality derived from its proposed physical causes. He is now beginning to realize his error and to understand that the world he lives in is one of psychic images. The East is wiser, for it finds the essence of all things grounded in the psyche. Between the unknown essences of spirit and matter stands the reality of the psyche. Psychic reality is held to be the only reality that we experience immediately.

000202 The stages of life. In: Jung, C., Collected Works of C. G. Jung, Vol. 8. 2nd Ed., Princeton University Press, 1972. 588 p. (p. 387-403).

The stages of life are discussed in terms of the problems they present to the individual. As the growth of consciousness is the source of all problems, only the second and third of the four stages of life, youth and middle-age, are discussed. The development of consciousness in the individual is traced from biological birth to psychic birth, which is said to occur at puberty. It is found to consist of three stages: the recognition of connections between two events, the development of the ego complex, and the awareness of the self's dual nature. Youth, the second stage of life, is defined as the years between puberty and the onset of middle-age at age 35 to 40. During this stage one's personality and place in society are established. At this stage problems revolve around either the individual's refusal to leave the conscious state of childhood or the crushing loss of cherished illusions through the contradiction of expectations of reality. At the onset of middle-age, man's values and even his body begin to change toward their opposites. Neurotic disturbances in adults all have one thing in common: the individual's attempt to carry over the psychology of youth into middle-age. He must, however, change his psychology or else risk damaging his soul. Middle-age is seen to have a cultural purpose as opposed to the individual purpose of youth. It is theorized that the value of religious beliefs in the supramundane is that they constitute a basis for living the second half of life with as much purpose and aim as the first. It is noted that the belief in life after death is a primordial image.

000203 The soul and death. In: Jung, C., Collected Works of C. G. Jung, Vol. 8. 2nd ed., Princeton University Press, 1972. 588 p. (p. 404-415).

The meaning of death is discussed in terms of its relation to the psyche. The view that death is simply the end of life, the period placed after an often uncompleted sentence, is countered by the view of death as the goal of life. Life is said to be an energy process that has rest as its goal. Its curve is parabolic: during youth, it ascends; it reaches its zenith at middle-age; then it sinks to the valley from which the ascent began. Man's problems begin when his psychological curve is out of phase with his biological curve. It is argued that this conception of death is not a mere syllogism on the grounds that, since man grants purpose and meaning to the ascent of life, he should also grant them to life's descent. It is stated that the consensus of the race, as expressed in the great religions of the world, is that there is some sort of continuation of life after death. In the West, however, religious belief has been devalued. Since the enlightenment, religions have come to be viewed as philosophical systems, as constructs of the intellect that amount to no more than a wish fulfilling fantasy. This view is countered by the contention that religious symbols are the products of the natural life of the unconscious and, as such, they are at least the essential truths of man's psychological nature. A final account of the meaning of death is held to be beyond the scope of an empirical science and the capabilities of the human intellect. Telepathy, and the various phenomena of parapsychology, are discussed as presenting evidence that the psyche is capable of transcending the space/time continuum. It is concluded that the psyche has a form of existence beyond space and time and thus partakes of what is inadequately and symbolically described as eternity.

000204 Synchronicity: an acausal connecting principle. Foreword. In: Jung, C., Collected Works of C. G. Jung, Vol. 8. 2nd ed., Princeton University Press, 1972. 588 p. (p. 417-420).

The paper on synchronicity is intended to systematize everything written on the subject in various papers of the past twenty years. It is warned that the subject plunges into regions of human experience which are dark, dubious, and hedged about with prejudice and intellectual difficulties. The phenomenon in question crops up frequently in the practice of psychotherapy as an inner experience that has great meaning and import for the patient concerned.

000205 Synchronicity: an acausal connecting principle. 1. Exposition. In: Jung, C., Collected Works of C. G. Jung, Vol. 8. 2nd ed., Princeton University Press, 1972. 588 p. (p. 421-458).

The concept of synchronicity as an acausal connecting principle is formulated and discussed. Evidence for the existence of complexes of noncausally yet meaningfully related events is presented. This evidence was developed by a survey and discussion of intuitive or "mantic" methods, such as the I-Ching, astrology, and alchemy, all of which take the existence of synchronicity for granted. A scientific rationale for accepting acausal explanatory principles is provided by modern physics which has demonstrated that natural laws, and their philosophical underpinning of causality, are relative and only statistically valid. Though acausal combinations of events are hard to detect in the macrophysical world there still exists a wealth of historical writings on the subject. Reference is made to a text by Albertus Magnus, circa 1485, and to Schopenhauer's treatise, "On the Apparent Design in the Fate of the Individual," among many others. Decisive evidence for synchronicity is found in J. B. Rhine's book "Extra-sensory Perception." His psychokinetic telepathic experiments are examined in detail and it is concluded that they reveal events which are related to one another experimentally and meaningfully but not causally. Furthermore his experiments indicate that, in relation to the psyche, space and time are "elastic." Several case histories from the author's clinical experience are presented to illustrate the psychological significance of synchronicity. From these it is deduced that synchronicity consists of two factors: an unconscious image that comes into consciousness either directly or indirectly, and an objective situation that coincides with this content. 16 references.

000206 Synchronicity: an acausal connecting principle. 2. An astrological experiment. In: Jung, C., Collected Works of C. G. Jung, Vol. 8. 2nd ed., Princeton University Press, 1972. 588 p. (p. 459-484).

The results of an astrological experiment conducted to test the empirical foundations of the intuitive method are discussed. It was hypothesized that, if astrological assumptions are at all correct, there would be several configurations in the individual's horoscope that would point to a predisposition in the choice of a marriage partner. To test this hypothesis the horoscopes of 180 married couples were plotted and then analyzed for the frequency of the conjunction and or opposition of certain preselected astrological characteristics. The results showed that the figures for all the analyzed characteristics fell well within the limits of probability. Their variance, however, corresponded surprisingly well with the psychic states of the individual subjects. This difference between the mass statistical result and the individual results is discussed at length. It is conceded that there is little hope of proving that astrology conforms to discoverable laws, however, it is maintained that statistics give merely an average picture and not a true picture of the world.

000207 Synchronicity: an acausal connecting principle. 3. Forerunners of the idea of synchronicity. In: Jung, C., Collected

Works of C. G. Jung, Vol. 8. 2nd ed., Princeton University Press, 1972. 588 p. (p. 485-504).

The intellectual history that forms the basis for the concept of synchronicity is examined. The fundamental idea underlying the concept of meaningful coincidence, i.e. synchronicity, is that all things contain a latent rationality. This latent rationality derives from the interconnection of all things and manifests itself in the explanatory principles of causality and synchronicity. The existence of this second explanatory principle alongside causality is traced through the primitive, classical, and medieval views of nature. Passages from texts by Theophrastus, Philo, Hippocrates, Pico, Agrippa, and Zoroaster are analyzed for their references to the "sympathy of all things," the principle of universal connection. Numerous parallels between these views and classical Chinese philosophy, as epitomized in the concept of the Tao, are drawn. Leibniz's theory of the preestablished harmony between both the inside and the outside of the monad, between psychic and physical events, is seen as the flowering of this philosophical tradition. Causality alone, however, was accepted, first by the natural sciences in the 18th century and then by the physical sciences in the 19th, as a valid explanatory principle. The principle of synchronicity would have vanished altogether had not the investigation of telepathic phenomena opened the question again. Synchronicity, therefore, has been revived by psychology to explain those events which, though relatively rare, are not amenable to explanation by the causality principle. 24 references.

000208 Synchronicity: an acausal connecting principle. 4. Conclusion. In: Jung, C., Collected Works of C. G. Jung, Vol. 8. 2nd Ed., Princeton University Press, 1972. 588 p. (p. 505-519).

The value of synchronicity as an explanatory principle and its impact on our conception of the world are discussed. It is argued that the coordination of psychic and physical processes in a living organism can be better understood as a synchronistic pheonomenon than as a causal relation. Several medical cases that involved the continuation of conscious processes during swoon states are detailed. The continuation of conscious processes during periods of cortical depression is interpreted as indicating that the mind and the body exist as an "acausal orderedness." Outside the realm of psychophysical parallelism, which, it is admitted, is not really understood, synchronicity is not easily demonstrated. The findings of modern physics, especially in the area of radioactive decay, suggest that the concept of "acausal orderedness" may replace causality as the principle underlying the ultimate laws of nature. The idea of synchronicity with its inherent quality of meaning produces a view of the world that is at first baffling. But added to the trinity of space, time, and causality it makes possible a view which includes the psychoid factor in our description and knowledge of nature. When this conceptual schema is modified into the quaternion of constant connection through effect (causality), indestructible energy, the space/time continuum, and inconstant connection through contingence, equivalence, or meaning (synchronicity), it satisfies the postulates of physics and psychology alike. 10 references.

000209 Appendix: On synchronicity. In: Jung, C., Collected Works of C. G. Jung, Vol. 8. 2nd ed., Princeton University Press, 1972. 588 p. (p. 520-531).

A transcript of a lecture delivered to the 1951 Eranos conference, gives a cursory sketch of the material contained in "Synchronicity: An Acausal Connecting Principle." Synchronicity is defined and several personal anecdotes that illustrate the concept are recounted. The experiments of J. B.

Rhine in telepathic phenomena and an astrological experiment are reviewed in detail. It is demonstrated that they provide empirical evidence for the usefulness of synchronicity as an explanatory principle. It is concluded that synchronistic phenomena prove the simultaneous occurrence of meaningful equivalences in heterogeneous, causally unrelated processes.

000210 On psychic energy. I. General remarks on the energic point of view in psychology. b. The possibility of quantitative measurement in psychology. In: Jung, C., Collected Works of C. G. Jung, Vol. 8. 2nd ed., Princeton University Press, 1972. 588 p. (p. 6-14).

The possibility of applying the principles used in measuring physical energy to the measurement of psychic energy is discussed. Although both the mechanistic/causal and energy/final viewpoints are required to explain psychic events, the decision to use one or the other viewpoint is determined by expediency, i.e.,the possibility of obtaining results. The question of whether or not the energic point of view is even applicable to psychic phenomena at all is raised along with the question of whether the psyche can be looked upon as a relatively closed system. Although these questions are controversial, they are answered in the affirmative. In order to apply the energic standpoint to psychology it is assumed that a quantitative estimate of psychic energy is possible. This assumption is based on the theory that the psyche actually possesses an extraordinarily well developed evaluatory system, namely the system of psychological values. An objective point of departure for estimating comparative value intensities is presented. Complexes are defined as constellations of psychic elements grouped around feeling toned contents, or complexes. These are said to consist of a nuclear element and a large number of secondarily constellated associations. The objective estimate of psychological value intensities is based on the assumption that the constellating power of the nuclear element corresponds to its value intensity, i.e.,to its energy. Three experimental methods for estimating the energic value of the constellating power are given. In addition, it is noted that a highly differentiated subjective system for recognizing and evaluating affective phenomena in others is present in everyone. 6 references.

000211 The structure of the psyche. In: Jung, C., Collected Works of C. G. Jung, Vol. 8. 2nd ed., Princeton University Press, 1972. 588 p. (p. 139-158).

The structure of the psyche is examined from the viewpoint of a practicing psychologist, as opposed to that of a researcher. The contents of consciousness are classified into seven groups: sense perception, the processes of instinct, evaluation, recognition, intuition, volition, and dreams. The last five of these are apperceptive, produced by a configuration of psychic (not physical) processes. The psyche is not composed wholly of consciousness. Its other side is the unconscious, which is not accessible to observation and can only be inferred from phenomena such as dreams, slips of the tongue, and various pathological states. It is believed that all activities ordinarily taking place in the consciousness can also proceed in the unconscious. An example of this is dreams, the most important and most obvious results of the unconscious intruding upon the conscious. Both analytical technique and a knowledge of mythology are deemed necessary for understanding a dream. This knowledge enables one to grasp the meaning of a content deriving from the deepest levels of the psyche, the collective unconscious. Evidence for the existence of the collective unconscious is found in several clinical cases; it is also reflected in the existence of several religious beliefs, especially in early and medieval Christianity. The collective unconscious consists of archetypes, primordial images, that are more or less fantastic analogies of regular physical occurrences. Man's psyche registers these images rather than the actual physical occurrences through the process of participation mystique, which refers to the lack of distinction primitive man makes between subject and object. The function of consciousness is seen not only as the recognition and assimilation of the external world through the senses, but also the translation into visible reality of the world within us, the unconscious. 1 reference.

000212 Instinct and the unconscious. In: Jung, C., Collected Works of C. G. Jung, Vol. 8. 2nd, ed., Princeton University Press, 1972. 588 p. (p. 129-138).

The terms instinct and the unconscious are defined and a distinction is made between unconscious processes and instinctive reactions. A review of the historical views of instinct is provided, and instinct is defined as those unconscious processes which are inherited, occur uniformly and regularly, and are of compelling necessity. The unconscious is then defined as a totality of all psychic phenomena that lack the quality of consciousness. Its contents are the product of associative activity, both personal and the collective. The latter contains inborn forms of intuition, namely archetypes of perception and apprehension which determine a priori all psychic processes. Archetypes and instinct, the two components of the collective unconscious, are defined and contrasted. Instincts are defined as typical modes of action, whether associated with a conscious motive or not. Archetypes are defined as typical modes of apprehension, whether the mythological character is recognized or not. It is concluded that it is impossible to determine whether the apprehension of the situation or the impulse to act comes first. 7 references.

000213 Psychological factors determining human behavior. In: Jung, C., Collected Works of C. G. Jung, Vol. 8. 2nd ed., Princeton University Press, 1972. 588 p. (p. 114-125).

The psychological factors determining human behavior are listed and examined. Chief motivating forces among these are the instincts. Though their characteristic compulsion is an ectopsychic stimulus, they do lead to the formation of structures or patterns that determine psychological behavior (psychization). The instincts: hunger, sexuality, the drive to activity, the reflective instinct, and creativity are all variable and lend themselves to different applications. In addition to the instincts there are the six modalities of psychic functioning that influence behavior in other ways. The first three: age, sex, and heredity of the individual, are primarily physiological; they are also psychological inasmuch as, like the instincts, they are subject to psychization. The other modalities: the conscious and the unconscious, extraversion and introversion, and spirit and matter, are considered to determine the most crucial problems of the individual and of society. These five instincts and six modalities are only general categories. In actuality, the psyche is a complicated interplay of all these factors with a marked tendency to split into autonomous parts or complexes that are not necessarily pathological but are often normal. The behavior of archetypes in the collective unconscious is analogous to that of the complexes in the psyche. The inherent tendency of the psyche to split is interpreted to indicate on the one hand, a capacity for dissociation into multiple structural units and, on the other hand, the capacity for change and differentiation of neurosis results from the observation that a differentiated part of the psyche sometimes becomes so powerful that it makes the personality onesided.

Of the four cognitive faculties, sensation, thinking, feeling, and intuition, one is usually more developed than the others, giving the personality its characteristic stamp. These faculties are contrasted: thinking vs. feeling, and sensation vs. intuition. It is recommended that the problem of opposites be made the basis for a critical psychology. All attempts at a comprehensive theory will be nessarily incomplete because of the tremendous complexity of psychic phenomena. The author's debt to William James is acknowledged.

000214 The significance of constitution and heredity in psychology. In: Jung, C., Collected Works of C. G. Jung, Vol. 8. 2nd ed., Princeton University Press, 1972. 588 p. (p. 107-113).

In a study of the typological method, the question of the relations of physical constitution, heredity and the psyche are examined. The psyche is viewed as relatively independent of the constitution, although certain physiological peculiarities are seen to determine psychic conditions. One of the difficulties in this or any other psychological research is that psychology has yet to invent its own specific language. Accordingly, many terms mean different things to different people. One factor not presently considered by those investigating the constitution is that the psychic process does not originate in individual consciousness but is rather a repetition of functions that have evolved over the ages and which are inherited along with brain structure. This gives rise to primordial images, or archetypes, which make up the collective unconscious. In acknowledging the existence of the collective unconscious, pure psychology is confronted by organic factors. Both the collective unconscious and the constitutional type are outside the control of the conscious mind; neglect of either leads to pathological disturbance, and therefore both are given attention in therapeutic work. 1 reference.

000215 A review of the complex theory. In: Jung, C., Collected Works of C. G. Jung, Vol. 8. 2nd ed., Princeton University Press, 1972. 588 p. (p. 92-104).

The nature and characteristics of feeling-toned complexes are presented and discussed in conjunction with methods of experimental psychology. The problem of assimilation is examined in terms of its interference with such experimental methods as association tests. It is shown that the experimental situation was disturbed by the autonomous behavior of the psyche. This leads to the conclusion that it is impossible to examine isolated psychic processes. Instead, certain constellations or complexes possessing their own psychic energy can be examined, especially if there is an awareness of resistance techniques used by the subjects to avoid revealing the psychic secret. A complex is described as an image of a certain psychic situation which is strongly accentuated emotionally and is incompatible with the habitual attitude of consciousness. This image has a powerful inner coherence, its own wholeness and a relatively high degree of autonomy. The feeling-toned complex is compared to the "splinter psyches" described by psychopathologists such as Janet Prince. It is considered to be certain their origin springs from a so-called trauma, an emotional shock for instance, that splits off a bit of the psyche. Since complexes produce such strong fear reactions, the conscious mind attempts to abolish them by declaring them "unreal" or "imaginary." Primitive man appears to have recognized the strength of the autonomy of complexes in that he posited the existence of demons as beings in their own right. When primitive magic means of apotropaic gestures and euphemisms fail to mask the complex, dissociative neurosis breaks out and attempts to assimilate the ego consciousness.

Freud's concept that the dream is the key to the unconscious is regarded as limited. The Jungian theory posits the complex as the architect of both dreams and symptoms. Despite the fact that, both historically and culturally, complexes were recognized, it has been difficult to regard them as characteristic expressions of the psyche. The theory of feeling-toned complexes is seen to arouse apprehension because these disturbing vestiges of the primitive state of mind are not yet understood.

000216 The transcendent function. In: Jung, C., Collected Works of C. G. Jung, Vol. 8. 2nd ed., Princeton University Press, 1972. 588 p. (p. 67-91).

The transcendent function, which arises from the union of the conscious and unconscious attitudes, is examined within the context of psychoanalytic practice. It is called "transcendent" because it makes organically possible the transition from one attitude to the other, without loss of either one. Modern life demands a kind of functioning which entails the risk of considerable dissociation from the unconscious. In discussing the aim and technique of therapy, it is stated that the reconciliation of the conscious and the unconscious is not an attempt at a permanent cure but rather at a psychological readjustment. The basic question for the therapist is not how to get rid of momentary difficulties, but how to help the patient successfully counter future difficulties. By means of transference, the patient may cling to the therapist, who seems to promise him a renewal of attitude. In the transcendent function the unconscious material must be brought to light because it exercises a regulatory influence that is necessary to our mental and physical health. There are several sources for this unconscious material, the most useful for the constructive method of therapy being spontaneous fantasies. The patient must give himself over to his mood and give form to his fantasies and other associations by writing, visualizing, or some form of artwork. The energy which the patient should have at his disposal to remedy the state of reduced adaptation is found in the intensity of the emotional disturbance itself. According to his personality, the patient will stress either creative formulation or intellectual understanding of his unconscious material. The opposite ego and the unconscious must be reconciled in order to bring about the transcendent function. At this stage it is no longer the unconscious that takes the lead, but the ego. Both sides, however, must be considered equally for the regulating factors to exert an influence on actions. The value of this transcendent function derives from the fact that it provides a way for the patient to break the dependence on the therapist and to attain liberation by his own efforts.

000217 On the nature of the psyche. IV. The primitive concept of the libido. In: Jung, C. Collected Works of C. G. Jung, Vol. 8. 2nd ed., Princeton University Press, 1972. 588 p. (p. 61-66).

In illustrations of the primitive concept of the libido, the intimate connection between the beginnings of religious symbol formation and the concept of energy is demonstrated. A list of names, given to mystical powers by North American Indians, primitive Africans and Australian Aborigines, are presented as examples of creative force and productivity expressed as a preliminary concretistic stage of the abstract idea of energy. The almost universal incidence of the primitive concept of energy is a clear expression of the fact that at early levels of human consciousness man felt the need to represent the sensed dynamism of psychic events in a concrete way. It is therefore concluded that the energic point of view in psychology has primordial roots. 7 references.

000218 On psychic energy. III. Fundamental concepts of the libido theory. d. Symbol formation. In: Jung, C., Collected Works of C. G. Jung, Vol. 8. 2nd ed., Princeton University Press, 1972. 588 p. (p. 45-61).

Symbol formation is presented as a bridge between man's instinctual and spiritual natures. The symbols primitive man formed through analogue building are examined and evaluated as an important means of utilizing instinctual energy for effective work. Since only a small part of man's total energy can be diverted from its natural flow. Most of it is not used up in symbol formation but goes to sustain the regular course of life, which consists of both instinctual and cultural functions. The transformation of the libido through symbols has occurred since the beginnings of humanity. Symbols were (and are) never devised consciously but always unconsciously. It is more than probable that most of the historical symbols derive directly from dreams or are at least influenced by them. This is evident in the symbol formation consistently encountered in patients. The two opposite forces, nature and spirit, are considered to exist together in the psyche and to be responsible for its self-regulation. Nature corresponds to the primitive mentality, that Freud called infantile sexuality. Freud is criticized for not recognizing that spirit is an equivalent counterforce to instinct. He is praised, however, for recognizing that instinct is the sine qua non of psychic energy. The conflict between ethics and sex today is analyzed as a struggle to give instinct its rightful place as a creative power in our lives. In a discussion of religion, the concept of one God, paradoxically both a creator and judge, is an expression of a profound psychological truth in its tension of opposites, a truth that defies logic. The function of all religions is viewed as providing a spiritual counterforce to instinctuality. In the first half of life, with its biological and instinctual orientation, man can usually afford to expand his life. The older man, on the other hand, is oriented toward culture, since the diminishing powers of his organism allow him to subordinate his instincts to cultural goals. It is observed that there is an almost total lack of guidance for this extraordinarily important transformation of energy from the biological to the cultural form. 4 references.

000219 On psychic energy. III. Fundamental concepts of the libido theory. c. The canalization of libido. In: Jung, C., Collected Works of C. G. Jung, Vol. 8. 2nd ed., Princeton University Press, 1972. 588 p. (p. 41-45).

The canalization of libido is defined as a transfer of psychic intensities or values from one content to another, a process corresponding to the physical transformation of energy. Examples chosen from primitive customs and ceremonies illustrate this process. Human culture is seen as the machine that provides for the canalization of libido as well as of mankind's physical and chemical energy. It is described as the means by which instincts are made productive. The transformation of instinctual energy is achieved by its canalization into an analogue of the object of instinct. An analogy is drawn to the manner in which a power station imitates a waterfall to gain possession of its energy, in order to explain how the psychic mechanism imitates the instinct and is thereby enabled to apply its energy for special purposes. Primitive man used complicated ceremonies to accomplish the canalization of libido; modern man does this by an act of will. Besides succeeding in taming external nature, man has succeeded in taming his internal nature to some extent. It is observed, that only slight threats to present conditions are needed to revive the magical ceremonies of our ancestors.

000220 On psychic energy. III. Fundamental concepts of the libido theory. b. Extraversion and introversion. In: Jung, C., Collected Works of C. G. Jung, Vol. 8. 2nd ed., Princeton University Press, 1972. 588 p. (p. 40-41).

The concepts of progression and regression are compared with those of extraversion and introversion. Although the two sets of concepts could be seen as parallels, they remain distinct from each other, since progression and regression are only vague analogies of extraversion and introversion, respectively. The reader is referred to "Psychological Types" for more information.

000221 On psychic energy. III. Fundamental concepts of the libido theory. a. Progression and regression. In: Jung, C., Collected Works of C. G. Jung, Vol. 8. 2nd ed., Princeton University Press, 1972. 588 p. (p. 32-40).

The progression and regression of libido are defined; their interrelation is described; and they are analyzed in terms of the flow of energy. Progression implies the continual satisfaction of the demands of environmental conditions. During progression, pairs of opposite attitudes in the psyche are united in the coordinated flow of psychic processes. During a conflict the pairs of opposing forces attempt to repress each other. If this repression occurs, it obstructs the progression of the libidio and regression sets in. The stalemated conscious opposites devalue one another, and there is an increase in the value of all those psychic processes which are not concerned with adaptation and therefore are seldom or never consciously employed. The unconscious begins to influence the conscious, as is evident in behavior disturbances. During regression, incompatible and rejected remnants of everyday life, as well as inconvenient and objectionable animal tendencies, rise to the surface. At first glance these elements appear to be undesirable; however, they contain the possibilities of new life, for they can reverse the stoppage of the libido caused by the failure of the conscious attitude. Regression, then, is not essentially a retrograde step but rather a necessary developmental phase. Frobenius's myth of the whale dragon is used to illustrate the principles of progression and regression and an argument is presented to defend the validity of using myths in support of psychological principles. It is noted that progression is a continuous process of adaptation to environmental conditions; regression, on the other hand, is an adaptation to the conditions of the inner world, to the demands of individuation. Man is capable of adapting to either set of conditions only when he is in harmony with both. From the energic standpoint, progression and regression are transitional stages in the flow of energy which, by allowing a manifestation of the inner world in the outer, enable man to adapt to his conditions.

000222 On psychic energy. II. Application of the energic standpoint. d. Energism and dynamism. In: Jung, C., Collected Works of C. G. Jung, Vol. 8. 2nd ed., Princeton University Press, 1972. 588 p. (p. 28-32).

The analysis of the pure concepts on which the energic and the causal/mechanistic views are based leads to an understanding of the differences between energism and dynamism. Dynamism corresponds to the causal/mechanistic view of psychic events and energism to the final/energic. The first view infers a dynamism from the causal effect observed, while the second observes the equivalence of the transformed effect rather than the effect of a cause. The concept of libido is clarified and related to the energic standpoint, with reasons given for choosing this term to express psychic energy. It is observed that the same process takes on different aspects according to the standpoint from which it is viewed. 1 reference.

000223 On psychic energy. II. Application of the energic standpoint. c. Entropy. In: Jung, C., Collected Works of C. G. Jung, Vol. 8. 2nd ed., Princeton University Press, 1972. 588 p. (p. 25-28).

Entropy, as important as equivalence in the practical application of the theory of energy to psychology, is explored. It is defined as a principle of partial processes that make up a relativey closed system. Since the psyche can also be regarded as a relatively closed system in which transformations of energy lead to an equalization of differences, the principle of entropy is applicable to psychic energy. Examples from daily psychological experience prove that an attitude that formed a far reaching process of equalization is a lasting one. The energic standpoint and the qualitative or causal/mechanistic, standpoint are compared and the dangers involved in substituting the latter for the former are reviewed. 1 reference.

000224 On psychic energy. II. Application of the energic standpoint. b. The conservation of energy. In: Jung, C., Collected Works of C. G. Jung, Vol. 8. 2nd ed., Princeton University Press, 1972. 588 p. (p. 18-25).

The necessity of testing the applicability of the energic standpoint to psychic life progress by using empirical evidence and by submitting it to the principle of conservation of energy is affirmed. The differences between the principles of equivalence and constancy are noted. The principle of equivalence which Freud demonstrated clearly in his investigation of the transformation of a given quantum of libido into another psychic force, is the only one necessary to empirical studies. The equivalence principle is of great heuristic value in the treatment of neuroses as is shown by examples given. The analogy with the theory of physical energy is further expanded by a discussion of the factors of intensity, and extensity. The latter is defined as the dynamic measure of energy present at any time in a given phenomenon. The energic viewpoint is also used to show how Freud's causal view of psychology, i.e.,reducing everything to its sexual component, inadequately explains the important idea of final development. Here again the conflict between the mechanistic/causal and energic/final views is evident, although both are necessary to explain development. The process of regression is used to illustrate the differences in the two viewpoints: what is fact to the causal view, is symbol to the final view and vice versa; everything that is real and essential to the one is unreal and inessential to the other. It is suggested, therefore, that this conflict be resolved by the antinomian postulate, since the psyche possesses both points of view.

000225 On psychic energy. II. Application of the energic standpoint. a. The psychological concept of energy. In: Jung, C., Collected Works of C. G. Jung, Vol. 8. 2nd ed., Princeton University Press, 1972. 588 p. (p. 14-18).

The term "psychic energy" as it appeared in the writings of Schiller, Lipps, von Grot and Stern is presented and the Jungian definition of this concept is discussed. The difficulties of delimiting this concept are explained as stemming from an inability to separate psychic from biological processes. It is hypothesized that it would be better to enlarge the narrower concept of psychic energy to a broader one of life energy. This life energy, of which psychic energy is a specific part, is called libido. This expanded definition expedites the study of quantitative relations and the discussion of "mind and body." It is concluded that, in all probability, the psychic and the physical are not two independent parallel processes, but are essentially connected through reciprocal action, although the actual nature of this relationship is still completely beyond experience. 5 references.

91 THE ARCHETYPES AND THE COLLECTIVE UNCONSCIOUS

000226 Archetypes of the collective unconscious. In: Jung, C., Collected Works of C. G. Jung, Vol. 9, Part 1. 2nd ed., Princeton University Press, 1968. 451 p. (p. 3-41).

The concept of archetypes as the mode of expression of the collective unconscious is discussed. In addition to the purely personal unconscious hypothesized by Freud, a deeper unconscious level is felt to exist. This deeper level manifests itself in universal archaic images expressed in dreams, religious beliefs, myths, and fairytales. The archetypes, as unfiltered psychic experience, appear sometimes in their most primitive and naive forms (in dreams), sometimes in a considerably more complex form due to the operation of conscious elaboration (in myths). Archetypal images expressed in religious dogma in particular are thoroughly elaborated into formalized structures which, while by expressing the unconscious in a circuitous manner, prevent direct confrontation with it. Since the Protestant Reformation rejected nearly all of the carefully constructed symbol structures, man has felt increasingly isolated and alone without his gods; at a loss to replenish his externalized symbols, he must turn to their source in the unconscious. The search into the unconscious involves confronting the shadow, man's hidden nature; the anima/animus, a hidden opposite gender in each individual; and beyond, the archetype of meaning. These are archetypes susceptible to personification; the archetypes of transformation, which express the process of individuation itself, are manifested in situations. As archetypes penetrate consciousness, they influence the perceived experience of normal and neurotic people; a too powerful archetype may totally possess the individual and cause psychosis. The therapeutic process takes the unconscious archetypes into account in two ways: they are made as fully conscious as possible, then synthesized with the conscious by recognition and acceptance. It is observed that since modern man has a highly developed ability to dissociate, simple recognition may not be followed by appropriate action; it is thus felt that moral judgment and counsel is often required in the course of treatment.

000227 The concept of the collective unconscious. In: Jung, C., Collected Works of C. G. Jung, Vol. 9, Part 1. 2nd ed., Princeton University Press, 1968. 451 p. (p. 42-53).

The definition, modes of manifestation and function of the collective unconscious are discussed. In addition to the personal unconscious generally accepted by medical psychology, the existence of a second psychic system of a universal and impersonal nature is postulated. This collective unconscious is considered to consist of preexistent thought forms, called archetypes, which give form to certain psychic material which then enters the conscious. Archetypes are likened to instinctual behavior patterns. Examples of ideas such as the concept of rebirth, which occur independently in various cultures and ages, are advanced as evidence for the collective unconscious. It is felt that there are as many archetypes as there are recurring situations in life, that when a situation occurs that corresponds to a particular archetype, the archetype presses for completion like an instinctual drive; resistance to its expression may result in neurosis. The existence of archetypes is demonstrated in the analysis of adult and childhood dreams, active imagination, psychotic delusions, and fantasies produced in the trance state. A case history of a paranoid schizophrenic is examined in terms of the manifestation of archetypes in the patient's delusional system.

000228 Concerning the archetypes, with special reference to the anima concept. In: Jung, C., Collected Works of C. G. Jung, Vol. 9, Part 1. 2nd ed., Princeton University Press, 1968. 451 p. (p. 54-72).

The formulation of the archetypes is described as an empirically derived concept, like that of the atom; it is a concept based not only on medical evidence but on observations of mythical, religious and literary phenomena, these archetypes are considered to be primordial images, spontaneous products of the psyche which do not reflect any physical process, but are reflected in them. It is noted that while the theories of materialism would explain the psyche as an epiphenomenon of chemical states in the brain, no proof has yet been found for this hypothesis; it is considered more reasonable to view psychic production as a generating rather than a generated factor. The anima is the feminine aspect of the archetypal male/female duality whose projections in the external world can be traced through myth, philosophy and religious doctrine. This duality is often represented in mythical syzygy symbols, which are expressions of parental imagos; the singular power of this particular archetype is considered due to an unusually intense repression of unconscious material concerning the parental imagos. Archetypal images are described as preexistent, available and active from the moment of birth as possibilities of ideas which are subsequently elaborated by the individual. The anima image in particular is seen to be active in childhood, projecting superhuman qualities on the mother before sinking back into the unconscious under the influence of external reality. In a therapeutic sense, the concept of the anima is considered critical to the understanding of male psychology. 16 references.

000229 Psychological aspects of the mother archetype. 1. On the concept of the archetype. In: Jung, C., Collected Works of C. G. Jung, Vol. 9, Part 1. 2nd ed., Princeton University Press, 1968. 451 p. (p. 75-80).

In a discussion of the concept of archetypes, Plato's concept of the Idea, a primordial disposition that preforms and influences thoughts, is found to be an early formulation of the archetype hypothesis. Other investigators such as Hermann Usener are also noted to have recognized the existence of universal forms of thought. Jung's contribution is considered to be the demonstration that archetypes are disseminated not only through tradition, language, or migration, but that they can arise spontaneously without outside influence. It is emphasized that an archetype is not predetermined in content; rather it is a possibility of representation which may be actualized in various ways. In this aspect the archetype is likened to the instincts; both are predetermined in form only, and both are only demonstrable through their manifestations.

000230 Psychological aspects of the mother archetype. 2. The mother archetype. In: Jung, C., Collected Works of C. G. Jung, Vol. 9, Part 1. 2nd ed., Princeton University Press, 1968. 451 p. (p. 81-84).

Some characteristic aspects of the mother archetype are delineated including the personal mother, grandmother, stepmother and mother-in-law figures; secondly, any woman with whom such a mother like relationship exists, such as nurse; and finally, figurative aspects of mother, such as a goddess. Symbols of the mother are seen in abstractions such as the goal of redemption, objects arousing devotion or awe, such as sea, moon, woods; and items representing fertility, such as a garden. The magical protection this archetype implies is similar to that of the mandala figure. The mother archetype has two aspects: she is both loving and terrible. Positively, the mother archetype has been associated with solicitude, wisdom, sympathy, spiritual exaltation, helpful instincts, growth and fertility; the negative or evil side of the mother archetype is associated with secrets, darkness, the world of the dead, seduction and poison. Because of the power of the mother archetype, it is suggested that the traumatic effects produced by a mother upon her children are of two kinds: first, those corresponding to traits actually present in the mother, and second, those due to traits which are archetypal projections on the part of the child. It is noted that even Freud admits of the importance of infantile fantasy in the development of neurosis. Automatically explaining a child's neorosis by means of unconscious archetypes leads to errors; instead, a thorough investigation of the parents is indicated. It is felt that the task of the therapist is not to deny the archetypes, but to dissolve their projections in order to restore their contents to the individual.

000231 Psychological aspects of the mother archetype. 3. The mother-complex. I. The mother-complex of the son. In: Jung, C., Collected Works of C. G. Jung, Vol. 9, Part 1. 2nd ed., Princeton University Press, 1968. 451 p. (p. 85-87).

The mother archetype is described as forming the foundation of the mother complex in sons; through the early influence of the actual mother, archetypal structure develops around the mother figure, producing fantasies which disturb the mother-child relationship. Typical effects of the mother complex include homosexuality, Don Juanism and sometimes impotence. An equal role is played by the anima and mother archetype in the formation of the mother complex, since for the male child the perception of the mother is complicated by sexual forces. In addition to its pathogenic properties, the mother complex is considered to have possible benefits for the male child in developing and refining in him certain essentially feminine qualities.

000232 Psychological aspects of the mother archetype. 3. The mother-complex. II. The mother-complex of the daughter. a. Hypertrophy of the maternal element. b. Overdevelopment of the Eros. In: Jung, C., Collected Works of C. G. Jung, Vol. 9, Part 1. 2nd ed., Princeton University Press, 1968. 451 p. (p. 87-89).

The possible effects of the mother complex in the daughter are described as the hypertrophy of the daughter's feminine instincts or its opposite, the atrophy of the feminine instincts. The exaggeration of the feminine aspect is manifested in the intensification of all female instincts, especially the maternal instinct; the negative aspect of this hypertrophy is seen in women to whom the husband is merely an object to be looked after, aside from his procreative function. Even her own life is of secondary importance, since the woman's children are the objects of her complex identification. The conscious development of the Eros in this type of woman is described as exclusively a maternal relationship. The personal Eros remains unconscious and is expressed in a will to power; this ruthlessness may result in the annihilation of her own personality and the lives of her children. When the maternal instinct is atrophied, an overdeveloped Eros forms and generally leads to an unconscious incestuous relationship with the father; the intensified Eros causes an abnormal emphasis on the personality of others. The woman of this type is often seen to engage in sensational behavior for its own sake.

000233 Psychological aspects of the mother archetype. 3. The mother-complex. II. The mother-complex of the daughter. c. Identity with the mother. d. Resistance to the mother. In: Jung,

C., Collected Works of C. G. Jung, Vol. 9, Part 1. 2nd ed., Princeton University Press, 1968. 431 p. (p. 89-91).

Two alternatives to the overdevelopment of the Eros in the mother complex of a woman are described as identity with the mother and resistance to the mother. In the former case, the daughter projects her personality completely on the mother, loses her own feminine instincts due to feelings of inferiority, and remains devoted to the mother in an unconscious desire to control her. It is noted that the submissive vacuousness these daughters display is often very attractive to men. The resistance to the mother is described as an example of the negative mother complex, in which behavior patterns of the daughter are formed exclusively in opposition to those of the mother. This complex is seen to result in marital difficulties, indifference to family based societal organizations, and sometimes an extreme intellectual development.

000234 Psychological aspects of the mother archetype. 4. Positive aspects of the mother-complex. I. The mother. In: Jung, C., Collected Works of C. G. Jung, Vol. 9, Part 1. 2nd ed., Princeton University Press, 1968. 451 p. (p. 92-94).

The importance of the archetypes in man's relationship to the world is emphasized; they are seen to express man's highest values, which would be lost in the unconscious if not for their projection onto the external environment. An example is the mother archetype, which expresses the ideal mother love. Although the projection of this archetpye on the actual mother -- an imperfect human being -- may lead to psychological complications, the alternative of rejecting the ideal is seen as even more dangerous; the destruction of this ideal and all other irrational expression is seen as a serious impoverishment of human experience. Further, archetypes relegated exclusively to the unconscious may intensify to the point of distorting perceptive and reasoning powers. The equilibrium of rational and irrational psychic forces is thus considered essential.

000235 Psychological aspects of the mother archetype. 4. Positive aspects of the mother-complex. II. The overdeveloped Eros. In: Jung, C., Collected Works of C. G. Jung, Vol. 9, Part 1. 2nd ed., Princeton University Press, 1968. 451 p. (p. 94-97).

The positive functions an overdeveloped Eros type of mother complex may fulfill are considered. This type of woman, whose behavior often develops in reaction to her own mother's instinctive and all devouring nature, tends to attract men in need of liberation from similar mothers or wives. Seen in this light, the wrecking of marriages which commonly results from such attraction has a positive aspect. Moreover, the moral conflict aroused in men who are the objects of the attraction is seen as conducive to increased self-knowledge and a higher degree of consciousness. It is suggested that even the woman with this type of mother complex may benefit from the same conflict, becoming more aware of her role of deliverer and possibly even consciously fulfilling it. 1 reference.

000236 Psychological aspects of the mother archetype. 4. Positive aspects of the mother-complex. III. The "nothing-but" daughter. In: Jung, C., Collected Works of C. G. Jung, Vol. 9, Part 1. 2nd ed., Princeton University Press, 1968. 451 p. (p. 97-98).

The possibility for positive development on the part of a woman who is so identified with her mother that her own instincts are paralyzed is seen to depend upon her emptiness being filled by a male anima projection. Once stolen from her mother, this woman may eventually come to self-awareness through utlimate resentment of her submissive role as a wife. If she remains unconscious of her own personality, however, she is considered capable of endowing her husband with her own undeveloped talents through projection. This type of woman is described as embodying the essential feminine attribute: emptiness (the yin).

000237 Psychological aspects of the mother archetype. 4. Positive aspects of the mother-complex. IV. The negative mother-complex. In: Jung, C., Collected Works of C. G. Jung, Vol. 9, Part 1. 2nd ed., Princeton University Press, 1968. 451 p. (p. 98-100).

The possibility for positive development of the woman with a negative mother complex is discussed. Although as a pathological phenomenon this type of woman is an unpleasant and exacting partner in marriage, it is felt that with experience this woman may actually have the best chance to make her marriage a success during the second half of her life. First she must give up fighting her mother in the personal sense; but she will always remain hostile to the feminine qualities of darkness and ambiguity, and will choose clarity and reason. Her cool judgment and objectivity can give this type of woman understanding of the individuality of her husband that goes beyond the erotic; she may become the friend, sister and competent advisor of her husband. All this can only be achieved if the complex is faced and lived out to its fullest. The Biblical character of Lot's wife is described as an example of this type of woman, who has an unconscious reactive view of reality, dominated by the exclusively feminine aspect. When this type of woman attains greater consciousness of herself, her rare combination of womanliness and masculine understanding is beneficial in the work environment as well as in intimate personal relationships. A man may project a positive mother complex on a woman with masculine qualities because she is easier to understand than one with another type of mother complex. Understanding this type of woman, moreover, is not seen as frightening to a man, rather it is conducive to confidence, a quality often absent in the relationship between men and women.

000238 Psychological aspects of the mother archetype. 5. Conclusion. In: Jung, C., Collected Works of C. G. Jung, Vol. 9, Part 1. 2nd ed., Princeton University Press, 1968. 451 p. (p. 101-110).

General observations on the mother complex and examples taken from mythology and history are used to support the concept of an unconscious origin for the mother archetype. The experience of the mother archetype is described as beginning in the state of unconscious identity in which the child first encounters the actual mother. Gradually, as the ego is differentiated from the mother, mysterious qualities originally attached to her are transferred to a female figure close to her, such as a grandmother; finally, as consciousness becomes clearer, the archetype recedes into the unconscious, assuming mythological proportions. Once the mother archetype is projected upon myth or fairytale, its opposite aspects may split apart, creating a good and an evil goddess, for example. The essential differnece between the operation of the mother image in a man's psychology and in a woman's is stressed: the mother typifies a woman's own conscious life, but is an alien figure to a man, and is surrounded with imagery from the unconscious. It is noted that the mythological projection of the mother archetype, the Great Mother, often appears with her male counterpart, creating the archetype of paired opposites which is the symbol of psychic individuation. The dogma of the Assumption is proposed as a modern effort to compensate

the dominance of rational and material science with its archetypal opposite, creating thereby a balanced world. It is suggested that this type of symbolic compensation and unity constitutes the only way man is able to organize and understand his role in the world. 2 references.

000239 Concerning rebirth. 1. Forms of rebirth. In: Jung, C., Collected Works of C. G. Jung, Vol. 9, Part 1. 2nd ed., Princeton University Press, 1968. 451 p. (p. 113-115).

Five different forms of rebirth are defined and described. Metempsychosis, or transmigration of souls, is described as life extended in time by passing through different bodily existences, an eternal life interrupted by different reincarnations. This concept does not require a continuity of personality, even in Buddhism where it is of particular importance, but only continuity of karma. In reincarnation, human personality is regarded as continuous; previous existences are at least potentially available to awareness, since the same ego is presumed to exist throughout the various lives. These lives are generally thought to be exclusively human. The third form of rebirth, resurrection, is defined as a reestablishment of human existence after death, with the implication of some change or transformation of the being. A different place or body may be involved in transformation; the change of body can be either in the carnal or the nonmaterial sense. Rebirth in its fourth form (renovatio) is described as rebirth within the span of individual life; this rebirth may either consist of some healing or strengthening of a part of the physical or psychological being without essential change of the whole, or of a profound basic change in the essential nature of the individual, called transmutation. Examples are offered such as the assumption of the body of the Mother of God into heaven after her death. The fifth form of rebirth is seen as an indirect one in which the individual witnesses or takes part in some rite of transformation and thereby shares a divine grace. It is exemplified by the witnessing of transubstantiation in the Mass, or the confession of the initiate in the Eleusinian mysteries. 1 reference.

000240 Concerning rebirth. 2. The psychology of rebirth. I. Experience of the transcedence of life. a. Experiences induced by ritual. In: Jung, C., Collected Works of C. G. Jung, Vol. 9, Part 1. 2nd ed., Princeton University Press, 1968. 451 p. (p. 116-118).

The psychic importance of the concept of rebirth and two main types of transformation experiences are discussed. It is felt that the rebirth concept can only be understood by examining history, since rebirth itself is a purely psychic reality transmitted only indirectly through personal statements. The affirmation of the concept of rebirth among many different peoples is taken as support for its archetypal quality. It is contended that psychology must deal with psychic events underlying the affirmations of rebirth, especially regarding the two main groups of transformation experiences: that of the transcendence of life, and that of individual transformation. The experience of the transcendence of life can be induced by ritual, in which the initiate takes part in some sacred rite revealing to him the continuity of life. The transformation does not take place within the initiate, but outside him, although he may become involved in the transformation. The experience of the Christian Mass is described as an example of this type of experience in which life, is transcended in a moment of eternity. 1 reference.

000241 Concerning rebirth. 2. The psychology of rebirth. I. Experience of the transcedence of life. b. Immediate experiences. In: Jung, C., Collected Works of C. G. Jung, Vol. 9, Part 1. 2nd ed., Princeton University Press, 1968. 451 p. (p. 118).

In addition to transcendence experienced through ritual, a second transcendence of life is described as a spontaneous, ecstatic or visionary experience of mystery without the aid of ritual. Nietzsche's Noontide Vision is discussed as a classic example of this type of transformation: in the myth of Dionysus-Zagreus, who was dismembered and returned to life, the Deity appears in the noon hour, sacred to Pan; Nietzsche's reaction is as though he had been present at a ritual. It is cautioned that these are more esthetic forms of experience, like dreams which have no lasting effect on the dreamer, and that they must be distinguished from those visions which involve permanent change in the individual. 2 references.

000242 Concerning rebirth. 2. The psychology of rebirth. II. Subjective transformation. a. Diminution of personality. In: Jung, C., Collected Works of C. G. Jung, Vol. 9, Part 1. 2nd ed., Princeton University Press, 1968. 451 p. (p. 119-120).

The diminution of personality as the result of a personality transformation is described as different from the changes produced by a mystical experience. It is noted that transformations of personality are already familiar to psychology, and appear in psychopathology. The primitive psychology refers to this diminution of personality as "loss of soul"; the impression that the soul has been suddenly lost is in accordance with the nature of primitive consciousness, which lacks the coherence of that of civilized man. The experience of civilized man is seen as similar to that of primitive man, but felt more as a lessening of conscious tonus; the consequent listlessness and loss of will advance to the point of distintegration, in which individual parts of personality escape from conscious control, as in the case of hysterical phenomena. This diminution of personality (abaissement du niveau mental) is described as resulting from physical or mental fatigue, physical illness, violent emotions, or shock, and leading to a narrowing of mental horizons and possibly to the development of a negative cast which falsifies the original personality.

000243 Concerning rebirth. 2. The psychology of rebirth. II. Subjective transformation. b. Enlargement of personality. In: Jung, C., Collected Works of C. G. Jung, Vol. 9, Part 1. 2nd ed., Princeton University Press, 1968. 451 p. (p. 120-122).

The transformation resulting in an enlargement of personality is described as the accretion of new experiences from without coupled with the response of some inner element to these experiences. New experiences cannot be assimilated unless the inner amplitude is equal to the incoming material; therefore, without psychic depth, an individual lacks the capacity to relate to the magnitude of experience, and a difficult task may destroy rather than benefit him. A literary example of such an enlargement is seen in Nietzsche's description of Zarathustra; religious and cultural illustrations of the process are found in the Christ figure, in Indian culture, and in the Islamic legend of Moses and Khidr. It is noted that the enlargement of personality can occur in smaller ways, as may be illustrated by the case histories of neurotic patients. 2 references.

000244 Concerning rebirth. 2. The psychology of rebirth. II. Subjective transformation. c. Change of internal structure. In: Jung, C., Collected Works of C. G. Jung, Vol. 9, Part 1. 2nd ed., Princeton University Press, 1968. 451 p. (p. 122-125).

Changes of personality are detailed that involve structural alterations in personality rather than enlargement or diminution. The phenomenon of possession, in which some idea, content or part of personality gains mastery of the individual, is characterized as one of the most important forms of change in

structure. Possession is described as identity of the ego personality with a complex, with no strict differentiation made between possession and paranoia. A common instance of possession and concomitant structural change in the personality is seen in an individual's identity with the persona, the manner the individual assumes in dealing with the world; life is then lived only as a public biography. Other examples of possession of parts of the personality are described as the possession by an "inferior function" which results in the individual's living below his own level, and possession by the anima or animus, which gives prominence in the personality characteristics of the opposite sex. In unusual cases states of possession may be observed to involve the soul of some forbear; evidence for this type of transformation is found in Leon Daudet's book "L'Heredo" and in the common importance of ancestral roles in society. 5 references.

000245 Concerning rebirth. 2. The psychology of rebirth. II. Subjective transformation. d. Identification with a group. In: Jung, C., Collected Works of C. G. Jung, Vol. 9, Part 1. 2nd ed., Princeton University Press, 1968. 451 p. (p. 125-128).

A form of transformation experience is described which occurs when an individual identifies with a group of people who have a collective experience of transformation. This type of experience is distinguished from participation in a transformation rite, which does not necessarily depend upon, or give rise to, a group identity. Transformation as a group experience is described as taking place on a lower level of consciousness than transformation as an individual, because the total psyche emerging from a group is more like the animal psyche than the human. Although the group experience is easier to achieve, it does not cause a permanent change once the individual is removed from the group. Events in prewar Germany are cited as typifying the results of inevitable psychological regression which takes place in a group when ritual is not introduced to counteract unconscious instinctuality. Although this evaluation of mass psychology is conceded to be essentially negative, it is pointed out that the mass can also have positive effects by fostering courage and dignity; however, these gifts are considered to become dangerous if they are taken for granted and stifle personal efforts to achieve them. 4 references.

000246 Concerning rebirth. 2. The psychology of rebirth. II. Subjective transformation. e. Identification with a cult-hero. In: Jung, C., Collected Works of C. G. Jung, Vol. 9, Part 1. 2nd ed., Princeton University Press, 1968. 451 p. (p. 128).

Identification with some god or hero who is transformed in a sacred ritual is discussed as an important form of personality transformation. The Metamorphosis of Apuleius, the Osiris cult of Egypt, and the Christian tradition are detailed as examples of this phenomenon. The latter is considered to represent a culmination of this transformation in the idea that everyone has an immortal soul and shares in the godhead; further development of this idea is seen to lead to the concept of Christ in each individual. Two forms of this indirect transformation process are described as dromenon, characteristics of the ritual of the Catholic Church, and the gospel, the Protestant preaching of the Word.

000247 Concerning rebirth. 2. The psychology of rebirth. II. Subjective transformation. f. Magical procedures. g. Technical transformation. In: Jung, C., Collected Works of C. G. Jung, Vol. 9, Part 1. 2nd ed., Princeton University Press, 1968. 451 p. (p. 128-130).

Two further forms of personality transformation beyond identification with a cult hero are suggested. Instead of the transformation occuring through an individual's participation in a sacred rite, the rite may be expressly utilized to effect the transformation, which takes place from the outside as an individual submits to a technique. Magical transformation techniques of primitive societies usually involve some physical procedure such as pulling a sick person through hole in the wall or through a leather cow, or a renaming, to give the individual another soul. Nonmagical techniques designed to produce psychic changes are exemplified by the practice of yoga. A fairy tale illustrates how spontaneous transformations are replaced by formalized techniques designed to reproduce the original transformation by imitating the procedure.

000248 Concerning rebirth. 2. The psychology of rebirth. II. Subjective transformation. h. Natural transformation (individuation). In: Jung, C., Collected Works of C. G. Jung, Vol. 9, Part 1. 2nd ed., Princeton University Press, 1968. 451 p. (p. 130-134).

In addition to technical processes of personality transformation, a natural individuation process is described as involving a spontaneous maturing of the personality. Natural transformation is evidenced in dreams symbolizing rebirth and in the intercourse between consciousness and some inner voice; this latter phenomenon, commonly described as talking to oneself, is seen as meditation in the alchemical sense. The inner voice is generally regarded as nonsense or as the voice of God; its real nature considered to be an unconscious counterpart to the ego. It is felt that if this psychic partner is recognized by the ego consciousness, the conflict between the two can have a positive effect. In alchemy, in ancient cults and in religion this inner presence is found personified as an external being such as Mercurius or Christ. 3 references.

000249 Concerning rebirth. 3. A typical set of symbols illustrating the process of transformation. In: Jung, C., Collected Works of C. G. Jung, Vol. 9, Part 1. 2nd ed., Princeton University Press, 1968. 451 p. (p. 135-147).

An example of the symbolism of transformation is found in the Khidr myth of Islamic mysticism which appears in the Eighteenth Sura of the Koran. The cave which appears in this text is seen as a symbol of the unconscious; the entry into the cave is the beginning of a process of psychic transformation which may result in a substantial personality change. Moral observations which follow the legend are considered as counsel to those who will not achieve transformation and who must substitute adherence to the law for true rebirth. The enusing story of Moses and his servant amplifies and explains the first tale; the catch and subsequent loss of the fish by Moses symbolizes an incomplete contact with the nourishing influence of the unconscious. The appearance of Khidr in the legend is felt to represent the greater self which can guide the ego consciousness (Moses) toward increased wisdom. An abrupt transition follows, and a story is told by Moses concerning Khidr and his friend Dhulguarnein, although it is in fact Moses who is interacting with Khidr; this substitution is interpreted in terms of a retreat from the psychic danger of a direct confrontation of the ego consciousness with the self. An allusion to the rebuilding of walls is seen as a symbol of the protection of the self and of the individuation process. It is concluded that the Khidr figure's significance in Islamic mysticism is due to this legend's complete expression of the archetype of individuation. 12 references.

000250 The psychology of the child archetype. I. Introduction. In: Jung, C., Collected Works of C. G. Jung, Vol. 9, Part 1. 2nd ed., Princeton University Press, 1968. 451 p. (p. 151-160).

A brief history of psychological philosophy is given to explain the long obscurity in regard to the unconscious as the essential nature of the psyche. In dream analysis, the existence of typical mythologems among individuals leads to the conclusion that myth forming structural elements must be present in the unconscious psyche. The child archetype is cited as an example of such a primordial image, called archetype, which may be found in myths, fairytales and psychotic fantasies as well as in dreams. Due to the undeveloped nature of primitive man, the unconscious and its archetypes are seen to intrude spontaneously into his conscious mind; thus primitive man does not invent myth but only experience it. In modern man, products of the unconscious may be divided into two categories: fantasies of a personal nature which can be traced to repression by the individual; and fantasies of an impersonal nature, not individually acquired, which correspond to inherited collective elements of the human psyche. This second category is given the name collective unconscious. It is explained that unconscious material can enter the consciousness during a state of reduced conscious intensity such as in dream, when the control of the unconscious by the conscious mind ceases. Archetypes are described as living psychic forces which can promote human growth and which, when neglected, may cause neurotic or even psychotic disorders. The archetype of the child god appears to be widespread: examples from myth and legend, such the Christ child, the alchemical child motif, and the figure of the dwarf or elf are cited. The most significant manifestation of the child motif in psychotherapy is described as occurring in the maturation process of personality induced by analysis of the unconscious or the individuation process. Here preconscious processes gradually pass into the conscious mind through dreams or through the active imagination. 17 references.

000251 The psychology of the child archetype. II. 1. The archetype as a link with the past. In: Jung, C., Collected Works of C. G. Jung, Vol. 9, Part 1. 2nd ed., Princeton University Press, 1968. 451 p. (p. 160-162).

The difficulty of completely explaining the meaning of an archetype, a psychic organ within every man, is acknowledged, with the warning that a poor explanation of it may result in injury to that psychic organ. It is felt that the explanation of the archetype should be such that an adequate and meaningful connection between the conscious mind and the archetypes is assured, and that the functional significance of the archetype remains unimpaired. The archetype's role in the psychic structure is described as representing or personsifying certain instinctive data from the unconscious. The preoccupation of the primitive mentality with magic, cited as evidence for the importance of the connection to primitive psychic contents, is seen as the basis of modern religion. The child archetype is defined as a representation of the preconscious childhood aspect of the collective psyche.

000252 The psychology of the child archetype. II. 2. The function of the archetype. In: Jung, C., Collected Works of C. G. Jung, Vol. 9, Part 1. 2nd ed., Princeton University Press, 1968. 451 p. (p. 162-164).

The function of the child archetype in regard to modern man is outlined. The purpose of the child archetype is seen as the compensation or correction of the inevitable onesidedness and extravagance of the conscious mind, the natural result of conscious concentration on a few contents to the exclusion of all others. Modern man's developed will is described as affording human freedom, but also the greater possibility of transgression against the instincts. Compensation through the still existing state of childhood is considered necessary to prevent the uprooting of modern man's differentiated consciousness. Symptoms of compensation, such as backwardness and regressive behavior, are evaluated negatively by modern man, whereas primitive man sees them as natural, in keeping with law and tradition. Dissociation of consciousness is seen to facilitate a separation of one part of the psyche from the rest, resulting in the falsification of the personality through the force of the separated part. Thus if the childhood state of the collective psyche is suppressed, the unconscious may inhibit or even overwhelm the conscious function.

000253 The psychology of the child archetype. II. 3. The futurity of the archetype. In: Jung, C., Collected Works of C. G. Jung, Vol. 9, Part 1. 2nd ed., Princeton University Press, 1968. 451 p. (p. 164-165).

Since the child is essentially a potential being, the child motif in the psychology of the individual signifies generally the anticipation of future, even though the motif appears to operate in a retrospective manner. In the same manner, the child in the individual is seen to pave the way for a future change of personality. The child motif is explained as a symbol that unites the opposites in one's personality, in that it anticipates the figure that comes from a synthesis of conscious and unconscious elements. The child as mediator of transformation is represented in numerous symbols, such as the circle or the quaternity; these symbols of wholeness are also identified with the self. The individuation process is concluded to exist in the child in a preconscious state, to be actualized in the adult psyche.

000254 The psychology of the child archetype. II. 4. Unity and plurality of the child motif. 5. Child god and child hero. In: Jung, C., Collected Works of C. G. Jung, Vol. 9, Part 1. 2nd ed., Princeton University Press, 1968. 451 p. (p. 165-167).

The child motif as an archetypal image is noted to manifest itself as unity or plurality. When a number of children appear with no individual characteristics, a dissociation of the personality such as is found in schizophrenia is indicated; while the appearance of the child as a unity is felt to represent a potential synthesis of the personality. The appearance of the child may be in the form of a god or hero, with the miraculous birth and early adversities common to both. The child god is seen as a symbol of the unintegrated unconscious; the child hero, combining human and supernatural qualities, is considered a symbol of the potential for individuation. The typical fates of the child figures are interpreted as symbols of psychic events which occur during the entelechy (genesis) of the self as the psyche struggles toward wholeness.

000255 The psychology of the child archetype. III. The special phenomenology of the child archetype. 1. The abandonment of the child. In: Jung, C., Collected Works of C. G. Jung, Vol. 9, Part 1. 2nd ed., Princeton University Press, 1968. 451 p. (p. 167-170).

Danger to and abandonment of the archetypal child figure are interpreted in psychological terms. The universal themes of the child's insignificant beginnings and miraculous birth are interpreted as psychic experiences whose object is the emergence of a new and as yet unknown content. Moments of psychic conflict from which there is no conscious means of escape are described as causing the unconscious to create a third presence of an irrational nature, which the conscious mind neither expects nor understands. One example of this unknown content is the symbolic emergence of the child figure. Since the child figure represents a moving towards

psychic independence, the symbol of abandonment is a necessary precondition for the detachment of the child motif from its origins. The symbol of the child anticipates a new higher state of consciousness which may remain only a mythological projection if it is not actually integrated in the being of the individual. It is noted that the moral conflict unique to modern man, like the physical conflict of primitive times, is still a life threatening situation affording no escape, as evidenced by the numerous child figures appearing as modern culture heroes.

000256 The psychology of the child archetype. III. The special phenomenology of the child archetype. 2. The invincibility of the child. In: Jung, C., Collected Works of C. G. Jung, Vol. 9, Part 1. 2nd ed., Princeton University Press, 1968. 451 p. (p. 170-173).

The psychological significance of the seemingly paradoxical invincibility of the child in myth is examined; although the child is often delivered into dangerous situations and is in continual danger of extinction, he possesses supernatural powers far beyond the human. Similarly, in situations of conflict within the conscious mind, the combatant forces are described as so overwhelming that the child as an isolated content bears no relation to the conscious elements present, and may easily return to unconsciousness; yet the child personifies the most vital urge to realize the self, and as such has great power. The development of the power of the child is traced through ancient myth and alchemical symbolism; Hindu thought is noted to recognize the psychological necessity of detachment and confrontation with the unconscious to make the progress of consciousness possible. It is considered necessary for modern medicine to realize that the archetypes underlying these fantasies cannot be dismissed as unreal. They arise from the depths of the psyche, having their ultimate source in the collective unconscious, identified by Kerenyi as the world itself. 1 reference.

000257 The psychology of the child archetype. III. The special phenomenology of the child archetype. 3. The hermaphroditism of the child. In: Jung, C., Collected Works of C. G. Jung, Vol. 9, Part 1. 2nd ed., Princeton University Press, 1968. 451 p. (p. 173-177).

The hermaphroditic nature of the child archetype and the majority of cosmogonic gods is interpreted as a symbol of the creative union of opposites, a dynamic symbol directed toward a future goal. The continuous renewal of this symbol from pagan mythology through Christian tradition is considered to support its identity as a universal primordial figure. In light of the recent development of psychology, the projection of the hermaphrodite figure is seen to symbolize the ideal psychic goal of self-realization through the unification of the psyche, which is in itself bisexual, consisting of a conscious, dominant gender and its unconscious opposite. 6 references.

000258 The psychology of the child archetype. III. The special phenomenology of the child archetype. 4. The child as beginning and end. In: Jung, C., Collected Works of C. G. Jung, Vol. 9, Part 1. 2nd ed., Princeton University Press, 1968. 451 p. (p. 177-179).

The association of the child archetype with both the beginning and end of life is interpreted psychologically in terms of the preconscious and postconscious essence of man; the preconscious state of early childhood is seen as repeated in the return to psychic wholeness after death. The evidence for this hypothesized psychic wholeness existing beyond the life of man is found in the analogous existence and activity of the unconscious beyond the conscious mind. This preexistent psychic whole is expressed in the symbol of the child, who is helpless but powerful, initially insignificant but ultimately triumphant.

000259 The psychology of the child archetype. IV. Conclusion. In: Jung, C., Collected Works of C. G. Jung, Vol. 9, Part 1. 2nd ed., Princeton University Press, 1968. 451 p. (p. 179-181).

The study of the nature and function of the archetype is described as inexact, in that archetypal symbols form such an interpenetrating network that it is difficult to separate one from the rest; the value of considering them is seen to lie more in their presentation as a whole than in the examination of a single one. Psychology itself is seen as a mythology, a system which can provide its believers with a means of counteracting dissociation from psychic origins. The therapeutic function of archetypes is described in terms of the patient's gradual confrontation with the self through the understanding and demystification of fantasy. The differentiation of conscious and unconscious processes through objective observation leads ideally to the synthesis of the two and to a shift in the center of the personality from the ego to the self.

000260 The psychological aspects of the Kore. In: Jung, C. Collected Works of C. G. Jung, Vol. 9, Part 1. 2nd ed., Princeton University Press, 1968. 451 p. (p. 182-203).

The result of a phenomenological study of psychic structure, consisting of the observance and description of the products of the unconscious, is described as the development of a psychological typology of situations and figures, called motifs, in the psychic processes of man. The principal types of motifs of the human figure include the shadow, the wise old man, the child, the mother as a supraordinate personality or a maiden, the anima in man and the animus in woman. One such motif is the Kore figure, belonging in man to the anima type and in woman to the supraordinate personality, or the self; like the other psychic figures, the Kore is observed to have both positive and negative manifestations. Images such as the Kore are considered to rise from an area of the personality which has an impersonal, collective nature, and to express this psychic material in the conscious. The experience of these archetypal expressions has the effect of widening the scope of consciousness. Several dream visions described by men and women are analyzed in their manifestations of the Kore symbol as supraordinate personality and anima. 1 reference.

000261 The phenomenology of the spirit in fairytales. I. Concerning the word "spirit." In: Jung, C., Collected Works of C. G. Jung, Vol. 9, Part 1. 2nd ed., Princeton University Press, 1968. 451 p. (p. 207-214).

A definition of the word "spirit" is proposed and a description of the historical and mythical characteristics of the spirit is presented. The great number of different definitions of the term in use today is considered to make it difficult to delimit any one concept; however, these definitions in combination are considered to provide a vivid and concrete view of the phenomenon. In the psychological sense, spirit is defined as a fundamental complex which was originally felt as an invisible but dynamic living presence; this concept is seen to precede the Christian view of the spirit as superior to nature. The contrasting materialistic view, developed under antiChristian influence, is based on the premise that the spirit is in fact determined by nature, just as the psychic functions are considered to depend on neurochemical phenomena. It is contended that while spirit and matter may eventually be revealed as identical, at present the reality of psychic contents and processes in themselves cannot be denied. The spirit is conceived as

originally external to man; now, although it has been internalized in the consciousness, it is still creative rather than created, binding man and influencing him just as the external physical world does. It is seen as autonomous and therefore capable of manifesting itself spontaneously in the conscious. 1 reference.

000262 The phenomenology of the spirit in fairytales. II. Self-representation of the spirit in dreams. In: Jung, C., Collected Works of C. G. Jung, Vol. 9, Part 1. 2nd ed., Princeton University Press, 1968. 451 p. (p. 214-217).

Interpretations and implications of the psychic manifestations of the spirit in dreams are discussed. The spirit is considered to depend on the existence of an autonomous, primordial, archetypal image in the preconscious makeup of mankind. The moral character of spirits in dreams is considered impossible to establish, since the unconscious process which produces the spirit is capable of expressing both good and evil. The figure of the wise old man is observed to appear where insight is needed that the conscious is unable to supply; thus the archetype compensates for conscious spiritual deficiency. Again, this insight is considered impossible to judge morally, as it often represents an interplay of good and evil. 1 reference.

000263 The phenomenology of the spirit in fairytales. III. The spirit in fairytales. In: Jung, C., Collected Works of C. G. Jung, Vol. 9, Part 1. 2nd ed., Princeton University Press, 1968. 451 p. (p. 217-230).

The positive and negative manifestations of the archetypal figure of the wise old man are demonstrated in various myths and fairytales. The old man in fairytales, like the old man of dreams, typically appears when the hero is in a hopeless or desparate situation from which he cannot extricate himself alone. The knowledge needed to overcome the hero's difficulties appears in the shape of a wise old man. The old men in fairytales often ask questions of the hero or heroine for the purpose of mobilizing their moral forces; another common function is to dispense some magic talisman. The old man figure is described as representing knowledge, reflection, insight, wisdom, cleverness, and intuition, as well as moral qualities such as goodwill and readiness to help, which make his spiritual character clear. Even in fairytales the old man has a clear link with the psychic unconscious, as in the case of a forest king connected with water and wood symbols, which are themselves symbols for the unconscious. The spirit archetype, like all other archetypes, is seen to have a negative as well as a positive aspect, expressed in the actions or appearance of the the wise old man figure. The manifestation of the good and evil aspects are often found combined in one fairytale, indirectly alluding to an inner relationship between the two. 14 references.

000264 The phenomenology of the spirit in fairytales. IV. Theriomorphic spirit symbolism in fairytales. In: Jung, C., Collected Works of C. G. Jung, Vol. 9, Part 1. 2nd ed., Princeton University Press, 1968. 451 p. (p. 230-242).

Descriptions, interpretations and examples of the manifestation of the spirit archetype in the form of an animal are presented. The assumption of animal form is seen as significant in that it shows the psychic contents in question to be beyond human consciousness, in the sense of the superhuman/demoniac or the subhuman/bestial. Thus in many fairytales helpful animals appear with a knowledge superior to man's, or wicked ones with superior power. A detailed analysis of one fairytale demonstrates the functioning of the animal figure in terms of its relationships with other archetypal symbols such as wholeness and polarity, and the priviledged number of the quaternity. The implication for psychology of triad and quaternity symbolism is discussed in terms of the four functions of consciousness, three of which are susceptible to differentiation, while one remains connected to the unconscious and inaccessible to the will. The complex relationships among these functions and their striving toward wholeness are seen to correspond admirably to the structure of the fairytale in question; this correspondence is seen as natural, given that fairytales as a whole are unusually naive and uncontrived products of the psyche. 2 references.

000265 The phenomenology of the spirit in fairytales. V. Supplement. In: Jung, C., Collected Works of C. G. Jung, Vol. 9, Part 1. 2nd ed., Princeton University Press, 1968. 451 p. (p. 243-252).

The methodology and results of a psychological investigation of the symbolism in a particular fairytale are discussed. Rational connections among the irrational data of the fairytale are first assumed to exist; the truth of the assumption is subsequently demonstrated by the results of study based upon it. For example, in a fairytale featuring threelegged and fourlegged horses, the threeleggedness is assumed to be a significant quality in itself; it is studied as a separate concept, and relationships to the archetypal triad and tetrad structures are revealed. The interpretation of symbols in the fairytale in question is discovered to be extremely complex, involving the animas and shadows of certain characters being personified in others; the representation of the instinctual unconscious, the animas and animal figures; and most important, the tension of opposites and their eventual resolution. A final interpretation of the fairytale portrays it as a representation of the unconscious processes that compensates the conscious Christian perspective; specifically, the fairytale demonstrates the attainment of wholeness or individuation through the union of negative and positive forces. 4 references.

000266 The phenomenology of the spirit in fairytales. VI. Conclusion. In: Jung, C., Collected Works of C. G. Jung, Vol. 9, Part 1. 2nd ed., Princeton University Press, 1968. 451 p. (p. 252-254).

The picture of the spirit that appears in dreams and fairytales is distinguished from the conscious idea of spirit. Originally the spirit was conceived as a demon which came upon man from the outside; those demon have been partially transformed into voluntary acts by the expansion of consciousness, which has begun to transform formerly unconscious areas of the psyche. It is felt that superhuman positive and negative qualities that the primitive man assigned to the demons are now being ascribed to reason, but that the historical events of modern times, such as war, point to a lack of reason. It is suggested that the human spirit is unaware of the demonism that still clings to him. The advanced technology and science of modern man is described as placing mankind in danger of possession. It is felt that mankind must escape from possession by the unconscious through a better understanding of it. Although Christianity is credited with the understanding that man's inner nature is of prime importance, this understanding is not considered to have penetrated deeply enough. 2 references.

000267 On the psychology of the trickster-figure. In: Jung, C., Collected Works of C. G. Jung, Vol. 9, Part 1. 2nd ed., Princeton University Press, 1968. 451 p. (p. 255-272).

A definition and history of the trickster figure as he appears in myth and in emotional disturbance are illustrated by examples of it in American Indian myth, alchemy, the Bible, and parapsychology. In his clearest manifestations the trickster figure is described as a faithful representation of the absolutely undifferentiated human psyche which has hardly left the animal level. In psychopathology the trickster figure is manifested in the split personality, in which a collective personification of traits which may be better or worse than the ego becomes active in the psyche. The trickster figure is represented in normal man by countertendencies in the unconscious that appear whenever a man feels himself at the mercy of apparently malicious accidents; this character component is the shadow. The myth of the trickster is explained to have been preserved and developed for its therapeutic effect: the earlier low intellectual and moral level is held before the consciousness of the more highly developed individual to remind him of the past. The trickster is defined as a parallel to the individual shadow, and the same trend toward meaning seen in the trickster figure is felt to exist for the shadow. Although the shadow appears negative, sometimes traits and associations arising from it can suggest a positive resolution to conflict. 5 references.

000268 Conscious, unconscious, and individuation. In: Jung, C., Collected Works of C. G. Jung, Vol. 9, Part 1. 2nd ed., Princeton University Press, 1968. 451 p. (p. 275-289).

Descriptions of the workings of the conscious, the unconscious and the individuation process, and their relationships to one another are discussed. Individuation denotes the process by which a person becomes a psychological unity or whole through conflict between the two fundamental psychic aspects, the conscious and the unconscious. This process is described as corresponding to alchemical symbols, especially the unity symbol. It is explained that many persons regard consciousness as the whole psychological individual, but that investigation of multiple personality has proved the existence of an unconscious area of personality in addition to the conscious area. There does not appear to be a ruling principle analogous to the ego in the unconscious, as unconscious phenomena are manifested in unsystematic ways. The conscious and unconscious may appear separate in that the conscious is unaware of the contents of the unconscious; yet cases are presented to demonstate that it is possible for the unconscious to swamp the ego, or that under the influence of strong emotion, the ego and the unconscious may change places as the unconscious becomes autonomous. The unconscious contains not only elements of a primitive world of the past, but is directed toward the future as well. The conscious mind is easily influenced by the unconscious, as in the case of intuition which is defined as perception via the unconscious. Elements which exist in the unconscious are described as the anima, that feminine personality hidden in a man, and the animus, the masculine personality hidden in a woman; the shadow, which pesonifies everything the subject does not wish to face in himself; the hero; and the wise old man. These elements are seen to exist in deep levels of the unconscious and bring into mankind's personality a strange psychic life from the remote past. The desired goal of harmony between conscious and unconscious comes about through the process of individuation, an irrational life experience also commonly expressed in symbols. The task of the analyst is defined as aiding in the interpretation of the symbols, in order to achieve a transcendent union of the opposites. The goal of psychotherapy is described as the development of the personality into a whole. 2 references.

000269 A study in the process of individuation. Introductory.
In: Jung, C., Collected Works of C. G. Jung, Vol. 9, Part 1.
2nd ed., Princeton University Press, 1968. 451 p. (p. 290-292).

Biographical data are presented on a patient who achieved
individuation through art therapy. In 1928 at the age of fifty-
five, the woman referred to as Miss X came to Europe to continue her studies under the guidance of Jung. She is described
as the daughter of an exceptional father, cultured, and with a
lively turn of mind. She is umarried, but living with an active
animus, considered typical of women with an academic education. This development of the animus was based on a positive
father complex, which did not a allow a good relationship with
her mother. Finding herself at an impasse, she felt she might
travel to Europe as a way out of her difficulties; her decision
to go to Europe was also based on a desire to expose herself
to her mother's Scandinavian heritage. Before coming to Zurich to see Jung, Miss X had visited Denmark, her mother's
country. Surprisingly, the landscape filled her with the desire
to paint, and she enjoyed her attempts at water color. On the
day before she visited for the first time, Miss X was beginning
a landscape from memory when a fantasy image intruded: she
saw herself buried to the waist in dirt in a region by the sea
filled with boulders. Jung appeared in the fantasy in the guise
of a medieval sorcerer, touched the rock with a magic wand,
and she escaped unharmed. This painting was subsequently
shown to Jung. 1 reference.

000270 A study in the process of individuation. Picture 1. In:
Jung, C., Collected Works of C. G. Jung, Vol. 9, Part 1. 2nd
ed., Princeton University Press, 1968. 451 p. (p. 292-294).

The first painting of a series, submitted by a female patient
during the initial stage of individuation in an art therapy program, is discussed. It is noted that drawing the picture was extremely difficult for the patient, and as it often happens with
beginners at art, it was easy for her to allow the unconscious
to intrude into awareness. Psychologically, the picture is seen
to show the patient caught in the unconscious; it is suggested
that her inadequate relationship with her mother left her with
psyche elements in need of development. It is emphasized that
the way of liberation is an individual one and that, since the
patient had discovered the method of the active imagination
independently, it remained for the therapist only to advise her
to continue on this path. The significance of various aspects of
the picture is interpreted in terms of the process of individuation. The only advice given the patient was to use her imagination to circumvent technical difficulties, in order to introduce
as much fantasy as possible into the pictures, and not to fear
bright colors, for the unconscious is felt to be attracted to
them.

000271 A study in the process of individuation. Picture 2. In:
Jung, C., Collected Works of C. G. Jung, Vol. 9, Part 1. 2nd
ed., Princeton University Press, 1968. 451 p. (p. 294-305).

A description and interpretation of the second of a series of
paintings submitted by a female patient in the psychic individuation process of an art therapy program is given. In contrast to the first picture, the boulders are still present, but they
have become abstracted into round circles; one of the forms
has been blasted by a flash of lightning, and the magician who
was Jung no longer enters into the picture. The picture is
showing an impersonal natural process: the circles are seen as
a rediscovery of the philosophical egg. Considerable historical
and mythological associations are noted for the flash of light-
ing, which is interpreted to signify a sudden, unexpected and
overpowering change of psychic condition. The work of
Bohme in particular is examined for its psychic and alchemical

connections with lightning. Although a Freudian explanation of
the picture would involve the concept of repression, it is suggested that a coming wholeness is marked by the function of
intuition, which seems to be the inferior, redeeming function of
the patients, whereas sensation is the superior function. The
circle is interpreted as a mandala, the psychological expression
of the totality of the self; other eggs appear as other selves
with whom the patient feels intimate. The pryamids found in
the first picture as rocks are seen again, but with their tops
gilded with light; these boulders are interpreted as contents of
the unconscious pushing upward for release in a positive
sense. 16 references.

000272 A study in the process of individuation. Picture 3. In:
Jung, C., Collected Works of C. G. Jung, Vol. 9, Part 1. 2nd
ed., Princeton University Press, 1968. 451 p. (p. 305-313).

The third picture in a series, painted by a female patient in
the process of psychic individuation as part of an art therapy
program, is analyzed. The primary distinguishing characteristic
of the third picture is its use of light colors. A dark blue
sphere is seen floating in space among clouds; around the middle of the sphere runs a wavy silver band which, the patient
explains, is keeping the sphere balanced by equal and opposite
forces. To the right above the sphere floats a snake with golden rings, its head pointed at the sphere. In the middle of the
band around the planet is the number twelve. Two dreams felt
by the patient to be influencing the painting are detailed and
interpreted as being of archetypal significance. The increase of
light in the picture symbolizes conscious realization; it is explained that the liberation concept has become integrated into
consciousness. The floating sphere represents the total personality, but at this time it is felt that Miss X does not know
of the relation of the ego to the total personality. The number
contained in the picture is discussed in terms of its connections to the concept of male and female in astrology and myth.
An analysis of the symbol of Mercury in the picture is also
made various symbolic significances of the colors used
together in the picture are proposed. 8 references.

000273 A study in the process of individuation. Picture 4. In:
Jung, C., Collected Works of C. G. Jung, Vol. 9, Part 1. 2nd
ed., Princeton University Press, 1968. 451 p. (p. 313-319).

The fourth picture of a series, painted by a female patient in
the process of psychic individuation as part of an art therapy
program, is described as showing a significant change. The
sphere has divided into an outer membrane and an inner
nucleus, the outer membrane is flesh colored, and a differentiated inner structure of a ternary character is seen. Lines
of force run through the whole nuclear body, indicating that
excitation has reached the innermost psychic core. The picture
is interpreted sexually to show the female organ in the act of
fecundation, with the sperm penetrating the nuclear membrane. The position of the snake on top of the picture is interpreted as representing the typical danger emanating from
the spiritual sphere, personified by the animus; for a man, the
danger is described as coming from the anima projected in to
the world. Picture four is described by the patient as the most
difficult of the series to execute, and that it seemed to denote
a turning point of the whole process. It is at this stage that the
ego is temporarily set aside, giving the unconscious the opportunity to manifest its oppositions clearly. It is noted that later
the will must protect itself in the midst of these opposites, so
that they be reconciled. 4 references.

000274 A study in the process of individuation. Picture 5. In:
Jung, C., Collected Works of C. G. Jung, Vol. 9, Part 1. 2nd
ed., Princeton University Press, 1968. 451 p. (319-323).

The fifth picture of a series, painted by a female patient during the process of psychic individuation as part of an art therapy program, is described by the patient as progressing naturally from picture four. The snake is sinking downward and seems to have lost its threatening power; the sphere has increased in size and blossoms in color. The division of the nucleus of the sphere falls into four parts; this division is interpreted by the patient as the division of consciousness into the four functions: thinking, feeling, sensation and intuition. A vortex is formed by the four divisions, apparently turning to the left, a phenomenon interpreted as a movement towards the unconscious. The colors of the picture are discussed in their mythological and alchemical significance. The snake is felt to represent the shadow, which can be compared with the principle of evil; the position of the snake is said to reflect the common view of evil as an external force. It is contended, however, that evil is the necessary counterpart of good within the psyche's dynamic structure. 3 references.

000275 A study in the process of individuation. picture 6. In: Jung, C., Collected Works of C. G. Jung, Vol. 9, Part 1. 2nd ed., Princeton University Press, 1968. 451 p. (p. 323-326).

An analysis is made of the sixth picture in a series of paintings done by a female patient during the process of psychic individuation as part of an art therapy program. This picture shows a mandala in bright colors against a grey background. Wings of Mercury reappear along with a striking swastika which is wheeling to the right. The mandala is interpreted as an attempt to unite the opposites red and blue, outside and inside; the rightward movement is explained as an attempt to bring material into consciousness. The black snake has disappeared, but the darkness of the background may have been caused by it. The picture is associated with a dream the patient had several days before, in which a tree was found in the middle of the room where she worked. Maternal significance is attributed to the tree; the painted mandala is given significance not only as a symbol of the self, but also as a God image. A brief discussion is offered of the mandala as it is manifested in religious practices from ancient Egypt onward. 11 references.

000276 A study in the process of individuation. Picture 7. In: Jung, C., Collected Works of C.G. Jung, Vol. 9, Part 1. 2nd ed., Princeton University Press, 1968. 451 p. (p. 326-335).

In the seventh picture of a series, painted by a female patient during the process of psychic individuation as part of an art therapy program, the entire background against which the mandala is painted is black, with all light in the picture concentrated within the sphere. The colors are less bright but more intense, and the blackness of the exterior has penetrated into the center of the mandala. This manifestation is interpreted as the penetration of the black snake from previous paintings of the series into the nucleus. The swastika of the previous picture has been replaced by an equal armed cross formed by the golden rays; four hooks suggest a rightward rotation, which appears to have come to an end with the attainment of absolute blackness penetrating the center of the mandala. The wings of Mercury are seen as having undergone extensive transformation, so that the sphere has the power to remain afloat without sinking into total darkness. The golden rays forming the cross produce an inner bond of consolidation as a defense against destructive influences. The picture is interpreted as portraying a mood of suffering and painful suspension over an abyss of inner loneliness. Alchemical symbols and biblical quotations are discussed in relation to the picture to demonstrate the universal nature of the ideas generated

by the patient. After painting this picture, the patient is reported as feeling a disturbing association with the color red, associated with the analyst, which leads to a feeling of self-pity over not having had any children. Only when she had recovered from these feelings could the patient paint again. It is explained that real liberation does not come from glossing over or repressing painful states of feeling, but only by experiencing them fully. 16 references.

000277 A study in the process of individuation. Picture 8. In: Jung, C., Collected Works of C. G. Jung, Vol. 9, Part 1. 2nd ed., Princeton University Press, 1968. 451 p. (p. 335-337).

The eighth picture of a series, painted by a female patient as part of an art therapy program, is considered to represent an advance in the psychic individuation process. Most of the interior of the picture is filled with darkness; the blue-green of the water has condensed to a dark blue quaternity, and the golden light in the center is turning counterclockwise. The mandala is interpreted as moving towards the chthonic depths, coming close to the darkness. An inner undifferentiated quaternity is seen to be balanced by an outer, differentiated one, equated with the four functions of consciousness. The colors assigned to each function are: yellow, intuition; light blue, thinking; flesh pink, feeling; and brown, sensation. Each quarter is again divided into three, producing the number twelve. The previous rejection of the tree as a symbol of the mother is now accepted and placed in the middle of the mandala. The cortices expand into the darkness as golden rings, interpreted as a far reaching effect on the environment coming from the self. A dream reported by the patient integrates her concepts and progressive development regarding her animus, with which she no longer identifies. The mandala is further described and interpreted as symbolizing the eye of God and having the purifying effect of consciousness. It is concluded from this painting that the patient has accepted her own psychic darkness. 6 references.

000278 A study in the process of individuation. Picture 9. In: Jung, C., Collected Works of C. G. Jung, Vol. 9, Part 1. 2nd ed., Princeton University Press, 1968. 451 p. (p. 338-342).

In an analysis of the ninth picture of a series, painted by a female patient during a final stage of the psychic individuation process of an art therapy program, the appearance is noted of a blue soul flower on a red background. In the center a golden light in the form of a lamp is found. The cortices are pronounced, consisting of light in the upper half of the mandala radiating outward. In the lower half of the mandala are rings of brown earth. Above are three white birds, symbolizing the Trinity; below the center a goat is rising, accompanied by two ravens and twining snakes. The black sky behind the three birds and the goat against the orange background are interpreted as indicating that there can be no white without black, and no holiness without the devil. The patient is deliberately stressing a connection with the East, painting into the mandala four hexagrams from the I-Ching. The sign in the left top half, "Yu, Enthusiasm," is interpreted as indicating a movement coming from the unconscious, the second hexagram at the top is "sun, decrease" which is taken to indicate the patient's insight into the conditional quality of all relationships, the relativity of all values, and the transcience of all things. The sign in the bottom right is "Sheng, pushing upward"; this hexagram is interpreted to mean there is no development unless the shadow is accepted. The final hexagram is "ting, the cauldron," which is taken to mean that through constant self-abnegation the personality becomes differentiated. The union of opposites achieved by the patient is seen to be manifested in the use of firm and yielding lines in the hexagrams. 2 references.

000279 A study in the process of individuation. Picture 10. In: Jung, C., Collected Works of C. G. Jung, Vol. 9, Part 1. 2nd ed., Princeton University Press, 1968. 451 p. (342-344).

The tenth picture of a series, painted by a female patient during the process of psychic individuation in an art therapy program, is divided into two parts, as is the ninth picture. The soul flower in the center still exists but is surrounded on all sides by a dark blue night sky, in which four phases of the moon appear. The three birds seen in picture nine have become two, and their plumage is darkened; the goat has become two semihuman creatures with horns and light faces, and only two of the four snakes remain. Two crabs appear in the lower chthonic hemisphere which represents the body. The symbol of the crab in myth and astrological functioning is discussed; its particular relevance to the patient appears to be that she was born in the first degrees of Cancer and wished to integrate her individual sign into the painting of her psychic self. The dualities that run through the picture are always seen to be inwardly balanced, so that they lose their incompatibility. The duplication motif is noted and explained as a phenomenon which occurs when unconscious contents are about to become conscious and differentiated. They are then split into two halves, representing the conscious and the still unconscious aspects of the material involved. 7 references.

000280 A study in the process of individuation. Picture 11. Pictures 12-24. In: Jung, C., Collected Works of C. G. Jung, Vol. 9, Part 1. 2nd ed., Princeton University Press, 1968. 451 p. (p. 345-348).

An analysis of paintings 11 through 24, the last in a series submitted by a female patient in art therapy, is presented, as the final phase in a psychic individuation process. Many of these, done after therapy ended, reveal the theme of psychic penetration by, and defence against, disrupting external elements. This struggle is seen to be resolved in an enantiodromia which restores equilibrium. Pictures 19 through 24 are not commented on due to lack of knowledge of the time and circumstances of their production.

000281 A study in the process of individuation. Conclusion. In: Jung, C., Collected Works of C. G. Jung, Vol. 9, Part 1. 2nd ed., Princeton University Press, 1968. 451 p. (p. 348-354).

The individuation process evidenced by a series of paintings submitted by a female patient in art therapy is discussed. The development of fantasy through painting in her case viewed as the renewal of contact with the unconscious and of a consciousness that has far outdistanced it. The whole of civilization is felt to be faced with the same task, due to a too rapid advance of technology and the inhibition of individual development. The initial paintings in the series illustrate the psychic processes set in motion when attention is given to a neglected area of the psyche. When contact is established, symbols of the self appear, representing the whole personality and exposing the individual to the archaic and alien situations which underlie faith and knowledge. The therapist's task is described as helping the patient to reach an adequate understanding of the new psychic material and to avoid dangerous misinterpretations. Caution is advised in the excessive consolidation of psychic forces, lest the patient identify completely with them at the expense of his ego. The spontaneous production of mandala symbols by individuals and cultures is stressed as evidence that they are not created by man, but preexistent. 7 references.

000282 Concerning mandala symbolism. In: Jung, C., Collected Works of C. G. Jung, Vol. 9, Part 1. 2nd ed., Princeton University Press, 1968. 451. p. (p. 355-384).

The symbol of the mandala is described and numerous examples of mandalas from various parts of the world are offered. The Sanskrit word mandala, meaning "circle," is identified as the Indian term for the circle drawn in religious rituals. The function of the mandala is described as a narrowing down of the psychic field of vision as an aid to intensification of concentration. The goal of the Yogi in contemplating the processes depicted in the mandala is to become inwardly aware of the deity; through contemplation, the practitioner may realize himself as God, and return from the illusion of individual existence into the universal totality of the divine. The basic psychological motif of the mandala is of a center of personality to which everything is related, by which everything is arranged, and which itself is a source of energy. The energy of the central point is manifested in the compulsion to become what one is, this desired presence may be called the self. The self is surrounded in the mandala by an area containing the paired opposites that make up personality; the totality of the mandala contains consciousness, a personal unconscious, and an indefinitely large area of collective unconscious whose archetypes are common to all mankind. Some of these archetypes are within the scope of personality and may acquire an individual stamp, such as the anima, the animus, and the shadow. Other religious mandalas and mandalas spontaneously produced by patients during the course of analysis are discussed. The production of mandalas in a therapeutic context is felt to occur in states of chaos or panic as a rearranging of the personality toward a new center. Patients are said to appreciate the soothing effects of these pictures, which emphasize wholeness, order and balance. It is noted that the reality of the collective unconscious is often first impressed upon a patient by means of his mandala productions. Numerous mandalas drawn by patients are reproduced and described. 11 references.

000283 Appendix: mandalas. In: Jung, C., Collected Works of C. G. Jung, Vol. 9, Part 1. 2nd ed., Princeton University Press, 1968. 451 p. (p. 385-390).

The meaning and function of the mandala is briefly described. The Sanskrit word mandala is defined as meaning "circle"; in religious practice and psychology the word refers to circular images which are drawn, painted, or danced. As psychological phenomena they appear spontaneously in dreams, certain states of mental conflict, and in schizophrenia. Often the mandala contains some figure in a multiple of four in the form of a cross or square. The mandala in Tibetan Buddhism is called a Yantra and aids in meditation and concentration; in alchemy, it represents the synthesis of the four elements which tend to fall apart. In psychology, the severe order imposed by a circular image of this kind compensates the disorder and confusion of the psychic state of the individual; this process is described as a natural and instinctive attempt at self-healing. Since the material expressed in them is essentially archetypal, there is fundamental similarity of mandalas regardless of origin; the mandala commonly represents psychic wholeness through the squaring of the circle. The object of individual mandalas is described as locating the self, which can be distinguished from the ego. Whereas the ego is described as the point of reference for consciousness, the self is at the midpoint of personality, and for this reason many mandalas show a dark and light half representing the conscious and unconscious divisions of personality. The therapeutic effect of mandalas is felt to consist in their spontaneous production; no therapeutic value is thought possible for the imitation or repetition of such iamges.

92 AION: RESEARCHES INTO THE PHENOMENOLOGY OF THE SELF

000284 The ego. In: Jung, C., Collected Works of C. G. Jung, Vol. 9, Part 2. 2nd ed., Princeton University Press, 1968. 333 p. (p. 3-7).

The concepts of self and unconscious as related to the ego are described. The somatic and psychic bases of the ego are said to contain both conscious and unconscious factors. Three levels of content are posited in the unconscious: that which can be produced voluntarily (memory); that which cannot be produced voluntarily but can be produced involuntarily; and that which can never be produced. From earlier discussions it is inferred that the ego is the center of consciousness but not the center of the personality, since it is but a part of the personality and so contained within it. The center of the personality is more properly labeled as "the self." The ego is viewed as arising from the continuous interplay of the person's inner and outer experiences. Its characteristics are unique to each individual, but its elements are common to all individuals. Its ability to change and develop in each person over a period of time is discussed. Finally, the notion of the collective unconscious is introduced and described as a subdivision of the extraconscious content of the psyche.

000285 The shadow. In: Jung, C., Collected Works of C. G. Jung, Vol. 9, Part 2. 2nd ed., Princeton University Press, 1968. 333 p. (p. 8-10).

From the contents of the collective unconscious, present from the beginning of life, the most accessible of the archetypes, the shadow, is examined and contrasted with the archetypes of the animus and the anima. The shadow is described as composed of the dark elements of the personality, having an emotional and primitive nature which resists moral control. The most resistant elements are usually associated with certain emotionally toned projections; since projections are attached to external objects, it is unlikely that the individual involved in them will recognize their source within his own unconscious. In extreme cases of projection, the individual may become completely cut off from his environment and will live in a self-perpetuating world of illusion. It is noted, however, that the most intense projections arise not from the shadow, but from the animus in a woman or the anima in a man. Since these archetypes are of a gender opposite that of the conscious individual their projections are even more difficult to recognize than those of the shadow, which represents primarily the personal unconscious.

000286 The syzygy: anima and animus. In: Jung, C., Collected Works of C. G. Jung, Vol. 9, Part 2. 2nd ed., Princeton University Press, 1968. 333 p. (p. 11-22).

The nature of the animus/anima archetypes and of the projections arising from them are described. These archetypes from the collective unconscious, reincarnated in each child, are seen to combine with the early experience of the child with the opposite gender parent to create the mother imago in boys and the father imago in girls. Because of the opposite sex nature of animus/anima projections, they are almost impossible to recognize as emanating from one's own psyche, whereas the shadow's same sex projections are considered to be more easily identified. The difficulty of dissolving such projections is seen to reside in the nature of archetypes as elements of the collective unconscious; although the contents of the animus/anima can be integrated into the conscious, they themselves remain separate as constituents of basic psychic structure. It is noted that the realization of the shadow, which makes possible a recognition of the animus or anima, is the first stage of the analytic process; recognition is only considered possible through an individual's relation to a partner and the formation of the quaternal marriage structure. This quaternion formed in the male of himself, his female partner, the transcendent anima, and the Wise Old Man archetype, and in the woman of herself, her male partner, the animus and the Chthonic Mother archetype, is noted to be the scheme for the structure of the self and for the structure of primitive society. 3 references.

000287 The self. In: Jung, C., Collected Works of C. G. Jung, Vol. 9, Part 2. 2nd ed., Princeton University Press, 1968. 333 p. (p. 23-35).

The self is defined in its relationship to the ego and the instincts, and the self's striving for wholeness is related to the parallel striving of the collective unconscious for wholeness as typified in the mandala symbols and ultimately in the figure of Christ. It is explained that the self is motivated by the unconscious, whereas the ego exists in the conscious; as long as the two are in equilibrium, the personality is functioning normally. However, when the self is assimilated by the ego or the ego by the self, the result is inflation of either the unconscious or the conscious to the detriment of the total personality. The striving of these forces is seen in individuals as instincts or natural forces; the need for equilibrium between them is felt as a need for wholeness. This conflict is seen to be represented throughout history by the quaternity or mandala symbols which are valued because of their similarity to the God image, the ultimate unity; understanding of the mandala is felt to grow from experiential rather than intellectual processes. The self is the basis of all theories of unity, which are part of all religions. Insofar as Christian symbols no longer express what is now welling up from the unconscious, the value of Christianity in the modern world is seen to be meaningless and hollow. 2 references.

000288 Christ, a symbol of the self. In: Jung, C., Collected Works of C. G. Jung, Vol. 9, Part 2. 2nd ed., Princeton University Press, 1968 333 p. (p. 36-71).

The archetype of the self as expressed in the image of Christ, including their respective opposites of shadow and Antichrist, is discussed in a critical review of Scripture and of the writing of the Gnostics. Christ is seen as a symbol of the archetypal God image, whose descent to hell and resurrection have psychological equivalents in the integration of the collective unconscious, which plays an essential part in the psychic individuation process. However, while the original Christian God image appears to have included even the dark animal side of man, the Christ symbol lacks wholeness because of the exclusion of this "inferior" aspect of the personality and its externalization in the form of the Antichrist. Christ, then, is an incomplete symbol of the self; to be whole the archetype must express both good and evil, the conscious as well as the unconscious. It is noted that in a pre-Manichaean Gnostic/Christian text dating from about A.D. 150, the equality of good and evil was recognized, and in fact creation as a whole was viewed as a structure of paired opposites (syzygies). A schema of the transcendental nature of Christ and the self is based upon a quaternion composed of opposites paired which apply to both; a similar quaternion illustrates the unity/opposition of good and evil, spiritual and material. Further analogies to the structure of Christian symbolism are found in alchemical texts and in psychological theory, particularly in regard to the impurity of the body and the opposing purity of the spirit. The distinction between the metaphysical and the psychological perspective in the study of the Christ image is emphasized. The psychological view is phenomenological; it is concerned with the description and analysis of archetypal images, not with their truth or falsehood as expressions of religious faith. It is in the psychological sense that Christ and the alchemical symbol of the lapis philosophorum may be identified as like symbolic expressions of the ideal wholeness of the self; the Christian concept of redemption is not devalued by this association, rather it is reinforced as an expression of the psychological imperative of reunion of opposites. It is felt that if this process is not realized by the individual and by civilization as a whole, world conflict will be the inevitable result. 31 references.

000289 The sign of the fishes. In: Jung, C., Collected Works of C. G. Jung, Vol. 9, Part 2. 2nd ed., Princeton University Press, 1968. 333 p. (p. 72-94).

Similarities between astrological and Christian symbolism are explored, with particular attention given to the historical evolution of the dual symbol of the fishes. The fish symbol is widely distributed throughout the mythologies and religions of ancient civilizations, especially in the Near and Middle East; however, suddenness of its activation in early Christian history is seen to have a more specific source in astrological symbolism. Christ was born under the sign of the Fishes, with the Sun in the sign of the Twins; the dual nature of both symbols is discussed as it relates to the Gnostic Christ/Antichrist myth. Other significant points in astrological chronology are explored in terms of their associations with the Christian movement. In particular, the dates of conjunction of opposing planets, events associated with new beginnings, are seen to correspond to the founding of new and historically influential religious orders. These new religious movements are in turn examined for the psychological impulses underlying their beliefs; the monastic Holy Ghost movement headed by Joachim, for example, is felt to be an expression of the vitalizing archetype of the spirit. This movement influenced some of the greatest religious and scientific theorists, but was elsewhere degraded and distorted by revolutionaries and anarchists in the antichristian era. The analysis of fish symbolism is resumed and related to the change in outlook which began with the Renaissance. In the astrological sense, whereas the age of the fishes is ruled by the conflict of opposite forces, the Aquarian age which follows it brings about the union of these opposites. The first fish is Christ, the second Antichrist, and the contact between them occurs at the time of the Renaissance; this contact of opposites (enantiodromia) is considered to have formed the spirit of the modern era. The Aquarian era of unification is yet to come in the third millennium. 24 references.

000290 The prophecies of Nostradamus. In: Jung, C., Collected Works of C. G. Jung, Vol. 9, Part 2. 2nd ed., Princeton University Press, 1968. 333 p. (p. 95-102).

The astrological prophecies made by Nostradamus in 1558 are considered in light of the accuracy in general of astrological prediction of historical and religious events. Nostradamus set the renovation of the age for the year 1792, which was in fact the year of the inception of the French Revolution's new calendar. The French Revolution is seen as the culmination of the spiritual and social enantiodromia (contact of opposing forces) which began with the Renaissance, parallelling the dynamic relationship of Christ and Antichrist, and of the two fishes in astrological symbolism. Nostradamus' identification

of the evil forces as coming from the North and the good as existing in the South is associated with the symbolism of earlier Christian texts, and with the fact that Luther, who was commonly seen as the Antichrist, came from Northern Europe. For his prediction of future revolution and reformation, Nostradamus is considered the foremost spokesman of the antichristian age. 1 reference.

000291 The historical significance of the fish. In: Jung, C., Collected Works of C. G. Jung, Vol. 9, Part 2. 2nd ed., Princeton University Press, 1968. 333 p. (p. 103-117).

The history of the astrological fish and ram symbols are compared to Christian symbolism and examined in terms of their associations with psychological premises. The dualism of the fish symbol in particular corresponds to the dual nature of Christ as the God image; as the God image is an archetype of the dual self, any imbalance in its expression, such as the suppression of the concept of evil in late Christianity, results in a profound uneasiness in the psyche. The destruction of the God image in the modern world has thus set in motion the destruction of the human personality. A comparison is made between the Christian and astrological interpretations of the fishes. Fishes of astrology are seen as Christ and the Virgin Mother, for in the astrological legend one fish becomes two, representing a mother/son relationship. In the astrological myth, the mother is a danger to her son; this destructive interpretation is related to the dangers in Christ's own childhood and the other Christian symbols and parables. The astrological characteristics of the fish are seen to contain the essential components of the Christian myth; however, no proof exists that Christian fish symbolism was derived from the zodiac, nor that the Christ/Antichrist polarity is causally related to the dualism of the Fishes. A more likely prototype for the Christ/fish symbol structure is considered to lie in pagan cults and myths. 8 references.

000292 The ambivalence of the fish symbol. In: Jung, C., Collected Works of C. G. Jung, Vol. 9, Part 2. 2nd ed., Princeton University Press, 1968. 333 p. (p. 118-125).

The dual symbol of the fish in astrological and Christian tradition is examined in its correspondences with psychic structure. The splitting of the monster who opposes God in early Jewish tradition into the two monsters Leviathan and Behemoth is compared to the doubling of the shadow figure in dreams: it is explained that in each case one of the forces in conflict -- the God image or the conscious ego personality -- is incomplete, necessitating that the dual symbol of the fish appears as well in ancient Middle Eastern symbolism, and is even found as an explicit symbol of the soul in Egyptian mythology. Another dual symbol, that of the North as source of evil and birthplace of God, traced through Arab, Babylonian and Mithraic texts, is discovered in Ezekiel's vision of God. This symbolic coincidence of opposites, with the similar dualism of the fish and other symbols, is discussed in terms of the incongruity of late Christianity's radical separation of the devil from God; the paradoxical symbolism of alchemy is seen as a more or less conscious compensation for this imbalance in the expression of the archetypal God image. 4 references.

000293 The fish in alchemy. 1. The medusa. In: Jung, C., Collected Works of C. G. Jung, Vol. 9, Part 2. 2nd ed., Princeton University Press, 1968. 333 p. (p. 126-137).

The associations of the fish in alchemical, Christian and psychological symbolism are discussed. The fish in alchemical texts prior to the 11th century is found to be identified with the lapis philosophorum, considered psychologically as a complex symbol of the self. Numerous references appear to the fish glowing from an inner fire of a dual nature represented both as the light of divine grace and as the fires of hell. This type of dualism is noted to have occurred frequently in medieval symbolism, but without any apparent awareness of the unity of opposing forces such a dual nature implies. An investigation of the complex network of archetypal symbols in alchemy reveals its close correspondence with the structure of the psyche; in particular, the unity of hell and God as the source of the world is seen to be parallel to the unified source of all disparate psychic operations, whether they are creative or destructive.

000294 The fish in alchemy. 2. The fish. In: Jung, C., Collected Works of C. G. Jung, Vol. 9, Part 2. 2nd ed., Princeton University Press, 1968. 333 p. (p. 137-145).

A distinction is drawn between the jelly fish in medieval symbolism and the alchemic cinedian fish with its relation to the lapis. Several texts concerning the nature of the fish are examined, the influence of the writings of Pliny is discussed, and the Messianic role attributed to it by Sir George Ripley is mentioned. To the alchemists the fish was a real fish of ancient times; it had legs and contained a dragon's stone, a white gem that acts as a alexipharmic. Its dual nature is emphasized; sometimes it was represented as white and sometimes as black, and from this union of opposites its magical powers were derived. The fish supposedly lived in the center of the ocean, or the center of the spirit of the world. For the alchemists the ocean was a symbol for the unconscious, hence the fish can be seen as a symbol of the self and, therefore, also of God. The power of the fish is defined as giving to the one who ate it the knowledge of all things. In this sense, it is compared to the eucharist. 2 references.

000295 The fish in alchemy. 3. The fish symbol of the Cathars. In: Jung, C., Collected Works of C. G. Jung, Vol. 9, Part 2. 2nd ed., Princeton University Press, 1968. 333 p. (145-153).

In the writings of the Cathars, the symbol of the fish was used in conjunction with beliefs about creation, power and the devil. These beliefs are examined and related to astrological, alchemical and Christian interpretations surrounding the fish. The interpretations are seen as figures representing the birth of consciousness under the control of the fish. A comparison is made between St. Augustine's interpretation of the multiplication of the loaves and fishes and the Cathars' perception of the fish; the former interpreted the fishes as symbolizing Christ's kingly and priestly power; the Cathars as the two ruling powers of Christ and devil. To the Cathars, it also meant that God knew and intended the enantiodromia of the world. The reappearance of the symbol of the fish in dreams, shown by means of a case study, illustrates the the unconscious "knowledge" of the individuation process and its historical symbolism.

000296 The alchemical interpretation of the fish. In: Jung, C., Collected Works of C. G. Jung, Vol. 9, Part 2. 2nd ed., Princeton University Press, 1968. 333 p. (p. 154-172).

The alchemical belief that the magical fish can be captured and used as a magnetic attraction to the prima materia is viewed as a secret doctrine rather than a chemical process. Since this doctrine could be taught, the alchemical symbols for the process represent two things: the chemical substance itself and the doctrine or theory of preparation. Analogies with the Holy Ghost archetype are discussed. From the writings of the alchemist Dorn, it is deduced that the arcane substance was the same whether it came from inside or outside of the seeker;

hence it can be concluded that Dorn recognized self-knowledge as the source of all other knowledge. The discussion turns to man's limited knowledge of himself, explained by showing that the majority of man's processes reside in the unconscious. The importance of Freud's and Adler's discoveries in this context are mentioned. It is felt that Freud delineated the elementary and Adler the final proof of these unconscious causal factors which are each person's individual potential. As is evident from this study, for the alchemists and for the modern psychologists, the self is not part of the ego but part of the unconscious. Alchemy, then, is credited with being the foundation for modern scientific thinking.

000297 Background to the psychology of Christian alchemical symbolism. In: Jung, C., Collected Works of C. G. Jung, Vol. 9, Part 2. 2nd ed., Princeton University Press, 1968. 333 p. (p. 173-183).

The widening chasm between faith and knowledge is discussed and related to modern man's reluctance to accept anything not based on objective fact. Scientific stress on objectivity and its neglect of the psyche until recently is contrasted with the Gnostic and alchemic recognition of the importance of the psyche and experiential knowledge. Modern man is perceived as scoffing at dogma which is based on faith and is subjective. It is noted that only a short time ago most of the world was pagan, and that Christianity has little power left, since modern man does not accept such notions as the Virgin birth as easily as did man at the time of Christ. The danger inherent in destroying tradition and myths is explained, and its importance is emphasized; since myths are part of the unconscious, they act as a bridge between the conscious and unconscious. Christ, as a combination of God and man archetypes, is part of this bridge. The fish symbol supports the importance of dogma and subjective experience or acts as an antidote for the fractionalizing tendencies of the modern mind. The psychological concept of human wholeness or individualization is seen as a modern replacement for the symbol of the fish. 1 reference.

000298 Gnostic symbols of the self. In: Jung, C., Collected Works of C. G. Jung, Vol. 9, Part 2. 2nd ed., Princeton University Press, 1968. 333 p. (p. 184-221).

The concept of the fish caught by magnetic attraction is extended to the image of Christ, who exerts a magnetic attraction on the divine nature of man. Three symbols of the magnetic agent -- water, the serpent, and the Logos -- found in Gnostic texts are considered symbols of assimilation corresponding to the assimilation of the ego psyche and the supraordinate self (individuation) which is the ultimate goal of the psychotherapeutic process. This process of individuation is related to the practices of the Gnostics and the alchemists, in which their awareness of the unconscious was formulated to suit the character of the age in which they lived. Meister Eckhart likened changes in the God image to changes in human consciousness, since God represented for him the ideal wholeness of man. The unconscious was expressed by the Gnostics in symbols of the universal ground as the beginning or source of perfection. Symbols found in dreams and visions are compared with the Gnostic association of sexual symbolism with Christ; the interpretation of the vision of John (John 3:12), which incorporates typical dream symbols of the mountain, Christ, woman figure and copulation is presented. The marriage quaternion and the figure of the perfect man in Naassene symbolism are found to parallel early Christian symbolism; both are seen to be closely connected with psychic realities. Two specific examples of second century formulations of the psychological nature of the self, conceived under the influence of Christian thought, are found in the conception of the perfect and complete man, the Monad, in Monoimos, and in the description by Plotinus of the soul as a dynamic process of circling around a central point. The latter concept is related to the similar structure of the mandala image, and to the alchemical image of the arcane substance as the invisible piont which is the center of all things. The assimilation of Christ to similar symbols, such as the mustard seed or the hidden treasure, is not seen as a devaluation of Christ's personality, but the desirable integration of Christ into the human psyche, and the resultant expansion of personality and consciousness. It is felt that the onesided rationalism of the modern world threatens this integration. 10 references.

000299 The structure and dynamics of the self. In: Jung, C., Collected Works of C. G. Jung, Vol. 9, Part 2. 2nd ed., Princeton University Press, 1968. 333 p. (p. 222-265).

A series of quaternions in ascending and descending arrangements are presented to show how similar symbols have been arranged by various philosophies and religions. Citing the Gnostics as among the first seekers of self-knowledge, and therefore as early psychologists, the idea of the importance of self-knowledge is traced historically. As self-knowledge seekers, the Gnostics were forerunners not only of psychological theory, but also of modern physiology and evolutionary theories. The symbols used to represent self-knowledge have varied but, as Freud has pointed out, the phallus as symbol becomes more important as sexuality is less valued. The snake and Paradise symbols, among many others, are discussed in their relationship to the structure of the self and the organization of symbols into circle and quaternion figures, the main quaternions being those of Anthropos and the shadow. Another quaternion is formed by the union of the four elements, producing the alchemical lapis. The numerous and varied arrangements of symbols used by the alchemists are listed: quaternions, pyramids, double pyramids, uroboros, and finally the rotundum. The beauty of such perfect geometric formulations graphically demonstrates the harmony of all existence. 13 references.

000300 Researches into the phenomenology of the self. Conclusion. In: Jung, C., Collected Works of C. G. Jung, Vol. 9, Part 2. 2nd ed., Princeton University Press, 1968. 333 p. (p. 266-269).

The purpose of the book, an exploration of the archetype of the self, is reiterated and its contents are summarized. An overview of the contents shows that the work began with an examination of the other archetypes that most affect the self, namely the shadow, the anima and the animus. A discussion of the positive and negative qualities of these archetypes follows. It is concluded that good and bad are relative and only meaningful when considered within the human sphere. The self is defined as the result of the union of these opposites and represents psychic totality. This unity is represented by the God image in religion. The Gnostics are credited with being among the first to seek systematically the symbols of the self, since they were ruled by their natural inner experiences.

10 CIVILIZATION IN TRANSITION

000301 The role of the unconscious. In: Jung, C., Collected Works of C. G. Jung, Vol. 10. 2nd ed., Princeton University Press, 1970. 609 p. (p. 3-28).

The unconscious is discussed not as a mere psychological construct but rather as an integral part of man's psyche, history and world view. The term "unconscious" was at first spurned by experimental psychologists who believed that everything psychic was conscious. Medical men treating severe forms of psychopathology, however, found the unconscious to be a useful construct. On the basis of empirical findings, the concept of the unconscious as the sum total of all repressed desires and forgotten memories gradually took form. Although Freud's observation that most of the repressed content of consciousness has to do with sexuality is accepted, his theory that sexuality is the fundamental instinct and activating principle of the psyche is rejected as an antiquated, reductionist, single forced approach to an explanation of the unconscious. It is suggested that such theories should be replaced by the view that psychological processes derive from a libidinal energy source that simply "is." The psyche is held to be no more explainable than life. The unconscious is divided into the personal and the collective unconscious: the personal unconscious consists entirely of material acquired during the individual's life whereas the collective unconscious is the psychic equivalent of the inherited brain structure. Not only does the unconscious store repressed material, but it also has a compensatory function: any complex of experience systematically denied by consciousness will build up in the unconscious and eventually force its way into consciousness, thus compensating for any onesidedness of conscious material. The unconscious is also seen to have a symbol creating function in that it is the wellspring of instinct and intuition. Evidence of the working of these two functions, compensation and symbol creation, are seen not only in the individual but in societies and nations. The French Revolution and the decline of Rome are used as examples of their occurrence on the national level.

000302 Mind and earth. In: Jung, C., Collected Works of C. G. Jung, Vol. 10. 2nd ed., Princeton University Press, 1970. 609 p. (p. 29-49).

The influence of the earth on man's mind is explored with the mind understood as a system of adaptation determined by the conditions of an earthy existence. Both the conscious and the unconscious parts of the mind are considered, and the latter is seen as the larger and more chthonic part. The contents of the unconscious, the archetypes, are considered to be the hidden foundations of the conscious mind. They are inherited with the brain structure and reveal the link with the earth as well as with the ancestral past, containing memories of experiences that have occurred over and over again. The suggestion is made that every psychic reaction that is out of proportion to its precipitating cause should be investigated in order to determine if it has been conditioned by an archetype. The investigation of a child's unreasonable fears leads to a discussion of fairytale motifs and childish fears as examples of the way in which the psyche expresses the biogenetic law that ontogeny recapitulates phylogeny. The same example is also used to illustrate the differences between the Freudian and Jungian views of the origin of neurosis in children: the former puts the onus on the child's sexual instincts while the latter sees the child's mind as a psychic appendage of the parents. The universal experience of the Mother and the Father is considered to be the most basic archetype, and the second most influential one is that of the opposite sex. As man has perceived and experienced woman throughout the ages, and vice-versa, so too will the individual man expect to encounter woman. A discussion of the animus in woman and the anima in man clarifies this theory. The colonization of North America is used to illustrate the way in which primitive archetypes have influenced the development of a specific culture and civilization. 1 reference.

000303 Archaic man. In: Jung, C., Collected Works of C. G. Jung, Vol. 10. 2nd ed., Princeton University Press, 1970. 609 p. (p. 50-73).

The psychology of primitive man is studied and his prelogical state compared to the conscious outlook of civilized man. From personal observations of primitive societies it is concluded that primitive men think, feel, and perceive in the same manner as civilized men, but differ from them in the way in which they account for events. The primary assumptions of primitive men place them in a different world. Primitives do not see things differently than we do; it is their presuppositions that are different. For the civilized man, all events can be explained by natural or perceptible causality; for the primitive man, events are explained in terms of invisible, arbitrary, supernatural powers. Primitive man is so strongly impressed by and adapted to things as they are that a transgression of the laws of his world frighten him and demand a better explanation than that afforded by mere happenstance or natural causality. Primitive man's belief in arbitrary, supernatural powers is considered to be based, in part, on his psychological tendency to project his own unconscious psychic contents onto the physical world so completely that they cannot be distinguished from objective, physical events. Thus through what Levy-Bruhl has termed the "participation mystique," primitive man is contained physically and psychically in his world. In constrast, civilized man believes that he is separate from nature and in possession of an individual soul. Thus modern man must deprive nature of psychic reality and, in order to see his world objectively, deny all his archiac projections. In considering primitives' belief in the supernatural, magic and mana, one is forced to ask if the psyche, the soul of the unconscious, originated in man or if, in early stages of conscious evolution, it existed in itself and was gradually embodied in what is called the human psyche. If the premise is granted that psychic contents once existed independently it is possible to conclude that human individuality is the accidental product of forces contained in the objective environment.

000304 The spiritual problem of modern man. In: Jung, C., Collected Works of C. G. Jung, Vol. 10. 2nd ed., Princeton University Press, 1970. 609 p. (p 74-94).

The spiritual crisis of post World War I Europe, evident in the widespread public interest in psychology and Eastern thought is recognized and analyzed. The recent emergence of the new science of psychology is explained as the result of the loss of a structure or external form to express the yearnings and hopes of the soul. In the past a living religion provided this form; consequently the psyche could appear to exist outside of man and psychological problems reduced to a minimum. World War I, however, not only shattered the European's illusion that the Christian millennium of peace and harmony could be attained and that psyic forces could be contained, but it also destroyed his faith in himself. The confrontation with unconscious psychic forces resulted in a quest for knowledge that led to a rediscovery of parapsychology, spiritualism, Eastern thought and astrology. Most importantly, it has stimulated an interest in psychology as a science that can assist man in dealing with the spiritual crisis that besets him. Other sociological signs of the psychological situation of modern man, such as the rediscovery of the body and the ideal of internationalism, are viewed as symptoms, along with his fascination with psyche, that will lead to a reassessment of fundamental human nature and a high level of consciousness.

000305 The love problem of a student. In: Jung, C., Collected Works of C. G. Jung, Vol. 10. 2nd ed., Princeton University Press, 1970. 609 p. (p. 97-112).

The numerous forms of love relationships and the various solutions to the problem of sex and love are surveyed. These questions are evaluated in terms of their contribution to the student's psychological development. Marriage, the most commonly accepted form of expression has traditionally been denied to the student for a number of reasons, the most immediate being that the student cannot support a family. The recent increase in student marriages is attributed to psychological changes in contemporary man and to the increased use of contraceptives. The psychological changes are traced to spiritual upheavals that resulted in a profound change in man's self-concept. Now viewing himself as part of nature, and therefore subject to scientific scrutiny, modern man has accepted the finding of analytic psychology that sexuality plays a major role in human psychology. The problems surrounding student marriages are discussed with emphasis placed on the sexual and psychological differences between young men and women. The importance of integrating the sexual complex into the whole personality is also noted. Other forms of relationships between the sexes during the student years are also examined. The psychological value of such liaisons is believed to depend on the existence of love along with sexuality whereas their transitoriness is seen as inhibiting the development of mature sexuality. The advantages and disadvantages of homosexual relations are discussed. The possible educative value of such a relationship between an older man and younger one, if accompanied with loyalty and steadfastness is acknowledged. Lesbian relationships are viewed as valuable in terms of affectivity and intimacy but dangerous to psychological development in reinforcing masculine traits. Liaisons between a young male student and an older woman are briefly commented on, as are platonic relationships, abstinence, and masturbation. The utopian solutions of free love and trial marriage are dismissed as wishful fantasies. It is observed that true love seeks commitments and sacrifices the illusion that other possibilities exist.

000306 Woman in Europe. In: Jung, C., Collected Works of C. G. Jung, Vol. 10. 2nd ed., Princeton University Press, 1970. 609 p. (p. 113-133).

The psychological change in post World War I European woman and its societal ramifications are examined. Modern woman is seen to be in a state of transition. The European psyche, torn to shreds by the war, is seeking to establish a new balance between the conscious and the unconscious. The modern woman's ego, conditioned over the ages by the sexual pattern to be submissive, is stimulated by the animus (unconscious masculine traits in the female psyche) to assert itself. This is manifested in the dramatic increase in the number of women pursuing masculine careers. The conscious reaction to the unconscious influence of the animus is a psychological need for a relationship. Traditional marriage, however, is too restrictive for modern woman and hence the marriage problem arises. The surplus of marriageable women, the spread of contraceptives, and the increasing demand by women to be free have all contributed to the weakening of the institution of marriage. What the future psychological relationship between the sexes will be is the fundamental question of the marriage problem. Eros, psychic relatedness, characterizes the feminine psyche; Logos, objective interest, characterizes the man's. Each, however, has elements of the other in him, which, previously unconscious, are now coming to the fore. Though harmful to the psychological development of the individual, this constitutes an evolutionary step for the species. Modern woman is thus seen as weakening marriage in order to change it. The woman who follows the law of her being and takes up this task of transforming society will find herself caught between two universals: historic inertia and the divine urge to create.

000307 The meaning of psychology for modern man. In: Jung, C., Collected Works of C. G. Jung, Vol. 10. 2nd ed., Princeton University Press, 1970. 609 p. (p. 134-156).

Popular misconceptions about psychology are discussed as a prelude to an exposition of the basic tenets of psychology. The common assumption that everyone's psychology is the same, contradicted by clinical experience, led to an investigation of the basis for this belief. It was discovered that primitive man is characterized by a group psychology. Though modern man has learned to differentiate himself from this group mentality, individual consciousness still must develop out of the collective unconscious. With individual consciousness, however, came discontent. This discontent is seen as an unconscious reaction to the stress produced by differentiation. It is an axiom of psychology that every psychic phenomenon is compensated for by another. Thus the discontent of the present age can be seen as the tension produced by evolution through the synthesis of opposites. The problem modern man has with psychology is that he refuses to admit its basic tenet: that the psyche transcends man and is, ultimately, unknowable. Instead of demanding from psychology a cure for his discontent, modern man is better advised to look within himself for the germ of unity. Dreams, the spontaneous products of the psyche that compensate for the onesidedness of the conscious mind, are guides to the workings of the unconscious. Their correct interpretation is an invaluable aid in the assimilation of unconscious contents by the conscious mind. The art of dream interpretation is discussed. It is concluded that no one method for interpretation is applicable to all dreams. 1 reference.

000308 The state of psychotherapy today. In: Jung, C., Collected Works of C. G. Jung, Vol. 10. 2nd ed., Princeton University Press, 1970. 609 p. (p. 157-173).

An overview of earlier psychotherapeutic techniques is provided and psychotherapists are challenged to reassess and change their methods of treatment in order to do full justice to the human psyche. Warring schools of psychology with their multiplicity of techniques are testimony to the multifaceted nature of psychology and the evils of the onesided, doctrinaire approach to psychotherapy. It is considered impossible for psychotherapeutic techniques to be uniformly applied to individuals. The fundamental rule of therapy is to consider each case as new and unique. To do this the therapist must be free of restrictive theoretical presuppositions. Reductionist theories concerning the nature of the unconscious and its role in neurosis (e.g.,Freudian, Adlerian) are criticized in that they view neurosis only as an aberration, thus depriving the patient of the compensatory function of the unconscious effected through neurosis. The art of the analyst lies in the ability to lead the patient to an understanding of his neurosis, thus allowing him to assimilate the appropriate contents from his unconscious. Religions are seen as psychoanalytic systems that express the whole range of psychic problems in mighty images; they are the avowal and recognition of the soul, the revelation of the soul's nature. This view of religion is contrasted with the view found in Freud's "Future of an Illusion."

000309 Preface to "Essays on contemporary events." In: Jung, C., Collected Works of C. G. Jung, Vol. 10. 2nd ed., Princeton University Press, 1970. 609 p. (p. 177-178).

In a preface to a series of essays on contemporary events, the psychotherapist's need to come to grips with world situations is explained in terms of the effects of social and political upheaval on the psychic life of the individual. In response to that need, these essays contain reflections on and reactions to the historical events and situations of the years between 1936 and 1946. Misunderstandings that arose over these essays are answered in an epilogue that collects fragments from other writings dealing with the same themes.

000310 Wotan. In: Jung, C., Collected Works of C. G. Jung, Vol. 10. 2nd ed., Princeton University Press, 1970. 609 p. (p. 179-193).

The National Socialist (Nazi) movement in Germany is explained in terms of the reawakening of the psychic forces symbolized by the ancient German god Wotan. Although it is admitted that political, economic, and psychological factors each explain certain facets of the movement quite well, it is maintained that the movement is best understood in terms of the repossession of the German soul by the archetype Wotan. This pre-Christian god of the German people was represented as a restless wanderer, an unleasher of passions and lust for battle, a magician's vessel in the occult, a god of storm and frenzy. The effects of such an archetypal, autonomous factor are examined in the collective life of a people. Several fragments from Nietzsche's writings are viewed as an anticipation of Wotan's return. Extensive references to books by Martin Nick and Wilhelm Hauer, dealing respectively with the myth of Wotan and the German Faith Movement, are used to explicate Wotan's origins and his impact on modern German religion. Members of the German Faith Movement were urged to recognize that Wotan, not Christ, is the true god of the German people. Hitler is seen as an agent of Wotan, as a possessed man who has infected a nation. Thus the German people are seen to be victims rather than active agents of evil. It is predicted that Wotan, in time, will show the other side of his nature -- the ecstatic, mantic side -- and that the National Socialist movement will not be the last word.

000311 After the catastrophe. In: Jung, C., Collected Works of C. G. Jung, Vol. 10. 2nd ed., Princeton University Press, 1970. 609 p. (p. 194-217).

In an attempt to explain the psychological factors responsible for the horrors of Nazi Germany, it is argued that Europe produced Germany, that Germany was but the crystallizing point for social and spiritual upheavals permeating all of Europe, and that all of Europe shares Germany's guilt. Certain social conditions, e.g. mass unemployment, urbanization, and dependence on the state, are seen to have exacerbated the German predisposition to feelings of inferiority. This inferiority complex was manifested in overcompensation and in a whole nexus of pathological features that were flagrantly displayed in the person of Adolf Hitler. Hitler is described as the incarnation of the average German. The German people saw in Hitler the reflected image of their collective hysteria. By hysteria is meant that the opposites, inherent in every psyche, are further apart than normal, resulting in a higher energic tension and a disposition towards inner disharmonies. Goethe's Faust is cited as a perfect example of this side of the German nature. Germany's pact with the devil is said to lie in her abandonment of the spiritual for the material. With Nietzsche's proclamation that God is dead the projected psychic image of God returned to its origin and produced a feeling of "God almightiness" that led the German people to disaster. The moral problem facing Europe is defined as a need to discover new sanctions for goodness and justice now that they can no longer be found in the metaphysics of religion. It is concluded that Europe must understandand accept its collective guilt and learn to live with the dark shadow that has been uncovered in its collective psyche. 1 reference.

000312 The fight with the shadow. In: Jung, C., Collected Works of C. G. Jung, Vol. 10. 2nd ed., Princeton University Press, 1970. 609 p. (p. 218-226).

The historical events in Germany from 1936 to 1946 are explained in terms of mass psychology and compensation. The former is viewed as the magnified psychology of the individual and is established as the starting point for this explanation; the latter, the concept of compensation, is then evoked to explain the disturbances that were noted in the unconscious of every single German patient from as early as 1918. The images of violence noted in the dreams of these patients are explained as an unconscious reflection of the many ills of German social life, e.g. mass unemployment, national humiliation, urbanization, etc. As the dark images of the unconscious broke into consciousness, archetypes of order were formed in the unconscious as compensation. It is predicted that this desire for order was exploited by National Socialism, and that Hitler's attraction resided in the fact that he symbolized something from everybody's unconscious: he represented the shadow, the inferior part of everyone's personality. The Germans did not recognize the incarnation of their shadow in Hitler since they denied its existence altogether. To avoid falling victim to the exteriorized shadow of the inner psyche in the form of demagoguery, it is considered essential to recognize one's own shadow and to fight against its overwhelming power drive, for both Society and State derive their quality from the mental condition of the individual.

000313 Epilogue to "Essays on contemporary events." In: Jung, C., Collected Works of C. G. Jung, Vol. 10. 2nd ed., Princeton University Press, 1970. 609 p. (p. 227-243).

In a series of quotes drawn from several sources such as: "The Role of the Unconscious," "The Structure of the Unconscious," "Two Essays," "The Meaning of Psychology for Modern Man," "Psychology an Religion," "Collected Papers on Analytical Psychology," "The Development of Personality," and various lectures, a coherent analysis of the psychological factors involved in the catastrophe of World War II is presented. The growth of the violent forces in the collective unconscious of the German people is traced from their inception in 1918 to their culmination in the mass psychosis of the National Socialist movement of the early 1930's. The animation of the dark forces of the collective unconscious is attributed to the breakdown of all conscious hopes in post World War I Germany. In responding to the criticism that he did not speak out strongly enough against National Socialism in the years prior to World War II, Jung contends that although prewar Germany was in the throes of a national psychosis, the role of a psychiatrist in such a situation is not to condemn but to help strengthen the conscious understanding of the process. It was hoped that the contents of the collective unconscious then breaking into consciousness could be properly assimilated. It is maintained that the National Socialist movement contained beneficial characteristics that were, unfortunately, never realized.

000314 The undiscovered self (present and future). 1. The plight of the individual in modern society. In: Jung, C., Collected Works of C. G. Jung, Vol. 10. 2nd ed., Princeton University Press, 1970. 609 p. (p. 247-255).

The threats to the individual in modern society are examined as coming from two sources: the latent psychosis of a subversive minority and scientific rationalism. The former are subject to collective excitement and are ruled by wish fantasies; the latter reduces all individual events, including man, to a conceptual average. The normal person's unconscious, that broad area of psychic activity that is immune to conscious control and criticism, is open to the influence of the subversive minority via unconscious psychic infection. The psychological effect of the scientific statistical world view is that the individual is replaced by conceptual units that are, in turn, lumped into mass forms. The state is an abstract entity constructed to represent the sum total of these forms. In the attempt to compensate for the chaotic formlessness of society an infalliable leader is produced, who then becomes a victim of his own inflated ego consciousness. This sequence of events is inevitable once the individual combines with the mass and suppresses the development of selfhood or individual uniqueness.

000315 The undiscovered self (present and future). 2. Religion as the counterbalance to mass-mindedness. In: Jung, C., Collected Works of C. G. Jung, Vol. 10. 2nd ed., Princeton University Press, 1970. 609 p. (p. 256-262).

The true nature of religion as an expression of an interpersonal relationship with an authority higher than that of the State is examined. This belief is seen as a thrust to mass mindedness and explains the attempts of totalitarian sociopolitical movements to supplant religion. Evidence for the function of religion as a counterbalance to mass mindedness is found in the attempts of all social/political movements to supplant religion. The State robs the individual of his dignity by depriving him of the metaphysical grounds for his existence. The individual, through awareness of a reciprocal relationship between man and an extramundane authority, receives the foundation for his freedom and autonomy. Parallels are drawn between the workings of the Soviet regime and established religions to illustrate how the State takes over religious functions. In general terms the state attempts to convert the masses from extramundane beliefs and goals to worldly ones.

000316 The undiscovered self (present and future). 3. The position of the west on the question of religion. In: Jung, C., Collected Works of C. G. Jung, Vol. 10. 2nd ed., Princeton University Press, 1970. 609 p. (263-268).

The totalitarianism of the communist state is examined in terms of individual development and is judged to be antithetical to such development. The main threat posed to the West by the communist countries is considered to be that of psychic infection. The ideological fanaticism displayed by communists is compared to religious fanaticism, and in fact, is seen as a substitute for religious faith. Idealism and reason are powerless in the face of such conviction. It is suggested that an equally potent faith is needed to check the spread of communism, a faith antithetical to materialism. Such a faith must be derived from inner experience in order to withstand critical examination. Modern Christianity's tendency to crumble under Marxist attack is seen as resulting from the uncritical acceptance by so many Christians of the literal interpretation of its mythology. A symbolic understanding of these myths, corroborated by experience and feeling, would enable Christianity to withstand the collision with rationalism. Unreflected belief and unqualified faith, be they in a religion or the state, are viewed as diminishing the individual's freedom and increasing his vulnerability to external controls. The West is seen as having nothing to offer modern man as a brace against materialism: America, with its educational system that places a premium on the scientific world view (the necessary precondition for materialism) and with its rootless population, is particularly vulnerable to communism; Europe, though possessing an historic and humanistic type of education, uses it to her own undoing in the form of nationalistic egoism and paralyzing skepticism. It is concluded that both need an idea that will reinstate the individual human being in the center as the measure of all things.

000317 The undiscovered self (present and future). 4. The individual's understanding of himself. In: Jung, C., Collected Works of C. G. Jung, Vol. 10. 2nd ed., Princeton University Press, 1970. 609 p. (p. 269-283).

The difficulties that man encounters in trying to understand himself are examined and the role of psychology in facilitating self-knowledge is assessed. Since man is a unique phenomenon with nothing to which he can compare himself, it is understandable that he knows so little of his true worth. The task then, of explaining man to himself has fallen to psychology. Two misconceptions about the psyche stand in need of correction before psychology can fulfill its purpose: it must be understood that the psyche is not merely a biochemical epiphenomenon nor an entirely personal phenomenon. An understanding of the psyche in its only apparent manifestation, the individual, is the prime goal of psychology. Obstacles to this understanding of the individual are seen to spring from both church and science: the former demands adherence to certain collective beliefs; the latter requires uniformity, thus making it more difficult to arrive at a correct appreciation of the human psyche. The greatest obstacle, however, is considered to be the individual's fear of discovering himself, particularly in the realm of the unconscious. This fear is evident in the founder of psychoanalysis, Freud himself, who defended the petrification of his sexual theory into dogma on the grounds that it was the sole bulwark of reason against a possible "eruption of the black flood of occultism" that might result from the complete investigation of the unconscious. Modern man cannot afford to avert his eyes from the unconscious if he is to discover the truth about himself and thus meet the spiritual challenge of his day. Medical psychology is seen as a means by which the individual, in his uniqueness, is able to arrive at knowledge and understanding of his impulses, his unconscious contents, his instincts and his inner experiences. It is necessary to take into account the archetypal elements of the individual psyche if medical psychology is to achieve its aim of revealing man to himself.

000318 The undiscovered self (present and future). 5. The philosophical and the psychological approach to life. In: Jung, C., Collected Works of C. G. Jung, Vol. 10. 2nd ed., Princeton University Press, 1970. 609 p. (p. 284-292).

The gap between faith and knowledge, religion and philosophy, the conscious and the unconscious is viewed as symptomatic of the split consciousness in modern society and explanatory of the search for a new life philosophy. The question of a philosophy of life only arises when conditions of existence change so rapidly that a tension between outer situations and inner beliefs is created. Neither denominational religions nor the increasingly rationalistic modern philosophy serves to resolve the tension; it is the psychologist who is faced with the task of uniting the opposites, of readapting the primordial images that maintain the flow of instinctive energy. Modern man, preoccupied with his conscious at the expense of his unconscious, is judged to have become estranged from his instincts. This separation from instinct leads to conflicts

between the conscious and the unconscious, spirit and nature, faith and knowledge. As a result of this rift between faith and knowledge within the individual psyche, most men suppress one or the other in order to establish a conscious harmony by artificial means creating fanatical alliance to political ideology on the one hand and blind adherence to the literal interpretation of religious mythology on the other. The unconscious is viewed as a counterbalance to the conscious. It is a second psychic authority that may very well provide the individual with the religious experience that would justify the religious attitude, and release modern rationalistic man from domination by the ego.

000319 The undiscovered self (present and future). 6. Self-knowledge. In: Jung, C., Collected Works of C. G. Jung, Vol. 10. 2nd ed., Princeton University Press, 1970. 609 p. (p. 293-301).

The necessity of understanding the role of the unconscious as a source of religious experience and of evil is examined in detail. The individual is encouraged to submit to rigorous self-examination and self-knowledge in order to discover the foundations of his consciousness; i.e.,the unconscious, the only medium in which one can experience God. Underestimating the psychological factor is considered harmful for the future of man. Not only will ignorance of the unconscious deprive him of the religious experience, it will also blind him to his capacity for evil, hence making it possible for this evil to be projected and depriving him of his capacity to deal with it. These reflections lead to the realization of the psychological duality of human nature. It is considered essential that he recognize the shadow side in order to promote real human relationships between individuals and inner cohesion within society. It is concluded that reason alone is not sufficient for accomplishing this task; a deeper self-knowledge, encompassing the entire psyche, is required.

000320 The undiscovered self (present and future). 7. The meaning of self-knowledge. In: Jung, C., Collected Works of C. G.Jung, Vol. 10. 2nd ed., Princeton University Press, 1970. 609 p. (p. 302-305).

The effect of genuine self-knowledge and recognition of the unconscious is described. The modern age is held to be a period of profound change for the unconscious within all men. The destruction and renewal accompanying this metamorphosis is evident in modern art, a symptom and a symbol of the age. As growth in self-knowledge has shown, the shadow or the inferior part of the psyche, contains great potentialities. Whether the irruption of these forces into the conscious mind will result in growth or catastrophe is seen to depend entirely upon the preparedness of the conscious mind to assimilate these forces. The task of the individual is to prepare himself for the acceptance of his totality. Only a genuine transformation of the individual will produce meaningful changes in the race, since the individual who has gained personal insight will influence others in achieving the same goal.

000321 Flying saucers: a modern myth of things seen in the skies. Preface to the first English Edition. Introductory. In: Jung, C., Collected Works of C. G. Jung, Vol. 10. 2ne ed., Princeton University Press, 1970. 609 p. (p. 307-313).

The rumors of unidentified flying objects (UFOs), and their possible existence, are seen to be events of such profound significance that an examination of their possible psychic consequences is deemed necessary. The public's prolonged uncertainty over the nature of UFOs is seen to have provoked conscious and unconscious fantasies. It is noted that it is hard to determine whether a primary perception is followed by phantasma or whether, conversely, a primary fantasy originating in the unconscious invades the conscious mind with illusions and visions. In addition to these two causal relationships, there is the third hypothesis that UFOs are a synchronistic phenomenon; i.e.,an acausal, meaningful coincidence. The work is not intended as an authoritative pronouncement on the physical reality of UFOs but rather an exploration of the psychic concomitants of this phenomenon. The question of why most men would prefer to believe that UFOs exist will be especially examined.

000322 Flying saucers: a modern myth of things seen in the skies. 1. UFOs as rumours. In: Jung, C., Collected Works of C. G. Jung, Vol. 10. 2nd ed., Princeton University Press, 1970. 609 p. (p. 314-329).

Flying saucers are treated and analyzed as products of the psyche (rumors). For the purposes of this chapter it is assumed that UFO reports are mistaken observations into which the observer has projected his own unconscious background. Since a psychic projection presupposes a psychic cause, it is deduced that the world wide occurrence of UFO sightings points to a universal psychic motive for the creation of the UFO rumor. This motive is held to be the extreme degree of emotional tension that all mankind feels as a result of today's precarious world situation. The principles of dream interpretation are applied to analyzing the details of the UFO rumor. It is concluded that UFOs represent a combination of man's archetypal images of both God and himself. It is then hypothesized that the world situation, which threatens man's survival as a species, has created a desire for a heavenly salvation. Modern man's rationalism will not allow him to voice this desire consciously and therefore has necessitated the projection of this unconscious material. The desire for supramundane salvation is expressed somewhat literally in the rumors of UFOs; these have just the right technological veneer to make them palatable to the mind of modern man. It is concluded, then, that UFOs are modern myths. As such they are essentially products of an unconscious archetype and, therefore, symbols that require psychological interpretation. 1 reference.

000323 Flying saucers: a modern myth of things seen in the skies. 2. UFOs in dreams. In: Jung, C., Collected Works of C. G. Jung, Vol. 10. 2nd ed., Princeton University Press, 1970. 609 p. (p. 330-382).

Seven dreams involving UFOs are presented and analyzed. The premise for this undertaking is that the analysis of dreams reveals the image in its unconscious associative context and thus aids in determining the meaning of the psychic phenomenon of the UFO myth. Both Freud's observations on the role of the sexual instinct in dreams and Adler's theories concerning the will to power are used in the analyses. The significance of the dreams is never reduced to the level of mere illusions begotten by repressed sexuality or an overcompensated inferiority complex. Each dream is interpreted in relation to the life situation of the dreamer. Many of the dream images reveal similarities to alchemical and religious symbols or contain instinctual and archetypal material. The dreams of all but one individual were observed to manifest some aspect of the spiritual crisis of our age; (the lone exception is included to illustrate that symbols cannot be interpreted in a uniform way). Generally the appearance of UFOs in dreams symbolizes some content of the collective unconscious trying to break into consciousness to compensate for a onesidedness that has developed there. It is concluded that the message that the UFO brings to the dreamer is a reminder of his own soul and

his own wholeness, a response to modern mass mindedness. 5 references.

000324 Flying saucers: a modern myth of things seen in the skies. 3. UFOs in modern painting. In: Jung, C., Collected Works of C. G. Jung, Vol. 10. 2nd ed., Princeton University Press, 1970. 609 p. (p. 383-400).

Three modern paintings, plates of which are included in the text, are analyzed in order to further clarify the psychic nature of the UFO phenomenon. Paintings were chosen for this investigation because they have traditionally given visible shape to the dominant trends of their age. The fragmentation of objects and loss of beauty in modern paintings, for example, are interpreted as the artists' response to the destructive forces at play in our age. It is suggested that these apocalyptic forces are the cause of modern man's desire for a heavenly intervention, symbolically expressed in the UFO myth. The central symbol of the second picture of a series, The Fire Sower by E. Jacoby, resembles the fiery ball of UFO reports. It is interpreted as a uniting symbol that brings together the desire for salvation and the fear of disaster. In the third picture, P. Birkhauser's The Fourth Dimension, the unconscious arrangement of the elements suggests that UFOs are subliminal contents or archetypal figures that have become visible. The abstraction of the fourth picture, an untitled painting by Yves Tanguy, is seen to have a psychological effect akin to that of a Rorschach test. By cutting off an objective understanding of the picture the artist has forced the viewer to fall back on his subjective feelings about it. The powers of the unconscious to which the picture appeals are thus strengthened. As though by chance, there appear in the chaos of possibilities unexpected ordering principles that have the closest affinities with the timeless psychic dominants of the unconscious.

000325 Flying saucers: a modern myth of things seen in the skies. 4. Previous history of the UFO phenomenon. In: Jung, C., Collected Works of C. G. Jung, Vol. 10. 2nd ed., Princeton University Press, 1970. 609 p. (p. 401-412).

A cursory survey of pre-20th century references to UFOs is presented along with an interpretive summary of the dreams and pictures of the two preceding chapters. Four illustrative plates reproducing two 16th century broadsheets, a 19th century woodcut and a 12th century manuscript illustration are included in the text; they all depict unusual celestial happenings taken as historical precedents for the modern UFO phenomenon. From these plates, the dream examples, and paintings presented earlier, it is concluded that the unconscious, in order to portray its contents, makes use of certain fantasy elements that resemble UFO phenomena. Their careful scrutiny reveals a meaningful content described as an epiphany. These epiphanies are expressed in symbols that unite antithetical pairs. Five such pairs that appear repeatedly in the examples of these three chapters are discussed. Reflections on their meaning leads to the conjecture that living matter has a psychic aspect, and that the psyche has a physical aspect. This hypothesis is said to be in accord with experience and to be a welcomed step away from psychophysical parallelism towards a model of the world that is closer to the idea of unus mundus.

000326 Flying saucers: a modern myth of things seen in the skies. 5. UFOs considered in a non-psychological light. In: Jung, C., Collected Works of C. G. Jung, Vol. 10. 2nd ed., Princeton University Press, 1970. 609 p. (p. 413-417).

The physical reality of UFOs is discussed, and implications are drawn for the psychological theories advanced in the previous chapters discussing the phenomena of unidentified flying objects. From information provided by Rupplet, former head of the American Air Force's UFO study group and from the failure of Professor Menzel, a UFO sceptic, to provide a scientific explanation for authentic UFO sightings, it is concluded that UFOs have some unknown physical basis. This claim does not negate the previous theories that assume UFOs to be mistaken observations; instead, their physical existence is understood to afford the opportunity for mythological projections. The UFO phenomenon is explained in terms of its significance in the current historical situation. Political, social, philosophical, and religious conflicts of unprecedented proportions are seen to have split the consciousness of our age. It is a psychological fact that, between opposites, a symbol of unity and wholeness arises spontaneously. When this symbol cannot reach consciousness it will be projected onto any extraordinary event that might occur in the external world. The carrier of this symbol is then invested with numinous and mythological powers. The UFO phenomenon is explained on this basis. It is concluded that the psychic situation of mankind and the UFO phenomenon as a physical reality bear no recognizable causal relationship to one another, but that they do seem to coincide in a meaningful manner.

000327 Flying saucers: a modern myth of things seen in the skies. 6. Epilogue. In: Jung, C., Collected Works of C. G. Jung, Vol. 10. 2nd ed., Princeton University Press, 1970. 609 p. (p. 418-433).

Three books dealing with UFOs and published while "Flying Saucers" was being written, are reviewed in the epilogue to a series of articles on flying saucers. The first work, "The Secret of the Saucers," is a description of Orfeo Angelucci's personal experiences with extraterrestrial beings. The author is said to have become a preacher of the gospel of UFOs. His account describes, unintentionally but perfectly, both the mystic experience associated with UFOs and the psychic process of individuation. The second book, "The Black Cloud" by astrophysicist Fred Hoyle, is admittedly a science fiction yarn. Viewed psychologically it is a description of fantasy content whose symbols demonstrate their origin in the unconscious. Interpreted symbolically its plot depicts the struggle of unconscious contents to become conscious. Its denouement is faithful to the psychological truth that failure to assimilate the contents of the unconscious into the conscious mind results in a return to one's former state. Both books, though totally different in their viewpoints and style, are judged to be activated by the same unconscious factor and to make use essentially of the same symbolism. The third novel is John Wynham's "The Midwich Cuckoos," also a science fiction story, in which man's reaction to the discovery of superior humanoids is portrayed. These more advanced beings are credited with increased knowledge without a correspondingly advanced higher level of feeling or morality. Paradoxically these more highly evolved people exhibit the primitive participation mystique; this lack of individuation is seen to reflect the condition of man in the uniform Marxist society. Hence, the seemingly negative ending may be open to positive interpretation. 1 reference.

000328 A psychological view of conscience. In: Jung, C., Collected Works of C. G. Jung, Vol. 10. 2nd ed., Princeton University Press, 1970. 609 p. (p. 437-455).

The concept of "conscience" is explored in terms of its relation to the moral code and to psychological reality. The etymology of the word conscience suggests a special kind of consciousness: a knowledge of the emotional value judgement attached to actions. However, it is suggested that it is not the empirical subject but an unconscious personality that is the knower and that behaves like a conscious subject. Conscience, then, is theorized to be an inherited archetypical behavior pattern. Freud's concept of conscience as the unconscious superego, uniquely acquired by each individual, is contrasted with this hypothesis and judged inadequate. Freud's superego is seen to be identical with the prevailing moral code and though it is admittedly difficult to separate the two, conscience operates autonomously and is considered to be anterior to the moral code. Material from a case history is presented, demonstrating that the conscience is a function of an autonomous psychic factor and has a dual nature, i.e.,a "right" and a "wrong" conscience coexist, showing more clearly than any other psychic phenomenon the polarity of the psyche. Conscience is explained as the collision of consciousness with a numinous archeytpe. As such it is both a moral and an ethical manifestation: moral, when it produces behavior that furrows the moral precepts of the community, ethical when it is in accord with the deepest foundations of the self, as in the case of conflict of duty. 1 reference.

000329 Good and evil in analytical psychology. In: Jung, C., Collected Works of C. G. Jung, Vol. 10. 2nd ed., Princeton University Press, 1970. 609 p. (p. 456-468).

The question of the meaning of good and evil and their role in psychotherapeutic treatment is discussed. Good and evil are defined as principles that are unknowable in their deepest reality and that form the basis of our ethical judgments. As principles, when reduced to their ontological roots, they are considered to be the beginning aspects of God, a supraordinate reality mightier than the individual. The psychotherapist is required to deal empirically with good and evil, although that does not imply relativizing the principles as such. Nevertheless, he must deal with good and evil in terms of the individual, not as a moral code, for the reality of these two concepts can only be perceived and apprehended in specific things and situations, whereas conventional morality, like the principles of physics, is only statistically valid. A brief discussion of the Eastern attitude towards good and evil leads to the conclusion that the healthy individual is one who is capable of seeing both the light and the dark side of his nature simultaneously, thus being freed of the control of the opposites.

000330 Introduction to Toni Wolff's "Studies in Jungian Psychology." In: Jung, C., Collected Works of C. G. Jung, Vol. 10. 2nd ed., Princeton University Press, 1970. 609 p. (p. 469-476).

In the introduction to Wolff's "Studies in Jungian Psychology," several of the problems discussed in the book as being endemic to analytic psychology are reviewed. One such problem is seen to arise from the fact that a large part of the therapeutic work in analytic psychology takes place on the collective level and thus avoids a discussion of individual differences. Another is that the analyst often uses his own prejudice as the criterion for normality. As president of the Psychological Club of Zurich, Wolff noticed that it is the nature of groups to entice their members into mutual imitation and dependence. She used observations of the workings of her own club as the basis for several essays that deal in general, with group psychology, and, in particular, with how the group reduces individual consciousness.

000331 The Swiss line in the European spectrum. In: Jung, C., Collected Works of C. G. Jung, Vol. 10. 2nd ed., Princeton University Press, 1970. 609 p. (p. 479-488).

Count Hermann Keyserling's book, "The Spectrum of Europe," is reviewed with special emphasis on his assessment of Switzerland. The chief value of this book is seen to be that it argues against the purely rational point of view. Keyserling advocates a return to a psychological view of the world, where nations are seen as functions of a great, indivisible man. This cosmic view of humanity is judged to be basically idealistic, not to say "metaphysical," and is indisputable proof of Keyserling's remoteness from the earth. Keyserling's criticism of Switzerland as the most backward, conservative, stiff-necked, self-righteous, smug, and churlish of all European nations is admitted to be essentially correct, however, as such it is the psychological and geographical center of the European. In its connection with the past and its neutrality, Switzerland is called the center of gravity for Europe. Keyserling's transformation of nations into functions destroys their fictitious substance and places them into the context of a functional system where the needs of the whole of Europe are to be considered. Men everywhere are urged not to attempt to change the character of their respective nations, but rather to transcend it.

000332 The rise of a new world. In: Jung, C., Collected Works of C. G. Jung, Vol. 10. 2nd ed., Princeton University Press, 1970. 609 p. (p. 489-495).

Count Hermann Keyserling's book, "America Set Free," is reviewed and judged to be as concerned with Europe as it is with America. Keyserling sees America with European prejudices and hence the objective accuracy of many of his observations and conclusions are considered suspect. Nevertheless they are viewed as important reflections about European sensibility. The book's subtitle, "The Rise of a New World," the theme of the work, is seen as referring not only to America but to the entire Western world. Keyserling is considered to be the mouthpiece of the collective spirit; his prophecy about the rise of a new consciousness, a new world view, is accepted as an accurate, though unintentional, assessment of the change taking place deep within modern man's unconscious. Many quotations from the book are included in the review to give the flavor and scope of Keyserling's observations. Particular attention is given to Keyserling's views that America does not yet have a soul; that it is a land of the overrated child; that the high living standard is the mainspring of its morality. It is suggested that the comments on the relation of the sexes, on the family and on the demasculization of men and the masculinization of women have much to contribute to the European views of these subjects. Keyserling is credited with having understood that the world is entering into an era that places understanding above faith and experience above creeds. What he has to say about the relation of the sexes in America is held to be particularly interesting.

000333 La revolution mondiale. In: Jung, C., Collected Works of C. G. Jung, Vol. 10. 2nd ed., Princeton University Press, 1970. 609 p. (p. 496-501).

Count Hermann Keyserling's book, "La Revolution Mondiale," is reviewed and though written in French, is judged to be German in spirit. Chinese characters with their capacity for vagueness and implications of the infinite are seen to be the best medium for expressing the flashes of intuition that are typical of his mind. The book is considered to be a record of Keyserling's reactions to contemporary events. The spiritual and the telluric are the contrapuntal poles of the book, and modern man is seen to be living through a "world change" effected by their reversal. Keyserling proposes that man saves what he can of his spiritual heritage by resurrecting the idea of

the cultural monastery. He is criticized for assuming that everything, in the end, can be understood. The spirit may have been overcome by the telluric in order to be reborn, but Keyserling must be understood symbolically and literally, for only then can he be recognized as the spokesman of the Zeitgeist of the spiritual man.

000334 The complications of American psychology. In: Jung, C., Collected Works of C. G. Jung, Vol. 10. 2nd ed., Princeton University Press, 1970. 609 p. (p. 502-514).

Explanations for the peculiarities of American psychology, as they appear to a European observer, are advanced. Americans are seen to have a tendency toward collectivity, sexual promiscuity, kinetic looseness, and emotional expressiveness. Not only are Americans observed to differ psychologically from their European ancestry but also anatomically. These differences are attributed to two factors: the coexistence of the Negro and the Caucasian races in America, and the influence of the land on its inhabitants. It is proposed that the temperament of a primitive race is highly contagious, in that it appeals to the unconscious of the more advanced race, and thus spreads through temperamental and mimetic infection. The Negro's influence is seen in the American style of laughter, love of noisy sociality, looseness of movement, dancing and music. It is noted that certain very primitive peoples believe that it is not possible to usurp territory since the children born there would inherit the wrong ancestral spirits. Parallels are drawn between the East's influence on ancient Rome and the influence of the Indian on America. The anatomical differences between Americans and Europeans, particularly noticeable in the shift from the European facial structure towards that of the Indian, are cited as concrete examples of this phenomenon. As a result of 25 years' work with American patients it is concluded that the guiding principle of the American spirit is the heroic ideal, an attitude typically characteristic of a sporty, primitive society. It is in this heroic attitude that the influence of the historical Indian spirit is considered to be most apparent. The maxim that the conqueror overcomes the body but succumbs to the spirits is applied to America, although no conclusions are drawn about the value of these influences. It is simply pointed out as an interesting fact that America has the most complicated psychology of all the nations.

000335 The dreamlike world of India. In: Jung, C., Collected Works of C. G. Jung, Vol. 10. 2nd ed., Princeton University Press, 1970. 609 p. (p. 515-524).

Impressions of India formed during the course of a six week tour are recorded. India is seen to possess a certain immutable core upon which all other events, whether they involve an individual life or the culture of a conquering civilization, unfold as if on film. Indian life is unimaginably rich in color and detail, but it seems essentially transitory, dreamlike, like a multicolored veil of maya. It is observed that in India one feels the presence of great age, but recognizes little history; history is seen as meaningless in India, for everything that exists there has existed a thousand times before, even the unique Gautama Buddha, who is but one of a succession of many Buddhas. The West is likened to a directional vector, India to that same vector extended infinitely until it returns to its origin. The differences between the Moslem and the Hindu temperament are noted as expressed even in their respective modes of dress: the one is active, warlike, and the other passive, submissive. The impression of softness that the Hindu displays indicates a predominance of the feminine element in the family. Family life and the relationship between the sexes in India are compared to their expression in the West and found to be superior in several regards; it is concluded that the Indians have found a degree of domestic belonging that we cannot attain.

000336 What India can teach us. In: Jung, C., Collected Works of C. G. Jung, Vol. 10. 2nd ed., Princeton University Press, 1970. 609 p. (p. 525-530).

The Indian mode of thought is compared to that of the West and found to be superior in certain respects. Indians are observed not to "think" as Western man thinks but rather to perceive their thoughts; this mode of cognition is seen as similar to the primitive thought process and a natural development in a civilization that has existed unbroken from primitive times. In the West, however, primitive man was confronted by an invasion of a psychology and spirituality that belonged to a much higher level of civilization. This invasion is seen to result in the fragmentation of Western man's psyche into a hyperdeveloped conscious mind and a suppressed primitive unconscious. It is felt that Western man needs to realize this unconscious darkness if he is to survive. India, on the other hand, is an example of a civilization that brought every essential trace of primitivity with it. India's civilization and psychology are symbolized in the carvings that decorate her temples with graphic depictions of man at his best and worst. It seems dreamlike to the Western observer precisely because its daily life gives expression to the unconscious world that we deny; India is seen to represent the other way of civilizing man, without suppression, violence, or rationalism. The Indian way of thinking typically results in an increase of vision as opposed to the West's tendency to scrutinize the details of nature, which results in the formulation of isolated facts. It is concluded that the Indian is capable of transforming his gods into thoughts, since the concept of God is ultimately based on instinctual thought patterns; thus the Indian, unlike Western man, has been able to rescue his gods and live with them.

000337 Editorial. (Remarks on Psychotherapy). In: Jung, C., Collected Works of C. G. Jung, Vol. 10. 2nd ed., Princeton University Press, 1970. 609 p. (p. 533-534).

General remarks on the course of psychotherapy are made in an address to the General Medical Society for Psychotherapy. It is noted that psychotherapy, like current politics, is marked by a confusion of conflicting doctrines. One-sided and mutually exclusive methods of observation are deplored, and an impartial appreciation of all objective contributions to psychotherapy is urged as the ideal. It is hoped that future theorists will go beyond the grounds of the pathological and the personal in constructing theories that will do justice to the whole psyche.

000338 A rejoinder to Dr. Bally. (Defense of political position). In: Jung, C., Collected Works of C. G. Jung, Vol. 10. 2nd ed., Princeton University Press, 1970. 609 p. (p. 535-544).

A rejoinder to Dr. Bally has the twin purposes of explaining how Jung's name became attached to a Nazi political manifesto, and to rebut the charge of antiSemitism which followed the manifesto's circulation. The manifesto was intended to appear in a special edition of the "Zentralblatt fur Psychotherapie," the journal of the International Society for Psychotherapy, which was to be circulated only in Germany; it consisted of a loyalty oath to the German government and a pledge to practice "Germanic psychotherapy" on the part of the German section of the Society. These promises were demanded of the German section under threat of disbandment. Against Jung's wishes the article was printed in the regular edition of the Zentralblatt and, as acting president of the Society, Jung's name appeared above it. It is remarked that, while it is easy to ridicule "Germanic psychotherapy," it is quite another matter entirely to deal with the demands of politics in an attempt to save medicine for the sake of humanity. It is not the role of doctors to oppose National Socialism as if it were a political party, but rather to heal the sick even if they are the enemy. The Jewish question is raised in Jung's early work, but such discussions on sensitive subjects are defended as the province of the psychotherapist. All psychological theories should be examined for their subjective premises; as these are identical with the individual's psychic idiosyncrasy, which is conditioned by the family, nation, race, locality and history, it is to be expected that the ethnic background of the individual theorist will color his theories. This natural bias is said to be the basis of Jungian criticism of Freud's and Adler's theories for their Jewish prejudice. It is pointed out that this question was first discussed in 1913, and that it is only now being exploited for political ends.

000339 Circular letter. (Invitation to Psychotherapists). In: Jung, C., Collected Works of C. G. Jung, Vol. 10. 2nd ed., Princeton University Press, 1970. 609 p. (p. 545-546).

A circular letter is reproduced in which all psychotherapists, regardless of creed, are invited to join the International General Medical Society for Psychotherapy. It is pointed out that the society is divided into national groups but that membership in the society is not contingent upon affiliation with a national group.

000340 Editorial. (Psychotherapy and Philosophy). In: Jung, C., Collected Works of C. G. Jung, Vol. 10. 2nd ed., Princeton University Press, 1970. 609 p. (p. 547-551).

The accusation that modern psychotherapy is too concerned with philosophical problems and too little with the minutiae of case histories is rebutted. It is maintained that therapy consists of helping the individual to adapt to both his interior and exterior situation, and therefore must take into account the political, economic, philosophical, and religious forces of the day. Psychotherapy cannot artificially separate its proper subject -- the sick psyche -- from its wider background, the human psyche in general. As a result of this, numerous theories concerning the nature of the psyche have sprung up as adjuncts to psychotherapy. The premises of these theories must, in turn, be critically examined in order to determine if they have been tainted by the subjective prejudices of the theoretician. It is pointed out that all sciences must criticize their assumptions; critical discussion of general assumptions is held to be particularly important for the present phase of psychotherapy, since it brings to light assumptions that exist tacitly and are therefore all the more dangerous.

000341 Editorial note. (International aspects of psychology). In: Jung, C., Collected Works of C. G. Jung, Vol. 10. 2nd ed., Princeton University Press, 1970. 609 p. (p. 552-553).

The inclusion of three articles by nonSwiss authors in the Swiss issue of the Zentralblatt is lauded as symbolizing the Swiss cultural characteristic of promoting international collaboration. It is noted that the greatest danger that threatens psychology is the onesidedness of a single viewpoint, and that these articles contribute to the enrichment of the Swiss outlook by contrasting it with those of other nations.

000342 Presidential address to the 8th General Medical Congress for Psychotherapy, Bad Nauheim, 1935. In: Jung, C., Collected Works of C. G. Jung, Vol. 10. 2nd ed., Princeton University Press, 1970. 609 p. (p. 554-556).

Two difficulties that have retarded the growth of the International Medical Society for Psychotherapy are discussed. The first problem is that psychotherapy is a young science and has not yet gotten completely out of the shadow cast by its two older sisters, psychiatry and neurology. As a rule it has existed only marginally under their auspices. It is maintained, however, that psychotherapy has advanced to the stage where its correct implementation requires a specialist and not a psychiatrist or neurologist. The second difficulty results from the doctrinairian approach to theory, observed in some psychotherapists who hold their theories to be indisputable with a conviction that is likened to religious faith. This opinion makes objective discussion among professionals, deemed necessary for the advancement of any science, impossible. It is concluded that in the face of these difficulties the International Society must maintain psychotherapy as an independent branch of medicine, and that scientific truths cannot be substantiated by uncritical and onesided convictions.

000343 Contribution to a discussion on psychotherapy. In: Jung, C., Collected Works of C. G. Jung, Vol. 10. 2nd ed., Princeton University Press, 1970. 609 p. (p. 557-560).

The reasons for Jung's acceptance of the presidency of the International Society, the difficulties involved with that post, and views on the future of psychotherapy are presented. It is stated that presidency was accepted in order to bolster the position of psychotherapy in Germany, and to help it maintain its international contacts. It is observed that from the first, opponents of the society have attempted to render impossible objective discussion -- considered the goal and purpose of the Society -- by sowing seeds of political suspicion and sectarian discord. Having overcome these problems, the society is now seen to be strong enough to assume its social responsibilities. It is warned that psychological problems are more deeply rooted in the public than is generally acknowledged. Psychotherapists are urged to accept lay assistants, as medical doctors have done, in order to multiply their own effectiveness.

000344 Presidential address to the 9th International Medical Congress for Psychotherapy, Copenhagen, 1937. In: Jung, C., Collected Works of C. G. Jung, Vol. 10. 2nd ed., Princeton University Press, 1970. 609 p. (p. 561-563).

The importance of cultivating a viewpoint that allows the psychotherapist to free himself from the artifical limits of national, political, religious, and philosophical prejudices is stressed. It is hoped that every professional opinion will be allowed expression and that as many nations as possible will make their contribution to the total picture of the European psyche.

000345 Presidential address to the 10th International Medical Congress for Psychotherapy, Oxford, 1938. In: Jung, C., Collected Works of C. G. Jung, Vol. 10. 2nd ed., Princeton University Press, 1970. 609 p. (p. 564-567).

The chief obstacle to collaboration in the field of psychotherapy is seen to be the doctrinairian disputes over theory which have divided psychologists into sectarian schools. Since the greater part of psychotherapy is not dependent on a particular theoretical base for its implementation, it is suggested that these warring schools stop debating the essence of the psyche and attempt to seek common ground in the areas of psychotherapeutic technique. The Swiss Committee of Psychotherapy, which was able to unite the various factions to aggreement, is advanced as a model for how to go about reaching a working harmony in psychology.

11 PSYCHOLOGY AND RELIGION: WEST AND EAST

000346 Psychology and religion. 1. The autonomy of the unconscious. In: Jung, C., Collected Works of C. G. Jung, Vol. 11. 2nd ed., Princeton University Press, 1969. 699 p. (p. 3-33).

In the Terry Lectures given at Yale University in 1937, a demonstration is proposed of the persective from which medical psychology views religion. Religion must be taken into account by psychologists, since it represents one of the most ancient and universal expressions of the human mind; but it is felt that the approach of psychology must be scientific, empirical and phenomenological rather than philosophical or metaphysical. Religion is defined for the purposes of this study as the belief in an external dynamic force which controls the human subject, and as the ritual acts carried out by men to produce the effect of this dynamic force, the numinosum. Religion is seen as an attitude of mind rather than any creed, although the creed is a codified form of the original religious experience. In the story of a patient who was convinced he had cancer, but whose real difficulty lay in obsessive drives he did not want to recognize, the desire of men in general to avoid revelatory contact with the unconscious is stressed; from primitive times to the present, man is seen to construct ritual and taboo to protect him from the voices of his dreams and the content of his unconscious. The definite forms and laws of the Church are seen in this light. Two dreams with specifically religious manifestations are briefly analyzed to demonstrate the existence of these inner voices and experiences, particularly the two figures of the anima and animus. Each is seen as a psychic representation of the minority of genes in the body; the anima, or female figure, appears in the imagery of the male's unconscious, and vice versa. It is felt that the processes of the unconscious are just as continuously active as those of the conscious mind, and that dreams are manifestations of this chain of events that can be experienced in the conscious. 1 reference.

000347 Psychology and religion. 2. Dogma and natural symbols. In: Jung, C., Collected Works of C. G. Jung, Vol. 11. 2nd ed., Princeton University Press, 1969. 699 p. (p. 34-63).

The importance of dream analysis as a means of contacting the unconscious is stressed in an account of the therapy of a particular patient, a scientist who had numerous dreams of a religious or mystical character. The unconscious is seen as the completion and enrichment of the personality, having a superior insight and knowledge lacking in the conscious self. The integration of all parts of the mind is considered the ideal goal of therapy. The Catholic defenses against immediate experience and its ambiguity in the particular case cited are similar to other religious dogma and pagan ritual which represent the formalized acting-out of psychic material so that the individual need not confront that material directly, immediately, in his own unconscious. It is observed that Protestantism, having divested itself of much of the ritual and codes of the Catholic Church, leaves the individual to confront his sins alone; this development has led to the uneasiness and anxiety, but also to the alertness and analytic nature of modern society. The dreams reported in the case study are examined for their archetypal material, those primordial ideas or tendencies of thought which are common to all human psychic experience. The significance of the number four, represented in one dream by a pyramidal shape, is discussed in its many manifestations in other dreams and in the history of myth and religious thought. Other alchemical symbols associated with the number four are the circle and the Philosopher's Stone. The latter symbol of the perfect living being is found to be an allegory of the Deity repeated by a number of early theorists. The Christian representation of God and the Trinity is compared to other systems in which the Deity is represented by the unity of four elements; the missing fourth element in religious doctrine is seen as the Devil. Although this fourth element is suppressed in the Christian religion in an expression of certain moral and mental attitudes of the practitioners, the unconscious supplies the fourth element in its various manifestations. 7 references.

000348 Psychology and religion. 3. The history and psychology of a natural symbol. In: Jung, C., Collected Works of C. G. Jung, Vol. 11. 2nd ed., Princeton University Press, 1969. 699 p. (p. 64-105).

Some of the archetypal symbols which have correlates in religion are discussed. A circle divided into four parts, the Philosopher's Stone, is a symbol that seems to recur throughout history. Four elements, four colors, and quaternity of gods correspond to the four parts of the circle; in the Western tradition the fourth part of these systems is earth, blue, and Mary respectively. The fourth part is slow in being accepted as it is part of the eternal duality of heaven and hell, air and earth, male and female; it is symbolized in dreams by the anima, that part of the unconscious suppressed by the male. The unconscious and the conscious striving for unity, are symbolized by the mandala and the squaring of the circle, collective symbols found in dreams. In modern times, no deity is observed to be symbolized in the center, but there is some representation of the center as the self. A self that has merged conscious and and unconscious has come to terms with its shadow. It is through knowing the dark side of of psyche -- the shadow -- that we find salvation, for the repressed or suppressed shadow fights to the surface in even more frightening forms. Gods are not created, they are taken on. There is no freedom of choice; if one has an unconscious desire, it is really the desire that possesses him. Part of accepting one's psyche as one's self is realizing what is there and reconciling it with one's consciousness. There is the symbolic circle holding together the four parts of the stone, or the realization of the wholeness of man. These symbols of wholeness and unity recur throughout history in dreams and other psychic manifestations seemingly without the influence of tradition or knowledge of religion of any type. Such a continuity can only exist if one assumes certain unconscious thought forms or archetypes to be an inherited a priori process. Accordingly, an archetype is a structural quality or condition peculiar to the psyche, but somehow connected with the brain. The mandala symbolizes belief, and neurosis is a lack of faith. The choice between mandala and neurosis is deeply personal and subjective, but the continual choice of the mandala throughout history is seen as an objective fact. 7 references.

000349 A psychological approach to the dogma of the Trinity. Introduction. In: Jung, C., Collected Works of C. G. Jung, Vol. 11. 2nd ed., Princeton University Press, 1969. 699 p. (p. 107-111).

It is contended that in a psychological study of Christian symbolism, which involves a dissection of the dogma of the Trinity, neither the validity nor the sacredness of the symbols examined is in question; they are studied in terms of their psychic function. This study, far from degrading the value of these symbols, is considered to be a confirmation of their essential nature as part of the human psyche.

000350 Psychological approach to the dogma of the Trinity. 1. Pre-Christian parallels. I. Babylonia. In: Jung, C., Collected Works of C. G. Jung, Vol. 11. 2nd ed., Princeton University Press, 1969. 699 p. (p. 112-115).

Primitive pre-Christian antecedents to the Trinity are explored. There have been many primitive symbolic triads, one of the most important being the Babylonian triad of Anu, Bel, and Ea. Anu was the lord of heaven; Bel was the lord of the lower realm, earth; and Ea was the god of the lower realm of the watery depths. In most of these primitive triads there were some family relationships, mostly father-son although there were others. Another theme involves one member of the triad being part man and part god. Analogies between Babylonian and alchemical symbols are mentioned.

000351 A psychological approach to the dogma of the Trinity. 1. Pre-Christian parallels. II. Egypt. In: Jung, C., Collected Works of C. G. Jung, Vol. 11. 2nd ed., Princeton University Press, 1969. 699 p. (p. 115-117).

An ancient Egyptian, archetypal, pre-Christian antecedent of the Trinity is described, in which three gods -- the homoousia of Father and Son, and ka, the procreative power of the deity -- form a triunity not unlike the Christian symbolic configuration. The passing of these ideas into the Hellenic Osiris/Horus/Isis myth is noted, as is its influence on Christian dogma. 1 reference.

000352 A psychological approach to the dogma of the Trinity. 1. Pre-Christian parallels. III. Greece. In: Jung, C., Collected Works of C. G. Jung, Vol. 11. 2nd ed., Princeton University Press, 1969. 699 p. (p. 117-128).

The mathematical speculations of the Greek philosophers are discussed as important pre-Christian antecedents of the number symbolism of the Trinity. One is the number from which all others have sprung and is perfect, being neither male or female, odd or even. Two or the "other" as it is called in some languages, divided the qualities into good and bad, male and female, heaven and hell. Both one and two are necessary because as a single element one would be shapeless and two nonexistent. On the second day of creation evil was made, making two a sinister number. The number three is the first uneven number and is a masculine number. Three defines form, whereas two only designates a two dimensional plane. The three points are combined into an equilateral triangle to symbolize the trinity. The number four is left out of Greek number symbolism and denied because it is a female number, and is not well understood. Plato tried to explain the creation in terms of mixing the divisible and the indivisible, and in terms of the mixing of the same with the different. It is the combination of these two pairs that gives us the combination mean and the third form. The description of this combination encircled is the sign for city and corresponds with the mandala. 2 references.

000353 A psychological approach to the dogma of the Trinity. 2. Father, Son and Spirit. In: Jung, C., Collected Works of C. G. Jung, Vol. 11. 2nd ed., Princeton University Press, 1969. 699 p. (p. 129-137).

The archetypal model for the Trinity (Father, Son, and Holy Spirit) is discussed as it manifests itself in Greek philosophy. The three Persons conceived by Plato are noted to be related by opposition, while the Christian Trinity is based on unity. It is concluded that the Christian symbol did not derive from the Greek, but rather that both were derived and conceptualized from more ancient archetypal elements. The relationship of the Holy Ghost in the Trinity, that of a life force proceeding from both Father and Son, is observed to resemble Egyptian kingship theology more than Greek. In both these symbolic systems the feminine element is excluded. The figure of the Son as the revealed God is seen also in the Persian symbol of Gayomart, the Original Man, and later in the Gnostic redeemer figures; but the archetype's actual origin is unknown, prehistorical. The other figures in the Trinity are considered to have the same eternal nature. It is noted that only recently has Christianity become aware of and accepted to some extent the similarities of their dogma with the dogma and ritual of other cults.

000354 A psychological approach to the dogma of the Trinity. 3. The symbola. I. The Symbolum Apostolicum. In: Jung, C., Collected Works of C. G. Jung, Vol. 11. 2nd ed., Princeton University Press, 1969. 699 p. (p. 138-141).

The unfolding of the archetype of the Trinity in Christian dogma is examined, and the various textual formulations of the Trinity relationship are mentioned as successive attempts to give rational symbolic expression to a primordial archetype. The first attempt to summarize these preconscious beliefs is the Apostle's Creed; in it the Trinity is latent, and its members are interchangeable in name and function. 1 reference.

000355 A psychological approach to the dogma of the Trinity. 3. The symbola. II. The symbolum of Gregory Thaumaturgus. In: Jung, C., Collected Works of C. G. Jung, Vol. 11. 2nd ed., Princeton University Press, 1969. 699 p. (p. 142-143).

The trinitarian philosophy of Gregory Thaumaturgus, revealed to him in a dream, held the figures of the Trinity to be equal to each other. According to his former teacher Origen, however, the Father had more power than the Son, who in turn was more powerful than the Holy Ghost.

000356 A psychological approach to the dogma of the Trinity. 3. The symbola. III. The Nicaenum. In: Jung, C., Collected Works of C. G. Jung, Vol. 11. 2nd ed., Princeton University Press, 1969. 699 p. (p. 143-144).

The text of the Nicene Creed is given as an example of one of the attempts to explain the relationship between the figures of the Trinity. It is noted that in this creed the Father and the Son have a homoousian relationship; that is, they are from the same substance. The Holy Ghost is not included in the creed. 1 reference.

000357 A psychological approach to the dogma of the Trinity. 3. The symbola. IV. The Nicaeno-Constantinopolitanum, the Athanasianum, and the Lateranense. In: Jung, C., Collected Works of C. G. Jung, Vol. 11. 2nd ed., Princeton University Press, 1969. 699 p. (p. 144-147).

Three explanations of the Trinity are represented by the Nicaeno-Constantinopolitanum, the Athanasianum, and the Lateranense creeds. The Holy Ghost is seen in the first as equal with the Father and the Son, but he proceeds from the Father only. The Athanasian creed insisted on the equality and eternality of the three persons. In the Creed of the Lateran Council, the three are declared equal but the Son is begotten by the Father, and the Holy Ghost comes from both the Father and the Son.

000358 A psychological approach to the dogma of the Trinity. 4. The three persons in the light of psychology. 1. The hypothesis of the archetype. In: Jung, C., Collected Works of C. G. Jung, Vol. 11. 2nd ed., Princeton University Press, 1969. 699 p. (p. 148-152).

According to the archetype hypothesis, which states that some tendencies of mind predate the conscious development of man, all religious theory and creed surrounding the Trinity has grown up around the archetypal idea of a triad. The statement that dogmas are inspired by the Holy Ghost indicates that they are not the product of conscious cogitation and speculation but are engendered by sources outside consciousness and possibly even outside man. The history of the Trinity is seen as the gradual crystallization of one of these archetypes.

000359 A psychological approach to the dogma of the Trinity. 4. The three persons in the light of psychology. II. Christ as archetype. In: Jung, C., Collected Works of C. G. Jung, Vol. 11. 2nd ed., Princeton University Press, 1969. 699 p. (p. 152-157).

Christ is seen as a major manifestation of the collective unconscious that is forced into a rational/religious structure. Christ, the God man, has little personal history; instead, history has forced itself on him. He is the archetypal hero, showing all the signs: improbable origin, divine father, hazardous birth, precocious development, conquest of the mother and of death, miraculous deeds, a tragic, early end, a symbolically significant manner of death, a wide range of consequences of his death. The symbol of self and the God image are indistinguishable. The self is thus synonymous with the inner Christ; it is the god within the psychic totality of the individual. Anything man postulates as being a greater totality than himself becomes a symbol of the self. The Christ figure itself is incomplete because it lacks evil, a necessary part of nature. It is through a blending of good and evil that self-realization is reached. The self embraces the inconceivable unconsciousness in the form of symbols, as the archetypal life of Christ is described in symbolic images.

000360 A psychological approach to the dogma of the Trinity. 4. The three persons in the light of psychology. III. The Holy Ghost. In: Jung, C., Collected Works of C. G. Jung, Vol. 11. 2nd ed., Princeton University Press, 1969. 699 p. (p. 157-163).

The Holy Ghost holds a unique position in the Trinity in that it is his function to propagate faith in man. It is through this faith engendering function, similar to the life engendering relationship between the Father and the Son that we are children of God. The Holy Ghost did not arise from the natural situation; rather he is a product of human reflection added on to the natural sequence of father and son. To try to understand the Holy Ghost as a feminine archetype would be to ignore the qualities of a life common to the Father and the Son and the Holy Ghost's role of procreating in man and bringing forth the works of the divine parentage. The forces that motivate trinitarian thinking are impersonal, arising from the collective psyche; they express an unconscious far surpassing all personal needs -- that of the integration of the unconscious with the conscious, which makes man a psychic whole.

000361 A psychological approach to the dogma of the Trinity. 5. The problem of the fourth. I. The concept of quaternity. In: Jung, C., Collected Works of C. G. Jung, Vol. 11. 2nd ed., Princeton University Press, 1969. 699 p. (p. 164-180).

The power of the dogma of the Trinity is readily acknowledged, but there seems to be a part that is missing. It is the fourth function of the conscious psyche, the feeling function, that does not cooperate. The other three: thinking, sensation, and intuition follow rational thought, but the fourth, feeling, is a regressive state allied with the unconscious. It can be suppressed but only at the expense of the conscious function. From this archetypal structure come other natural quaternities into which the world seems to be divided according to various philosophies; others are the four elements, four prime qualities, four colors, four castes, etc. Already in the Trinity there are three parts to the quaternity: Father, Son, and Holy Ghost. The fourth part must be the devil or Lucifer, since in the basic duality of the structure of nature, good must have evil to have substance. The relationship among the elements of the Trinity and the fourth element is explored. It is from the Father that Satan sprang, for he is called the first Son, and Christ the second Son. This places Christ, who stands for all that is good, in opposition to Satan, who is evil. Christ cannot overcome Satan on his own, instead he requires the ministrations of the Holy Ghost, a reconciliation of opposites and hence the answer to the human suffering that Christ personifies. In the diagram of the quaternity, man's salvation is shown in the form of the cross, itself a quaternity. It is contended that there can be no such thing as "beyond good and evil," that the notion only encourages self-deification, and that what is needed to reconcile the two is the holy and unifying spirit and comfort of the Holy Ghost. 1 reference.

000362 A psychological approach to the dogma of the Trinity. 5. The problem of the fourth. II. The psychology of the quaternity. In: Jung, C., Collected Works of C. G. Jung, Vol. 11. 2nd ed., Princeton University Press, 1969. 699 p. (p. 180-187).

To interpret the Trinity symbol psychologically it is considered important to begin at the individual level and to regard the symbol as an expression of the psyche. It is possible to do this because the collective ideas represented in religious dogma are derived from the individual consciousness. The Father represents the early state of development of consciousness. This consciousness is a passive unreflecting state of awareness without any intellectual or moral judgment. In a second transformation, the Son usurps the Father's role by forming a violent identification with the father and by subsequently killing the father. This is not in itself an advancement, but it does force the isolated individual to discriminate and reflect rather than to simply act out of necessity or ignorance. The third transformation is the recognition of the unconscious and subordination to it through the union of psychic opposites with no personal designation.

000363 A psychological approach to the dogma of the Trinity. 5. The problem of the fourth. III. General remarks on symbolism. In: Jung, C., Collected Works of C. G. Jung, Vol. 11. 2nd ed., Princeton University Press, 1969. 699 p. (p. 187-192)

The fourth element of the archetype of unity and redemption, missing in the Christian concept of Trinity, is characterized as the element of oppositon, which alone can give the triad reality. No other formulation will satisfy the needs of the unconscious. This, then, is the function of all symbols; they are allegorical representations of the unconscious processes, accepted universally because they are recognized by the unconscious. The quaternity symbol as one of these archetypal manifestations is seen to occur in dreams as well as the consciously constructed dogmas and rituals; some typical appearances of four figures in dreams are reviewed. Since the unity of the four is completion of the religious and psychic experience, the imago Dei aspect of the quaternity may be identified with the self. The implications of these archetypal symbol structures for the psychotherapist are considered; it is felt that neurotic dissociations cannot be repaired by intellectual or purely practical methods, but rather by the integration of symbolic dream images into the patient's consciousness.

000364 A psychological approach to the dogma of the Trinity. 6. Conclusion. In: Jung, C., Collected Works of C. G. Jung, Vol. 11. 2nd ed., Princeton University Press, 1969. 699 p. (p. 193-200).

The Trinity expresses man's need for spiritual development and independent thinking, but this is not the only activity of the psyche. It is through the essential unity of the three part process (Father, Son, and Holy Ghost) that unconscious maturation occurs in the form of instinctive, psychic, and regularly timed occurrences. The symbolic expression of the trinity is seen as a continuing conscious realization that has occurred over the centuries. The three forms of God differ in that the Son proceeds from the Father, and the Holy Ghost comes from both the Father and the Son; the Son is understood as the symbol of self and the Holy Ghost as the self's actualization in man where man enters in unity with the substance of God. A fourth and largely ignored symbol is the first Son or the fallen angel; he is eternal and autonomous. He is the Antichrist; it is the oppositon between the trinity and the first Son that makes a whole. This symbol is the realization of evil that completes the self. Individuation requires the realization of the shadow as a part of one's personality and the integration of it into one's consciousness. Religion is the revealed or dogmatic way to individuation; it is a formalization of preconscious knowledge valid for the unconscious even if our intellect does not grasp it. 1 reference.

000365 Transformation symbolism in the Mass. 1. Introduction. In: Jung, C., Collected Works of C. G. Jung, Vol. 11. 2nd ed., Princeton University Press, 1969. 699 p. (p. 201-207).

In the introduction to the topic of sources of the Mass, several references to transformation in the Bible are cited, particularly in I Corinthians. Two distinct ideas are seen to be blended in the Mass: the first idea is thysia, from the word to slaughter or sacrifice, means the flaring of the sacrificial fire when the gift offered to the Gods is consumed; the second is deipnon, meaning a meal at which sacrificial food is eaten. Hebrews 13:10-15 is also considered a possible source for the Mass. In it are the ideas of perpetual sacrifice and eternal priesthood, both essential in the Mass. However, it is the transformation that is the miracle of the Mass. Its ritual amplifies this transformation step by step until the climax is reached -- the consecration. It is at this moment that Christ is present in time and space as the revelation of something existing in eternity. The rite is necessarily and in each of its parts a symbol seeking to describe the mystery of the human psyche.

000366 Transformation symbolism in the Mass. 2. The sequence of the transformation rite. I. Oblation of the bread. In: Jung, C., Collected Works of C. G. Jung, Vol. 11. 2nd ed., Princeton University Press, 1969. 699 p. (p. 208).

In a discussion of the symbolic value of the Mass, the lifting up of the Host is seen as a sacrifice which is made sacred by exaltation. Analogies are mentioned between this ritual, the account in Justin of the cleansed lepers in the Temple, and the later alchemical idea of the naturally imperfect substance made perfect by alchemical art.

000367 Transformation symbolism in the Mass. 2. The sequence of the transformation rite. II. Preparation of the chalice. In: Jung, C., Collected Works of C. G. Jung, Vol. 11. 2nd ed., Princeton University Press, 1969. 699 p. (p. 209-211).

The symbolic value of that part of the Mass in which water and wine are mixed in the chalice is examined. It is noted that in many early rituals the chalice contained only water; this fact is taken to indicate that the interest of the Mass lies in the symbolism rather than in the strict observation of the sacrament.

000368 Transformation symbolism in the Mass. 2. The sequence of the transformation rite. III. Elevation of the chalice. IV. Censing of the substances and the altar. In: Jung, C., Collected Works of C. G. Jung, Vol. 11. 2nd ed., Princeton University Press, 1969. 699 p. (p. 212-213).

Religious acts of the Christian Mass are explained psychologically and symbolically. After the lifting of the chalice in the Mass, the Holy Spirit is considered to be infused in the wine; the priest then makes the sign of the cross three times. It is noted that he signs twice from right to left, in a counterclockwise movement which corresponds psychologically to a movement downwards toward the realm of the unconscious; he then signs once left to right, or upward in the direction of the conscious. The censing is the last act in the preparation of priest and congregation for the transubstantiation.

000369 Transformation symbolism of the Mass. 2. The sequence of the transformation rite. V. The Epiclesis. In: Jung, C., Collected Works of C. G. Jung, Vol. 11. 2nd ed., Princeton University Press, 1969. 699 p. (p. 213).

The Epiclesis, final act in the Christian Mass, is described as it was practiced in different times and by different peoples. At the end of the Mass ritual everything has been prepared for the appearance of the Lord, and the invocation is said naming or summoning the Lord. The actual manifestation of the Lord was the culminating point of the Mass.

000370 Transformation symbolism of the Mass. 2. The sequence of the transformation rite. VI. The consecration. In: Jung, C., Collected Works of C. G. Jung, Vol. 11. 2nd ed., Princeton University Press, 1969. 699 p. (p. 214-216).

The significance and symbolism of the Consecration, the climax of the Roman Mass in which the transubstantiation of bread and wine into the body and blood of Christ is believed to occur, are examined. Particular attention is given to the words of Consecration showing that, since they represent the actual words of Christ speaking in the first person, Christ becomes both the gift and giver in this ritual act. References to the explanations of the Consecration provided by John of Damascus, Duns Scotus and the Council of Trent reveal the belief that, at this moment, Christ renews, in a bloodless fashion, His sacrificial death on the cross. The sacramental words are examined as a metaphor for the sacrificial sword or knife by which this death was accomplished. It is concluded that several of the ritual acts of the Roman Mass, as well as the Consecration rite of the Greek Orthodox Church, are symbols of the death of Christ.

000371 Transformation symbolism of the Mass. 2. The sequence of the transformation rite. VII. The greater elevation. VIII. The post-consecration. In: Jung, C., Collected Works of C. G. Jung, Vol. 11. 2nd ed., Princeton University Press, 1969. 699 p. (p. 216-218).

The symbolism of the greater elevation and the post-consecration prayers in the Roman Mass is examined. The elevation of the consecrated substances and the prayers that follow this portion of the mass are seen as symbolic representation of Christ's sacrificing himself to God. The prayer itself is cited and the Scriptural allusion to the sacrifices of Abel, Abraham and Melchisedec, contained therein, are explained.

000372 Transformation symbolism of the Mass. 2. The sequence of the transformation rite. IX. End of the Canon. X. Breaking of the Host ("fractio"). In: Jung, C., Collected Works of C. G. Jung, Vol. 11. 2nd ed., Princeton University Press, 1969. 699 p. (p. 218-219).

The ritual acts of the Roman Mass that occur at the end of the Canon and after the recitation of the Our Father are examined. The sign of the cross made with the Host over the chalice is seen as an affirmation of the unity of all parts of the sacrifice; the fractio or breaking of the Host over the chalice is considered to be symbolic of Christ's death. Differences in the Byzantine and Mozarabic rituals of fractio are described in terms of the symbolic significance of the number of parts into which the Host is broken.

000373 Transformation symbolism of the Mass. 2. The sequence of the transformation rite. XI. Consignatio. XII. Commixtio. In: Jung, C., Collected Works of C. G. Jung, Vol. 11. 2nd ed., Princeton University Press, 1969. 699 p. (p. 219-220).

The symbolism of the consignatio and commixtio portions of the Roman Mass is discussed. After making the sign of the cross with a fragment of the Host over the chalice, the particula is dropped into the wine, symbolizing the reunion of soul and body. Earlier rites involving the use of water or honey and milk instead of wine are mentioned and the interpretation of commixtio in the "Leonine Sacramentary" is described. The relationship of the commixtio and the baptism rituals is discussed showing that the former reverses the symbolism of the latter and becomes a symbol of the resurrection.

000374 Transformation symbolism in the Mass. 2. The sequence of the transformation rite. XIII. Conclusion. In: Jung, C., Collected Works of C. G. Jung, Vol. 11. 2nd ed., Princeton University Press, 1969. 699 p. (p. 220-221).

The Christian religious Mass as a whole is described as a codification of the life and sufferings of Christ: the prefiguration, the incarnation, the passion and death on the cross, the descent into hell, and the resurrection. The archetypal symbol of unity is found in the mingling of wine and bread, as is the symbol of the androgynous character of Christ (the wine and bread are seen as masculine and feminine, respectively). Thus the essential symbol of the Mass is that of transformation of the imperfect parts into the perfect whole.

000375 Transformation symbolism in the Mass. 3. Parallels to the transformation mystery. I. The Aztec "teoqualo." In: Jung, C., Collected Works of C. G. Jung, Vol. 11. 2nd ed., Princeton University Press, 1969. 699 p. (p. 222-225).

Antecedents and parallels are found for the ritual of the Christian religious Mass in Aztec, Mithraic and pagan religious practices. The Aztecs make a dough figure of the god Huitzilopochtli, which is then symbolically killed, divided and consumed. In the Mithraic ritual of sacrificing a bull, which represents Mithras himself, symbols of transformation and resurrection are noted. All these symbolic structures featuring young gods who die and rise again are seen as manifestations of preconscious archetypes; the commonly held conception that they were invented and somehow passed from one cult to the other is rejected.

000376 Transformation symbolism in the Mass. 3. Parallels to the transformation mystery. II. The vision of Zosimos. In: Jung, C., Collected Works of C. G. Jung, Vol. 11. 2nd ed., Princeton University Press, 1969. 699 p. (p. 225-246).

Examples of pre-Christian antecedents of the symbolism of the Christian religious Mass are found in the dream visions of the alchemist Zosimos. Numerous allusions to sacrificial rites are found in the visions of the priest Hiereus and the sacrificer Hierourgon, in which the priest submits voluntarily to various types of torture, ritual dismemberment (deipnon), and burning on the altar (thysis). Through these sacrifices the priest is transformed. Similar sacrificial transformations are noted in the Scythian flaying and scalping rituals, and the custom of head shaving among ancient and contemporary religious sects; the shaving of the head is associated with a return to the new-born state, a rebirth into purity. Throughout the vision it is observed that sacrificer and sacrificed are identical; this unity is one of the basic themes of alchemical thought, and is found symbolized in different ways in different alchemical traditions. This symbolic division, transformation and reunion of a new and more perfect substance are found in the sacrificial sword of alchemical and Christian tradition which both kills and brings to life, and in the dismemberment and decapitation formulae of ancient pagan ritual. The decapitated head as oracle (transformation into higher knowledge) appears in Greek as well as ancient pagan and modern Bantu symbolism. The unconscious origin of these dream visions and of alchemical and religious symbolic structure in general is stressed. However, in ancient times the idea of an unconscious psychic process had not yet been formulated; the visions were considered by ancient theorists to spring from natural forces and spirits outside of them rather from their own psyches. It is only in man's recent history that science has demystified nature, compelling men to look into themselves for the origins of universal symbols. 2 references.

000377 Transformation symbolism in the Mass. 4. The psychology of the Mass. I. General remarks on the sacrifice. In: Jung, C., Collected Works of C. G. Jung, Vol. 11. 2nd ed., Princeton University Press, 1969. 699 p. (p. 247-252).

The psychological and the metaphysical or religious interpretations of the Roman Mass are discussed and compared. It is the view of the Church that human consciousness, represented by the priest and congregation, is confronted in the Mass with an autonomous force that transcends and transforms it. The psychological view of the Mass as the psyche's symbolic self-transformation through an acting-out of unconscious drives on the conscious level is seen as complementary rather than contradictory to Christian dogma. The mystery of transubstantiation is considered no less miraculous for being human as well as divine. The belief in the dual nature of God and the God-man, well substantiated in Scripture and Christian tradition, itself supports this dual interpretation of the Mass.

000378 Transformation symbolism in the Mass. 4. The psychology of the Mass. II. The psychological meaning of sacrifice. In: Jung, C., Collected Works of C. G. Jung, Vol. 11. 2nd ed., Princeton University Press, 1969. 699 p. (p. 252-273).

Through the sacrifice in the Mass Christ is eternally redeemed and man can reach salvation. In the Mass the sacrifical offering is bread and wine, symbolizing male and female, spiritual and earthly elements. As the raw substances of grain and grapes are transformed by special processes into bread and wine, so too are the participants in the Mass refined and transformed by its ritual. It is in identifying a person's property as a projection of himself that the giving of a gift (a sacrifice) is giving of part of that person. Thus in sacrificing an object one sacrifices oneself. This act of giving part of oneself reflects the knowledge that one does have some control and understanding of the self. Thus by giving up the self

one comes to truly possess it. Man is forced to make this effort of sacrificing himself by the power of the unconscious, which constantly drives for union with the conscious. It is through self-awareness, self-reflection and individuation that all psychic parts are integrated. The immature ego nature is abolished by the widening of the circle of consciousness, making psychic paradoxes conscious and resolving sources of psychic conflict. The comparison between the vision of Zosimos and the Mass seem superficially unrelated, though in the deeper symbolism of the Mass as a sacrifice they are very similar. The basic difference in the two is that Zosimos took his vision literally rather than symbolically.

000379 Transformation symbolism in the Mass. 4. The psychology of the Mass. III. The Mass and the individuation process. In: Jung, C., Collected Works of C. G. Jung, Vol. 11. 2nd ed., Princeton University Press, 1969. 699 p. (p. 273-296).

Manifestations are found in Christian literature and tradition of Christ as the total man symbolizing the total personality, or the self. The round dance alluded to in the Acts of John is an example of the symbolic individuation process seen in the Mass. It is through the circle in the round dance that the relationship in nature of the parts to the whole is symbolized. Here the world is not an antithetical dichotomy of good and evil, but is much more appropriately understood as conscious trying to comprehend unconscious. The circle again is in the form of mandala, the center symbolizing the idea of totality and finality. In the hymn that accompanies the dance the dual nature of Christ is revealed in a series of paradoxes; each paradox is explicated as a symbol of Christ's role as man and God, and of the ideal reunion between the two. The nature of the cross as instrument of torture and as divine symbol further support this identity/duality. The cross is the center, but it also represents division; it is a counterpart of the mandala symbolizing the division of the world into a polarity of right and left. The cross is one of the prime symbols of order where opposing sides meet and a third force is found. This force has the nature of both of the opposing sides but is itself free of opposition. In like manner the unconscious contains both the nature of unity and multiplicity at once; without the psyche man could not establish the existence of the world, let alone know it. It is through selfhood that man finds relief from the chaotic conditions in the world. The tremendous polarities in man can only be overcome by the terrifying psychic process of understanding the unconscious, an act whereof man is the object and the subject. It is the act of becoming aware of the unconscious and the preconscious that is symbolized in the Mass by the crucifixion and redemption. 1 reference.

000380 Foreword to White's "God and the unconscious." In: Jung, C., Collected Works of C. G. Jung, Vol. 11. 2nd ed., Princeton University Press, 1969. 699 p. (p. 299-310).

In the foreword to White's work, "God and the Unconscious," the relationship between the theological and the psychological concern for sick and suffering human beings is analyzed with emphasis on the need for cooperation and understanding between the two approaches. That an idea is not liked and that its implications falsify some basic idea underlying society is not considered to negate the idea; nor should the discoverer be criticized for the content of the discovery. The archetype privatio boni does not give man the choice between good and evil, instead the evil works upon man without his permission, making him the object of the deed rather than the subject. White is seen as a theologian seeking to define God in terms of empirical fact. This procedure is one of the tenets of therapy: examination of the spiritual side of the patient is recommended as a means of cure. It is also suggested that each patient be treated individually, as many have the spiritual maturity of the early Christians or primitives and their cures will be found in those terms.

000381 Foreword to Werblowsky's "Lucifer and Prometheus." In: Jung, C., Collected Works of C. G. Jung, Vol. 11. 2nd ed., Princeton University Press, 1969. 699 p. (p 311-315).

Although Werblowsky's "Lucifer and Prometheus" is primarily a work of literary criticism, this introduction to it examines the poetic, religious and artistic significance of the Satan image and traces the numerous changes in the interpretations of this symbolic figure. Satan first emerged as the shadow, the symbol of the opposite of good; the Catholic Church made him the left hand of God and the first Son; in medieval times the Cathars believed Satan to be the creator of all things; and in modern times he is seen as a personification of all that is evil. It is a psychological rule that when an archetype such as Satan has lost its metaphysical hypostasis it becomes operative in the conscious mind of the individual. As it still contains some numinosity, it generally produces an inflation of the subject leading to moral irresponsibility.

000382 Brother Klaus. In: Jung, C., Collected Works of C. G. Jung, Vol. 11. 2nd ed., Princeton University Press, 1969. 699 p. (p. 316-323).

The visions of Brother Klaus, recorded by Father Stoeckli, Heinrich, Wolflin and Karl Bouillus, are analyzed as examples of a genuine primordial experience expressed in an archetypal symbol. Brother Klaus, a 15th century Swiss hermit, renounced his family and withdrew into solitude as a result of the overpowering force of his visions which he interpreted to be a representation of God himself, the Absolute Good. The predominance of light in both the adult vision of the Trinity and in the vision of a star that Brother Klaus believed to have had while he was still in his mother's womb are taken as indications of an irrupting illumination, a primordial religious experience of God that can neither be assimilated nor denied. The whirl symbol used by Brother Klaus to elucidate his vision is interpreted as a mandala symbol, whereas his vision of the woman is considered to be a reflection of the androgynous nature of mystic experience and a parallel to the Tantric philosophy of Shiva and Shakti.

000383 Psychotherapists or the clergy. In: Jung, C., Collected Works of C. G. Jung, Vol. 11. 2nd ed., Princeton University Press, 1969. 699 p. (p. 327-347).

A brief overview of the development of theories of neurosis is provided and the relationship between psychotherapeutic treatment and man's spiritual suffering is examined. Freudian, Adlerian and purely neurological theories of neurosis are rejected in favor of the view that psychoneurosis must be understood as the suffering of a soul that has not yet discovered its meaning. By defining neurosis in these terms, the religious nature of the problem becomes apparent. The inability of the clergy to deal with the psychological dimensions of the suffering person is analyzed as in modern man's unwillingness to seek help from the clergy. Thus it is the doctor who is confronted with the questions concerning ultimate meaning -- questions formerly answered by theologians and philosophers. In order to liberate the sufferer from the interior conflict he is experiencing, the doctor is urged to recognize that he is dealing with the fundamental problem of good and evil. To deal effectively with this problem certain basic attitudes are required: unprejudiced objectivity, a willingness to allow the patient to experience his capacity for evil, a recognition of his own

shadows on the part of the doctor. Healing is defined as a reconciliation of the conflicting forces and the patient's egoism; a symptom of neurosis is viewed as useful in allowing the neurotic to experience his own loneliness and isolation. When the archetypes of the unconscious are awakened and take over the guidance of the psychic personality, replacing the futile striving and will of the ego, the cure begins. In religious terms, the patient may describe the experience as guidance from God; in psychotherapeutic language, it may be described as the psyche's awakening to its own spontaneous activity. It is concluded that the cure involves a true, primordial experience of the spirit.

000384 Psychoanalysis and the cure of souls. In: Jung, C., Collected Works of C. G. Jung, Vol. 11. 2nd ed., Princeton University Press, 1969. 699 p. (p. 348-354).

The approaches to the cure of souls employed by Catholic and Protestant clergy are examined and and compared to the work of the psychoanalyst. It is the job of the psychoanalyst to lay bare the unconscious and integrate it with the conscious mind, while the clergyman's cure is based on the Christian confession of faith. The methods of Adler and Freud are analyzed in the light of their usefulness in the pastoral cure of souls and rejected as inadequate. Rather than to treat the conscious mind, Freudian psychoanalysis seeks to lead the contents of the unconscious over into the conscious mind, whereas Adlerian pedagogies are seen to aim at the normalization and adaptation of the individual, neglecting the unconscious. The advantages of the Catholic confession as a means of understanding unconscious control are pointed out. The Protestant minister, not having the confessional, has turned to analytical psychology: the cure of souls, through the soul of the minister working on the soul of the troubled person. Objections to this analytical method are raised much faster than to the confessional method because the former is more formalized and dogmatic. Further, the Protestant minister, who lacks the ritual forms for channelling clients' psychic conflicts, runs a greater risk of personal involvement in these conflicts, to the detriment of his professional and family situation. However, the intimate contact with the world this curing of souls provides is seen as a challenge and an adventure as well as a danger for the Protestant minister.

000385 Answer to Job. Prefatory note. In: Jung, C., Collected Works of C. G. Jung, Vol. 11. 2nd ed., Princeton University Press, 1969. 699 p. (p. 355-358).

In the preface of "Answer to Job," the sources and motives that fashioned this work are stated. It is, in part, an answer to the problems raised by the Christ/Antichrist antagonism found in the "Aion" as well as a examination of the religious question concerning the origin of evil. The aim of this book is to trace historically the evolution of the idea that God is a consortium of opposites from the time of Job through the centuries to its most recent symbolic manifestations. The work itself is not a definitive statement of eternal truth but rather an expression of the questions of a single individual, based on personal experience and subjective emotions.

000386 Answer to Job. Lectori benevolo. In: Jung, C., Collected Works of C. G. Jung, Vol. 11. 2nd ed., Princeton University Press, 1969. 699 p. (p. 359-363).

The "physical" as the only criterion of truth is compared with "psychic" truths. That which we consider real in physical terms ignores the half of the world that is psychically real. The archetypes found throughout history are part of our unconscious and are unknowable in a physical sense; rather they are founded in psychic fact. These psychic facts are not constructed by deduction; instead they enter the conscious as complete thoughts in the form of symbols from the unconscious.

000387 Answer to Job. In: Jung, C., Collected Works of C. G. Jung, Vol. 11. 2nd ed., Princeton University Press, 1969. 699 p. (p. 365-470).

The representation of the god Yahweh in the Book of Job is examined in terms of the amorality of Yahweh's dealings with humanity. In this text Yahweh appears as much more human than divine; he is unjust, selfish, irrational, and capable of much less moral consciousness than Job. The fact that Job asks God to defend against God himself is taken as a symbol of the dual nature of God as protector and persecutor, as good and evil simultaneously. The character of God is clearly an antinomy, a unity of opposites, and it is from this inner conflict that the dynamism, the omniscience and the omnipotence of God are seen to derive. This view of God is seen as a reflection of the realization on the part of the author of the Book of Job in particular, and of metaphysical theorists in general, that the concept of God is a relative one, dependent not upon facts but upon interpretations. However, this suspicion did not lead to the devaluation of the God figure until the modern age, when the dual nature of God and its implication for the mind of man is being seriously analyzed. The state of religious thought and tradition at the time of the writing of the Book of Job is examined in terms of the dual nature of God. The figure of Sophia, a feminine force coeternal with God, is seen as a derivation of Greek symbolic tradition and a parallel of Indian mythology; she is the gentle and wise counterpart to the ruthlessness of Yahweh. The assimilation of Sophia and Yahweh is observed to take place at the moment when man's rationality and sense of justice had matured beyond the point of accepting an unjust God. A further humanization of God is His coming to earth in the form of man, prefigured in the Cain and Abel story where the one pleasing to God's eye is slain. The Son of God is seen as a quality desired by both man and God. The inclusion of the feminine with the masculine as a part of the concept of God unites conflicting entities; a similar unification is seen in the awareness of the unconscious by the conscious through symbols. It is through an analysis of his unconscious that man becomes aware of the God archetype. God is not identified with the unconscious; rather it is an archetypal image that arises from the unconscious and aids in man's search for wholeness. 2 references.

000388 Psychological commentary on "The Tibetan Book of the Great Liberation." 1. The difference between Eastern and Western thinking. In: Jung, C., Collected works of C. G. Jung, Vol. 11. 2nd ed., Princeton University Press, 1969. 699 p. (p. 475-493).

A comparison is made between Eastern and Western views of psychic reality in a psychological interpretation of the "Tibetan Book of the Great Liberation." The former is considered to be basically introverted; the latter, extraverted. In his objective attitude towards experience Western man finds meaning in his everyday world and his life. Western man bombards himself with facts, the meaning of which is unintelligible, yet it is through the accumulation of countless facts that he hopes to find meaning. He then looks outward to Christianity for meaning and purpose. The psyche is considered by modern man as an untrustworthy part of the mind that must be suppressed as completely as possible. Partial expressions of his incompletely suppressed psyche are perceived by the ego centered Western man as sinful. Eastern man finds

his religion in his subjectivity. He looks inward and becomes totally aware of his unconscious, and thus of his successes and failings. In so doing the conscious becomes identical with the unconscious, and every unconscious thought can be controlled. Both Eastern and Western religions fail by refusing to take the other's facts as evidence; psychic events, which are not considered facts by Western man, constitute the basic facts of existence for Eastern man. 1 reference.

000389 Psychological commentary on "The Tibetan Book of the Great Liberation." 2. Comments on the text. In: Jung, C., Collected Works of C. G. Jung, Vol. 11. 2nd ed., Princeton University Press, 1969. 699 p. (p. 494-508).

A commentary on the text of "The Tibetan Book of the Great Liberation" is provided in order to show the parallels between Eastern metaphysical thought and the discoveries of modern psychology. The universal mind of Tibetan lore and the collective unconscious are seen as the same; they are the root of the experience of validity oneness, the interrelation of all archetypes, and the validity of the phenomenal world. Here gods exist as thought forms, as the one and the opposite, yin and yang. By exploring the unconscious, man finds oneness, indefiniteness, and timelessness. Knowledge of the One Mind is necessary in order to know one's self and to compensate for a onesided adjustment to the world. Man cannot compel unconscious compensation for his onesidedness; instead he must wait for it with a comtemplative attitude that is in itself healing. The transcendental "At-one-ment" is attained by withdrawing into the undifferentiated unconscious where nothing is distinct enough to cause conflict. It is felt that Western man must carefully explore his unconscious before attempting to experience the subjectivity of Eastern religions; it will do him little good to attempt yoga if he is unconsciously a medieval Christian. He must be able to put aside his history to accept this introspective Eastern outlook, part of which involves existing and not existing at the same time. 1 reference.

000390 Psychological commentary on "The Tibetan Book of the Dead.' In: Jung, C., Collected Works of C. G. Jung, Vol. 11. 2nd ed., Princeton University Press, 1969. 699 p. (p. 509-526).

Thi tripartite division of "The Tibetan Book of the Dead" is presented and a psychological commentary on its contents is provided with comparisons made between the Eastern and Western views of the psyche or soul. It is through the Bardo Thodol in "The Tibetan Book of the Dead" that the dead are guided through the 49 days' transition. The instant of death is the highest, most glorious moment; it is from this point that the soul descends until it reaches physical rebirth 49 days later. At the moment of death one is part of the mind of Buddha; this state is called Chikhai, of which a major symbol is the mandala with Buddha in the middle. The second state is the Chonyid, or the Bardo of the experiencing of reality. It is in this state that man finds out what is good and evil, precious and worthless, subject and object, and that the ego is sacrificed and the soul enters a form of psychosis and torment. The third state is Sidpa, or the Bardo of seeking rebirth. In this state sexual fantasies occur, and the soul is drawn toward mating couples until it focuses on one and is drawn toward rebirth in that couple. It is possible for the soul to reach the Dharmakaya by transcending the four face Mount Meru, providing it does not follow its reason and dim the guiding lights. There is no similar symbolism in the West, only Catholicism has named a place for souls to go after death; for this reason Freud could not have patients regress back farther than the intrauterine stage.

000391 Yoga and the West. In: Jung, C., Collected Works of C. G. Jung, Vol. 11. 2nd ed., Princeton University Press, 1969. 699 p. (p. 529-537).

In a comparative study on Eastern and Western mentality, the basic duality of the Western mind is seen to negate the value of yoga. Western man has divided his world into two distinct natures, the scientific and the religious; the two are separate entities, but neither makes any sense without the other. Western man divested yoga of its religious implications, making it just another system to be followed -- for physical rather than psychic hygiene. Western man does not have the same history as Eastern man, and the implications of these differing histories have not carried over in the use of yoga, in that western man cannot understand the concept of prana and therefore cannot unite the psychological with the physiological.

000392 Foreword to Suzuki's "Introduction to Zen Buddhism." In: Jung, C., Collected Works of C. G. Jung, Vol. 11. 2nd ed., Princeton University Press, 1969. 699 p. (p. 538-557).

The satori, the original religious experience of the East, is described as a natural occurrence that cannot be communicated verbally. It is through the enlightenment of satori that man sees the nature of the self and frees himself from its illusions. Having once had this experience, man can begin to see things in terms of nonego. He does not see new ideas or things; instead, he sees them differently. Satori is found through the Koan, an ambiguous question with no formulated answer; it is through studying the many koans that the answer breaks through. The answer is not formulated by the conscious mind, but is found in nature and in the unconscious. This belief, the satori experience, is similar to that of Western thought in terms of the transformation of unconscious processes into conscious thought. This also means that man is not born in a state of tabula rasa, but with preconscious or innate ideas. In man's search for wholeness he bursts through to his unconscious, the recognition of which enables him to comprehend the uncomprehensible unconscious. In the modern West, it is the psychotherapist who smooths the path for those seeking wholeness. 2 references.

000393 The psychology of Eastern meditation. In: Jung, C., Collected Works of C. G. Jung, Vol. 11. 2nd ed., Princeton University Press, 1969. 699 p. (p. 558-575).

The Indian religious practice of yoga is examined as an expression of the Indian view of the mind and as an instrument for attaining a certain state of being with attention given to the subtle differences between Indians and Western mandala symbols. Buddhism arose from yoga, a form of meditation, which existed long before Buddha, who merely followed the path of meditation. Certain meditations are listed through which Indians find themselves in Buddha; the meditations begin with looking at the setting sun, a circular symbol of life, God, and unity, a symbol found in both Western and Eastern cultures. The second object of meditation is water, the symbol of life, knowledge, and grace. The water solidifies and becomes ice, and then lapis lazuli: the stone then becomes transparent and visible, under which the Buddha is sitting on a lotus with the eight demarcations of direction around him. It is at the point of solidification that Western man cannot follow the symbolism any longer; it is here that the unconscious becomes real and concrete, and more importantly, known by the conscious. Western man finds his peace in rising above the unconscious, while Eastern man delves into the unconscious to find enlightenment. Western man cannot reach beyond his personal unconscious to the collective unconscious and his enlighten-

ment. In Eastern culture Buddha is found in man, whereas in the West, man is found in Christ. Even though the West cannot find enlightenment in Eastern meditation, the symbolism behind both religions is seen to be the same. It is here that the collective unconscious is seen in the archetypal symbols.

000394 The holy men of India. In: Jung, C., Collected Works of C. G. Jung, Vol. 11. 2nd ed., Princeton University Press, 1969. 699 p. (p. 576-586).

The thought of the Indian holy man, Shri Romana and Rama Krishna, is examined as an expression of the conflict between ego and self. The Indian problem of self and ego parallels the Western man's God/man dichotomy. The Indian problem appears merely psychological in comparison to the Western metaphysical problem. Yet the goal of both is to shift the center of being from the ego or man to the self or God. For the Indian this is accomplished by submerging the ego in the self, and for Western man, the submerging of his self in God. The goal of psychic development is for the self to encompass the conscious and unconscious, a goal attainable in Indian culture. But this idea is seen to be threatened in India because of the westernization that comes with statehood. It is felt that Western man's ways of concerning himself with only the conscious and not the unconscious will take its toll spiritually in India. 1 reference.

000395 Foreword to the "I-Ching." In: Jung, C., Collected Works of C. G. Jung, Vol. 11. 2nd ed., Princeton University Press, 1969. 699 p. (p. 589-608).

In the foreword to the English edition of the "I-Ching" (Book of Changes), a demonstration of how the I-Ching functions in the Chinese mind is presented instead of a psychological commentary on the whole book. The goal of this demonstration is to help the reader to form a tentative judgment on the operation of the I-Ching. In order to understand the use of the I-Ching, it is considered important to distinguish between the Chinese synchronistic approach to events and the Western causal approach: the former interprets events in terms of coincidence and chance. Consequently the 64 hexagrams of the I-Ching indicate the essential situation that prevailed at the moment of the origin of each hexagram. These hexagrams, in turn, are the instruments by which 64 different yet typical situations can be determined. Two experiments are described which illustrate the workings of the I-Ching. The book was personified; i.e.,considered as a speaking subject, and certain questions were addressed to it. In keeping with Chinese tradition, three coins were tossed and the pattern that they formed was used as a guide to the hexameters to be consulted. An analysis of the hexameters is provided and the methods used in interpreting their significance are discussed with attention given to the importance of lines designated by the numbers 6 and 9. It is concluded from this experiment that the I-Ching, as if speaking for itself, faced its future on the American book market calmly and optimistically. A second experiment is described that demonstrates how the I-Ching can elucidate the subjective attitude of the user. Although it is acknowledged that the Western mind has great difficulty in accepting the psychological phenomenology of the I-Ching, the discussions and prophecies of this work are felt to have a wisdom and knowledge that can be attributed to more than chance.

12 PSYCHOLOGY AND ALCHEMY

000396 Introduction to the religious and psychological problems of alchemy. In: Jung, C., Collected Works of C. G. Jung, Vol. 12. 2nd ed., Princeton University Press, 1968. 571 p. (p. 1-37).

A study of the relationship between alchemy and the psychic process of individuation is presented. The need to address the problems of the psyche is based on the fact that the psyche is still one of the most mysterious regions of experience. Observation of people points to the mystery of the psyche, and the psychotherapeutic process itself constantly reveals that the object of the search, for both doctor and patient, is the discovery of the whole man, a greater man in the future. The difficulty and dangers of this search are explored and the potentiality for wholeness in the true Christian "imitatio Christi" is explained. An exhaustive discussion of the relationship between religion and the psyche is included, with emphasis on the religious nature of the soul and on the contribution that psychology can make to arriving at a better understanding of religious truths. A comparison is made between the archetypes of the unconscious and religious dogmas, with stress on the importance of the Christ symbol as an expression of the union of opposites. The alchemic view of the soul and the Godhead is presented and contrasted with the Christian view. In alchemy, the search was also directed toward the discovery of the seed of unity as is the psychotherapeutic process. The goal of this latter process is stated as enabling the patient to be alone with the self. The methods, dangers and difficulties of arriving at this goal are discussed. Reference is made to a dialogue between the patient and his shadow, which is to be followed by the study of a series of dreams containing mandala symbols of the center or the goal. It is in developing these symbols that the healing process or the solution for this particular person emerges. An attempt is made to introduce the symbolism of alchemy and to relate it to Christianity, Gnosticism and the psychotherapeutic process.

000397 Individual dream symbolism in relation to the alchemy: a study of the unconscious processes at work in dreams. 1. Introduction. I. The material. II. The method. In: Jung, C., Collected works of C. G. Jung, Vol. 12. 2nd ed., Princeton University Press, 1968. 571 p. (p. 39-46).

In introducing a study of symbols of the individuation process as gathered from dream material, their nature as images of an archetype depicting the production of a new center of personality is reasserted. This center is called the self; i.e.,the center of the psyche containing both the conscious and the unconscious. The images that refer directly and exclusively to this new center as it comes into consciousness belong to a category referred to as mandala symbolism. A series of such symbols arranged in chronological order and taken from over a thousand dreams and visual impressions produced by a young man educated as a scientist is presented. For purposes of this study the first 400 dreams and visions covering a period of nearly 10 months are examined. In order to provide conditions of unprejudiced observation and recording, a student undertook the observation of the process with the young man. The belief that interpretation of dreams cannot be approached with preconceived notions about what is meant by any unconscious expression is repeated here. It should be assumed that every dream, and every part of a dream, is unknown at the outset; therefore, attempts at interpretation can be made only after making a careful examination of the context in which it appears.

000398 Individual dream symbolism in relation to the alchemy: a study of the unconscious processes at work in dreams. 2. The initial dreams. In: Jung, C., Collected Works of C. G. Jung, Vol. 12. 2nd ed., Princeton University Press, 1968. 571 p. (p. 47-93).

Extracts from 22 initial dreams and visual impressions obtained from the analysis of a young man are presented. These extracts are interpreted in terms of their relation to the emergence into consciousness of archetypal images referring to the self, the new center of the personality that results from the dialectical process of individuation. These archetypal images are referred to as mandala symbolism. The purpose of interpreting these initial dreams is to indicate the way in which the mandala symbolism makes a very early appearance in the dream material and remains imbedded in it throughout. 11 references.

000399 Individual dream symbolism in relation to the alchemy: a study of the unconscious processes at work in dreams. 3. The symbolism of the mandala. I. Concerning the mandala. In: Jung, C., Collected Works of C. G. Jung, Vol. 12. 2nd ed., Princeton University Press, 1968. 571 p. (p. 95-102).

An explanation of the origin of the mandala is given, and reasons are provided to justify the choice of this term in describing dreams and visions in which the self is symbolized. The mandala is the ritual or magic circle used in Lamaism; in Tantric yoga it is a yantra, or aid to contemplation. The Lamaic view of the mandala is presented by means of a report of a conversation with a Lamaic priest that took place in 1938. According to this view, a mandala is a mental image that can be created only by an instructed Lama through the power of imagination. No mandala is like any other; all are individual. Thus, physical representations of the mandala found in monasteries and temples have no real significance; the true mandala is always a mental image. Despite the alleged individual formation of Lamaic mandalas it is noted that a certain unmistakable style and structure predominate. For example, they are all based on a quaternary system and their contents are derived from Lamaic dogma. A strict distinction is made between the Lamaic mandala, the khilkor, and the sidpe-korlo, or Buddhist world wheel. The latter is based on a tertiary system in which the three world principles are represented. It is asserted that these Eastern symbols were not invented by religious leaders but that they originated in dreams and visions. Their widespread distribution across cultures is cited as evidence. Mandalas used in ceremonies are of great significance because their centers usually contain important religious figures, e.g. Shiva or the Buddha. If, as surmised, mandalas symbolize a psychic center of the personality that is separate from the ego, the high value placed on them is justified. 1 reference.

000400 Individual dream symbolism in relation to the alchemy: a study of the unconscious processes at work in dreams. 3. The symbolism of the mandala. II. The mandalas in the dreams. In: Jung, C., Collected Works of C. G. Jung, Vol. 12. 2nd ed., Princeton University Press, 1968. 571 p. (p. 103-202).

Extracts of 59 dreams and visions, out of a continous series of more than 400 dreams obtained from the analysis of a young man are presented. These excerpts were chosen for interpretation because they provide clear evidence of mandala symbolism. Images of the circle frequently recur and are interpreted as the symbol for the center of the personality; the mirror image is seen as a simile for the intellect. Several of the symbols lend themselves to division into a quaternity which suggests a relation to alchemical symbols. For this reason, alchemic writings are cited to show the connections between the meaning behind the dream symbols and the meaning of such alchemical terms as lapis philosophorum, king, sol niger and others. The progress of the striving of the unconcious to reach consciousness is charted by means of the dream symbols, with special attention given to the symbols of conflict that this emerging of the unconscious evokes. In the dream references to a glass containing gelatinous material and to the uterus, an acceptance of the anima as part of the dreamer's own psyche is seen. The approach to reality takes the form of images related to specific time and place. The conclusion is drawn that the symbols, eagle and ship, depict the consciousness transcending self. 37 references.

000401 Individual dream symbolism in relation to the alchemy: a study of the unconscious processes at work in dreams. 3. The symbolism of the mandala. III. The vision of the world clock. In: Jung, C., Collected Works of C. G. Jung, Vol. 12. 2nd ed., Princeton University Press, 1968. 571 p. (p. 203-214).

The Great Vision of a young man underlying analysis whose 400 dreams (5 of which are recorded in this volume) were analyzed by a student of Jung's is examined in detail because of the impression of most sublime harmony that it produced in the dreamer. Two heterogeneous systems interesting in the self and standing in a functional relationship to one another are revealed, indicating the dreamer's desire for the most complete union of opposites that is possible. The vision, that of a "world clock," is described as a three dimensional mandala, a symbol of realization of the self. It is hypothesized that disparate and incongruous elements have combined in this vision to produce an image that realizes the "intentions" of the unconscious in the highest degree. Material from astrology, myth and religion is used in the interpretation of the vision. Special reference is made to the writings of Guillaume de Digulleville, a Norman poet, in explicating the significance of the world clock image. 5 references.

000402 Individual dream symbolism in relation to alchemy: a study of the unconscious processes at work in dreams. 3. The symbolism of the mandala. IV. The symbols of the self. In: Jung, C., Collected Works of C. G. Jung, Vol. 12. 2nd ed., Princeton University Press, 1968. 571 p. (p. 215-223).

The development of the central symbol in a dream series produced in analysis is discussed. This process might be described in terms of a spiral process with the unconscious moving around a center, gradually coming closer to it, while the characteristics of the center grow more distinct. On the other hand, the center, in itself virtually unknowable, might be seen as a magnet acting on the disparate elements and processes of the unconscious. The apparent quaternity of the central symbol is discussed with reference to numerous historical and ethnological parallels. Upon examining such evidence, it is concluded that there is some psychic element expressing itself through the quaternity. The element is named the "self." The archetypal nature of mandala symbolism is examined. It is felt that the facts are better served if it is assumed that the increase in the clarity and frequency of the mandala motif is due to a more accurate perception of an already existing "type" rather than to something generated in the course of the dream series.

000403 Religious ideas in alchemy: an historical survey of alchemical ideas. 1. Basic concepts of alchemy. I. Introduction. II. The alchemical process and its stages. III. Conceptions and symbols of the goal. In: Jung, C., Collected Works of C. G. Jung, Vol. 12. 2nd ed., Princeton University Press, 1968. 571 p. (p. 225-241).

A brief review of the causes for the demise of alchemy is presented, followed by a description of the alchemical process and goal. Although the 18th century spirit of enlightenment and the scientific discovery of chemistry could be applied to explain the death of alchemy, the real cause resided in its own

increasing obscurity, resulting from devotion to the allegories and speculations of Hermetic philosophy. Despite its inability to survive into the scientific ages, alchemy is seen to merit attention because of the psychic projections contained in the writings of its practitioners. That the art was filled with psychic projections is evidenced by the fact that, although alchemy was a chemical process, the description and ingredients of this process varied from author to author. There were, however, four stages posited by all the alchemists in the beginning, and these were characterized by the four colors: black, white, yellow, red. In the 15th century yellow was eliminated. The initial state, nigredo may be produced by the separation of elements, then the union of opposites (coniunctio) is performed, followed by the death of the product of this union (mortificatio). From this the washing (baptisma) leads to the albedo or whiteness and the release of the soul at the death of the last stage and its reunion with the body. This was considered to be the first goal of the process: the silver or moon condition. Red was produced by intensifying the fire, and the gold or sun was the result of the "chymical wedding" of red and white, symbolic of the King and Queen. Just as the processes varied, so did the conceptions and symbols of the goal. Certain characteristics were held by all, however: fire and water and the Hermetic vessel, for instance, were commonly associated with the prima materia and the stone. The characteristics of each of these symbols were often paradoxical and even antithetical to one another, yet all had a symbolic significance. In 1576, Joseph Quercetanus established a sequence of twelve operations but, since each of the twelve was open to multiple definition, the variations remained almost infinite. It is concluded that, although alchemy produced very little in terms of the knowledge of modern chemistry, it was a process filled with a sense of adventure due to the constant excitement of the quest and the hope of discovering the precious gold. 11 references.

000404 Religious ideas in alchemy: an historical survey of alchemical ideas. 2. The psychic nature of the alchemical work. I. The projection of psychic contents. In: Jung, C., Collected Works of C. G. Jung, Vol. 12. 2nd ed., Princeton University Press, 1968. 571 p. (p. 242-254).

It is asserted that the alchemical opus deals less with chemical experiments as such than with what is described as "something resembling psychic processes expressed in pseudochemical language." It is proposed that the real root of alchemy lies not in philosophical doctrine but in the projections of the individual investigator. By this is meant that the investigator, while working on his chemical experiments, had certain psychic experiences that appeared to him as part of the actual chemical process. As this is a matter of psychological projection, and therefore unconscious, the alchemist would experience his projection as a property of matter. Thus, he was in reality experiencing his own unconscious. Excerpts from several alchemic manuscripts are presented in support of the notion that psychic projection of unconscious material onto chemical substances is the key to understanding the alchemic opus. 19 references.

000405 Religious ideas in alchemy: an historical survey of alchemical ideas. 2. The psychic nature of the alchemical work. II. The mental attitude toward the opus. In: Jung, C., Collected Works of C. G. Jung, Vol. 12. 2nd ed., Princeton University Press, 1968. 571 p. (p. 255-274).

The psyche's relation to alchemical work in terms of the psychological requirements of the individual alchemist is examined. A number of passages from alchemic literature are presented. These examples indicate that, in order for the opus to be successful, the operator must be in possession of a proper "psychological set." This evidence is interpreted as indicating that the alchemic authors believed the essential secret of their art to lie hidden in the human mind, or what is termed the unconscious in analytical psychology. It is observed that the texts stress the importance of understanding and intelligence, not only because superior intelligence is needed in the performance of the art, but because "it is assumed that a species of magical power capable of transforming even brute matter dwells in the human mind." It is pointed out that alchemy, from its beginning, had a dual nature: on the one hand it was a chemical work; on the other it was a psychological process. Its psychic nature was partially conscious and partially the result of unconscious projections, as is seen in the various transformations of matter. This close connection between the psyche of the investigator and the alchemical work can also be seen in the emphasis placed on the mental attitude of the worker and on the virtues he was exhorted to cultivate. 23 references.

000406 Religious ideas in alchemy: an historical survey of alchemical ideas. 2. The psychic nature of The alchemical work. III. Meditation and imagination. In: Jung, C., Collected Works of C. G. Jung, Vol. 12. 2nd ed., Princeton University Press, 1968. 571 p. (p. 274-280).

An explication of the specific uses of the terms meditatio and imaginatio is undertaken with special reference to Ruland's "Lexicon alchemiae." Ruland's definition of meditatio proves beyond doubt that when alchemists speak of meditari they do not simply mean meditation or cogitation but explicitly an inner dialogue implying a living relationship with the "answering voice of the 'other' in ourselves," i.e. of the unconscious. Several other texts are cited to substantiate this explanation. Ruland's Lexicon also provides clarification of the particular importance of the term imaginatio in the alchemic opus. The act of imagining (imaginatio) was perceived as an activity that did not simply create fantasy but rather as producing something more corporeal, a "subtle body," semi-spiritual in nature. The imaginatio was thus a physical activity that could be fitted into the cycle of chemical or material changes. In this way the alchemist related himself not only to the conscious but directly to the very substance which he hoped to transform through the power of imagination. 3 references.

000407 Religious ideas in alchemy: an historical survey of alchemical ideas. 2. The psychic nature of the alchemical work. IV. Soul and body. In: Jung, C., Collected Works of C. G. Jung, Vol. 12. 2nd ed., Princeton University Press, 1968. 571 p. (p. 280-287).

The meaning of the terms, soul and body, and their relation to each other in alchemical thought are examined. The soul, or anima corporalis, is seen as corresponding to the unconscious, if this is understood to be the psychic phenomenon that mediates between consciousness and the physiological functions of the body. The fusion of opposites is characteristic of every psychic event in the unconscious state, thus the anima corporalis is also spiritualis. According to alchemical literature, the soul is only partly confined in the body, an analogy to God being only partly enclosed in the body of the world. As God's "imagining" is seen as the act of creation, the imaginatio, in alchemic terms, gives the key to the goal of alchemy: to project and make actual those contents of the unconscious which do not exist in nature. The contents of the unconscious have an a priori archetypal character. The medium through which

this goal is realized is neither mind nor matter, body nor soul, but a realm of subtle reality adequately expressed only by the symbol, since the latter is neither abstract nor concrete, rational nor irrational, real nor unreal, but both. 2 references.

000408 Religious ideas in alchemy: an historical survey of alchemical ideas. 3. The work. I. The method. In: Jung, C., Collected Works of C. G. Jung, Vol. 12. 2nd ed., Princeton University Press, 1968. 571 p. (p. 288-295).

The nature of the alchemical work is described and reasons are given to explain its obscurity. Part of work, the operatio, was practical in the sense that it dealt with a series of chemical experiments, yet it remained shrouded in obscurity due to the fact that each alchemist built an individual edifice of ideas composed of the sayings of the philosophers and analogies to the basic tenets of alchemy. At the same time, the alchemist was interested in creating a nomenclature that would describe psychic as well as physical transformations. The resulting amplification (amplificatio) of the procedures, which consists primarily of philosophical and religious analogies, is the second part of the opus, and was termed the theoria. The illustration on the title page of the "Tripus aureus" (1618) provides a graphic illustration of this alchemic duality. Special attention is given to Mercurius and to the circular nature of the alchemic work. 5 references.

000409 Religious ideas in alchemy: an historical survey of alchemical ideas. 3. The work. II. The spirit in matter. In: Jung, C., Collected Works of C. G. Jung, Vol. 12. 2nd ed., Princeton University Press, 1968. 571 p. (p. 295-306).

The alchemic notion of the spirit in matter is discussed with particular reference to the writings of Zosimos. Nietzschean metaphors are also used to express the idea that, in antiquity, the material world was considered to be filled with "the projection of a psychic secret, which from then on appeared as the secret of matter and remained so until the decay of alchemy in the 18th century." The alchemists searched for this secret spirit in the marvellous stone (lapis lazuli) that transforms base metals into noble ones by a process of coloration. As quicksilver approximates this process, this spirit substance was called Mercurius. The possessor of this penetrating Mercurius can "project" it into other substances and transform them from the imperfect to the perfect state. The analogy between alchemical work and the projection of unconscious psychic content is explored. The point is made that this unconscious content, up to the present, has rarely been attributed to any human personality, the notable exception being Christ. Pagan projections on the other hand go beyond man to the material world, the realm of inanimate matter. The alchemical work reflects the influence of both Pagan and Christian traditions. 9 references.

000410 Religious ideas in alchemy: an historical survey of alchemical ideas. 3. The work. III. The work of redemption. In: Jung, C., Collected Works of C. G. Jung, Vol. 12. 2nd ed., Princeton University Press, 1968. 571 p. (p. 306-316).

The nature of man as both the one to be redeemed and the redeemer is discussed. Man as the one to be redeemed is the Christian formulation; man as redeemer is alchemical. The symbolism and language of the Mass is examined in some detail. It is pointed out that, when the priest pronounces the consecrating words to bring about the transformation that redeems the bread and wine from their elemental imperfection, he is, in essence, an alchemist and not a Christian. The point is made that in both the Church and in alchemy the work is that of redemption, with the alchemist participating in two roles: that of the redeemer as well as that of the redeemed. 12 references.

000411 Religious ideas in alchemy: an historical survey of alchemical ideas. 4. The prima materia. I. Synonyms for the materia. In: Jung, C., Collected Works of C. G. Jung, Vol. 12. 2nd ed., Princeton University Press, 1968. 571 p. (p. 317-320).

In the discussion of the prima materia, the basis of the alchemical work, it is proposed that this prima materia represents the unknown substance embodying or carrying the projection of psychic content. For this reason, the substance cannot be specified because the projection emanates from the individual and is thus necessarily different in each case. It is incorrect to maintain that alchemists never defined the prima materia. On the contrary, all too many proposed their definitions. As a result, there exist many synonyms for this term, including words for chemical, mythological, and "philosophical" substances, that are briefly examined here. 8 references.

000412 Religious ideas in alchemy: an historical survey of alchemical ideas. 4. The prima materia. II. The increatum. In: Jung, C., Collected works of C. G. Jung, Vol. 12. 2nd ed., Princeton University Press, 1968. 571 p. (p. 320-323).

The nature of the prima materia as radix ipsius (root of itself) is discussed with special reference to the Paracelsan idea of the increatum; i.e.,that the prima materia is unique and mysterious in that it is "uncreated." The philosophical implications of this view, especially the implied equality of the prima materia with the Deity, enabled alchemists to project the highest value -- God -- into matter. This elevation of matter is seen as the starting point for the development of both modern chemistry and philosophical materialism. 2 references.

000413 Religious ideas in alchemy: an historical survey of alchemical ideas. 4. The prima materia. III. Ubiquity and perfection. In: Jung, C., Collected Works of C. G. Jung, Vol. 12. 2nd ed., Princeton University Press, 1968. 571 p. (p. 323-327).

The nature of the prima materia is discussed in terms of the qualities of ubiquity and perfection. With the writings of George Ripley, an English alchemist, as a primary source, passages are quoted describing the prima materia as being in every place and in every time, eternal and limitless. Comment is made on the views held by Ripley and other cosmological theorists, who maintained that the prima materia had a perfect spherical nature, a nature acquired when it emerged from the swirling chaos. It is this perfect "roundness" which resulted in the prima materia being often referred to as lapis. As the lapis is initially in the hidden state and can be transmitted through "the art and the grace of God" into the second manifest state, it is often seen as coincidental with the initial stage of the alchemical process, the nigredo. 8 references.

000414 Religious ideas in alchemy: an historical survey of alchemical ideas. 4. The prima materia. IV. The king and the king's son. In: Jung, C., Collected Works of C. G. Jung, Vol. 12. 2nd ed., Princeton University Press, 1968. 571 p. (p. 327-332).

The mythical theme of the king and the king's son is discussed as it relates to the prima materia. Basic to this myth are the images of the inanimate king in whose land nothing is begotten and the king's son is trapped at the bottom of the sea. This first image is interpreted as a description of the latency and potentiality of the hidden state. The darkness of the sea is seen as a representation of the depths of the uncon-

scious. Thus, when the king cries for help from his unconscious (dissociated state), it is to the conscious mind that this plea is addressed. The "rescue" necessitates a descent into the dark world of the unconscious, the dangerous night sea journey whose end and aim is the restoration of life and triumph over death. The legend of Arisleus is cited as an example of this theme, with attention given to the incest theme; i.e.,the union of opposites, which is the cause of the death. This death was interpreted by the alchemists as the completion of the spirit's descent into matter. 3 references.

000415 Religious ideas in alchemy: an historical survey of alchemical ideas. 4. The prima materia. The myth of the hero. In: Jung, C., Collected Works of C. G. Jung, Vol. 12. 2nd ed., Princeton University Press, 1968. 571 p. (p. 333-339).

The myth of the hero, with examples taken from the Arisleus legend, is presented as an analogy of the "descent into the unconscious" with all its attendant danger. The purpose of the descent, as universally exemplified in the myth of the hero, is to demonstrate that only in the region of great danger can one find the "treasure hard to attain" (the jewel, the life potion, lapis, triumph over death, etc.). The dread and resistance that arise when any normal human being begins to delve deeply into himself is analogous to the mythical journey to Hades with its attendant fear. The disintegration described in the myth of Gabricius is a repetition of the coniunctio of Nous and Physis, expressed in terms of a personal crisis brought about by the intervention of the alchemic philosophers. The philosopher makes the descent into hell as a redeemer. 6 references.

000416 Religious ideas in alchemy: an historical survey of alchemical ideas. 4. The prima materia. VI. The hidden treasure. In: Jung, C., Collected Works of C. G. Jung, Vol. 12. 2nd ed., Princeton University Press, 1968. 571 p. (p. 340-344).

Some of the various ways in which alchemists symbolized the "hidden treasure" or the "treasure hard to attain," believed to be present in the dark prima materia, are examined. Among these are Christopher of Paris' notion that this substance is potentially present in the chaos of the prima materia as a mass of all the elements combined into one. Johannes Grassens held that the white dove called "the salt of the metals" was contained within the lead (plumbum) of the philosophers. Valentinus believed that, like a reflection in a mirror, the treasure is an invisible spirit, intangible, yet, the root of all substances necessary for alchemy. In a similar view Michael Maier expressed the belief that the sun, in its revolutions, spins gold into the earth. As the sun is the image of God, the heart is the sun's image in man, and God is known in the gold. This golden image of God is the anima aurea which, when breathed into common quicksilver, changes it into gold. 7 references.

000417 Religious ideas in alchemy: an historical survey of alchemical ideas. 5. The lapis-Christ parallel. I. The renewal of life. In: Jung, C., Collected Works of C. G. Jung, Vol. 12. 2nd ed., Princeton University Press, 1968. 571 p. (p. 345-355).

The nature of the spirit hidden in the prima materia is discussed in light of Christian mysticism. This divine spirit is seen as the psychological equivalent of the projection of unconscious content. The task of alchemy was to make visible this hidden spirit. Since this work was contaminated by the unconscious projection of the alchemist, it was at the same time a psychic activity compared to what is termed active imagination. The parallel is drawn between the legend of Arisleus, in which salvation is obtained from an immortal fruit possessing miraculous regenerating effects, and the ecclesiastic symbolism of the Mass. This parallel eventually breaks down in that the Christian receives the fruit of the Mass for his own personal redemption whereas the alchemist receives the "immortal fruit" not merely for himself but first and foremost for the king or the king's son, that is, in order to perfect the coveted substance. It is asserted that without knowing it the alchemist carries the imitation of Christ (imitatio) a stage further and in a sense assimilates the Redeemer. As this process is carried out on the unconscious level, the alchemist can be said to project this correspondence to the Redeemer onto his "wondrous stone," the lapis. 1 reference.

000418 Religious ideas in alchemy: an historical survey of alchemical ideas. 5. The lapis-Christ parallel. II. Evidence for the religious interpretation of the lapis. a. Raymond Lully. In: Jung, C., Collected Works of C. G. Jung, Vol. 12. 2nd ed., Princeton University Press, 1968. 571 p. (p. 357-358).

It is proposed that, although alchemical symbolism is suffused with ecclesiastical allegory, the roots of this art can be traced back to origins in pagan thought, especially in Gnosticism. The assertion of A. E. Waite that Heinrich Khunrath, in his "Amphitheatrum" (1598) was the first author to identify the stone or lapis with Christ is disputed and Raymond Lully is credited with being the first to make this comparison in his work, "the Codicillus." 3 references.

000419 Religious ideas in alchemy: an historical survey of alchemical ideas. 5. The lapis-Christ parallel. II. Evidence for the interpretation of the lapis. b. Tractatus aureus. In: Jung, C., Collected Works of C. G. Jung, Vol. 12. 2nd ed., Princeton University Press, 1968. 571 p. (p. 358-360).

The "Tractatus aureus" is considered to be the oldest source of the lapis/Christ parallel. This source, ascribed to Hermes and regarded as Arabic in origin even in the Middle Ages, does not mention Christ directly by name. Yet, it is felt that it presented a God/man analogy very closely approximating the lapis/Christ parallel. 2 references.

000420 Religious ideas in alchemy: an historical survey of alchemical ideas. 5. The lapis-Christ parallel. II. Evidence for the religious interpretation of the lapis. c. Zosimos and the doctrine of the Anthropos. In: Jung, C., Collected Works of C. G. Jung, Vol. 12. 2nd ed., Princeton University Press, 1968. 571 p. (p. 360-372).

Gnostic texts ascribed to Zosimos are quoted at length as evidence for the lapis/Christ parallel. Although the "Christ" of this text is a Gnostic son of God, the parallel seems to be evident. For instance, the son of God, (a term used by the alchemists to signify sublimation) in both Zosimus' text and alchemic literature is identical with Adam who is a quaternity compounded of four different earths. He is the Anthropos, the first man, symbolized by the four elements, as is the lapis. Similar analogies are found in the myths of Osiris, Herakles and Enoch. Prometheus and Epimetheus, like Christ and Adam, correspond to the inner and outer man while the ability to become all, attributed by the Gnostics to the son of God, is reflected in the alchemical Mercurius. These numerous parallels indicate that the lapis/Christ motif of alchemy had its roots in Gnosticism, even to the point where the alchemic meaning of the opus can be compared with the Gnostic mystery of redemption. 7 references.

000421 Religious ideas in alchemy: an historical survey of alchemical ideas. 5. The lapis-Christ parallel. II. Evidence for the religious interpretation of the lapis. d. Petrus Bonus. In:

Jung, C., Collected Works of C. G. Jung, Vol. 12. 2nd ed., Princeton University Press, 1968. 571 p. (p. 373-375).

An extract from the text "Pretiosa margarita novella," written by Petrus Bonus of Ferrara between 1330 and 1339, is presented as the oldest source of the explicit identity of Christ with the lapis. It is noted that the parallel of the mystery of Christ and the mystery of the lapis is so clear that the alchemical opus might be seen as a continuation of the divine work of redemption. 1 reference.

000422 Religious ideas in alchemy: an historical survey of alchemical ideas. 5. The lapis-Christ parallel. II. Evidence for the religious interpretation of the lapis. e. Aurora consurgens and the doctrine of Sapientia. In: Jung, C., Collected Works of C. G. Jung, Vol. 12. 2nd ed., Princeton University Press, 1968. 571 p. (p. 376-396).

The "Aurora consurgens," a manuscript tentatively dated in the first half of the 14th century, is presented as evidence for the lapis/Christ parallel. The author of this text was apparently a cleric whose idiom was full of biblical quotations and who also was quite familiar with alchemic philosophy. This manuscript is analyzed at length because of its subject matter and language: it combines Christian and alchemic language, and it illustrates the lapis/Christ parallel. 20 references.

000423 Religious ideas in alchemy: an historical survey of alchemical ideas. 5. The lapis-Christ parallel. II. Evidence for the religious interpretation of the lapis. f. Melchior Cibinensis and the doctrine of the alchemical paraphrase of the Mass. In: Jung, C., Collected Works of C. G. Jung, Vol. 12. 2nd ed., Princeton University Press, 1968. 571 p. (p. 396-406).

A document written at the beginning of the 16th century by Nicholas Melchoir of Hermannstadt is cited as a source for the lapis/Christ identity. This document, part of which is reproduced, is an exposition of the alchemic process in the form of a Mass. Special note is taken of the implied identity of the Virgin Mary with the arcanum of the alchemical art. It is evident that Melchoir felt the alchemical process to be the equivalent of the transubstantiation in the Mass, and that he had the need to express his experience precisely in that form. Though Christ is not mentioned as the lapis, the identity of the two seems apparent in the whole drift of the text. 2 references.

000424 Religious ideas in alchemy: an historical survey of alchemical ideas. 5. The lapis-Christ parallel. II. Evidence for the religious interpretation of the lapis. g. Sir George Ripley. In: Jung, C., Collected Works of C. G. Jung, Vol. 12. 2nd ed., Princeton University Press, 1968. 571 p. (p. 406-422).

Two of Sir George Ripley's (1415-1490) works, the "Liber duodecim portarum" and the "Cantilena Riplaei" are cited as evidenc for the lapis/Christ parallel. Special emphasis is given the "Cantilena," a recounting of a legend involving the themes of the king, the king's son, the hero, and the virgin mother, all of which have parallels with certain ideas of Christian dogma. The discussion of the Cantilena is expanded in order to uncover the allusions to the unconscious, the conflict of opposites, mother incest, dissolution of the domineering conscious mind and the rebirth through a kind of resurrection. 5 references.

000425 Religious ideas in alchemy: an historical survey of alchemical ideas. 5. The lapis-Christ parallel. II. Evidence for the religious interpretation of the lapis. h. The Epigoni. In: Jung, C., Collected Works of C. G. Jung, Vol. 12. 2nd ed., Princeton University Press, 1968. 571 p. (p. 423-431).

The "Epigoni" refers to a group of 17th century alchemists who wrote during the full flowering of the alchemic tradition as well as the beginnings of its downfall. It was in this century that the physical aspects of alchemy began to split from its more philosophical and mystical elements. Examples of the lapis/Christ parallel from this literature are presented. It is noted that in addition to providing evidence for this parallel, the Epigoni make clear that the real aim of alchemy was to produce a corpus subtile, a transfigured and resurrected body; a body that was at the same time spirit. This is compared with Chinese alchemy with its main concern for the "diamond body"; that is, the attainment of immortality through the transformation of the body. The rise of secret societies in the 17th century, e.g. the Rosicrucians, is mentioned as evidence of the decline of alchemy. Such societies are seen as no more than guardians of "a secret that has lost its vitality and can only be kept alive as an outward form." 7 references.

000426 Religious ideas in alchemy: an historical survey of alchemical ideas. 6. Alchemical symbolism in the history of religion. I. The unconscious as the matrix of symbols. In: Jung, C., Collected Works of C. G. Jung, Vol. 12. 2nd ed., Princeton University Press, 1968. 571 p. (p. 432-434).

The symbolism that remained prevalent even after the scientific break between alchemy and chemistry is seen as an indication that such symbolism is an expression of an essential part of the psyche. It is seen as fitting that the relationships of this symbolism to the psyche was unknown, for the paradoxical statements made in the literature of alchemy on the prima materia are intuitions about the paradoxical nature of the unconscious. It follows then, that "the only place where intuitions of this kind could be lodged was in the unknown aspect of things, be it matter or man." Alchemic literature often indicated that the secret, the prima materia, might be found in some strange creature or in part of man's brain. It was thought of as an ever changing substance or as the essence of such a substance. This substance was designated "Mercurius" and was thought to be a paradoxical double substance known variously as monstrum, hermaphroditus, or rebis. The lapis/Christ parallel can be seen as establishing an analogy between this substance and Christ. 2 references.

000427 Religious ideas in alchemy: an historical survey of alchemical ideas. 6. Alchemical symbolism in the history of religion. II. The paradigm of the unicorn. a. The unicorn in alchemy. In: Jung, C., Collected Works of C. G. Jung, Vol. 12. 2nd ed., Princeton University Press, 1968. 571 p. (p. 435-438).

The example of the unicorn is chosen to illustrate how the symbolism of Mercurius is intermingled with the traditions of pagan Gnosticism and of the Christian Church. As the unicorn is not a single, clearly defined entity, more specific concern is centered on the theme of the beast with a single horn (the alicorn). Examples are given from the literature (esp. the Chymical Wedding of Rosencreutz) in which the unicorn, the lion and the white dove appear, all of these beasts being symbols of Mercurius. Reference is also made to medieval art in which images of the unicorn and the virgin appear. These images are said to represent the dual aspect of Mercurius: the virgin as the passive, feminine aspect and the unicorn (or the lion) the wild, rampant, masculine force. Because the symbol of the unicorn as an allegory of Christ and the Holy Ghost was also current in the Middle Ages, it is felt that alchemical literature of this period, in using this symbol, establishes the Mercurius/Christ identification. 5 references.

000428 Religious ideas in alchemy: an historical survey of alchemical ideas. 6. Alchemical symbolism in the history of religion. II. The paradigm of the unicorn. b. The unicorn in ecclesiastical allegory. In: Jung, C., Collected Works of C. G. Jung, Vol. 12. 2nd ed., Princeton University Press, 1968. 571 p. (p. 439-447).

The appearance of unicorn symbolism in ecclesiastical allegory is examined. The basis for unicorn allegories in the Church is in the Psalms, where the horn of the unicorn signifies the health, strength, and happiness of the blessed. References from writings of Church Fathers are noted in which the unicorn is variously identified with the God of the Old Testament and with Christ. It is pointed out that there are ecclesiastical quotations in which the unicorn is said to contain the element of evil. It is this inner contradiction that makes the unicorn an appropriate symbol to be used by the alchemists' monstrum hermaphroditum. In these examples the close connection between alchemical symbolism and ecclesiastical language becomes evident. 13 references.

000429 Religious ideas in alchemy: an historical survey of alchemical ideas. 6. Alchemical symbolism in the history of religion. II. The paradigm of the unicorn. c. The unicorn in Gnosticism. In: Jung, C., Collected Works of C. G. Jung, Vol. 12. 2nd ed., Princeton University Press, 1968. 571 p. (p. 449-452).

Parallels between the language of the Church and pagan Gnostic symbolism and Mercurius are examined. The serpent in Gnostic Literature is described as a "moist element" without which nothing, animate or inanimate, can exist. This description corresponds to the alchemical description of Mercurius in several ways. The serpent is also compared with the alicorn in terms of its being able to transform and perfect unripe or imperfect bodies, i.e. the alchemical salvator and servator. 1 reference.

000430 Religious ideas in alchemy: an historical survey of alchemical ideas. 6. Alchemical symbolism in the history of religion. II. The paradigm of the unicorn. d. The one-horned scarabaeus. In: Jung, C., Collected Works of C. G. Jung, Vol. 12. 2nd ed., Princeton University Press, 1968. 571 p. (p. 452-453).

The "Hieroglyphica" of Horapollo is cited as an important source of information concerning the unicorn symbolism of Mercurius. According to this work there exists a genus of scarab which is unicorned and thus sacred to Mercurius. In addition to being one horned this scarab is described as being "born of itself." In Paracelsus, the prima materia is also depicted as "uncreated" and is directly linked with Mercurius. A further parallel found in the Hieroglyphica is the dismemberment of the scarab. Such a dismemberment was undergone by the dragon, a common symbol of Mercurius, in what is referred to in Egyptian alchemic literature as the "separation of the elements." 5 references.

000431 Religious ideas in Alchemy: an historical survey of alchemical ideas. 6. Alchemical symbolism in the history of religion. II. The paradigm of the unicorn. e. The unicorn in the Vedas. In: Jung, C., Collected Works of C. G. Jung, Vol. 12. 2nd ed., Princeton University Press, 1968. 571 p. (p. 453-456).

The symbolism of the unicorn in pre-Christian Indian religious tradition is examined. Particular attention is given to the legend of Manu as recounted in "Shatapatha-Brahmana." According to legend, Manu hooked a one horned fish that grew larger and larger. Eventually this fish saved Manu from a flood by allowing him to tie his ship to its horn. The fish is an incarnation of Vishnu and Manu means "man." The parallels between Manu and the Greek Anthropos are noted: he is a God man, father of humanity, and is descended directly from God, i.e. Brahma. Manu is also considered the father of medicine, and in Buddhist tradition, "Lord of the Golden Age." The virgin and the unicorn motif are also present in Indian literature. 8 references.

000432 Religious ideas in alchemy: an historical survey of alchemical ideas. 6. Alchemical symbolism in the history of religion. II. The paradigm of the unicorn. f. The unicorn in Persia. In: Jung, C., Collected Works of C. G. Jung, Vol. 12. 2nd ed., Princeton University Press, 1968. 571 p. (p. 456-460).

An account of the unicorn in Persian tradition, taken from the Bundahish (Ch. XIX), is presented. In it, the Persian monster described is a cosmological being whose nature is based on the number three; it is compared to the personifications of the prima materia in Arabic alchemy. References to the ass and the tree, also found in Arabic alchemy, are noted. The tree's peculiar power to change into any animal shape is also attributed to Mercurius versipellis. 4 references.

000433 Religious ideas in alchemy: an historical survey of alchemical ideas. 6. Alchemical symbolism in the history of religion. II. The paradigm of the unicorn. g. The unicorn in Jewish tradition. In: Jung, C., Collected Works of C. G. Jung, Vol. 12. 2nd ed., Princeton University Press, 1968. 571 p. (p. 460-465).

References to unicorns in the Talmud and in Jewish legend are presented, and the similarity between the descriptions of the gigantic unicorn (re'em) and of Og, the King of Bashan are noted. Special attention is paid to Jewish literature in which the unicorn and the lion appear together. These beasts are both symbols of Mercurius in alchemy as well as being allegorical Christ figures in the Church. The lion and unicorn are seen as standing for the inner tensions in Mercurius and, by extension, the tensions between the Christian's interpretation of God as all good and his experience of the demonic forces of nature. 7 references.

000434 Religious ideas in alchemy: an historical survey of alchemical ideas. 6. Alchemical symbolism in the history of religion. II. The paradigm of the unicorn. h. The unicorn in China. In: Jung, C., Collected Works of C. G. Jung, Vol. 12. 2nd ed., Princeton University Press, 1968. 571 p. (p. 465-466).

The appearance of the unicorn in Chinese Literature is noted and related to alchemic symbols. According to the "Li Chi," or Book of Rites, the four spiritual animals are the unicorn, the phoenix, the tortoise, and the dragon. The unicorn is considered to be the chief among these beasts, and is reported to appear in conjunction with perfect rulers or kings. According to legend a unicorn appeared to the mother of Confucius during her pregnancy; and the death of this philosopher was said to have been presaged by the wounding of a unicorn. The androgynous quality of the unicorn as well as its inclusion with the phoenix and the dragon, is noted as being parallel with the alchemists' view of Mercurius, especially since the dragon represents Mercurius in his lowest form and the phoenix in his highest form. The use of the horn of the rhinoceros (an alicorn) as an alexipharmic is briefly discussed. 2 references.

000435 Religious ideas in alchemy: 6. Alchemical symbolism in the history of religion. II. The paradigm of the unicorn. i. The unicorn cup. In: Jung, C., Collected Works of C. G. Jung, Vol. 12. 2nd ed., Princeton University Press, 1968. 571 p. (p. 466-471).

References to the cup made from the horn of the unicorn in Greek, Chinese, and Christian traditions are presented. It is noted that the unicorn cup is related in some way to both the Eucharistic Chalice and the vessel used in divination. The secret of the cup is also the secret of the unicorn horn and stands for the essence of the unicorn as bringer of health, strength, and life. The dual nature of the horn is analyzed. As a symbol of vigor and strength it has a masculine character; as a cup it is also a feminine symbol. Thus the cup becomes a "uniting symbol" expressing the bipolarity of the archetype. 5 references.

000436 Epilogue. (Psychology and alchemy). In: Jung, C., Collected Works of C. G. Jung, Vol. 12. 2nd ed., Princeton University Press, 1968. 571 p. (p. 473-483).

The relationship between the mysteries of alchemy and the psychology of the unconscious are discussed. The latter is considered to be the only source for understanding the meaning of the alchemic lapis. In attempting to understand the psychology of alchemical thought it is necessary to begin from the standpoint of the psyche. The contents of the chemical research of the alchemists were a projection of empirical, collective archetypes. The alchemic need for a "redeeming substance" reflected the psychological necessity of uniting the opposites. This alchemic need is contrasted with the Christian view of the Redeemer: the former sought its solution in the individual or the personality; the latter in the collective or society. Goethe's Faust and Nietzsche's Zarathustra are given as examples of what happens when identification with the thing to be transformed takes place. The result was an inflation of ego consciousness, a paradoxical regression into unconsciousness that is produced when the ego consciousness takes too many unconscious contents upon itself and loses the power of discrimination. To avoid such a catastrophe (a catastrophe that can take on universal form as is evidenced in the second World War), it is deemed necessary to recognize that there are contents of the unconscious which do not belong to the ego consciousness but to a psychic nonego, a collective unconscious apparent in the archetypes of poets and philosophers. The alchemists' attempts to find a panacea is regarded as a projection of the process of individuation, a process that is still shrouded in mystery, since it is concerned with the centralizing processes in the unconscious that go to form personality. It is considered doubtful that reason alone will be capable of resolving this mystery; only experience can grasp the significance of these processes. The study of dream symbols, with which this volume was concerned, is an example of how this experience looks in reality. It is one way of showing what happens when an earnest inquiry is turned upon the unknown regions of the soul.

13 ALCHEMICAL STUDIES

000437 Commentary on "The secret of the golden flower." In: Jung, C., Collected Works of C. G. Jung, Vol. 13. Princeton University Press, 1967. 444 p. (p. 1-5).

The text of "The secret of the golden flower," a Taoist text and an alchemical treatise, is cited as the major source of the discovery of the connecting link between Gnosis and the collective unconscious, a link that had been impossible to establish due to the absence of a history of psychic experience. Certain misunderstandings concerning the use of this text are corrected: it is neither a recipe for happiness nor is the commentary on it a description of Jungian psychotherapeutic method. Instead, it is stressed that the idea of the collective unconscious is an empirical concept to be put alongside the concept of libido.

000438 Commentary on "The secret of the golden flower." 1. **Difficulties encountered by a European in trying to understand the East.** In: Jung, C., Collected Works of C. G. Jung, Vol. 13. Princeton University Press, 1967. 444 p. (p. 6-10).

Eastern and Western approaches to the understanding of life are compared and contrasted. Without disparaging the Western reliance on science and its necessary dependence on intellect, it is acknowledged that Eastern knowledge has been grounded in the awareness of psychic processes and the experiences of life for thousands of years. In order for the West to advance to a higher state of life, it is necessary to balance intellect and psychic knowledge, hence the turning toward the East in search of a way in which to achieve this balance. Western man is cautioned not to mistake imitation for true understanding and growth. It will be only in combining the insights gained from the East with the highly developed intellectual function of the Western psyche that the full understanding of the human psyche will be achieved.

000439 Commentary on "The secret of the golden flower." 2. **Modern psychology offers a possibility of understanding.** In: Jung, C., Collected Works of C. G. Jung, Vol. 13. Princeton University Press, 1967. 444 p. (p. 11-19).

Clinical observations of patients opened a new approach to the concepts of Chinese philosophy, which is explained in terms of the theory of the collective unconscious, a common substratum in the human psyche transcending all differences in culture and consciousness. The contents of the collective unconscious are expressed in archetypes that come into the consciousness in the form of symbols. The dependence of conscious ideation and action on these common instincts is explored and attention is given to the neuroses that appear whenever the unconscious has been repressed to the point where it is completely out of touch with the primordial images. The unconscious appears to be in full revolt against the consciousness and the unity of the personality seems to have disappeared. It is at this point that one is encouraged to turn to the Chinese philosophy for a way to resolve the conflict. Certain insights concerning this conflict gained from clinical observation are discussed and three observations are made: 1) that patients do not solve the problem but outgrow it, i.e.,arrive at a new level of consciousness; 2) that a new potential was discovered stemming either from an outer happening or inner experience; 3) that this new potential was uncovered only by letting things happen, i.e.,allowing the fantasy function free reign so that the conscious mind can develop a new attitude towards the activity of the unconscious. Western man is again cautioned to avoid denying his own heritage in favor of the Eastern solution or turning back to the medievalism of the Christian Church; the search is directed to discovering one's inner integrity.

000440 Commentary on "The secret of the golden flower." 3. **The fundamental concepts. a. Tao. b. The circular movement and the center.** In: Jung, C., Collected Works of C. G. Jung, Vol. 13. Princeton University Press, 1967. 444 p. (p. 20-28).

The psychological meanings of the concept of Tao and the mandala symbols are discussed. Tao is explained as a conscious way of uniting opposites, a reunion of life and consciousness that can only be accomplished by realization of the unconscious law of being. This union of opposites is neither rational nor relational, but a process of psychic development. Mandala symbols, produced by fantasies, are examined, and the frequent recurrence of the symbol of the circle is documented by reference to medieval Christian, Buddhist, American Indian and Eastern mandalas, such as the cross, flower and wheel. The golden flower, the Taoist mandala that expresses the secret of the Tao, is analyzed as a symbol of the beginning of life where everything is as one. In studying the mandala as it appears in the drawings of patients it is noted that the very expression of the symbol also produces a unifying effect, bringing the patient back to the inner unconsciousness that is the source and goal of the psyche. The circular characteristic of the mandala is examined and the texts from the writings of Chivard Maitland and Hildegard of Bingen are cited as examples illustrating this characteristic. It is concluded that symbols are the key to the unconscious and hence that the individuation process can never be obtained without the symbol. 6 references.

000441 Commentary on "The secret of the golden flower." 4. **Phenomena of the way. a. The disintegration of consciousness.** In: Jung, C., Collected Works of C. G. Jung, Vol. 13. Princeton University Press, 1967. 444 p. (p. 29-38).

The dangers inherent in the meeting between the conscious and the collective unconscious are due to the autonomous psychic contents of the latter. It was the recognition of this danger that produced the symbolic figure of the protecting circle. At the outset these fragmentary systems are seen as affects; as they grow more complicated they assume the character of personalities and are encountered as such in cases of psychologic splitting of the personality, in mediumistic phenomena and in the phenomenology of religion. Thus it can be said that the activated unconscious psychic contents first appear as projections but are gradually assimilated into consciousness reshaped into conscious ideas. The denial of the existence of the unconscious is seen as particularly dangerous not only to this individual in whom this denial leads to neurosis, but also to nations where the collective delusions take the form of destructive mass psychoses. Insanity is defined as possession by an unconscious content that cannot be assimilated into consciousness since the very existence of the former is denied. Western man is counseled to acknowledge the existence of these dissociative tendencies and to consciously detach himself from their power in order to free himself from subservience to them. 1 reference.

000442 Commentary on "The secret of the golden flower." 4. **Phenomena of the way. b. Animus and anima.** In: Jung, C., Collected Works of C. G. Jung, Vol. 13. Princeton University Press, 1967. 444 p. (p. 38-43).

The figures of animus and anima as they appear in the Secret of the Golden Flower are analyzed and compared to the present concepts of these terms. Animus (hun) is the masculine principle, (yang) a higher breath soul that rises, after death, to the position of spirit or god (shen). Anima (p'o) is a feminine principle (yin) that descends to the earth after death and becomes a demon (kuei). The Chinese philosphy recognized these two principles as distinguishable psychic factors united in the one human nature. The psychologist recognizes the anima as an autonomous unconscious principle identifiable with the affective side of the masculine psyche and the archetype of all the experiences of man with woman. The term Logos is preferred to that of animus in defining the clarity of consciousness and rationality of the masculine psyche since these characteristics are universal, not personal, and are in sharp contrast to the personal anima. In discussing the psychology of women, the term animus is retained to indicate the quasi-intellectual factor in the feminine psyche, consisting of inferior judgments or opinions. Animus is seen as an inferior Logos just as anima in masculine psychology is best described as an inferior Eros. The characteristics of Logos are defined as differentiation, clarification, discrimination and detachment; those of Eros as interweaving and relatedness. Anima is further defined as a personification of the unconscious in general, a bridge between the conscious and the unconscious. Eastern and Western views of the source of consciousness are contrasted: the former sees consciousness as an effect of anima whereas the latter sees the unconscious as a derivative of consciousness. Fantasies and their place in Eastern and Western thought are also examined; both reject fantasies: the former because they have already extracted their essence and condensed it in their teaching; the latter because they have not even allowed themselves to experience these fantasies. 3 references.

000443 Commentary on "The secret of the golden flower." 5. The detachment of consciousness from the object. In: Jung, C., Collected Works of C. G. Jung, Vol. 13. Princeton University Press, 1967. 444 p. (p. 44-48).

The process of differentiating conscious and unconscious, subject and object, unconscious and world is reviewed. The primitive mentality is characterized by nondifferentiation between subject and object, referred to by Levy-Bruhl as participation mystique. Civilized man retains his own form of nondifferentiation as is evident in an extended identification with parents, affects or prejudices. The resolution of this state of nondifferentiation is seen to require a recognition that both the unconscious and the conscious are determining factors in one's psyche and that the demands of both must be taken into account. The center of gravity of the total personality is then no longer the ego but the self, a hypothetical point between, conscious and unconscious. The arrival at this state of consciousness detached from the world is viewed as originating in middle life and intending to offer a natural preparation for death, seen as the goal of life in the psychological perspective.

000444 Commentary on "The secret of the golden flower." 6. The fulfilment. In: Jung, C., Collected Works of C. G. Jung, Vol. 13. Princeton University Press, 1967. 444 p. (p. 49-54).

The relationship of psychology to metaphysics and religion is discussed. Eastern philosophers are described as symbolical psychologists; metaphysics is criticized for ignoring the validity of the psyche. The West neither can nor should deny its religious history in its search for enlightenment: there is a vast difference in religious experience between Eastern lack of personification and inwardness and the Western emphasis on the human incarnation of Christ. It is suggested, however, that the Eastern belief that redemption depends on self-realization be applied to the imitation of Christ; rather than aping Christ's actions, one should emulate the courage and self-sacrifice with which Christ arrived at his own self-realization. This goal, this evaluation of a higher consciousness, is seen to involve a recognition of instincts and the unconscious. 1 reference.

000445 Commentary on "The secret of the golden flower." 7. Conclusion. In: Jung, C., Collected Works of C. G. Jung, Vol. 13. Princeton University Press, 1967. 444 p. (p. 55-56).

The basic agreement of psychic states and religious symbolism of the East and West is emphasized here. It is through these analogies that the East can be understood without a denial of the Western history and heritage. In exploring the analogies between East and West, conciousness will be broadened and a development in our own psyche will occur. This brief conclusion is followed by illustrations of the European mandalas.

000446 The visions of Zosimos. I. The texts. In: Jung, C., Collected Works of C. G. Jung, Vol. 13. Princeton University Press, 1967. 444 p. (p. 57-65).

The strange dreams recorded by the Gnostic alchemist Zosimos are interpreted by the dreamer as clues to the alchemical art, the composition of liquids and the art of metals. The images of men being boiled in water, dismembered or consumed by flames are interpreted to refer to the casting off of the body in order to be transformed into spirit. A philosophical interpretation of the dreams is also cited, indicating that the purpose of this vision is to provide the key to the investigation of the arts, wisdom, reason and understanding of alchemy. 1 reference.

000447 The visions of Zosimos. II. Commentary. 1. General remarks on the interpretation. In: Jung, C., Collected Works of C. G. Jung, Vol. 13. Princeton University Press, 1967. 444 p. (p. 66-69).

Zosimos' visions are interpreted as the recording of a single highly significant experience or dream that may have occurred during the work and revealed the nature of the psychic processes in the background. All the psychic contents that the alchemists projected into the chemical process are present in the vision, especially the emphasis on the miraculous water (aqua divina) which was extracted from the lapis through the torment of fire. The importance given to these dreams and alchemical texts is explained by recalling that the symbolism of alchemy has a great deal to do with the structure of the unconscious and the biological compensation produced by dreams.

000448 The visions of Zosimos. II. Commentary. 2. The sacrifical act. In: Jung, C., Collected Works of C. G. Jung, Vol. 13. Princeton University Press, 1967. 444 p. (p. 70-90).

The numerous symbols, in Zosimos' dream, many of which are details of archetypes, are examined and compared with similar symbols in Christian literature as well as in other alchemical texts. The image of the sacrificer who is also the sacrificed relates to the concept of Christ sacrificing himself and to the image of the dragon biting his own tail. It is a continuous circle of creation and destruction. The head is a symbolical circle housing the soul. It was thought that by scalping or skinning the head the soul could be released from the body. The circle consists of two parts: outwardly it is water; inwardly it is the arcanum. The head is the symbolic essence of consciousness which must be sacrificed for greater consciousness. The images of the hermetic vessel and of the divine water are also explained: the bowl shaped altar represents a wonder working vessel in which immersion takes place and transformation into a spiritual being is effected, a symbol of renewal or rebirth; the water, commonly associated with spirit or soul, is capable of transforming matter. Zosimos' image of the temple built of a single stone is an obvious illusion to the lapis, the wholeness to be achieved by integrating the contents of the unconscious into consciousness with its corresponding enlightening effect -- an increase in consciousness. It is concluded that the alchemists chose the symbolism of metals to express the concept of the inner man and his spiritual growth. 56 references.

000449 The visions of Zosimos. II. Commentary. 3. The personifications. In: Jung, C., Collected Works of C. G. Jung, Vol. 13. Princeton University Press, 1967. 444 p. (p. 90-94).

The portion of the Zosimos' text called the introduction is examined as an example of a conscious allegory expressed in alchemical language. The abstracted spirits of the metals are pictured as suffering human beings, a remnant of the primitive and archaic psychology that personified lifeless things because of an unconscious identity with them. This identification is the result of projection, a process that allows the contents of the unconscious to become accessible to consciousness by representing them as qualities apparently belonging to the object. The difference between primitive and modern psychology is said to be qualitative as well as one of degree: whereas civilized man develops consciousness by the acquisition of knowledge and withdrawal of projections recognized as psychic contents to be integrated into the psyche, the alchemists personified all of their important ideas. Thus man is represented as a microcosm representing the earth and the universe and as a macrocosm of the whole of nature. 8 references.

000450 The visions of Zosimos. II. Commentary. 4. The stone symbolism. In: Jung, C., Collected Works of C. G. Jung, Vol. 13. Princeton University Press, 1967. 444 p. (p. 94-101).

The significance of the symbol of the stone and its attributes is explored. The alchemical lapis is seen as a complementary image of the Christ figure, a symbol of the inner Christ, of God in man. An overview of the stone symbol as it appeared in primitive societies is given. It was as an image of the birthplace of the gods, a container of children's souls, a source of fertility and healing. In a myth originating among the Navaho Indians, the stone took the form of a matriarchal goddess, an anima figure representing the self, particularly the self of a man living in a matriarchal society who is still immersed in his unconscious femininity as can be seen even today in cases of masculine mother complexes. The connection with immortality is also shown to be very ancient. The stone is a panacea, an alexipharmic, a cure for melancholy, a symbol of the Savior and of the Anthropos. 11 references.

000451 The visions of Zosimos. II. Commentary. 5. The water symbolism. In: Jung, C., Collected Works of C. G. Jung, Vol. 13. Princeton University Press, 1967. 444 p. (p. 101-104).

The correlation between historical or ethnological symbols and those spontaneously produced by the unconscious is evident in the lapis as symbol of the self. The principle personified in the visions of Zosimos, the divine water, is analyzed as a representation of the death, rebirth cycle. The dialogue between Christ and Nicodemus is referred to as a possible parallel with Zosimos' vision. It is concluded that the alchemist's symbol of divine water is a reference to the deus absconditus, the god hidden in matter. 2 references.

000452 The visions of Zosimos. II. Commentary. 6. The origin of the vision. In: Jung, C., Collected Works of C. G. Jung, Vol. 13. Princeton University Press, 1967. 444 p. (p. 105-108).

Zosimos' dream and its predominant symbol of the divine water is seen as reflecting both an alchemical preoccupation and a psychological drama. In the image of the divine water one finds the expression of the alchemical goal; in the punishment, torment, death and transfiguration motif, one discovers how the process of change is manifested to human understanding. It is in the mystical side of alchemy that parallels can be drawn to the psychological problem of individuation. In the projections of the alchemists is seen a medieval method for allowing the inner factors to come to consciousness. Alchemy is described as a philosophy that provides a valuable source for a psychological understanding of psychic experience. 1 reference.

000453 Paracelsus as a spiritual phenomenon. 1. The two sources of knowledge: the light of nature and the light of revelation. In: Jung, C., Collected Works of C. G. Jung, Vol. 13. Princeton University Press, 1967. 444 p. (p. 109-116).

The contributions of Paracelsus to medicine and philosophical alchemy are noted and source of his knowledge examined. The goal of Paracelsus' life was helping and healing; its driving force was compassion. The source of this motivating dynamism is considered to have derived from two feminine figures: his mother and Mother Nature. In addition, he remained faithful to Mother Church despite the criticisms he levelled against her during the Protestant Reformation. Paracelsus himself expressed the conflict he experienced between Nature and Church: one, the source of natural knowledge; the other, of divine. Because of his fidelity to the light of nature, he judged his writings to be pagan. He is praised for his recognition of the authenticity of one's own experience of nature, and credited with liberating science from the authority of tradition. His writings are seen to reflect the knowledge of the dual nature of man, a duality derived from the unity of God. 11 references.

000454 Paracelsus as a spiritual phenomenon. 1. The two sources of knowledge: the light of nature and the light of revelation. a. Magic. In: Jung, C., Collected Works of C. G. Jung, Vol. 13. Princeton University Press, 1967. 444 p. (p. 116-122).

A second duality in the life of Paracelsus, his fidelity to the Church yet his wholehearted devotion to magic, is discussed. In many ways, his words can be seen not only as a reflection of the times in which he wrote, but also as an expression of a great tension of inner opposites: that of the man who serves God and he who commands God. The former side of his nature was revealed in his spirituality; the latter, in his use of manticism, magic, amulets, spells and talismans. Although Paracelsus believed that he was at one with himself, the analysis of his writings, both in their style and their vocabulary, is seen to reveal the unconscious conflict that made him war against his opponents, unaware that the enemy was within. 2 references.

000455 Paracelsus as a spiritual phenomenon. 1. The two sources of knowledge: the light of nature and the light of revelation. b. Alchemy. In: Jung, C., Collected Works of C. G. Jung, Vol. 13. Princeton University Press, 1967. 444 p. (p. 122-124).

Paracelsus' use of alchemy for the purpose of curing the sick is discussed, and a brief review of the major tenets of this secret doctrine is provided. It is obvious from the writings of Paracelsus that he understood the Hermetic literature without being aware of the true nature of alchemy. For him, alchemy consisted of a knowledge of the materia medica and a chemical procedure for preparing medicine as well as a belief in the possibility of making gold and engendering the homunculi. It is concluded that Paracelsus was not only familiar with the teachings but was convinced of their rightness as well. 5 references.

000456 Paracelsus as a spiritual phenomenon. 1. The two sources of knowledge: the light of nature and the light of revelation. c. The arcane teaching. In: Jung, C., Collected Works of C. G. Jung, Vol. 13. Princeton University Press, 1967. 444 p. (p. 124-129).

The study of Paracelsus' writings is seen to reveal many similarities with alchemical concepts. Greek terms in his writings, composed etymologically of the terms for star and matter, allude to the spirit of life in classical alchemy; others are embellishments of the alchemical flores. His philosophical concepts, such as his doctrine of the astrum, again lead back to established alchemical and astrological traditions. It was his belief in the light of nature that links him most closely with the aim of alchemy: to beget this light in the shape of the filius philosophorum. This idea of light coincides with the concept of Sapientia or Scientia. Although Paracelsus is judged to have been unaware of the ultimate insidiousness of this doctrine in which man takes the place of God and the forces of nature serve man as never before; nevertheless, the influence of this doctrine is seen to be evident in his pride and arrogance, a result of his feelings of inferiority springing from his unconscious guilt. 8 references.

000457 Paracelsus as a spiritual phenomenon. 1. The two sources of knowledge: the light of nature and the light of revelation. d. The primordial man. In: Jung, C., Collected Works of C. G. Jung, Vol. 13. Princeton University press, 1967. 444 p. (p. 129-132).

Paracelsus' idea of primordial man, that he was the son of God manifested in the form of man, and made up of four elements, is discussed. Paraculsus, the Theophrastus school, and alchemy in general were criticized and accused of Arianism by Conrad Gessner. Although this accusation was unwarranted, other texts of Paracelsus are shown to reveal the use of the Cabala and his belief in the alchemical primordial man, the one through whom the God or the word creating principle was made manifest. Several other names of the primordial man are given and it is concluded that for Paracelsus, as for the Gnostics, this concept was also connected with that of creation and redemption. 9 references.

000458 Paracelsus as a spiritual phenomenon. 2. "De vita longa": an exposition of the secret doctrine. a. The Iliaster. In: Jung, C., Collected Works of C. G. Jung, Vol. 13. Princeton University Press, 1967. 444 p. (p. 133-137).

The conditions for Paracelsus' ideas on longevity which, he maintained, last up to one thousand years, are presented. Life is defined by Paracelsus as nothing more than a certain embalsamed Mumia, preserving the body by means of a mixed saline solution. Incorruptibility was attributed to a special balsam or elixir that keeps the body alive or, if dead, incorruptible. Several arcane remedies were also included in Parascelsus' work on longevity, with special healing powers attached to certain gems. The life principle or balsam corresponded to the balsam or the concept of Iliaster; i.e.,that which was considered to be higher than the four elements and determines the length of life. The Iliaster was thought to have three forms subordinate to man and sorted by means of a chymical wedding. Since there were supposed to be as many Iliastri as there were men, it seems to be a kind of universal formative principle and principle of individuation. 2 references.

000459 Paracelsus as a spiritual phenomenon. 2. "De vita longa": an exposition of the secret doctrine. b. The Aquaster. In: Jung, C., Collected Works of C. G. Jung, Vol. 13. Princeton University Press, 1967. 444 p. (p. 137-140).

The Iliaster and the Aquaster are compared, and the latter is described as a spiritual principle whose characteristics correspond to the alchemical concept of the water in prima materia. Christ is said to have taken his body from the celestial Aquaster; Mary, from the iliastric Aquaster. The Aquaster is interpreted as a psychic principle, closely related to the modern concept of the unconscious. In Paracelsus' writings, it was personified as the homunculus. Both Iliaster and Aquaster were believed to extend upwards and downwards, assuming a spiritual form as well as a quasi-material one; in this respect they are seen to resemble the alchemical prima materia. 15 references.

000460 Paracelsus as a spiritual phenomenon. 2. "De vita longa": an exposition of the secret doctrine. c. Ares. In: Jung, C., Collected Works of C. G. Jung, Vol. 13. Princeton University Press, 1967. 444 p. (p. 140-142).

The alchemical concept Ares is discussed and compared to the Paracelsan Aquaster. In the alchemic view, Ares is presented as the determiner of individual form and species, hence, an intuitive concept for a preconscious, creative and formative principle to individual creatures. Paracelsus endowed Ares with a watery character, bringing it into relationship to the body. The Paracelsan concept of Ares is seen to be scarcely distinguishable from that of Aquaster, a situation not uncommon in alchemy where concepts are seen to take the place of one another ad infinitum. 3 references.

000461 Paracelsus as a spiritual phenomenon. 2. "De vita longa": an exposition of the secret doctrine. d. Melusina. In: Jung, C., Collected Works of C. G. Jung, Vol. 13. Princeton University Press, 1967. 444 p. (p. 142-144).

The nature, characteristics and psychological significance of Melusina are presented. Melusina is in the same category as the nymphs and sirens who dwell in the "Nymphidida." Melusines, on the other hand, dwell in the blood. These fabulous nymph-like, sexless creatures belonged to the watery realm, were paradisal creatures with no genitals, who after Adam and Eve's Fall went on living in the human blood in their paradisal state. Melurina can be interpreted as a spirit, an anima figure, whose birthplace was the unconscious. 3 references.

000462 Paracelsus as a spiritual phenomenon. 2. "de vita longa": an exposition of the secret doctrine. e. the filius regius as the arcane substance. (Michael Maier). In: Jung, C., Collected Works of C. G. Jung, Vol. 13. Princeton University Press, 1967. 444 p. (p. 145-148).

The concept of filius regius as it appears in several alchemical texts is examined and explained. It is pointed out that the longing of the Paracelsan Melusines for a soul and redemption is similar to the alchemical idea of the kingly substance hidden in the sea. This substance, in Michael Maier's work, was antimony, a secret transformative substance which had fallen into the darkest depths of matters and was awaiting deliverance. Many Biblical passages are cited to show parallels to the idea of an interior being longing for a redemption and deliverance, although the alchemical vision of the king who was capable of redemption was more positive than that of the Church Fathers, who saw the dark depths as evil itself to which the king had been attached by his own sinfulness. 10 references.

000463 Paracelsus as a spiritual phenomenon. 2. "De vita longa": an exposition of the secret doctrine. f. The production of the one, or center, by distillation. In: Jung, C., Collected Works of C. G. Jung, Vol. 13. Princeton University Press, 1967. 444 p. (p. 148-152).

The process of distillation as a means of extracting the spirit from the body is presented in both Paracelsan and alchemical writings and related symbolically to the psychic concept of the self. The distillation, which in some way turned back upon itself after starting from the center, was intended to purify the human body so that it would unite with the inner spiritual man and partake of its longevity. The emphasis on the center is seen to reflect a fundamental alchemical idea akin to the gold, paradise, fire, God. The terms spogyric process, fetus and birth are explained and shown to relate to the creation of the inner, eternal man in the shell of the outer, mortal man, the filius philosophorum. The importance of fire and balsam in maintaining longevity is explored and it is concluded that the distillation process was intended to activate and develop a psychic center, -- in psychological terms, the self. 8 references

000464 Paracelsus as a spiritual phenomenon. 2. "De vita longa": an exposition of the secret doctrine. g. The coniunctio in the spring. In: Jung, C., Collected Works of C. G. Jung, Vol. 13. Princeton University Press, 1967. 444 p. (p. 152-156).

The Paracelsan description of the transformation process is likened to the gathering together of all psychic processes for the transformation. It follows the separation of Saturn from Sol, a separation produced through the drug Melissa. When the separation has been completed and the body purified, the coniunctio can take place within the inner man. From this union comes Enochdianus whose power or virtue is called Iloch or Anindus. In the connection between this process and the spring, the renewal of life is perceived, and several references to other associations with spring are mentioned: the hierospamos of Poliphilo, and the reign of Venus, and the power of the nettles (youthful lust). The Aniada or Anachnus (indistinguishable in Paracelsus' work) are said to be extracted at this time in order to enjoy longevity. Several photographs and drawings are given as illustrations of some alchemical concepts. 3 references.

000465 Paracelsus as a spiritual phenomenon. 3. The natural transformation mystery. a. The light of the darkness. In: Jung, C., Collected Works of C. G. Jung, Vol. 13. Princeton University Press, 1967. 444 p. (p. 157-163).

The importance of Paracelsus' contributions to psychology and the use of symbolic language as a means of expressing these psychic experiences are discussed. Although Paracelsus recognized that he was not completely following the doctrinal order that Christianity had set up, he was naive about the substantial differences implicit in his views. In reality, he can be considered the forerunner of the new religion of nature that was not only chemical and physical but also psychical. As a physician he is credited with recognizing the important role that psychic occurrences play in diseases and in their cures. The goal of Paracelsus and of all the philosophical alchemists is seen as an attempt to grasp the nature of the soul, interwoven with the world and matter, filled with demonical figures and the source of life shortening diseases. Unlike the church with its attempts to exorcise and banish demons, the alchemists sought to unite the conscious with the unconscious. This goal reflects the light of nature with its own transformation of death and rebirth, unifying the opposites rather than denying the validty of one of them. It is considered appropriate that Paracelsus and the alchemists expressed themselves in parables and symbols when describing their work. Since they were probing the depths of the psyche, the use of symbols and mythologems allowed not only a visualization of the psychic experience, but more significantly, a reexperiencing of it. 4 references.

000466 Paracelsus as a spiritual phenomenon. 3. The natural transformation mystery. b. The union of man's two natures. In: Jung, C., Collected Works of C. G. Jung, Vol. 13. Princeton University Press, 1967. 444 p. (p. 163-167).

Man is said to have two life forces: one natural and one aerial, corresponding to the modern terminology physiological and psychic. Longevity is perceived by Paracelsus as the result of having led the aerial life. The explanation given by Paracelsus is clarified by analysis: psychic means the soul is not only prevented from escaping from the body, but also brought back to the center of the heart, where it enjoys freedom from bondage of the body and a certain tranquility; in this state the soul can echo the higher entities: Aniadus, Adech, and Endochinum -- designation for the inner homo maximus, the deathless original man. 7 references.

000467 Paracelsus as a spiritual phenomenon. 3. The natural transformation mystery. c. The quaternity of the homo maximus. In: Jung, C., Collected Works of C. G. Jung, Vol. 13. Princeton University Press, 1967. 444 p. (p. 167-170).

In discussing the Paracelsan concept of the homo maximus, it is concluded that Paracelsus discovered the quaternity symbol in man by introspective intuition rather than by rational conscious thought. The union of four seasons, the four gates of heaven and the four elements are viewed as a quaternity expressing totality. This is viewed as an archetypal arrangement of the four aspects of consciousness: thinking, feeling, sensation and intuition. A comparison is drawn between Ruland's and Dorn's perception of this quaternity and that of Paracelsus. The difficulties and dangers that the alchemists experienced in their attempt to discover the prima materia are explained by analogy to the difficulties encountered whenever an attempt is made to come to terms with the unconscious, the dark or shadow side of man. 1 reference.

000468 Paracelsus as a spiritual phenomenon. 3. The natural transformation mystery. d. The rapprochement with the unconscious. In: Jung, C., Collected Works of C. G. Jung, Vol. 13. Princeton University Press, 1967. 444 p. (p. 170-172).

The alchemical opus of Paracelsus and others is viewed as an attempt to come to terms with the unconscious, to understand the archetypal world of the psyche and, at the same time, to avoid the sanity threatening fascination with the depths, paradoxes and heights of psychic truths. At the point where the conscious mind meets the unconscious, an encounter between mortal ego and immortal self, finite consciousness and its archaic foundations, is felt. The doctrine of the Anthropos, the collective preconscious state from which the individual ego arose, was considered dangerous because it was at variance with the teachings of the Church. 1 reference.

000469 Paracelsus as a spiritual phenomenon. 4. The commentary of Gerard Dorn. a. Melusina and the process of individuation. In: Jung, C., Collected Works of C. G. Jung, Vol. 13. Princeton University Press, 1967. 444 p. (p. 173-180).

Paracelsus' concluding chapter in the Vita longa is presented and followed by a commentary by Dorn in which the obscurities of the former text are explained. Further clarification is provided by an analysis of the functions of consciousness (Scaiolae) and the role of the anima (Melusina). The figure of Melusina, part fish and part human, is shown to have appeared in many legends and myths, one of which is recounted. She appears at the moment of catastrophe, as a vision or dream, to guide the adept out of the darkness of not-knowing. Many qualities attributed to her were also characteristic of the alchemical mercurial serpent, or the Wise Old Man and Mercurius. It is the inner man guided by the conscious functions and in search of the self that gives rise to the fantasy images of Melusina. The adept, however, must apply critical judgment to the visions and acts of Melusina (anima) in order to extract wisdom from the deceptive phantasms she presents. 6 references.

000470 Paracelsus as a spiritual phenomenon. 4. The commentary of Gerard Dorn. b. The hierosgamos of the everlasting man. In: Jung, C., Collected Works of C. G. Jung, Vol. 13. Princeton University Press, 1967. 444 p. (p. 180-183).

The process of reuniting the conscious and unconscious in order to produce the one man is presented as it appears in Paracelsus' writings. Melusina, the anima, must not remain in the projected state but must become integrated into the conscious mind of the adept, thus producing the longed after coniunctio of conscious and unconscious. This union is defined as an experience that cannot be stated in words but that is accompanied by a sense of eternity or timelessness. Allusion is made to the Paracelsan description of the characters of Venus, and a comparison is drawn between the union with the feminine personification of the unconscious and the sacred marriage of the Lamb and the Virgin found in the Apocalypse. The experience of unity is seen to include an awareness of atonement, not only within the self, but also with the multiplicity of all being.

000471 Paracelsus as a spiritual phenomenon. 4. The commentary of Gerard Dorn. c. Spirit and nature. In: Jung, C., Collected Works of C. G. Jung, Vol. 13. Princeton University Press, 1967. 444 p. (p. 183-185).

The reasons for Parcelsus' choice of the pagan images of Venus and Mars to describe the union of the conscious and the unconscious are discussed. Despite the fact that Paracelsus lived in a Christian age, he chose pagan symbols to express his thoughts. It is proposed that in an era that neglected the natural spirit and expressed everything in the light of culture or reason, nature was making her own demands. Paracelsus is credited with having recognized the light of nature and with raising it to a principle, in which the workings of the unconscious can be observed. The importance of attending to the unconscious is stressed: it is an autonomous entity capable of extending beyond consciousness and, with its symbols, anticipates future consciousness; it is capable also of correcting the biases and aberrations of the conscious attitude. 1 reference.

000472 Paracelsus as a spiritual phenomenon. 4. The commentary of Gerard Dorn. d. The ecclesiastical sacrament and the opus alchymicum. In: Jung, C., Collected Works of C. G. Jung, Vol. 13. Princeton University Press, 1967. 444 p. (p. 185-188).

Paracelsus' work is assessed in terms of its relation to Christianity. As an alchemist, his language is seen to be an expression of renewed archetypal experience, resulting from the projections of his own unconscious. Despite the fact that the procedure he was describing was clearly intended to attain immortality, his belief in the light of nature enabled him to express himself in terms of Venus and Amor rather than in the Christian language of the sacraments of the Church. Nevertheless, though an alchemical philosopher, he is judged to be a Christian who saw his art as a means of bringing the divine will implanted in nature to perfection. 4 references.

000473 Paracelsus as a spiritual phenomenon. 5. Epilogue. In: Jung, C., Collected Works of C. G. Jung, Vol. 13. Princeton University Press, 1967. 444 p. (p. 189).

The value of Paracelsus' contributions to modern psychology are assessed. Although the preceding pages have neglected Paracelsus the Christian and physician, they have not denied that, in Paracelsus, the Christian and primitive pagan lived together to form a conflicting whole. Despite the conflict, Paracelsus is seen to have been spared the split between faith

and knowledge that was to afflict later generations. In the person of Paracelsus can be seen the division which would lead to a higher consciousness, a greater synthesis. He is considered, then, the forerunner of the modern psychology of the unconscious.

000474 The spirit Mercurius. Part I: 1. The spirit in the bottle. In: Jung, C., Collected Works of C. G. Jung, Vol. 13. Princeton University Press, 1967. 444 p. (p. 191-198).

Grimm's fairytale, "The Spirit in the Bottle" is analyzed in terms of its psychological content and its relation to the teachings of the alchemists. In the tale, certain spontaneous statements of the unconscious about itself are disclosed: the forest is the synonym for the unconscious; the oak, a prototype of the self, the still unconscious core of the personality. It is concluded that the hero of the tale is profoundly unaware of his self. The key to the personality of the hero is buried and imprisoned against its will. Several of the symbols are interpreted as references to the alchemical concepts of the four elements, the spiritus vegetativus, the alchemist magician who has imprisoned Mercurius. The fact that Mercurius, i.e.,the principle of individuation, has been confined against his will is taken as an indication that this principle was considered to be a source of evil, a view held by Schopenhauer and Buddhist philosophy, as well as by the Christian doctrine of original sin. However, in that the spirit is only contained not banished, it is concluded that the intent was to isolate the spirit from the surrounding medium. Insofar as the spirit is called by the alchemic name Mercurius, identical with the German Wotan, it is concluded that the tale was of alchemical origin, interpreting the evil spirit as a pagan god forced into the underworld by Christianity and morally disqualified. In this sense, identification is established between Mercurius of this tale and the devil. 4 references.

000475 The spirit Mercurius. Part I: 2. The connection between spirit and tree. In: Jung, C., Collected Works of C. G. Jung, Vol. 13. Princeton University Press, 1967. 444 p. (p. 199-201).

The connection between the mythical symbol of the voice in the oak tree and psychological facts is established and analyzed. The evil spirit confined under the oak tree is, in psychological terms, a reference to the evil spirit hidden in the roots of the self, in the principle of individuation. Five stages of consciousness, progressing from primitive times to the present, are charted. In the primitive the contents of the unconscious were projected on the object, making them appear as one; in the second stage a differentiation was made between object and unconscious content, achieving an act of enlightenment. At the third level, evil was attributed to the psychic content, separated from the object; in the fourth level, that of the present day, the objective existence of the spirit is denied. However, it is proposed that, at the fifth level, the existence of a phenomenon arising from the unconscious is recognized and real existence is granted to the unconscious. This final view requires the acceptance of the spirit as a reality and accepts the necessity of examining the problem of good and evil in relation to the unconscious.

000476 The spirit Mercurius. Part I: 3. The problem of freeing Mercurius. In: Jung, C., Collected Works of C. G. Jung, Vol. 13. Princeton University Press, 1967. 444 p. (p. 202-203).

In conclusion of the tale of the spirit of Merurius, the freeing of Mercurius, frustrated evil in man, is examined in the light of the alchemical process. Although the tale reveals the subsequent good fortune of its hero, nothing is said about the consequences of freeing Mercurius by any voluntary alchemical process. The experienced alchemist would have wished, at all costs, to retain the elusive Mercurius in captivity in order to transform him, so great was the association between Mercurius and the demonic arcane substance. It is concluded then that the ending of the tale is to be regarded as alchemically incorrect. 1 reference.

000477 The spirit Mercurius. Part II: 1. Introductory. In: Jung, C., Collected Works of C. G. Jung, Vol. 13. Princeton University Press, 1967. 444 p. (p. 204-206).

The alchemical spirit Mercurius is studied with the intention of elucidating some of the psychological phenomena contained in alchemy. The philologist Reitzenstein is credited with having discovered the mythological and Gnostic ideas imbedded in alchemy, particularly the doctrine of the Anthropos with its redemptive role. Through practical experience and observation with the projections of patients, it was possible to understand the primitive state of identity between subject and object, or, in the case of the alchemists, the projections of the collective unconscious on metals. The original sources for this study are fourfold: the texts by ancient authors, especially Greek and Arabic texts dating from first to eighth centuries and edited by Berthelot; Latin texts, translated from Arabic or Hebrew, dating from the ninth to the 13th centuries; later Latin texts, the principal source, ranging from the 14th to 17th centuries; and some texts in modern European languages from the 16th to 17th centuries, with a few references to 18th century texts. 2 references.

000478 The spirit Mercurius. Part II: 2. Mercurius as quicksilver and/or water. In: Jung, C., Collected Works of C. G. Jung, Vol. 13. Princeton University Press, 1967. 444 p. (p. 207-208).

The numerous names given to Mercurius are cited and explained. The first and widely accepted term applied to Mercurius was quicksilver, crude or philosophic, the latter being the arcane substance to be produced by alchemy. Because of its fluidity, quicksilver was also defined as water, with many variations in its description to point to the spiritual nature or golden tincture of this arcane substance. 8 references.

000479 The spirit Mercurius. Part. II: 3. Mercurius as fire. In: Jung, C., Collected Works of C. G. Jung, Vol. 13. Princeton University Press, 1967. 444 p. (p. 209-210).

The alchemical definitions of Mercurius as fire are presented, and the paradoxical nature of this designation indicated. As natural or elemental fire, he was considered to be the source of mystical knowledge, a kinsman of the ancient Hermes. Although not ungodly by nature, the mercurial fire was believed to contain the fires of hell, which was considered to be a component of the deity since God was a coincidence of opposites. The locus of this mercurial fire was thought to be the center of the earth where the heavenly spiritual powers are rearranged in the chthonic world of matter. Therefore this evil hell fire was considered to be identical in substance with its spiritual counterpart. Mercurius, of course, could not be destroyed by fire, but because of his fiery nature, he rejoiced in it. 3 references.

000480 The spirit Mercurius. Part II: 4. Mercurius as spirit and soul. In: Jung, C., Collected Works of C. G. Jung, Vol. 13. Princeton University Press, 1967. 444 p. (p. 211).

The contradiction between the fiery nature of Mercurius that fire itself does not change and the vaporous nature of quicksilver under heat is examined and explained as an indica-

tion of the highly specialized projection of psychic content. Since the alchemists themselves identified this arcane substance as spirit or soul, it is evident that they too recognized its psychic nature. However, because of the ambiguous nature of the these concepts, it is necessary to proceed slowly in order to understand the full import of these alchemical terms.

000481 The spirit Mercurius. Part II: 4. Mercurius as spirit and soul. a. Mercurius as an aerial spirit. In: Jung, C., Collected Works of C. G. Jung, Vol. 13. Princeton University Press, 1967. 444 p. (p. 212-213).

The aerial aspect of Mercurius, the counterpart of Hermes and the Egyptian Thoth, is discussed. The terms -- pneuma, spiritus, volans, spiritualis -- applied to the aerial aspect of Mercurius indicate a gaseous state of aggregation. Other terms, combining an understanding of Mercurius as visible yet impalpable, suggest the contamination of the two separate realms of spirit and matter: he was considered to be the spirit of the world embodied in the earth. 5 references.

000482 The spirit Mercurius. Part II: 4. Mercurius as spirit and soul. b. Mercurius as soul. In: Jung, C., Collected Works of C. G. Jung, Vol. 13. Princeton University Press, 1967. 444 p. (p. 213-214).

The basic duality of Mercurius is most apparent in the designations of spirit and soul that are discussed. In that the basic characteristic of "breath soul" is to animate and be animated, Mercurius can be considered a life principle, as the term anima, a feminine being, also suggests. Several other terms referring to Mercurius as spirit are given with attention drawn to the identification between Mercurius and the anima mundi. In this latter appellation, the alchemists were combining the Platonic concept of world/soul and the Christian concept of the Holy Spirit to emphasize the identity of matter and spirit as well as the procreative quality of Mercurius. 9 references.

000483 The spirit Mercurius. Part II: 4. Mercurius as spirit and soul. c. Mercurius as spirit in the incorporeal, metaphysical sense. In: Jung, C., Collected Works of C. G. Jung, Vol. 13. Princeton University Press, 1967. 444 p. (p. 215-216).

The specifically spiritual nature of Mercurius is examined, showing that the alchemists did associate him with the pure world of spirit -- hyperphysical and incorruptible, incorporeal and of celestial or possibly demonic origin. The association of this arcane substance with the goddess of love is also noted. It is concluded that the alchemists themselves conceived Mercurius as a psychic phenomenon and never ceased drawing attention to the psychic nature of Mercurius. The nomenclature suggests a union of opposites; hence, the psychologem Mercurius indicates an essentially antinomian dual nature. 6 references.

000484 The spirit Mercurius. Part II: 5. The dual nature of Mercurius. In: Jung, C., Collected Works of C. G. Jung, Vol. 13. Princeton University Press, 1967. 444 p. (p. 217-220).

Numerous names indicating the dual nature of Mercurius are listed, among them such opposites as waking/sleeping, dry/moist, good/evil, water/fire, male/female, husband/wife, lover/beloved. He was identified with hermaphroditic first man, the Adam Kadmon, and the Gnostic Anthropos -- a concept that coincides with the psychological concept of the self. Mercurius is undoubtedly identified with the most extreme opposites. 30 references.

000485 The spirit Mercurius. Part II: 6. The unity and trinity of Mercurius. In: Jung, C., Collected Works of C. G. Jung, Vol. 13. Princeton University Press, 1967. 444 p. (p. 221-224).

The symbols and terms referring to the alchemical concept of the unity of Mercurius are examined and the relationship between his triadic nature, and the Christian dogma of the Holy Trinity is explored. Several references to earlier triads are given of the underworld and of ancestors, which are most often associated with attributes of the gods. From all of the alchemical names referring to the threefold nature of Mercurius, it is concluded that he corresponds not only to Christ but to the triune divinity as well, a parallel most clearly seen in the name Azoth applied to Mercurius in the "Aurelia occulta." In addition, he is considered to be the Logos (Christ) become word, an indication of his identification with the collective unconscious. Another attribute of Mercurius that relates him to the Godhead is his ability to beget himself like the uroboros dragon. This identification with trinity does not exclude his continued sharing of the quaternity of the lapis, thus causing him to exemplify the axiom of Maria Prophetissa, the dilemma of the three and four. 17 references.

000486 The spirit Mercurius. Part II: 7. The relation of Mercurius to astrology and the doctrine of the archons. In: Jung, C., Collected Works of C. G. Jung, Vol. 13. Princeton University Press, 1967. 444 p. (p. 225-229).

The identification of Mercurius with the planets -- Mercury, Venus and Saturn -- is discussed in terms of the attributes he was to have shared with them. The most important astrological relationship was with Saturn through associaition of lead, prima materia, with both the planet and Mercurius drawing the eternal water and being hermaphroditic in nature. The spirits of Saturn and of Mercurius were also linked, particularly in terms of the transformation of the lion. In addition, Saturn was perceived as the dwelling place of the devil, a parallel to the alchemical belief that the masculine principle of Mercurius was diabolus. Mercurius' nature is described as beginning with evil and ending with good. In the poem Verus Hermes, the transformation of Mercurius is described as a projection of the individuation process which takes place even without the participation of consciousness, however when consciousness does participate in the process, all the emotions associated with a religious revelation are experienced; hence the identification of Mercurius with Sapientia or the Holy Ghost. 25 references.

000487 The spirit Mercurius. Part II: 8. Mercurius and Hermes. In: Jung, C., Collected Works of C. G. Jung, Vol. 13. Princeton University Press, 1967. 444 p. (p. 230-234).

The similarity between Hermes and Mercurius is discussed by showing the resemblance between the values and ideas attributed to both as well as by the numerous names ascribed to Mercurius in the alchemical texts. Both are described as pointing the way, revealing divine secrets, and being transformed from evil into good. The dark Mercurius, associated with the demiurgic principle and the mother/son incest, is interpreted as an allusion to the initial nigredo state. His transformation or redemption is contrasted with that of Christ: the latter descends from heaven and then ascends; Mercurius is raised from earth to heaven and then returns to earth. His nature is circular, like the uroborous, and symbolized by the circulus simplex. It is suggested that the union of Hermetic and Aristotlean philosophy may be possible in the future but only if a psychological definition of religious and scientific views has been completed. 15 references.

000488 The spirit Mercurius. Part II: 9. Mercurius as the arcane substance. In: Jung, C., Collected Works of C. G. Jung, Vol. 13. Princeton University Press, 1967. 444 p. (p. 235-236).

The complex nature of Mercurius is illustrated by the identification with the arcane substance, prima materia, lapis. He is not only the beginning and end of the alchemical opus but the process in between, hence the names Mediator, Servator, Salvator that are applied to him and the parallel drawn to Christ. In the macrocosm of nature he holds the position that Christ holds in the world of reason of divine revelation. In his capacity for self-generation, self-transformation, self-reproduction and self-destruction, he is considered to be a principle coeternal with God. 15 references.

000489 The spirit Mercurius. Part II: 10. Summary. In: Jung, C., Collected Works of C. G. Jung, Vol. 13. Princeton University Press, 1967. 444 p. (p. 237-250).

A summary of the multiple aspects of Mercurius is provided; a comparison is made between the figure of Christ and that of Mercurius; and the psychological significance of this alchemical figure is explored at length. Mercurius is presented as a symbol of all conceivable opposites, as a process of transformation, as a dual God/devil image, and as a representation of the self, the individuation process and the collective unconscious. Both Christ and Mercurius are viewed as archetypes: the former of consciousness; the latter, of the unconscious; both are preconscious, autonomous images from which knowledge of psychic conditions can be derived. Since the development of the Christ image resulted in a strengthening of consciousness and a neglect of the unconscious, the compensatory tendencies of the latter created the figure of Mercurius, who stands in compensatory relation to Christ and whose object is to bridge the abyss separating the conscious from the unconscious. It is this new knowledge springing from the unconscious that must be integrated into consciousness in order to complete the individuation process, allow the emergence of the self, and reveal the collective nature of the self. The evil, dark side of Mercurius is not to be interpreted as an image of the Christian devil but of the shadow side of the self. The alchemists' discoveries in terms of metals is not considered unusual since the concentration on one topic or problem causes the psyche to express itself in terms of the material under observation. 6 references.

000490 The philosophical tree. I. Individual representations of the tree symbol. In: Jung, C., Collected Works of C. G. Jung, Vol. 13. Princeton University Press, 1967. 444 p. (251-271).

Thirty-two descriptions of a series of pictures drawn by patients to express their inner experiences are given. The symbol of the tree as it appears in all of the pictures is analyzed in terms of the expression of psychic content with references made to the similarities between these spontaneously created symbols and alchemical or mythical concepts. Many of the descriptions reveal allusions to psychological processes: the union of opposites, the awareness of the value of the unconscious, regression, the danger of identification with the self, the process of individuation or discrimination between self and ego, the personification of animus, and several others. 6 references.

000491 The philosophical tree. II. On the history and interpretation of the tree symbol. 1. The tree as an archetypal image. In: Jung, C., Collected Works of C. G. Jung, Vol. 13. Princeton University Press, 1967. 444 p. (p. 272-274).

The history and interpretation of the tree as a symbol are examined. As an archetypal image, the symbol of the tree has undergone changes of meaning throughout the centuries. As a whole, however, the tree is associated with growth, protection, life, unfolding of form, old age, personality, death and rebirth. Despite the amount of material derived from myth, fairytale and poetry, the patients who drew them were unaware of the sources of their images. Three explanations for this lack of awareness are given: little thought is ever given to dream images or myth motifs; sources have been forgotten; or the sources sprang from archetypes and are, therefore, of a collective nature. The collective nature of the image makes it difficult to establish its full meaning from the associative material of a single individual. Since this awareness is important for therapy, comparative research into symbols is encouraged. Medieval natural philosophy, alchemy and Hermetic philosophy are believed to be a reservoir of the most important and enduring mythologems of the ancient world. 3 references.

000492 The philosophical tree. II. On the history and interpretation of the tree symbol. 2. The tree in the treatise of Jodocus Greverus. In: Jung, C., Collective Works of C. G. Jung, Vol. 13. Princeton University Press, 1967. 444 p. (p. 274-278).

The central positon of the tree in mythology is illustrated in the work of the 16th centruy writer Greverus. His tree stands in a well tended garden grown in soil of the purified Mercurius. Planets form the trunk; the moon and sun supply its seeds. The planetary names correspond both to metals and temperaments or psychic factors. Greverus sees his work as having a universal purpose, containing the secret of the undivided oneness of the holy trinity. The alchemists' insistence that a parallelism existed between their ideas and those of religion is noted and interpreted as a recognition that ideas are organized by the same psychic laws, the archetypes. In the process of synthesis, the triad of sun, moon and Mercurius combines in a fourth, tetrasomia. The four elements then become joined in the union of persons. 5 references.

000493 The philosophical tree. II. On the history and interpretation of the tree symbol. 3. The tetrasomia. In: Jung, C., Collected Works of C. G. Jung, Vol. 13. Princeton University Press, 1967. 444 p. (p. 278-283).

The historical background of the tetrasomia, the reduction or synthesis of a quaternio to unity, is studied. Two dyads -- one benevolent, the other maleficent make up the quaternion to be synthesized. The fourfold Mercurius, the four forms of the Hellenistic Hermes, Ezekiel's vision of four cherubim, the cross, the four gospels as pillars of Christ's throne, and the four animals in Daniel's vision are all considered to be images of the quaternity. It is shown that the incest motif, which extends into Christian tradition and medieval alchemy, had its origins in the Egyptian myth that Horus begat his four sons with his mother Isis. The images of quaternity are considered to represent the self or man's wholeness in the symbolism of the unconscious. It is concluded that the alchemical tetrasomia and its reduction to unity form an archetype of a totality divided into four parts but possessing one central nature. 6 references.

000494 The philosophical tree. II. On the history and interpretation of the tree symbol. 4. The image of wholeness. In: Jung, C., Collected Works of C. G. Jung: Vol. 13. Princeton University Press, 1967. 444 p. (283-285).

The image of wholeness in mythology and alchemical symbolism is reviewed: water, Mercurius, lapis are all totality images with their own wholeness. Zosimos's whole is a microcosm, a reflection of the universe. Here, microcosm and macrocosm are identical: the microcosm attracts the macrocosm in a restoration of individual elements to the original wholeness. The outline of the associative background of the tree is considered a necessary prelude to explaining the place of the tree in alchemy. 5 references.

000495 The philosophical tree. II. On the history and interpretation of the tree symbol. 5. The nature and origin of the philosophical tree. In: Jung, C., Collected Works of C. G. Jung, Vol. 13. Princeton University Press, 1967. 444 p. (p. 286-289).

The nature and origin of the philosophical tree are outlined in the work of the 17th century Platonist, Gerard Dorn. He drew a vivid picture of the growth, expansion and death of the tree. He envisaged it as a system of blood vessels -- with the branches as veins -- extending throughout the earth. Its blood like liquid coagulates into its fruit which dies only to create new life. To Dorn, the archetypal tree was projected on the empirical world. His view is totalistic, embracing the whole of organic and inorganic nature as well as the spiritual world. The battle between those who advocate objectivity and those who support a psychology based on pyschic premises is seen as a parallel to Dorn's opposition to the scientific empiricists of his time. 5 references.

000496 The philosophical tree. II. On the history and interpretation of the tree symbol. 6. Dorn's interpretation of the tree. In: Jung, C., Collected Works of C. G. Jung, Vol. 13. Princeton University Press, 1967. 444 p. (p. 289-292).

Dorn's description and interpretation of the philosophical tree as a living thing, a metaphorical form of hidden substance, is quoted and criticized. His distinction between living things of nature and material organisms is not clear. It is suggested that he may be referring to the existence of archetypes in the comprehensive Platonic nature which he envisages. 1 reference.

000497 The philosophical tree. II. On the history and interpretation of the tree symbol. 7. The rose-coloured blood and the rose. In: Jung, C., Collected Works of C. G. Jung, Vol. 13. Princeton Univefsity Press, 1967. 444 p. (p. 292-297).

Historical precedents for Dorn's rose-colored blood and the rose are examined. The alchemists conceived of a body as composed of the four elements and capable of uniting all opposites. The stone was a primordial religious experience to be reconciled with Christian beliefs and hence the parallel between it and Christ. It was this lapis/Christ parallel that introduced the mystique of the rose into alchemy. To the alchemists, the rose-colored blood of the alchemical redeemer was derived from rose mysticism and expressed the healing effect of a certain kind of Eros. This alchemical redeemer (servator cosmi) is seen as a representation of the still unconscious idea of the whole man. Christianity's call to practice love of neighbor is viewed as a compensation for a corresponding social defect and an attempt to educate man to consciousness and responsibility, thereby illuminating the interior world of the psyche. 8 references.

000498 The philosophical tree. II. On the history and interpretation of the tree symbol. 8. The alchemical mind. In: Jung, C., Collected Works of C. G. Jung, Vol. 13. Princeton University Press, 1967. 444 p. (p. 297-302).

The significance of the alchemists' efforts to discover the stone is discussed. According to Petrus Bonus, the alchemical opus anticipated throughout history the sacred myth of the generation, birth and resurrection of the Redeemer, although they could not resolve the lapis/Christ parallel, little by little the meaning of the stone and its relationship to man himself became clear. Only in later centuries was their projection into and from matter abolished with the recognition of the psyche. Dreams, along with mythologems and alchemical symbols, are viewed as attempts to translate unconscious thought forms, the common property of mankind, into the language of consciousness. This new consciousness is seen as threatening and isolating; hence, collective or archetypal images are produced as compensations. Religion is seen as one way of linking the individual to the instinctual powers of the unconscious. In the absence of religion, compensating primordial images appear in the form of mythologems or dreams. The alchemist reduced his symbols to chemical substances, modern man to personal experiences. Freud is criticized for reducing everything to the archetype of incest. Instead, it is suggested that the meaning of symbols be explored, recognizing that they compensate an unadapted attitude of consciousness. Consequently, the analyst is exhorted to give full attention to the symbolic aspects of his patient's problems, since healing comes only from what leads the patient beyond himself and beyond his entanglement in his own ego. 2 references.

000499 The philosophical tree. II. On the history and interpretation of the tree symbol. 9. Various aspects of the tree. In: Jung, C., Collected Works of C. G. Jung, Vol. 13. Princeton University Press, 1967. 444 p. (p. 302-308).

In an effort to determine the meaning of the tree to the alchemists, many sources are compared. The tree of paradise, both as an abstraction and as a living plant, the magical tree, and the truncated tree all appear in alchemical symbolisms representing the alchemical process, the journey of shaman, and transformation. The motif of the dead tree, prefiguring the tree of the forbidden fruit, is not common in alchemy but does appear in the Judaeo-Christian tradition. Four elements -- the quaternity, the symbol of wholeness -- are often associated with the flowering and fruit bearing tree. In alchemical traditon, God appears as the fruit of the philosophical tree, the product of the opus whose goal is to liberate the world creating spirit of God. 19 references.

000500 The philosophical tree. II. On the history and interpretation of the tree symbol. 10. The habitat of the tree. In: Jung, C., Collected Works of C. G. Jung, Vol. 13. Princeton University Press, 1967. 444 p. (p. 308-311).

The various habitats of the philosophical tree, especially the sea and the mountain, are considered. Mountain and tree are seen as symbols of personality, of the self, and of Christ. The association of the tree and water suggests an allusion to Mercurius, who unites the opposites in himself since he is metal and liquid. The symbolism of fire and metal is found in many philosophies. The golden tree is related to the seven metals, seen as the seven planets. In such a connection, it becomes a world tree.

000501 The philosophical tree. II. On the history and interpretation of the tree symbol. II. The inverted tree. In: Jung, C., Collected Works of C. G. Jung, Vol. 13. Princeton University Press, 1967. 444 p. (p. 311-315).

Numerous examples from medieval, Indian and Cabalistic sources are cited as illustrations of the inverted tree. Man is perceived as an inverted tree rooted in paradise. Both in East and West, the tree symbolizes a living process as well as a process of enlightenment. To the alchemists, it represented their opus. It also appears as having various substances, all of which have some moral significance. 13 references.

000502 The philosophical tree. II. On the history and interpretation of the tree symbol. 12. Bird and snake. In: Jung, C., Collected Works of C. G. Jung, Vol. 13. Princeton University Press, 1967. 444 p. (p. 315-317).

The significance of birds and snakes associated with the tree is explored in the context of Biblical, alchemical and classical quotations. The stork in alchemical literature stands for the opus and its consummation just as the ingrown leaves represent the opus contra naturam and introversion. The snake, with its obvious reference to the Biblical story of the Fall, is also seen as the mercurial serpent or arcane substance, transforming itself and giving life. A quotation from the "Scriptum Alberti" reveals analogies to Christ and to the transformation process in the symbols of the dragon and the stork. This latter symbol is also viewed as an allegorical representation of piety and of Christ the judge. Just as the snake is the chthonic numen of the tree, so that stork is its spiritual principle and a symbol of Anthropos. 5 references.

000503 The philosophical tree. II. On the history and interpretation of the tree symbol. 13. The feminine tree-numen. In: Jung, .C., Collected Works of C. G. Jung, Vol. 13. Princeton University Press, 1967. 444 p. (p. 317-319).

The feminine and maternal significance of the tree, as the seat of transformation and renewal, is discussed. This symbolism is found in both ancient and biblical tradition as well as in alchemical texts. The dual nature of the tree is identified by the alchemists: the division of the tree soul into a masculine and feminine figure is said to correspond to the alchemical Mercurius, the hermaphrodite, as life principle of the tree. 7 references.

000504 The philosophical tree. II. On the history and interpretation of the tree symbol. 14. The tree as the lapis. In: Jung, C., Collected Works of C. G. Jung, Vol. 13. Princeton University Press, 1967. 444 p. (p. 319-322).

The significance of lapis, the philosophical stone, as both first and last matter, is investigated. The stone, as prima materia, is an oily water. Since oil and water do not mix, the oily water represents the double or contrary nature of Mercurius. The stone is seen as identical with the tree and both are identified as symbols of wholeness or self, as proven by quotations from Arabic and Persian writings. Psychologically, the first meeting with the self may be accompanied by all those negative qualities which characterize an unexpected encounter with the unconscious. It is concluded that a psychosis could result if the conscious mind were unable to assimilate, either intellectually or morally, the contents of the unconscious. 7 references.

000505 The philosophical tree. II. On the history and interpretation of the tree symbol. 15. The dangers of the art. In: Jung, C., Collected Works of C. G. Jung, Vol. 13. Princeton University Press, 1967. 444 p. (p. 322-326).

The quotations from several alchemical texts are examined and the dangers of practicing the alchemical art are explored. Death, either physical or spiritual, and demonic agents are cited among the dangers for those who lacked spiritual understanding. Since the mystery of the stone pervades alchemy and was considered by the alchemists as a miracle, it was frequently associated with a fear of mental disturbance. A second century Chinese alchemist's warnings of the dire consequences of making mistakes during the opus are described both in their physiological and psychic manifestations. The alchemist was involved in the development of his own individuation, in a difficult process of unifying consciousness with the shadow and the anima. He was exposed to the dangers of the demands made on both his intelligence and moral qualities. 10 references.

000506 The philosophical tree. II. On the history and interpretation of the tree symbol. 16. Understanding as a means of defence. In: Jung, C., Collected Works of C. G. Jung, Vol. 13. Princeton University Press, 1967. 444 p. (p. 327-328).

The need to defend against the power of the philosophical stone was recognized by the alchemists. They realized that the stone was stronger than they and sought to try to understand it. By attempting to guess the secret name, the alchemists sought to gain power of the dangerous force. This process is seen to have its parallel in psychotherapy: neurotic symptoms can often be rendered harmless by conscious understanding and experience of their contents. However, it is important to remember the autonomous nature of these contents and recognize them as the source of individuation. Just as the alchemists attempted to use the symbols produced by the unconscious as spellbinding names, so does modern man use intellectual concepts for the purpose of denying the unconscious, hopeful that reason and intellect can destroy its reality. 1 reference.

000507 The philosophical tree. II. On the history and interpretation of the tree symbol. 17. The motif of torture. In: Jung, C., Collected Works of C. G. Jung, Vol. 13. Princeton University Press, 1967. 444 p. (p. 328-333).

The ambiguous meaning of torment in alchemical work is explored. It afflicts both the body and the soul, the raw materials and the arcane substance of the alchemists. In their most important discovery, the alchemists projected their own psychic processes into chemical substances. Therefore, it is not surprising that suffering and sadness should have been associated with the Christ's cross and its connection with the tree. Quaternity, the symbol of the cross, also applies to the tree wherein four elements are united. The analogies of the sword on the tree and the serpent on the cross in mythological and Christian tradition are discussed. The snake represents two aspects of the unconscious: its cold and ruthless instinctuality and its quality of natural wisdom. In the snake symbolism, Christ personifies the unconscious, hung on the tree in sacrifice, a sacrifice in which the unconscious is overcome.

000508 The philosophical tree. II. On the history and interpretation of the tree symbol. 18. The relation of suffering to the coniunctio. In: Jung, C., Collected Works of C. G. Jung, Vol. 13. Princeton University Press, 1967. 444 p. (p. 334-337).

The relation of suffering to union -- coniunctio -- is examined. According to Gnostic tradition the feminine figure of wisdom, not primordial man, was cast out into darkness. The masculine element thereby escaped the danger of being swallowed up by the dark powers and from the sufferings of wisdom arose the entire created world. This creation myth is interpreted as psychological representation of the separation of the female anima from the masculine, spiritually oriented consciousness which is seeking the victory of the spirit over the world of the senses. Wisdom's unconscious state, its formlessness and darkness characterizes the anima of man who identifies himself absolutely with his reason and spirituality. By his separation from the anima he risks the loss of the compensat-

ing powers of the unconscious. In such a case, the latter makes itself felt with violent emotions and man loses touch with reality. In the language of myth, Christ -- the principle of masculine spirituality -- perceives the suffering of Wisdom -- the psyche -- and thereby gives her form and existence. She is, however, left to suffer. In a parallel with masculine neuroses, a man can perceive psychic suffering but may not become conscious of its reasons in the unconscious. Masculine spirituality withdraws into the light and shuts out the darkness. Wisdom will not give up her dark emotions with the result that original unity is split into irreconcilable halves. In this symbolism, the quaternity of two pairs of opposites again appears.

000509 The philosophical tree. II. On the history and interpretation of the tree symbol. 19. The tree as man. In: Jung, C., Collected Works of C. G. Jung, Vol. 13. Princeton University Press, 1967. 444 p. (p. 337-341).

A concern with the conceptual relationship of tree to man has recurred throughout history. The tree is seen as an intermediate form of man since, on the one hand, it springs from primordial man and, on the other, grows into a man. The feminine tree numen is an accurate symbol of the self for women, but for the alchemists it represented a projection of the anima figure. When the anima, (man's femininity) or the animus, (woman's masculinity) is not sufficiently differentiated and integrated into consciousness, the self is only potentially present. The spontaneous products of the unconscious in modern man depict the archetype of the tree and the historical parallels, not the biblical associations. Instead, the tree image seems to portray an inner process of development independent of consciousness or will. 7 references.

000510 The philosophical tree. II. On the history and interpretation of the tree symbol. 20. The interpretation and integration of the unconscious. In: Jung, C., Collected Works of C. G. Jung, Vol. 13. Princeton University Press, 1967. 444 p. (p. 341-349).

The origins and treatment of psychic disturbances are reviewed. Treatment of such disturbances involves the integration of contents which have become dissociated from consciousness. The more negative the conscious attitude, the more aggressive the dissociated content becomes. To be effective, the therapy must establish communication with the split-off part. In attempting to interpret a complex dream in which an eagle reappeared recurrently, it was discovered that the eagle was associated with the patient's experiences in a concentration camp and with his basic beliefs. Since neuroses are symptoms of maladjustment the neurotic regression into an infantile state can be analyzed by means of the symbols produced by the unconscious to compensate this regression. When these symbols are understood objectively a change in attitude occurs whereby the dissociation between man as he is and man as he ought to be is bridged. The psyche needs to know the meaning of its existence, of the images and ideas originating in the unconscious. The conscious psyche is of a personal nature but it is not the whole of the psyche. Dream symbols have a reality that reveals unknown factors of the unconscious. When their meaning is understood, the unconscious can be integrated and the dissociation overcome. The study of the alchemical laboratory experiences, of the theories and the "philosophic tree," is considered important because of the relevance of these discoveries to the modern psychological study of the unconscious.

14 MYSTERIUM CONIUNCTIONIS

000511 The components of the coniunctio. 1. The opposites. In: Jung, C., Collected Works of C. G. Jung, Vol. 14. 2nd ed., Princeton University Press, 1970. 702 p. (p. 3-6).

The alchemical duality of opposites, the symbols used to express them, and their significance in terms of psychology are briefly presented. A list of the factors coming together in the coniunctio, such as heat/cold, moist/dry, spirit/soul, active/passive, etc.,are provided. It is noted that these polarities are often arranged into a quaternity, usually symbolized by a Physis (a cross.)Both personified and theriomorphic examples of symbolic representations of the coniunctio are given. A brief analysis of the astrological fishes and the stag/unicorn/forest symbols from Lambspringk's "Symbols" is provided. The elevation of the human figure to a king or divinity is explained as an indication of the transconscious character of the pair of opposites showing the relation of the opposites to the ego personality and the self.

000512 The components of the coniunctio. 2. The coniunctio and the mediating role of Mercurius. In: Jung, C., Collected Works of C. G. Jung, Vol. 14. 2nd ed., Princeton University Press, 1970. 702 p. (p. 6-17).

Through examples from several alchemical texts, the significance of Mercurius as the synthesizing or union of the pairs of opposites in the quaternio is discussed. These texts are then related to their Christian religious background. The arrangement of opposites into a quaternity is illustrated by an analysis of the four goddesses in Stolcenberg's Viridarium chymicum and the Abu'l-Qasim. In the latter example, Ostanes stands between masculine/feminine, good/evil opposites and is subject to the compulsion of the stars; i.e.,a transconscious factor beyond the reach of the human will. As a result he is a diversity of persons, whereas he should be one. Hermes points out that he (Oranes) shares something incorruptible in his nature, a unity symbolized by a crown or kingly totality. The quaternio of the Consilium coniugii is cited, and the ogdoad or double quaternio of Bernardus Trevisanus is illustrated by a diagram. In this instance, the center of unity is expressed symbolically as being in the Indian Ocean (the unconscious). It symbolizes the microcosm, the mystical Adam, and bisexual original man, where he is identical with the unconscious. The quaternio of the scholia to the "Tractatus aureus Hermetis" is presented, illustrated by a diagram, and analyzed, with the spirit of Mercurius representing the unifying agent of the opposites. Mercurius is seen as both the original man discriminated in crude form through the physical world, and as the reconstituted totality in sublimated form. He is likened to the matrimonium or coniunctio of opposites. The alchemical terms: Pelican, Mercurius, Lapis, Circle and Hermetic Vessel, are related to the mandala and to symbols for Christ found in the Epistles, the Gospels and the Shepherd of Hermas. The goal of the alchemists' endeavour was to arrive at an Ecclesia spiritualis, above all creeds, and subject solely to Christ. 4 references.

000513 The components of the coniunctio. 3. The orphan, the widow, and the moon. In: Jung, C., Collected Works of C. G. Jung, Vol. 14. 2nd ed., Princeton University Press, 1970. 702 p. (p. 17-37).

The alchemical symbols: orphan, widow and moon, are related to the images found in classical mythology, the Patristic writings, and the Cabala. A link between the precious stone, orphan, found in the writings of Albertus Magnus and the lapis Philosophorum mentioned in Carmen Helviodori, Petrus Bonus and Dorn is established. This analysis of orphan leads to a discussion of the term widow as a symbol of alchemic prima materia, mother of the lapis philosophorum. Parallels are drawn between the myth of Isis and the synonyms used for prima materia or the feminine principle in alchemy. The paradoxical joy/bitterness; destroyer/healer roles of both are emphasized and related to the Christian belief in transubstantiation, as well as to Aztec and Egyptian myths. It is shown that alchemy replaced the sponsus/sponsa Christian image with one of material and spiritual totality personified by Mercurius, the union of Sapientia and matter (feminine) with the Holy Ghost and the devil. The Cabalan Malchuth is recognized as having been assimilated into the alchemical imagery of the widow as was the Patristic sponsus/sponsa symbol. The paradoxical symbol of the moon as source of light and also destroyer of light (sol, sun) is traced through alchemical writings, the writings of Augustine and motifs from Aztec and Egyptian writings. The motif of wounding, associated with the eclipse, with Christ and the Church, Hecate and Persephone, and the writings of Zosimos and Philaletha, show that the goal of the alchemist was to root out the original sin with the balsam of life, a mixture of natural heat and radical moisture. This "redemption" was to be accomplished through the art of alchemy. Further elucidation of this redemptive role, accomplished by kinosis (emptying), is provided by quotations from Rahner, St. Ambrose, and St. Hilary, with a reference to the alchemical text of the Scrutinium. 5 references.

000514 The components of the coniunctio. 4. Alchemy and Manichaeism. In: Jung, C., Collected Works of C. G. Jung, Vol. 14. 2nd ed., Princeton University Press, 1970. 702 p. (37-41).

A parallel is drawn between Manichaean and alchemic views on the sources of evil, the method of salvation, and dualistic nature of the savior figure (Anthropos - Mercurius). The story of Manes or Cubricus the son of the widow, is recounted and he is identified with the alchemic Kyrius, Gabricius, a name derived from an Arabic word meaning sulphur. The term black sulphur used in the alchemists' texts to refer to the active, masculine substance of Mercurius is compared to the Manichaean term hyle or matter, the dark, fluid human body of evil principle. The Manichaean dualistic Christ figure, the Anthropos, is likened to the alchemic dualistic redeemer of the microcosm (Christ) and of the macrocosm (lapis philosophorum). The role of sweat as rain in Manichaean teaching as a means of freeing light material from dark bodies is compared to the dew or arcanum of alchemy. The Acta Archelai of Manichaeism with its saving wheel is seen to be reflected in the rota of alchemy. The comparison of these two systems reveals the death-rebirth drama hidden in the coniunctio. It is stated that the moral task of alchemy was to bring the feminine, maternal background of the masculine psyche into harmony with the spirit. 5 references.

000515 The paradoxa. 1. The arcane substance and the point. In: Jung, C., Collected works of C. G. Jung, Vol. 14. 2nd ed., Princeton University Press, 1970. 702 p. (p. 42-48).

An overview of several alchemic writings indicates the prevalence of paradoxes and the importance of the point in alchemy. The paradox is a natural result of the alchemists' attempts to visualize the opposites together and to express them in the same breath as the adjectives used to qualify arcane substance (lapis, prima materia and Mercurius) indicate. They are at one and the same time base and noble, precious and cheap, one and many, visible to all and unknown. The paradox of Mercurius is presented as the paradox par excellence. Citations from John Dee, the Turba, Dorn, Paracelsus, Steeb, Maier and others, illustrate the significance of the point in alchemy. The point is the smallest written sign, used to symbolize the mystery of four elements, the center of nature, the "sun point" in the egg; it corresponds to fire, light, world's center, the Godhead: it is the mode of the perfect form. The properties of gold are listed as they relate to the point, the circle, eternity, the Godhead, and indivisible substance.

000516 The paradoxa. 2. The scintilla. In: Jung, C., Collected Works of C. G. Jung, Vol. 14. 2nd ed., Princeton University Press, 1970. 702 p. (p. 48-56).

The alchemical doctrine of the scintilla or spark is presented, the symbol of the eye is examined and its significance is explained in psychological terms. The concept of spark or scintilla is found in the writings of Meister Eckhart, Heraclitus, Hippolytus and Simon Magus as well as in those of the alchemists. Alchemists defined the spark as Archaeus, the fiery centre of the earth which is hermaphroditic, consisting in a conjunction of male and female. The parallel to Adam Kadmon, the original man of Jewish Gnosis and the product of the conjunction of sun and moon, is noted. The significance of the eye as a symbol of the scintilla is discussed and related to the doctrine of Gnosticism and Manichaeism. The psychological analysis of the eye and sun as symbol and allegory of the consciousness, which is the mark of the ego complex, is compared to the alchemists' view of the union of the scintillae to form gold (sol) and the Gnostic goal of reintegrating atoms of light. Dorn's concept of the scintilla, an invisible sun in the centre of man and a fire point created by tension of masculine and feminine principles in Mercurius, is examined as in Khurach's description of the scintilla as elixir. The resemblance between Khurath's concept and that of Monoimos is noted.

000517 The paradoxa. 3. The enigma of Bologna. In: Jung, C., Collected Works of C. G. Jung, Vol. 14. 2nd ed., Princeton University Press, 1970. 702 p. (p. 56-88).

An epitaph found in Bologna and known as the Aelia-Laelia-Crispis Inscription is cited, and it is demonstrated that both the epitaph, which was in reality a joke, and the numberless interpretations of it reveal the workings of the collective unconscious. A review of the interpretations is provided with special attention given to those of Barnaud, Maier, Malvasius, Senior, Richard White, Veranius and Schwartz. The interpretations of Barnaud and Maier are based on alchemical concepts of prima materia, lapis, dismemberment, panacea and coniunctio. The interpretation of Malvasius reveals anima projections and feminine archetypes: the oak, a feminine numes, is seen to be the source of the fountain, a vessel, mother, and the source of life. Attention is drawn to similar images in modern dreams. The motif of the oak tree is examined in the light of the Cadmos myth with its symbols of loss of anima in the realm of the unconscious, incest relationship, transition to exogamy, the battle of split off complex and the moral problem of opposites. This same myth is given an alchemic interpretation: Cadmos is Mercurius in his masculine form (Sol) in search of his feminine counterpart (Luna); in order to destroy the chaos he must kill the serpent to allow the coniunctio or harmony of elements to occur. The spoils of the battle are offered to the oak tree, representative of the unconscious, the source of life and harmony. Both the enigma and the commentaries are seen as perfect paradigms of the method of alchemy in general. Analogies are found in medieval literature in Vita Merlin, the epigram of the Hermaphrodite attributed to Mathieu de Vendome and in the Niobe epigram. Richard White's definition of the soul as the selfness of all mankind is

interpreted as a possible reference to the collective unconscious; attention is given as well to his discovery of the androgynous nature of the human soul. Comment is made on the Veranius' interpretation as a forerunner of Freud's sexual theory of the unconscious. Schwartz's interpretation, in which the monument is understood as the church, is considered significant in that the symbol of the church expresses and substitutes for all the secrets of the souls which humanistic philosophers projected into the Aelia inscription. The study of both the inscription and its interpretation leads to the conclusion that the collective unconscious, through archetypes, provides a priori conditioning for the assignment of meaning. 2 references.

000518 The personification of the opposites. 1. Introduction. In: Jung, C., Collected Works of C. G. Jung, Vol. 14. 2nd ed., Princeton University Press, 1970. 702 p. (p. 89-92).

The fundamental opposition, seen by the alchemists as a male/female opposition, is analyzed in terms of the incest conflict described by Freud. The expression of the conflict as male/female opposition is explained by reference to the primal guilt mentioned in Genesis and the opposition in nature between the physical and the spiritual; the goal of the former is viewed as union, that of the later, discrimination. The alchemists' awareness of this problem is shown by an analysis of their myth of the King of the Sea and a description of the dual goal of alchemy: the discovery of gold as a panacea for the physical and the rebirth of light from the darkness of Physis: healing self-knowledge and the deliverance of the pneumatic body from the corruption of the flesh. The Christian attempt to restore the state of innocence through monasticism and celibacy is contrasted with that of the alchemists'. The former used the image of the Christian spiritual marriage of Sponsus (Christ) and sponsa (Church) and offered a purely spiritual solution; the latter used the image of chymical marriage, coniunctio of Sol and Luna, and exalted incest. It is shown that both attempts fail because the image of the oppositon of the sexes must be resolved in another realm, the soul of man. The reason for the difficulty of this solution is explained, and Freud's discovery of the Oedipus complex as a universal problem is analyzed as a psychopathological form of the natural problem of the union of opposites.

000519 The personification of the opposites. 2. Sol. In: Jung, C., Collected Works of C. G. Jung, Vol. 14. 2nd ed., Princeton University Press, 1970. 702 p. (92 -110).

The alchemical attributes of Sol are presented, analyzed, and related to the psychological concept of the ego. Sol is perceived as a virtuous or generative and transforming power found both within man and in the universe. Since it was considered to be a single element, it was to be the source of universal power of growth, healing, magic, and prestige from which the gold could be generated. However, it too had its shadow, capable of destroying. Symbolically then, the Sol image is seen as an expression of the physiological and psychological drama of return to prima materia, a death necessary for returning to the incorrupt preworldly paradise. The coniunctio of Sol and Mercurius is discussed, and an analogy is drawn to the Christ/Mary relationship. The differences between the Christian dogmatic schema and that of the alchemical schemes are illustrated with quaternal diagrams. The contrast between the upward movement of the alchemical drama, from darkness of earth to spiritual light, and the downward movement of the Christian drama, the scent of the Kingdom of heaven to earth, is presented. It is concluded that alchemical projections sketch a picture of certain fundamental psychological facts, one being the primary pair of opposites: consciousness and unconsciousness, symbolized by Sol and Luna. Sol is interpreted as a projection of the ego, since the latter is the indispensable condition for all consciousness. A distinction is drawn between the concept of the self as the suprapersonal atman, the totality of conscious and unconscious, and the ego, the personal atman, the central reference point of the unconscious. The alchemists came close to recognizing that the arcane substances and the longed for lapis were the ego. 1 reference.

000520 The personification of the opposites. 3. Sulphur. In: Jung, C., Collected Works of C. G. Jung, Vol. 14. 2nd ed., Princeton University Press, 1970. 702 p. (p. 110-128).

The alchemical attributes and effects of sulphur are presented and related both to the Christ image as a psychic archetype and to the structure of the psyche as perceived in modern psychology. Citing several texts, some alchemical qualities are attributed to sulphur: it is the prima materia of Sol and the companion of Luna. It possesses a psychic double nature: burning and corrosive, healing and purifying, corporal and spiritual, earthly and occult, the source of all living things and the end product. Its effects are shown to be equally dualistic: it consumes and purifies; it is a coagulating, tincturing, maturing principle. On the one hand it is identified with Diabolus, on the other with Christ; it is a synonym for the mysterious transformative substance. A parallel is drawn between properties of sulphur as they appear in the texts of Dorn, Paracelsus, the Turba and the Consilium coniugii and the role of Christ as Redeemer. Basic to both conceptions is the Jungian concept of the self which is defined as the human totality, greater than the ego conscious personality and embracing ego consciousness, the personal shadow and the collective unconscious. The discoveries of the alchemists are considered to be more important to psychology than to chemistry, since they revealed the psychological existence of the shadow which opposes and compensates the conscious, positive figure as well as the hidden structure of the psyche. This latter discovery is illustrated by means of the Christ/lapis/unconscious equation in which the unconscious is considered as the medicine for the untrustworthy sulphur, a symbolic representation of the motive factor in consciousness. Sulphur is compared to unconscious dynamism or compulsion which springs from both shadow and Anthropos contained in the unconscious. 3 references.

000521 The personification of the opposites. 4. Luna. a. The significance of the moon. In: Jung, C., Collected Works of C. G. Jung, Vol. 14. 2nd ed., Princeton University Press, 1970. 702 p. (p. 129-146).

From the texts of Dorn, Khunrath, Ruland, Macrobius, Simon Magus and the Allegoriae super librum Turbae among others, the alchemical characteristics of Luna are presented and analyzed. As the counterpart of Sol, Luna is cold, moist, dark, feminine, corporeal, passive and a partner in coniunctio. Luna is personified as sister, bride, mother, and spouse. Symbolized as the vessel of the sun and funnel of the earth, she is responsible for the conception of the universal seed of the sun in the belly and womb of nature. The symbol of the moon as a tree or plant is discussed and related to the tree symbols of Arabic alchemy, the Cabala, Christianity, and Hinduism. The connection of Luna (moon) to intellect and to the contrasexual archetypes in the unconscious is presented along with an analysis of the Gnosis of Simon Magus as an example of the description of a masculo/femina pneuma. The neotic qualities of Luna, the Luna/Mercurius relation and the role of Luna in

transformation mystery are examined in the light of the alchemic texts. The negative aspects of Luna are evident in the disadvantageous position given to Luna compared to that of Sol and in the attribution of appetites or sensual powers the sphere of the moon. The psychological interpretation of the Luna indicates that the alchemists perceived the union of Sol (consciousness) and Luna (unconscious) to be dangerous and productive of poisonous animals: first cold blooded, then warm blooded predators, and finally birds of prey. The alchemical role of Luna is compared to that of the Virgin Mary and the Church in that it partakes of earth's sufferings, standing on the borderline between etheral, eternal things and the earthly sublunar sphere.

000522 The personification of the opposites. 4. Luna. b. The dog. In: Jung, C., Collected Works of C. G. Jung, Vol. 14. 2nd ed., Princeton University Press, 1970. 702 p. (p. 146-160).

The process of uniting the contents of the unconscious with the conscious mind is presented through the analysis of imagery in alchemic texts. In these texts both Sol (conscious) and Luna (unconscious) are represented theriomorphically as dog and bitch, respectively, indicating the awareness that both the conscious and the unconscious have negative, fearsome aspects. Several texts are examined, showing a linking of three forces: flying bird, house, and stone; Hermaphrodite, doves, and rabid dog; Winged Youth, Diana and thief. Numerous functions of the dog as symbol in alchemic texts are explained, with particular attention given to the rabid dog as a symbol of the unconscious that turns into a winged eagle, a symbol of the transformation process involved in the healing of the psyche. The archetype of incest is examined as it appears in dreams and in the alchemic images. It is explained as a parable for the preliminary form of the union of opposites.

000523 The personification of the opposites. 4. Luna. c. The alchemical allegory. In: Jung, C., Collected Works of C. G. Jung, Vol. 14. 2nd ed., Princeton University Press, 1970. 702 p. (p. 160-173).

It is suggested that dreams, or alchemical parabales, which constitute the daily fare of the psychotherapist, can be translated into rational speech through knowledge of the dreamer's (alchemist's) personal situation or symbolic assumptions. Although it is conceded that dream interpretation can hardly ever be convincingly proved, the second of Philaletha's texts is examined as a dream, and the question is raised whether the author really had such thoughts and ideas concealed in ornate metaphors. In the dream the thief or robber of the self is contrasted with the winged youth, who represents the spirit of inner truth that measures man not by his relation to the mass, but by his relation to the mystery of the psyche. It is the age old struggle of evil versus good expressed in alchemical language, just as today the struggle is expressed in conflicting ideologies. Good and evil are seen as spiritual forces outside of man, who is caught in the conflict. We learn that the winged youth is espoused to the "central water." But he will become real only if he can unite with Luna, the "mother of mortal bodies." It is concluded that psychology can unravel the secrets of alchemy, but not lay bare the secret of its secrets.

000524 The personification of the opposites. 4. Luna. d. The moon-nature. In: Jung, C., Collected Works of C. G. Jung, Vol. 14. 2nd ed., Princeton University Press, 1970. 702 p. (173-182).

In a further discussion of the personification of the opposites, a psychological evaluation of the luminaries Luna and

Sol is presented, with considerations of the astrological and mythological disciplines included. The psychology of the moon is complex, and alchemical texts written exclusively by men are often observed to neglect women's role in alchemy. In the metaphorical descriptions of the alehcmists, Luna is primarily a reflection of a man's unconscious femininity, but she is also the principle of the feminine psyche in the sense that Sol is the principle of a male psyche. For purely psychological reasons, it is suggested that the name Logos equate the masculine consciousness characterized by discrimination, judgement, and insight; and Eros, the feminine consciousness, with the ability to relate. The common occurrence of a psychically predominant contrasexuality is seen as the chief psychological source for the alchemical concept of the hermaphrodite. Consciousness is seen as influenced by lunar anima in a man and solar animus in a woman. It is concluded that evil and good must find a balance, and that good forces are not sufficient to produce a national world order nor faultless ethical behavior. The forces of evil are so great that an individual can become imprisoned in them and commit crimes even if he is an ethical man. It is felt that the conflict between evil and good can not be eradicated, and that casuistic subtlety is indicated, as it is no longer a question of extirpating evil but of the difficulty of putting a lesser evil in place of a greater one.

000525 The personification of the opposites. 5. Sal. a. Salt as the arcane substance. In: Jung, C., Collected Works of C. G. Jung, Vol. 14. 2nd ed., Princeton University Press, 1970. 702 p. (p. 183-192).

Salt and a number of symbols closely related to salt, such as sea water and the baptismal quality and "bitterness" of the sea, are discussed as aspects of the unconscious. Sal is associated with lunar symbolism and is a member of the triad sulphur/Mercurius/sal, which from the time of Paracelsus was seen as corresponding to the Trinity; since Mercurius has both masculine and feminine qualities, this triad, like the Trinity, is really a quaternity. The fourth figure in alchemy, the dark, lunary, feminine side of Mercurius, is identified with the devil in Christian tradition. The Assumption of Mary in Catholic doctrine is discussed as an example of the ultimate acceptance of this necessary fourth figure lacking in the Trinity. Salt in alchemical philosophy is identified as the symbol of the arcane substance; this concept is traced to early Arabic influence on Latin texts such as the "Turba," where salt water is a synonym for the aqua permanens. This association with the arcane substance is found to be more clearly supported in the later alchemical texts. 6 references.

000526 The personification of opposites. 5. Sal. b. The bitterness. In: Jung, C., Collected Works of C. G. Jung, Vol. 14. 2nd ed., Princeton University Press, 1970. 702 p. (p. 192-198).

Associated with salt and sea is the quality of bitterness, an alchemical term connoting not only the sharp salt taste of the sea water, but also corruption and imperfection. This corruption is the quality of the prima materia, which is synonymous in alchemical and mythological tradition with chaos and the sea. It is noted that the sea was often characterized as something impure in ancient cultures, especially that of Egypt and Greece; in the same cultures and in ancient China as well, salt is often found characterized as a spirit and identified with a bird. This bird represents the spirit of corruption expelled from an impure substance which is made pure thereby; it is usually said to have many colors. This and other spirits of impurity constitute that part of the universe which is still chaos, and in the psychological sense, that part of the psyche which remains unconscious. As the spirit of chaos is indispensable to

the alchemical world order, so the unconscious is essential to the balanced working of the mind. 1 reference.

000527 The personification of the opposites. 5. Sal. c. The Red Sea. In: Jung, C., Collected Works of C. G. Jung, Vol. 14. 2nd ed., Princeton University Press, 1970. 702 p. (p. 199-210).

The Red Sea has a unique symbolic value; in contrast with the bitterness and impurity usually associated with the sea, it represents the healing and transforming properties of baptismal waters. The destruction of the Egyptians trying to cross the Red Sea is seen as an allegory of the inability of the unenlightened or unaware to be transformed; more specifically, it is the inability of the incomplete psyche to find wholeness. The resistance of Christian tradition to the acceptance of the "other," the unconscious and primitive, as part of the order of life, is viewed as a barrier to the very salvation it purports to seek. Numerous references to the significance of the Red Sea in alchemical thought are examined. Allusions are found to a symbolic vehicle which is immersed in the Red Sea and purified; the vessel is commonly characterized as combining the four elements as a reflection of the unity of the world. In psychological terms, the vessel symbolizes the psyche, combining the four functions of consciousness, which goes through a period of introversion leading to the ideal integration of the personality. Similar chariot figures are discovered in Indian mythology and in the Song of Songs. The frequent association of a serpent with the chariot is discussed in terms of the serpent as the anima mundi, an image of the arcane substance, and the relationship of chariot wheels as points of consciousness to the symbol of the eye is noted. 7 references.

000528 The personification of opposites. 5. Sal. d. The fourth of the three. In: Jung, C., Collected Works of C. G. Jung, Vol. 14. 2nd ed., Princeton University Press, 1970. 702 p. (210-217).

The symbolic value of the privileged alchemical number four is examined as representative of the four functions of consciousness. The fourth function is described as the most unconscious of all; it is usually symbolized as a great animal such as Leviathan, or a whale, a wolf, or a dragon. In Maier's text in particular, the fourth function is identified with Africa, the dark and mysterious continent. In the story of a mystical journey whose goal is the understanding of the world, the fourth place visited -- Africa -- is the site of revelation to the traveler. A fabulous animal combining the four alchemical colors appears; through interpretation of this quaternity symbol and of the animal soul of the Ortus, Maier finds new meaning and self-knowledge. Associations of the Ortus symbol with other figures of the self are mentioned. 2 references.

000529 The personification of the opposites. 5. Sal. e. Ascent and descent. In: Jung, C., Collected Works of C. G. Jung, Vol. 14. 2nd ed., Princeton University Press, 1970. 702 p. (p. 217-224).

The tale by Michael Maier of the quest for knowledge covering four continents is examined for its allegorical content. In particular, Maier's comparison of the seven mouths of the Nile to the seven planets, and his description of an ascent and descent through these seven planetary spheres, is seen in terms of a reunion of higher and lower powers. It is noted that in Christian/Gnostic tradition this symbolic transformation involves descent and subsequent ascent (resurrection), while in the text in question and in alchemical interpretation in general the reverse process operates. The soul in alchemical thought rises into the spiritual realm, but is not made whole until its descent into the center of the earth. This ascent and descent are seen to represent the realization of psychic opposites, a realization which leads to their integration and to a complete personality.

000530 The personification of the opposites. 5. Sal. f. The journey through the planetary houses. In: Jung, C., Collected Works of C. G. Jung, Vol 14. 2nd ed., Princeton University Press, 1970. 702 p. (p. 224-235).

In a psychological interpretation of Michael Maier's symbolic journey to the seven mouths of the Nile, the theme of individuation is traced in its correspondences with alchemical tradition. The mystic journey through the planets is associated with the archetypal voyage of the hero, particularly as it is expressed in the "Shepherd of Hermas." Further comparison of the two texts reveals a number of analogies in the stages and events of the journey toward enlightenment; both are seen to symbolize the psychological motif of the search for psychic wholeness through confrontation of conscious process and unconscious content. The original state of spiritual confusion experienced by the seekers leads in modern therapy to an analysis and interpretation of irrational thoughts expressed in dreams and fantasies (anamesis). The acceptance of this material from the unconscious widens the perspective and awareness of the conscious mind, and enables the enriched personality to better cope with its environment. It is noted that the seven spheres had great significance for ancient astrologers as well, and that a journey through the planets meant to them a systematic shedding of character traits ordained by each planet. Another model for the journey is found in the Gnostic redeemer. The peculiar reticence of Maier to describe the last conversation of the searcher with Mercurius is explained as a sign of the excruciating psychic conflict experienced in the process of individuation. 1 reference.

000531 The personification of the opposites. 5. Sal. g. The regeneration in sea-water. In: Jung, C., Collected Works of C. G. Jung, Vol. 14. 2nd ed., Princeton University Press, 1970. 702 p. (p. 235-239).

A philosophical discussion on sea water (salt water) is presented from the viewpoints of alchemy, symbolism, and baptism in the Christian religions. The principal function of sea water is cleansing the sinner. In the ritual of baptism it becomes symbolically synonymous with fire, which is itself a cleansing agent recommended for baptism in certain parts of the Christian Bible. The alchemists professed to a transformation between fire and water, which they regarded as baptism. Sources from various cultures are cited, from literature, mythology, and religious writings -- ancient, medieval, and modern -- in which sea water is held to possess certain powers, esoteric meanings, and special symbolic and spiritual allusions to other substances, processes, or phenomena. Thus the treatise of Ostanes says that when preparing the baptismal vessel, it should be immersed in sea water in order to perfect the divine water within. In sea water baptism, as the liquid evaporates from the body, the salt (symbol of wisdom) remains. While the impurities have left the body, it is volatated and sublimated. Psychologically the process corresponds to the conscious realization and integration of the unconscious. 10 references.

000532 The personification of the opposites. 5. Sal. h. The interpretation and meaning of salt. In: Jung, C., Collected Works of C. G. Jung, Vol. 14. 2nd ed., Princeton University Press, 1970. 702 p. (p. 239-257).

A variety of alchemical significations for the substance salt are examined; the link between the several different motifs is seen to be the association of salt with soul. Salt is a transcen-

dental substance which coagulates and transforms other substances; like the word soul, it pervades all substances. Salt is associated with the Christ figure in that both are identified with the anima mundi, the creative substance. Scriptural references are cited in which salt is synonymous with wisdom, in the form of Godly revelation or human insight. The psychological interpretation of salt as a symbol of the self finds support in the dream material and drawings of patients, in which a crystalline substance is commonly seen to represent the center, the self; the duality of bitterness and wisdom reflects the struggle of the psyche. Salt is further associated in alchemical tradition with the moon, the earth, and the feminine nature. The duality in the nature of salt is expressed by a number of different alchemical and religious symbols. However, the alchemists appear to have had considerably more understanding of the imagery involved than did the later Christians; they recognized the dark part of the psyche and of the world, whereas the Church demanded -- and demands -- a kind of blindness to the limitations of its dogma, refusing the shadow a place in the order of things. 2 references.

000533 Rex and regina. 1. Introduction. In: Jung, C., Collected Works of C. G. Jung, Vol. 14. 2nd ed., Princeton University Press, 1970. 702 p. (p. 258-261).

The symbolism of Christ as King, and the idea of kingship in general, is seen as an expression of an archetypal figure. Highly developed social and theological structures based on the idea of kingship are noted in Oriental, Egyptian and Greek cultures; the trinity symbol is also found in these traditions.

000534 Rex and regina. 2. Gold and spirit. In: Jung, C., Collected Works of C. G. Jung, Vol. 14. 2nd ed., Princeton University Press, 1970. 702 p. (p 261-265).

The similarity between certain alchemical and Christian symbols is explained by their common source in primitive mysticism. The king imagery in particular is traced from alchemical literature of the first and third centuries; in them the king is identified with the metal gold, which is produced through the liberation of the soul from the flesh. This chrysopoeia (goldmaking) was thought of even then as a psychic operation, a moral and spiritual transformation from the fleshly to the pnenumatic. References to the birth of the king in Egyptian and alchemical literature are mentioned. 1 reference.

000535 Rex and regina. 3. The transformation of the king. In: Jung, C., Collected Works of C. G. Jung, Vol. 14. 2nd ed., Princeton University Press, 1970. 702 p. (p. 265-274).

The king as a dynamic symbol of transformation is examined in alchemical literature, either in the description of his birth or in his rebirth into perfection. In the medieval treatise "Allegoria Merlini" the primitive symbol of the sacrificed king being resurrected in new strength is elaborated; in this and other similar parables the agent of resurrection is the sweet water, the aqua permanens. Citations from several alchemical treatises demonstrate the importance of water in the symbolic process of transformation; in the writings of Dorn, it is clear that the solution process was viewed as more a spiritual phenomenon than a physical one, a psychic union of conflicting elements into one substance. Although it is not evident in the "Allegoria Merlini," in later alchemical literature the rebirth process commonly leads to a higher moral and spiritual state as well as -- or instead of -- a merely physical one.

000536 Rex and regina. 4. The regeneration of the king (Ripley's "Cantilena"). In: Jung, C., Collected Works of C. G.

Jung, Vol. 14. 2nd ed., Princeton University Press, 1970. 702 p. (p. 274-330).

The "Cantilena" of Sir George Ripley is analyzed relative to the symbolic revitalization of the sick king. From the beginning of the "Cantilena" the imperfect, corrupt nature of the king is stressed, as is his need for renewal through the aqua permanens. Identification of this transformative substance with God is hinted at in the text, with its corresponding allusions to imperfection as a part of God's character. This representation of God appears to be a combination of Christian and pagan influence, since Christian theology does not recognize weakness or corruption in God. In order to enter the kingdom of God, the king of the Cantilena must return to the initial world state of massa confusa, where all elements are in conflict. This transformational process is accomplished through a return to the mother and through her to the original substance of the lapis of seven symbolic colors. Both the lapis and peacock figures symbolize the reunion of all elements in alchemical tradition. The great amount of overlap in the symbolic structure of alchemical beliefs, exemplified in the Cantilena, is considered due to the archetypal nature of the symbols which arise from a comingling (homoousia) in the unconscious. The numerous appearances of animals as symbolic motifs in the Cantilena represent the return of the king to the animal state, the psychic source of revitalization; for this reason images of savage animals predominate. The animals are often associated with feminine figures, again symbolizing the dark unconscious aspect of the king which must be assimilated. The transformation itself is seen as taking place in isolation; it is a dissolution, a very similar process to that symbolically described by the Mass. The historical development of the ancient art of alchemy into modern analytical science is not considered surprising in view of the enormous enthusiasm of the alchemists for research. Further, the alchemists are felt to have been much more in touch with psychic reality than many later philosophers, particularly in their realization of the importance of assimilation of conflicting elements.

000537 Rex and regina. 5. The dark side of the king. In: Jung, C., Collected Works of C. G. Jung, Vol. 14. 2nd ed., Princeton University Press, 1970. 702 p. (p. 330-343).

The phase of decay and death (nigredo) leading to the rebirth of the king is examined. It is noted that the common symbol of immersion or sinking into the depths had a distinctly paradoxical character in alchemical literature, signifying both a return to the corruption of the sea and a purification through its renewing powers. This and other paradoxes were basic to alchemical thought, which carefully preserved the idea of the polarity of all things; this perspective is considered a healthy one, whereas extreme onesidedness developed in the name of clarity is seen as a dangerous imbalance in both the psychic and the social sense. The reborn king is frequently symbolized by the Mercurial serpent figure and the phoenix, regenerated (first as a worm) from its own destruction. In alchemical symbolic structure Mercurius is synonymous with the life force which connects and thus transforms the chaos. The appearance of the serpent allegory in Christian as well as alchemical allegory is explored. 16 references.

000538 Rex and regina. 6. The king as Anthropos. In: Jung, C., Collected Works of C. G. Jung, Vol. 14. 2nd ed., Princeton University Press, 1970. 702 p. (p. 343-355).

The correspondences between the alchemical figure of the king and the Christ figure are discussed in terms of their source in the archetypal projections of the unconscious. The alchemical motif of the dissolution of the kingly "matter" and

its eventual generation has many parallels in the passion of Christ; however, the psychic connotations this symbolic configuration had for the alchemists is much closer to the Basilidian conception of the redeemer than to the Christian. It is felt that this image of Christ as inner man, suppressed by Christianity, reflects a primordial and preconscious archetype expressed by many early cultures. The fact that Christian tradition even partially manifests this archetype is considered to be the reason for the widespread acceptance of the dogma; the archetype is recognized subliminally by the practitioner of the rite. The Gnostic symbol of the inner man was the Anthropos; he is Chinese alchemy's chen-yen, Dorn's "vir unus," and the lapis philosophorum. He is characterized as an integrated individual rather than a redeemer of others. The struggles of the hero figures in alchemical texts are similar in form to the Passion of Christ, but not in purpose, for the hero in the former sacrifices the self to redeem the self in an allegory of the psyche's struggle for wholeness. This emphasis on the psychological theme in alchemical tradition is supported by citations from Dorn and Chinese alchemist Wei Po-yang. 4 references.

000539 Rex and regina. 7. The relation of the king-symbol to consciousness. In: Jung, C., Collected Works of C. G. Jung, Vol. 14. 2nd ed., Princeton University Press, 1970. 702 p. (p. 355-365).

The constellation of alchemical symbols surrounding the rebirth of the king is discussed in terms of the integration of the psyche through conscious acceptance of unconscious material. The female symbol of Luna/mother is identified with the unconscious in the psychological sense, and with the Virgin Mother in Christian tradition. The king is seen as synonymous with the sun and with the light of consciousness, or more specifically the subjective ego personality which is consciousness. The deterioration of the king personality occurs as the psychic process becomes more and more limited to the conscious functions, repressing the vast unconscious and unaware of its dynamic nature. It is at this point in the psychic process that dreams and fantasies abound, created by the strain of imbalance between the two functions; if the unconscious is still not confronted and analyzed, neurotic symptoms follow. A historicoreligious analogy to psychic decadence and reintegration is seen in the dominant Christian view of the world in the Middle Ages, and in the changes Christian doctrine underwent under the influence of Protestantism. The shedding of Catholic ritual and dogma, and particularly the rejection of the feminine element (the cult of the virgin), led to the dominance of the rational in Protestantism. The spirituality of the dogmatic image receded into the unconscious; it is suggested that the popularity of alchemy in the 16th and 17th centuries is due to the surviving psychic need for contact with the complete archetype, a need unfulfilled by Protestant doctrine. As the dominance of the conscious at the expense of the unconscious leads to neurosis in the individual, so it led to the religious wars and bloody conflicts of the Age of Enlightenment. In light of these observations, the importance of conscious acceptance of eternal images is emphasized on the social as well as the individual level. 11 references.

000540 Rex and regina. 8. The religious problem of the king's renewal. In: Jung, C., Collected Works of C. G. Jung, Vol. 14. 2nd ed., Princeton University Press, 1970. 702 p. (p. 365-376).

The belief systems of alchemy and Christianity are considered in light of medical psychology, particularly as they relate to the conflict between the conscious and the unconscious. It is felt that a thorough understanding of archetypal symbolism in Christian dogma would be especially beneficial to the psychotherapist whose patient develops an unexpected interest in religious questions during the course of therapy; these patients are seen as having spiritual demands which sometimes necessitate the analyst's involvement in purely theological matters. The renewal of the aging king and the death and resurrection of Christ are seen as expressions of the archetypal myth; further the Christ figure is a symbol of the unity of conscious and unconscious in which neither contains the other, but rather a totality is formed. Christ and Buddha are similar in that they reintroduced the mythologem Anthropos, the human figure, into religions dominated by gods. However, the androgynous nature of Christ has been largely suppressed, whereas in alchemical and psychological symbolism the male/female conflict and union is essential to the renewed king personality. Moreover, the ideal interpenetration of divine and human, a symbolic expression of the union of psychic opposites, is alluded to in Christian texts but not made explicit in the doctrine. It is concluded that the mystics, among them the alchemists, have contributed most to the widening of dogmatic boundaries and to the conservation of the true, fulfilling and unbiased expression of archetypal images. 6 references.

000541 rex and Regina. 9. Regina. In: Jung, C., Collected Works of C. G. Jung, Vol. 14. 2nd ed., Princeton University Press, 1970. 702 p. (p. 376-381).

Some of the mythological and religious forms in which the archetypal symbol anima has appeared throughout history are briefly discussed. The anima is seen as forming the archetypal syzygy with the animus in the figures of Luna, the Queen of Sheba and, in the Christian symbolic organization, the Church, the vessel of Christ. The image of Christ as essentially androgynous, uniting the anima (soul) and the animus (consciousness), is stressed. In the human psyche, the animus is still seen to symbolize consciousness, while the anima personifies the unconscious. The negative aspect of the anima/unconscious is seen as the power it can exert on the conscious subject, aiding and strengthening the ego to the detriment of the persona. The renunciation of the nefarious forces of the anima is seen as redemptive, leading to a more perfectly balanced psyche. It is emphasized that the animus/anima figure is a psychological concept derived not at all from mythology, but from practical investigation and case material; it is an intuitive representation of a psychological process the real mechanism of which cannot be conceived.

000542 Adam and Eve. 1. Adam as the arcane substance. In: Jung, C., Collected Works of C. G. Jung, Vol. 14. 2nd ed., Princeton University Press, 1970. 702 p. (p. 382-390).

The mythicoreligious figures of Adam and Eve are seen as alchemical symbols expressing the relationship of opposites. Adam is seen as the arcane, transformative substance, the prima materia. The importance of the transformational process is illustrated by the multitude of symbols of the bath as rebirth; all symbolic material dealing with the bath, baptism, submersion, and drowning are included in this representation of the unconscious process of rebirth of the self. It is felt that the reason the figure of Adam is associated with this primordial material is that he was made out of clay, viewed by alchemists as the prima materia; this substance was regarded as a piece of the original massa confusa, primordial but capable of organization and transformation. As the ordering of the universe is symbolized as a unity of the four elements, so Adam is found to represent the compositio elementorum throughout religious literature; he is seen as composed of the

four corners of the earth, and the four colors and elements are part of him. Psychologically, Adam's quaternary nature corresponds to the four functions of consciousness, two of them perceptive/irrational, and two discriminative/rational. He represents the total and unified psyche. The importance of these early representations for the interpretation of dreams is stressed. 10 references.

000543 Adam and Eve. 2. The statue. In: Jung, C., Collected Works of C. G. Jung, Vol. 14. 2nd ed., Princeton University Press, 1970. 702 p. (p. 390-397).

The alchemical symbol of the statue is considered in its early religious philosophical and mythological manifestations. It is first noted to be associated with the figure of Adam; in him and in other figures the statue is characterized as a lifeless body into which life is placed. Another common symbolic configuration is the image of some precious substance being hidden in the statue -- water, sacred oil, or figures of the gods. In each case the bringing to life of the statue is seen as a sublime and mysterious work of redemption, admired in particular by the alchemists as the highest form of transformation/creation. It is noted that the living statue is often represented as the end state of the creative work; it is sometimes found in symbolic representations of the end of the world, when all life is transmuted into a perfect state. This representation is found in Manichaean as well as Christian symbol structures. In the latter the statue is often a pillar of glory, the perfect human; thus the figure of the complete primordial man (Adam) is found at both the beginning of creation (the prima materia) and its end (the lapis philosophorum). The frequent appearance of sun imagery in association with the statue is felt to support is character of perfection and divinity. 6 references.

000544 Adam and Eve. 3. Adam as the first adept. In: Jung, C., Collected Works of C. G. Jung, Vol. 14. 2nd ed., Princeton University Press, 1970. 702 p. (p. 397-406).

The characterization of Adam in early religious and philosphical writings as the personification of intelligence by virtue of his perfection and original righteousness is associated with the alchemical notion of the lapis philosophorum. The legend of Adam as the inventor of all the arts and professions through his diachronous knowledge is traced to Jewish tradition, which represents Adam as the first of eight incarnations of the true prophet, the last being Jesus. This concept of the primordial seer is also observed to exist in ancient Chinese mythology; the light prophets appear in the Taoist series of the eight immortals, but in this particular legend the eighth saint is a girl. These serial configurations and others found in literature and philosophy are associated with the concept of concentric circles appearing in Herodotus and in Persian and Mithraic mysteries as well as in Christian symbolism. The nature of Adam as the first prophet, like that of Christ as the eighth, is seen as the male/female duality of the androgyne, in which Adam is the spirit and Eve the flesh. 18 references.

000545 Adam and Eve. 4. The polarity of Adam. In: Jung, C., Collected Works of C. G. Jung, Vol. 14. 2nd ed., Princeton University Press, 1970. 702 p. (p. 406-415).

The dual nature of Adam is described as it appears in early philosophical and religious thought, and its associations with alchemical symbolism are considered. The foremost manifestation of this duality is the hermaphroditism of Adam which appears in Jewish tradition and among the Naassenes. Examples of primordial androgynous beings are also found in Plato's spherical Original Being, in the Persian Gayomart and in Arabic Hermes mythology; however, few traces of this idea are found in alchemical treatises. Numerous other symbolic constructs aside from the androgyne are observed to represent the basic polarity in Adam's physical and spiritual nature; he is often represented as having two faces and as being composed of evil as well as good forces. The inner connection of Adam and Satan is stressed as an integral part of Adam's being; Adam is in fact the source of the macrocosm, the prima materia from which all force and substance derives, whether it is evil or good. A great deal of support is found in alchemical symbolism for this expanded form of dualism/unity in the primordial man figure. Sources for the image appear very early in Jewish, Christian and pagan thought; later the Christian element is seen to dominate and the syncretistic pagan concepts diminish in force. Christian mysticism and Jewish gnosis (Cabala) are seen to perpetuate the image of Adam as the embodiment of the universe in a similar manner; Jewish/Gnostic antecedents for the Song of Songs, and midrashic sources for the distinction found in I Corinthians between the heavenly and earthly Adam. As he unites both the body and soul of the Israelite people, so in the psychological sense Adam is the total psyche, embodying both the conscious and unconscious elements. The process of psychic integration in which all unconscious elements become conscious, and which can redeem the inner man is seen as a correlation of the Christian symbolism of the redeemption of the world through the coming of the Messiah (the second Adam). 27 references.

000546 Adam and Eve. 5. The "old Adam." In: Jung, C., Collected Works of C. G. Jung, Vol. 14. 2nd ed., Princeton University Press, 1970. 702 p. (p. 415-420).

A discussion of the probable referent for the "old Adam" in Eleazar's text "Uraltes Chymisches Werck" leads to a consideration of the eternal opposition/union of the spiritual and physical in human nature. The old Adam corresponds to the sinful Adam who issued from the Shulamite; he is the primitive man, far removed from present day consciousness and having his roots in the animal world. The Primordial Man, on the other hand, embodies perfect wisdom and intelligence in Christian and other ancient symbolic systems. But as the Adam figure is ultimately seen as uniting both the sinful and pure elements of the universe, so the human psyche is discovered through analytical psychology to contain much archaic, unconscious, instinctual material in addition to its conscious rational content. These psychic forces are seen as complementary but conflicting; the tension between them creates the energy for the extension and differentiation of consciousness. However, if the tension becomes too intense, a countermovement becomes operative to reconcile the conflicting elements. This mechanism is seen to operate on a social as well as on a psychic level, in the development throughout history of rites and customs (anamnesis) designed to ameliorate states of distress through divine intervention. If no intervention is forthcoming, the distressful life situation deteriorates; and if no reconciliation is made, the individual psyche degenerates, losing forever the image of the homo maximus, the Anthropos. 2 references.

000547 Adam and Eve. 6. The transformation. In: Jung, C., Collected Works of C. G. Jung, Vol. 14. 2nd ed., Princeton University Press, 1970. 702 p. (p. 420-434).

The alchemical and Christian symbolic expressions for the transformation from a defective to a perfect state are compared. By eating from the tree of knowledge, Adam and Eve gained a moral consciousness which opened the polarity between divine and human; humanity degenerated steadily until the Deluge, which can be seen as the destroying and puri-

fying waters of alchemical symbolism, the nigredo. In Eleazar's "Uraltes Chymisches Werck" the Shulamite as the symbol of decay and corruption must be crucified to be transformed; this crucifixion is compared to that of Christ and to the transformation of Parvati. Certain quaternary relationships in the text -- the quaternion of the Black/Illuminated Shulamite to Old Adam/Adam Kadmon, for example -- are found to correspond to psychic as well as alchemical structures. However, one significant difference in the psychological transformation is stressed: while the goal of perfection is possible, in the myths and doctrines which are archetypal projections of the psychic drive for unity, this ideal psychic union has never been approached in reality. In the light of scientific objectivity, man has had to set his sights considerably lower than did the medieval romanticists. The incomplete transformation of the Shulamite and of Old Adam in Eleazar's text are considered to express a realization by the author that wholeness for man is only imperfectly achieved. 6 references.

000548 Adam and Eve. 7. Rotundum, head and brain. In: Jung, C., Collected Works of C. G. Jung, Vol. 14. 2nd ed., Princeton University Press, 1970. 702 p. (p. 434-438).

Various symbolic representations of the head and brain in alchemical and religious symbolism are examined. The motif of the golden head is found in the Song of Songs and in alchemical texts; in alchemy the arcane substance, the corpus rotundum, is also associated with gold. References to the brain in alchemical treatises and in the Scriptures portray the brain as the source of infernal as well as divine forces. This similarity in symbolic expression, manifesting itself in extremely diverse belief systems, is considered to strongly support the hypothesis of archetypal image projection. 4 references.

000549 Adam and Eve. 8. Adam as totality. In: Jung, C., Collected Works of C. G. Jung, Vol. 14. 2nd ed., Princeton University Press, 1970. 702 p. (p. 438-456).

The transformation symbolism seen in Eleazar's "Uraltes Chymisches Werck" is discussed in terms of its correspondences with Christian symbolism. It is felt that Eleazar had in mind the apocalyptic figure of the Son of Man when he referred to the duality and union of earth and fire, sun and moon, in the transfiguration process. Allusions to the quaternity and to multiples of the quaternity, essential to alchemical structures, are found in early Christian texts such as Ezekiel as well as in 17th and 18th century alchemical treatises. The figure of Yesod in Revelations is considered to correspond with Mercurius, the creative force which mediates the resolution of polarity. The alchemical symbol of the lapis, which is the sapphire in the Cabala, are also found in Ezekiel, Exodus and Deuteronomy to be closely associated or identified with God. It is concluded that the alchemical symbol network represents an effort to express the integration of evil as a necessary part of redemption on the individual human level; the ultimate source for the symbolism is the psychic individuation process. The nigredo in Eleazar's text represents the darkness of the unconscious, or the shadow. The first transformation, represented by the Black Shulamite, is the rise to consciousness of the feminine aspect, the anima; the second is the differentiation within the consciousness (the Primordial Man) of the masculine and feminine aspects. But the final transformation is not complete in the Shulamite nor in the Old Adam; neither is it in the psyche of man. It is emphasized that this and other studies of the dynamics of psychic processes are scientific and not theological, although they may make use of theology during their development. 13 references.

000550 The conjunction. 1. The alchemical view of the union of opposites. In: Jung, C., Collected Works of C. G. Jung, Vol. 14. 2nd ed., Princeton University Press, 1970. 702 p. (p. 457-469).

The symbolic as well as chemical nature of alchemical procedures and goals is described. It is felt that the coniunctio in alchemical tradition represented more than the attempt to produce gold by a combination of other substances; it was the expression of a world view which included both the exterior and interior universe of man. It is for this reason that one finds such an aggregation of symbols representing the transformative process; all the symbols ultimately describe a psychic rather than a physical reality. The alchemical description of the beginning of the world, for example, describe as well the primitive state of consciousness on the point of differentiation into its affective processes (represented alchemically by the four elements). Deterioration accompanies this differentiation, and the elements must be reunited into one world consciousness. The alchemists themselves are observed to associate the physical with the psychic union, since they commonly considered self-knowledge a requisite for the production of the Philosopher's Stone. Mercurius, both the agent and the object of unification, is the collective unconscious, the undifferentiated Being. Just as many alchemical symbols are found to signify certain archetypes, so too the archetypes are united in that each reflects an aspect of the ego. This ultimate center is itself symbolized by the mandala, or in alchemy by the lapis or the Microcosm. It is noted that alchemical theorists, lacking any real knowledge of psychic and chemical processes, believed in the symbol rather than the thing symbolized, although the texts do sometimes demonstrate an intuitive association of the two. The progressive social function of symbol is proposed as a counterpart to its reflect function; symbols move the conscious toward a definite, but undefined, psychic goal. 11 references.

000551 The conjunction. 2. Stages of The conjunction. In: Jung, C., Collected Works of C. G. Jung, Vol. 14. 2nd ed., Princeton University Press, 1970. 702 p. (p. 469-477).

A comparison is made between the voluntary death and reunion of opposites, expressed symbolically in alchemy, and the processes of individuation in psychotherapy. Since the soul is an organ of the spirit and the body an instrument of the soul, it is deemed necessary to become aware of the elements of the composite. This dissolution and discrimination is akin to a dissociation of the personality, a violation of the mere natural man, perceived by the alchemists as a kind of death. The next step in individuation is presented as a reunion of the spirit with the body, symbolized by the chymical marriage in alchemy and parallel to the Christ image in theology. Dorn is credited with recognizing the psychological implications of this reunion. The insights from this union must be made real, making a reality of the man who has acquired knowledge of his paradoxical wholeness. This last step is considered to be the crux of the individuation process, a stage which is not yet fully understood. 2 references.

000552 The conjunction. 3. The production of the quintessence. In: Jung, C., Collected Works of C. G. Jung, Vol. 14 2nd ed., Princeton University Press, 1970. 702 p. (p. 477-482).

Texts cited from the writings of the alchemist, Dorn, serve to illustrate the belief that a "balsam" or quintessence, hidden in the human soul, is necessary for the uniting of the opposites, soul and body, the second stage of the coniunctio. The nature of this balsam is defined and several synonyms for it are given. The result of this balsam (truth) is described as self-knowledge which enables one to know what he is rather than who he is. It is felt that from this knowledge will spring knowledge of God, of others and of the world. 4 references.

000553 The conjunction. 4. The meaning of the alchemical procedure. In: Jung, C., Collected Works of C. G. Jung, Vol. 14. 2nd ed., Princeton University Press, 1970. 702 p. (p. 482-487).

The ingredients used by the alchemists in preparing the quintessence are listed and their properties described. Honey, celandine, dog's mercury, the lily, and human blood were among the ingredients used to produce caelum, a purified liquid that, in Dorn's view, corresponded to the celestial substance, the secret truth, the hidden treasure in man. This product is interpreted to mean the kingdom of heaven on earth. In this chemical procedure, fraught with mystery and magic overtones, the fantasy of the alchemist was given free play. In considering the role of fantasy, the psychological meaning of the procedure can be revealed. 1 reference.

000554 The conjunction. 5. The psychological interpretation of the procedure. In: Jung, C., Collected Works of C. G. Jung, Vol. 14. 2nd ed., Princeton University Press, 1970. 702 p. (p. 487-496).

The alchemical identification of the body with the chemical preparation caelum is discussed as a projection of psychic contents into chemical substances. The significance attached to the ingredients: sweetness of life in honey, accentuation of value in celandine, and the power of binding in rosemary, are examined in order to show the nature of the psychic contents projected on the caelum. It is believed that the alchemists worked both with a mixture of herbs and with ideas, psychic processes and states referred to under the name of the corresponding substances. The purpose of this symbolic rite is seen as being the creation of the God image or life principle that, if interpreted psychologically, represents the individuation process by means of active imagination. A therapeutic method of allowing the patient to create a series of images that reveal the contents of the unconscious is described; this coming face to face with the other by dealing with the contents of the shadow is considered a positive way of gaining insight into the complex nature of the personality. 1 reference.

000555 The conjunction. 6. Self-knowledge. In: Jung, C., Collected Works of C. G. Jung, Vol. 14. 2nd ed., Princeton University Press, 1970. 702 p. (p. 497-505).

The method and meaning of arriving at self-knowledge, in alchemy and in psychology, are discussed. The alchemical term meditation is seen to correspond to the psychological process of getting in touch with one's unconscious. A distinction is made between this type of meditation and that of the Spiritual Exercises of St. Ignatius or other forms of religious meditation that reflect on the conscious ego or on objective events. The first effect of confrontation with the shadow is called chaos, melancholy nigredo, for at this point there is a dead balance, an absence of any moral decisions. A distinction is made between the meditation of the alchemists, the confronting of the shadow, and that type of meditation practiced by philosophers or religious people. The latter is used to develop concentration and consolidate consciousness. It has no therapeutic value, except in those instances where the conscious is overwhelmed by the unconscious. Critical introspection, on the other hand, is considered necessary to allow the subject to establish and recognize his projections and to integrate the material discovered in them into his personality. From an examination of the text of Dorn, the role of Mercurius in the unio mentalis is described, and the alchemical view of selfeknowledge is seen to correspond to the psychological definition of it. The process of arriving at this self-knowledge involved a union of opposites from which union sprang a third principle free from the opposites. The writings of Albertus Magnus reveal insight into the psychological meaning of this transcendental third principle, creating a quaternion that corresponds to modern representations of the self. 2 references.

000556 The conjunction. 7. The Monocolus. In: Jung, C., Collected Works of C. G. Jung, Vol. 14. 2nd ed., Princeton University Press, 1970. 702 p. (p. 505-519).

Through the examination of an illustration found in an 18th century French manuscript, the images used for expressing the alchemical concepts of the stages of conjunction are explained. The colors, symbols and positions of the figures in the illustrations are shown to represent the initial separation (stage of chaos or melancholy), the extraction of the contents of the shadow, and the union of the opposites. The coniunctio appears here as the union of a consciousness (spirit), differentiated by self-knowledge, with a spirit abstracted from previously unconscious content. Although the alchemical images of these stages seem far removed from the terminology of modern psychology, it is stated that, if analyzed as one would analyze a fantasy, the images of the alchemists correspond strikingly to images produced in psychoses, dreams and active imagination. The philosophy of the alchemists is therefore described as projected psychology.

000557 The conjunction. 8. The content and meaning of the first two stages. In: Jung, C., Collected Works of C. G. Jung, Vol. 14. 2nd ed., Princeton University Press, 1970. 702 p. (p. 519-533).

The process of self-knowledge as a step toward psychic union is discussed in historical and psychotherapeutic terms. Direct confrontation with the self, without the aid of projections, was as difficult in ancient times as it is now, and for this reason primitive man constructed all sorts of rituals and religious experiences to make contact with the unconscious while still being protected from it. Today this function is performed by the formalized religions. When certain archetypal expressions become ineffective through social or scientific progress, new formulations evolve which represent the archetypal myth according to the mores and attitudes of the new culture; a prime example of this process is considered to be the progressive reinterpretation of the Christian doctrine throughout its history. Since Christianity has traditionally denied the body, however, other compensatory belief systems grew with it which concerned themselves with natural bodies as well; such a system was alchemy, which began to flourish as early as the 13th century. The dilemma of the analyst is seen to be his inability to provide his patients with more than partial solutions; he can effectively cure certain aberrations in their behavior or thought patterns, but he cannot solve the everyday human problems with which he himself struggles. Real self-knowledge must by achieved by the individual; although the analyst may provide the initial insight, the experience of self is the patient's alone. The second stage of self-knowledge, in which the patient progresses from the mere appreciation of his fantasies to the moral and intellectual judgment of them, is considered possible and even essential in some cases, though dangerous. 4 references.

000558 The conjunction. 9. The third stage: the unus mundus. In: Jung, C., Collected Works of C. G. Jung, Vol. 14. 2nd ed., Princeton University Press, 1970. 702 p. (p. 533-543).

The alchemical idea of unus mundus, the last stage of conjunction, is considered in terms of the psychic process of self-knowledge. In alchemical terms this final union produces the undifferentiated world of before the Creation; in the psychic sense it is the union of the liberated and assimilated unconscious with the collective unconscious. This process, which forms an essential part of Eastern belief, is seen as an alien concept to the Western mind. The assimilation of the physical with the spiritual that such a union would involve is conceded to be unfathomable with man's present understanding of the world; but it is felt that in light of the numerous relationships already discovered between psychic and physical processes, the actual identity of the two beyond our present experience can be justifiably proposed. That the two aspects of man strive for union is considered demonstrable, however; it is a tendency evidenced by the discontent of the alchemists under the purely spiritual doctrine of Christianity. The intolerable dissociation of conscious/spiritual at the expense of the unconscious/physical led them to attempt a union through the alchemical coniunctio. The exploration of psychic and physical union is observed to have come the full circle from alchemy through chemistry to the empirical study of the chemistry and physics of the brain.

000559 The conjunction. 10. The self and the bounds of knowledge. In: Jung, C., Collected Works of C. G. Jung, Vol. 14. 2nd ed., Princeton University Press, 1970. 702 p. (p. 544-554).

The recent advances in psychological understanding and the self-knowledge that has accompanied it are discussed in terms of their ethical and therapeutic consequences. The increased understanding an individual has of his own psychic processes, if it is used at all leads to a confrontation between the expanding self and the structure of ego consciousness, necessitating a moral judgment of the ego personality, which is always disturbing to the ego. The psychological interpretation of the archetype of unification alluded to intuitively by the alchemists, is seen to have therapeutic value in the portrayal of an ideal psychic state in which the gap between conscious and unconscious is bridged. The reality of the confrontation becomes manifest in the process in which the conscious must strain to resolve the psychic conflict. This struggle is considered the source of the numinous experiences of some patients in the course of their therapy; the historical acceptance of these intimate psychic experiences as spontaneous expressions of religious or mystical truths make them difficult to explain in purely scientific terms. Nonetheless, it is contended that numinous experiences, whether they are interpreted as merely pathological or as divine inspirations, derive from an overwhelming breakthrough of unconscious material into consciousness. The metaphysical interpretations ascribed to these psychic happenings are seen as consciously elaborated hypotheses; gods, then, are not external forces but images projected by the psychoid realm. The validity of the inner experience of transcendental reality remains, but as a product of man himself.

000560 Epilogue. In: Jung, C., Collected Works of C. G. Jung, Vol. 14. 2nd ed., Princeton University Press, 1970. 702 p. (p. 554-556).

Psychology is described as the philosophical successor of alchemy in that the harmonious union of opposites is the goal of each. It is noted that the psychology of the unconscious began with C. G. Carus, who based his theory on essentially the same basis as the alchemists: out of corruption, wholeness can be made. Herbert Silberer is credited with actually discovering the link between alchemy and modern psychology in the richness of archetypal symbols of synthesis and renewal to be found in alchemical treatises. Further, the legacy of alchemical symbolism is considered invaluable in the understanding of the psychic individuation process, since case histories can provide only partial and biased portrayals of the process as a whole.

15 THE SPIRIT IN MAN, ART, AND LITERATURE

000561 Paracelsus. In: Jung, C., Collected Works of C. G. Jung, Vol. 15. Princeton University Press, 1966. 160 p. (p. 3-12).

The life, philosophy, and contributions to modern science of the medieval Swiss physician Paracelsus are discussed in an address presented at Paracelsus' birth place. Shadowed by the Alps, it is considered to have had an importantly early biographical influence on Paracelsus, which gave him the typical Swiss qualities of self-reliance, obstinacy, and pride. The most important influence on Paracelsus, however, was his father, whose fate he set out to avenge. Paracelsus' revenge took the form of withholding love from everyone except his father, for, as far as is known, he never loved anyone else. After extensive travel and study, Paracelsus achieved fame as a self-taught and excellent physician who offended everyone with his arrogance. Toward middle age he became interested in philosophy and medicine. Although emotionally Paracelsus remained a good Catholic, intellectually he embraced a pagan philsophy influenced by the Neoplatonist Marsilio Ficino. To designate his highest cosmogonic principle, Paracelsus coined the word "Yliaster," or "Hylaster," which might be translated as "cosmic matter." For him, the spiritual principle took second place to cosmic matter; man and the world were both seen as parts of animate matter. Thus while being a medieval animist who believed nature is full of witches, incubi, and other spirits, Paracelsus was at the same time a modern materialist. According to him, everything consists of animate particles, or entia, diseases included. Diseases, therefore, are natural, necessary constituents of life rather than hated and foreign ones. The sources of Paracelsus' thought and work were his own psyche, which he probed in depth, and superstitious pagan beliefs which he collected extensively. While working within the confines of existing medieval knowledge, he used the methods of scientific empiricism, thus adding to the modern understanding of the nature of disease and of life itself.

000562 Paracelsus the physician. In: Jung, C., Collected Works of C. G. Jung, Vol. 15 Princeton University Press, 1966. 160 p. (p. 13-30).

A summary of Paracelsus's ideas about the nature of the physician's science is presented, although it is noted that his prodigious literary output, much of it obscure, contradictory, and colored by his abrasive personality, makes interpretation difficult. Quotations from his own work are used extensively in outlining his conservatism, evident in his Catholicism, his belief in alchemy and astrology and emphasis on folklore, as well as his rebellion against academic medicine. Paracelsus's central idea is the importance of understanding external things as a way to understanding the internal. The physician is seen as gaining his knowledge of disease not from the patient but from the study of external phenomena, particularly the study of alchemy, which enables the physician to diagnose diseases from their analogy with the diseases of minerals. Astrology is considered to be the other important source of the physician's knowledge, in that each organ of the body corresponds to a

star, a relationship that must be considered during treatment. Paracelsus' belief in magic is considered to foretell the place of chemistry in modern medicine. The psychotherapeutic aspect of Paracelsus's work is discussed with examples of his compassion toward his patients. 49 references.

000563 Sigmund Freud in his historical setting. In: Jung, C., Collected Works of C. G. Jung, Vol. 15. Princeton University Press, 1966. 160 p. (p. 33-40).

Freud's work is evaluated in the light of the influence of its historical conditioning, that of the transition from the Victorian age to the 20th century. The main thrust of Freud's thought, that pathology results from unnecessary sexual repression, is seen as a necessary antidote to Victorian morality. On the other hand, Freud's commitment to rational explanations is considered an outgrowth of 18th century thought. It is considered more accurate to view Freud as an exemplar of the resentment of the new century for the old than as a harbinger of new truths. Freud's emphasis on sexual repression as the cause of neurosis at the expense of other psychological phenomena, and his firm roots in the 19th century European doctor's consulting room, are viewed as causes of the seemingly parochial nature of his work. It is concluded that, although Freud did not penetrate the deeper truths common to all peoples, he did admirably fulfill his historical task. 1 reference.

000564 In memory of Sigmund Freud. In: Jung, C., Collected Works of C. G. Jung, Vol. 15. Princeton University Press, 1966. 160 p. (p. 41-49).

The course of Freud's career and his contributions to psychology are reviewed. Beginning with his initial work on hysteria and hypnosis under Charcot, the development of Freud's theory of neurosis is traced. The repression of sexual trauma, stemming from the existence of infantile sexuality, is considered to be at the root of all neuroses. This theory, together with the unorthodox idea put forth in "The Interpretation of Dreams", namely that dreams are an important source of knowledge about the unconscious, are seen as being Freud's most significant contributions. Freud's later excursions into philosophy, religion, and primitive psychology are viewed negatively. Since he saw everything through the eyes of a physician and was inadequately trained in other fields, Freud was unable to transfer successfully his views on neurosis to other areas. In addition, he saw only the unfavorable or ambiguous aspects of the unconscious at the expense of its creative and healing powers. Freud's psychology is considered an important contribution toward destroying the false ideals of the 19th century, but inadequate in fulfilling the needs of the 20th. 2 references.

000565 Richard Wilhelm: in memoriam. In: Jung, C., Collected Works of C. G. Jung, Vol. 15. Princeton University Press, 1966. 160 p. (p. 53-62).

The sinologist Richard Wilhelm's creation of a bridge between Eastern and Western cultures is discussed in an address originally delivered at a memorial service for him. Wilhelm's greatest achievement is seen to be his translation of, and commentary on, the I-Ching. Through this work, Wilhelm opened to the European world a different view of science, one based not on the causality principle but on what is tentatively called the synchronistic principle. This term and its relationship to astrology comprise the basic formula of the I-Ching, which is accepted in this address as a premise. It is considered the purest expression of Chinese thought, a badly needed alternative to Western intellectualism and rationalism. A danger is seen nonetheless in embracing this new philsophy too enthu-siastically, since its true value lies not in blindly accepting it but in integrating it into our own culture. Wilhelm's ability to approach an alien culture freely, modestly, and without preju-dice is admired, and his clarification and confirmation of much of Jung's own work is noted. In conclusion, more was learned from Wilhelm than from any other man. 2 references.

000566 On the relation of analytical psychology to poetry. In: Jung, C., Collected Works of C. G. Jung, Vol. 15. Princeton University Press, 1966. 160 p. (p. 65-83).

The relation between psychology and art is discussed in a study of the creative process in poetry and its connection to analytical psychology. The essential definition of art is not discussed here since it is considered to belong to esthetics, not psychology; rather, the emotions and symbols surrounding art are explored. The discussion begins with a criticism of the medical reductionism practiced by Freud. Although Freud is correct in maintaining that a poet's biography illuminates his work, it does not totally explain it. Analytical psychology is seen as different from medical psychology. The latter must be discarded when examining a work of art, for a work of art is not a disease, and requires a different analytical approach. Two basic types of art are identified and some criteria pro-vided for differentiating between them. The first (introverted) is the result of the artist's assertion of his own conscious aims upon his material; the second (extraverted) is characterized by the artist's complete identification with his work. In the second instance, the artist seems to cease being an individual and becomes a nutrient medium for the creation of his art. The creative process is described as a living thing implanted in the human psyche, an autonomous complex which has a life of its own outside ordinary consciousness. The autonomous com-plex, and specifically the autonomous creative complex, are further defined. The latter arises from the collective uncon-scious, which consists of primordial images, or archetypes. The emotional impact of these images, when they are present in a work of art, is described. In conclusion, the creative process is defined as the unconscious activation of an archetypal image and the shaping of this image into a finished work. The social significance of art is derived from its rediscovery of lost primordial images which are brought up from the deepest unconscious. An analogy is drawn between the role of the unconscious in individual development and that of art in the development of a nation: just as reactions from the unconscious correct the onesideness of an individual's at-titude, so too does art represent a process of self-regulation in the life of nations and epochs.

000567 Psychology and literature. Introduction. 1. The work of art. 2. The artist. In: Jung, C., Collected Works of C. G. Jung, Vol. 15. Princeton University Press, 1966. 160 p. (p. 84-105).

The reasons for approaching literature from the viewpoint of analytical psychology and the role of the human psyche in both disciplines are outlined. Psychology, a study of psychic processes, can be applied to the study of literature, for the human psyche is the womb of all the arts and sciences. This approach takes two different forms. In the first instance, the object of analysis is a concrete artistic achievement; in the second, it is the creative human being as a unique personality. Although these two aspects of creativity are intimately related, neither can explain the other. Two modes of artistic creation are described: the psychological, dealing with familiar materi-als drawn from man's conscious life; and the visionary, deal-ing with primordial images that transcend human understand-ing. The first mode is seen as a reduction of the artist's vision

to personal experience, a reduction that deflects our attention from the psychology of the work of art and focuses it on the psychology of the artist. Some examples of literary works using the second, visionary mode are given. This mode brings out night fears to our conscious mind. From the beginnings of human society we find traces of man's efforts to banish his fears by expressing them in magical or propitiatory forms. It is to be expected, therefore, that the poet will turn to these mythological images to give suitable expression to his own ex-perience. Since these images arise from the collective uncon-scious, the psychologist can do little to elucidate them other than to provide comparative material and a terminology for their discussion. What is important for the study of literature is that the manifestations of the collective unconscious are compensatory to the conscious attitude. A review of Freud's ideas on creativity in the artist is provided, and their short-comings are pointed out. The dual nature of the creative per-sonality is noted: the artist is both a human being with a per-sonal life and an impersonal creative process. This dual nature puts great strain on the artistic personality, arousing the professional interest of the psychologist. Since the artist's work responds to the needs of his society, it has implications greater than those involving his own personal fate. The archetypal images that the artist uses are morally neutral; therefore a great work of art is always morally and intellec-tually ambiguous. To grasp its meaning, we must allow it to shape us as it shaped the artist. It is suggested that this par-ticipation mystique is the secret of artistic creation and of the effect which great art has on the perceiver. 11 references.

000568 Ulysses: a monologue. In: Jung, C., Collected Works of C. G. Jung, Vol. 15. Princeton University Press, 1966. 160 p. (p. 109-134).

The subjective monologue of James Joyce's Ulysses, a book that arouses the psychologist's interest because of its con-troversial initial reception and its considerable subsequent in-fluence on contemporary authors, is analyzed. The reader's frustration in trying to decipher this book, whose dominant note is utterly hopeless emptiness, is described. It is suggested that the work is an example of visceral thinking, a process severely restricting cerebral activity and confining itself to in-formation provided by the perceptual processes. Certain similarities with schizophrenia are described. Ulysses, how-ever, is no more a pathological product than is modern art as a whole. The schizophrenic qualities of the latter do not reflect the disease in any individual artist but are a collective manifes-tation of our time. In the insane, distortions of meaning and reality are a consequence of the destruction of their personali-ty. The distortion present in the artist's work is not destruc-tive, but rather creative. It is suggested that, despite his seem-ing paganism, Joyce is actually very much an Irish Catholic. Instead of generating only local interest, as might be expected, Joyce's Irish Catholicism may account for his book's popular appeal, as all of us are still citizens of the Catholic Middle Ages. The book's negativism presents a counterforce to that age's high moral ideals, whereas the atrophy of feeling in it is explained as a reaction against too much sentimentalism. Detachment of consciousness is seen as the goal, the Ithaca, of the whole book. All the negative aspects of Joyce's book, all that is cold-blooded, bizarre and banal, grotesque and devilish, is in fact a positive virtue that deserves praise. At the end, Ulysses's masculine creative power turns into feminine acquiescence -- "The Eternal Feminine/Still draws us on." Ulysses is considered the distillation of a new, universal con-sciousness. 7 references.

000569 Picasso. In: Jung, C., Collected Works of C. G. Jung, Vol. 15. Princeton University Press, 1966. 160 p. (p. 135-141).

The psychology, not the esthetics, of Picasso's art is discussed. By viewing his art as a pictorial representation of psychic processes, analogies may be drawn between Picasso's work and the art done by mental patients. Both these are forms of nonobjective art that draws its contents from the unconscious. The pictorial expression of these unconscious contents makes them more accessible to the patient's understanding. The two different types of art produced by neurotic and schizophrenic patients are described and the similarities between Picasso's work and that of the second group of patients are noted. These similarities do not imply that Picasso is schizophrenic. The two types of art have one thing in common: their symbolic content. In either type of art a series of images begins, as a rule, with the symbol of the Nekyia, the journey to Hades, the descent into the unconscious. Examples of the Nekyia in Picasso's work are pointed out. The symbol of the Harlequin, whose journey through the psychic history of mankind has as its object the restoration of the whole man by awakening the memories of the blood, is examined. The symbols of madness experienced during a schizophrenic's period of distintegration are usually followed by images that represent the coming together of opposites. It is noted that in Picasso's latest paintings this motif is seen very clearly. No predictions are made about Picasso's future work, although the basic tragedy of the Harlequin figure is noted and compared with a similar figure in Nietzsche's Zarathustra.

16 THE PRACTICE OF PSYCHOTHERAPY

000570 General problems of psychotherapy. I. Principles of practical psychotherapy. In: Jung, C., Collected Works of C. G. Jung, Vol. 16. 2nd ed., Princeton University Press, 1966. 384 p. (p. 3-20).

Psychotherapy is defined as a kind of dialectic process, a dialogue and discussion between two persons. The various schools of thought on psychotherapy are examined and it is concluded and that their variety does not necessarily invalidate their divergent premises. The interdependence of psyche and body is established as a basic theoretical principle. Initially, the psychotherapist cannot judge the whole of his patient's personality. Although the patient can be seen as approximating the universal man, his individuality is his own and must be allowed expression without being hampered by the doctor's assumptions. Since the individual signifies nothing in comparison with the universal, and the universal signifies nothing in comparison with the individual, methods such as suggestion and "mana," the universal healing power, can have some success. This success, however, is believed to be limited by the contradictions of the individual/universal antinomy. Psychoneuroses can be divided into two main groups: collective types with underdeveloped personality and individualists with atrophied collective adaptation. Therapists are cautioned to treat their patients in accordance with the unique and unpredictable individuality of the latter; the cure should not alter the patient's personality but lead to individuation. It is noted that the dialectic procedure calls for the most unbiased attitude possible on the part of the therapist who is a fellow participant in the therapeutic discourse with his patient. Freud's concept of depth dimension logically resulted in the involvement of the doctor's own personality as well as that of the patient in the psychotherapic treatment. Because the conscious attitude of the neurotic must be balanced by compensatory or complementary contents from the unconscious, the continuity of dreams, a source of unconscious content, is stressed. In a 2

month dream series, for example, a water motif, symbolic of the collective unconscious, was recurrent. Another dream series centered around various forms of woman, representing the mythological personification of the unconscious, the "anima." It is justifiable to resort to mythological ideas to assist the patient. Religious beliefs are viewed as forms of psychotherapy which treat and heal the suffering of the soul and the suffering of the body caused by the soul. Since many patients do not have such beliefs, for them, dialectic developments of the mythological material within them is indicated. Various types of people for whom different treatment is required are distinguished. Aim of the therapeutic process is to enable the patient to assimilate the unconscious elements in his psyche, thus achieving the ultimate integration of his personality and the removal of the neurotic dissociation.

000571 General problems of psychotherapy. II. What is psychotherapy. In: Jung, C., Collected Works of C. G. Jung, Vol. 16. 2nd ed., Princeton University Press, 1966. 384 p. (p. 21-28).

The nature of psychotherapy as a science requiring the use of scientific methods and new forms of treatment is discussed. A glance at former methods shows that suggestion therapy had given way, and that Freud's demands that the causes of neuroses be brought to consciousness were heeded. The trauma theory, originally intended to explain the cause of neuroses is rejected as a hasty generalization, and it is shown that even Freud abandoned this theory for that of repression. It became evident that modern psychotherapy cannot be generally applied but must give undivided and general attention to the individual. This theory goes beyond Freudian psychoanalysis and Adler's individual psychology in that it emphasizes the need for more extensive individualization in the method of treatment. The doctor is cautioned to avoid influencing the patient in the direction of his own bents for only when a man lives in his own way can he be responsible and capable of action. Methods of treatment recommended show that, in all clear cases of neuroses, reeducation and regeneration of personality are essential. It is considered essential that modern psychotherapeutic methods take into account the philosophy of the humane sciences and be based on a thorough knowledge of psychiatry. For adequate study of dreams, a study of primitive psychology, comparative mythology and religion is required.

000572 General problems of psychotherapy. III. Some aspects of modern psychotherapy. In: Jung, C., Collected Works of C. G. Jung, Vol. 16. 2nd ed., Princeton University Press, 1966. 384 p. (p. 29-35).

Freud's theories concerning the unconscious are examined and evaluated. His assumption that bringing the causes of neuroses into consciousness will cure them is rejected as is his view that dreams are a facade. Instead, dreams are considered to be a reflection of basic elements in an individual's psyche, and regression to childhood is seen as a sign of a patient's efforts to find himself. The negative conception of the unconscious held by Freud is rejected in favor of the belief that the unconscious is a creative factor as well as the stronghold of ancestral conservatism. By discerning the true reasons for his childhood longings, and by penetrating the wide realm of the collective psyche, the patient is enabled to enter into the healthy and natural matrix of the human mind.

000573 General problems of psychotherapy. IV. The aims of psychotherapy. In: Jung, C., Collected Works of C. G. Jung, Vol. 16. 2nd ed., Princeton University Press, 1966. 384 p. (p. 36-52).

Divergent opinions concerning the structure of neuroses and principles of therapy are examined and compared to those derived from clinical observations of patients. Although Freud's explanation of neurosis in terms of sexual causation and Adler's viewpoint based on the will to power are considered to correspond to psychic realities, nevertheless, their methods cannot be applied indiscriminately. Because individual life is extraordinarily diverse, the psychotherapist is exhorted to abandon too fixed an aim and to be aware of the patient's own unconscious nature and will to live. A distinction is made between young patients who must shape their conscious ego and older ones who are more concerned with understanding the meaning of their inner life. Dream analysis is recommended when rational methods of treatment are not successful since, though not scientific, it provides a practical method of showing the patient the trend of his unconscious. It is deemed necessary for the doctor to know as much as possible about primitive psychology, mythology, archaeology and comparative religion in order to enrich the associations of his patients by analogy. Fantasy, the maternally creative side of the masculine mind, is judged to be bound to the taproot of human and animal instinct; therefore, it is considered valid to encourage the patient in his fantasies without going beyond the meaning which is effective for the patient. Painting is encouraged, not for the sake of art, but in order to aid in the development of independence and psychological maturity, freeing the patient from dependence on dreams or the doctor's knowledge. Painting alone is not sufficient, however; it must be accompanied by synthetic interpretation that will allow the patient, in collaboration with the doctor, to attain intellectual and emotional understanding. The problems of dealing with this process of psychic life that lies outside consciousness are stressed; since psychic reality is not commensurate with conscious reality, the observation of the psyche can only be indirect, yet it is this independent psychic reality that the therapist must plumb.

000574 General problems of psychotherapy. V. Problems of modern psychotherapy. In: Jung, C., Collected Works of C. G. Jung, Vol. 16. 2nd ed., Princeton University Press, 1966. 384 p. (p. 53-75).

The use of the term psychoanalysis to describe many different approaches to the study and treatment of the psyche is discussed and alternate therapeutic methods, such as Freudian psychoanalysis, Adlerian individual psychology, medical psychology and anlytical psychology are examined. The diversity of professional opinions implied by the various methods indicates the difficulty inherent in gaining access to the psyche. Analytical psychology is defined as embracing both psychoanalysis and individual psychology. This approach includes four stages: confession, elucidation, education and transformation. Each of these stages is subsequently analyzed. In the first stage, the secrets or inhibited emotions, analogous to repressed sins that lead to neuroses, must be confessed to enable the patient to regain his wholeness, and his dependence on the doctor, transference, must be severed. Next the elucidation of this transference must take place and the patient's fixation analyzed. The theories of Freud and Adler are examined in their relation to this stage. The importance of drawing the patient out of himself in a process of education in order to attain normal adaptation is stressed. The fourth stage, transformation, is seen to affect both patient and doctor, whose personalities have interacted throughout the treatment. Emphasis is placed on the doctor's need to engage in self-education and to understand that both he and the patient are in search of a cure that involves not just the body but the entire psyche.

000575 General problems of psychotherapy. VI. Psychotherapy and a philosophy of life. In: Jung, C., Collected Works of C. G. Jung, Vol. 16. 2nd ed., Princeton University Press, 1966. 384 p. (p. 76-84).

The theme that the psyche must be treated with sufficient attention given to physiological and spiritual factors is expanded. The difficulty of the psychotherapeutic task lies in the concept that the psyche, influenced by both physiological and psychological factors, has a contradictory structure giving rise to the problem of opposites. This problem, once brought to consciousness, is seen as capable of threatening the philosophy of life of both therapist and patient. Since man's philosophy of life, the most complex of psychic structures, forms the counterpose to the physiologically conditioned psyche, it ultimately determines one's fate. Hence the psychotherapist needs to have well developed, valid convictions of his own, yet be open to search with the patient for the latter's religious and philosophical ideas. Both religious and philosophical convictions are considered extremely valuable for the psychotherapeutic process, especially the Christian view of original sin and suffering. In an analysis of a patient's neurosis, the psychotherapist is advised to explore both pre-Christian and non-Christian concepts in order to deal with archetypal symbolism in the unconscious. The psychotherapist is enjoined to be aware that the neurosis is not a separate thing but rather the whole of the pathologically disturbed psyche, hence it is not the neurosis but the whole man who should be treated.

000576 General problems of psychotherapy. VII. Medicine and psychotherapy. In: Jung, C., Collected Works of C. G. Jung, Vol. 16. 2nd ed., Princeton University Press, 1966. 384 p. (p. 84-93).

In a 1945 meeting of the Swiss Academy of Medical Science, the differences between medicine and psychotherapy are analyzed. The three stages of medical procedure -- anamnesis, diagnosis and therapy are examined and compared to psychotherapeutic procedures. In psychotherapy, anamnesis, the reconstruction of historical facts in the case, must be supplemented by a consideration of the patient's whole environment. Accordingly the psychotherapist's task involves asking questions seemingly unrelated to the patient's psychoneurosis and applying his professional skill and his intuition to draw out facts about an illness that involves the whole man. In contrast to medical cases, diagnosis is considered irrelevant since in psychotherapy the discovery of facts does not lay the basis for specific treatment but only gives indications of the direction therapy should take; recognition of disease rests much less on the clinical picture than on the content of complexes. Every psychotherapist not only has his own method -- he himself is that method. The subject of psychotherapy, unlike that of medicine, is not the disease but the human being psychically defined. These views lead to the important conclusion that the real and authentic psyche is the unconscious, whereas ego consciousness can be regarded only as an epiphenomenon. The belief that there are certain prenatal modes of behavior and function which bear on the individual psyche, as indicated by the recurrence of common themes in mythology and other folklore, is discussed, and it is determined that neuroses must be considered by the psychotherapist according to their connection with instinctual disturbances and their situational patterns. It is concluded that psychotherapy must go beyond medical symptomatology since it deals with the psyche behind the symptoms and requires knowledge gained from humane sciences, as well as from natural sciences.

000577 General problems of psychotherapy. VIII. Psychotherapy today. In: Jung, C., Collected Works of C. G. Jung, Vol. 16. 2nd ed., Princeton University Press, 1966. 384 p. (p. 94-110).

The relationship between the individual psyche and the suprapersonal world of the patient is discussed. This relationship is first experienced within the family but must be broadened to include the entire world into which one must enter as a whole person. Projection, the extension of the parental images to the whole of external reality, is considered to be a major cause of neurosis, and withdrawal of projection of the parental image from external reality one of psychotherapy's most difficult tasks. The recognition of the need to facilitate the transition from child to adult is evident in both primitive and Christian ceremonies. The psychotherapist is warned that he must reckon with the patriarchal orientation of the psyche which tradition has encouraged, and also guard against transference whereby the patient develops too great a dependence on the doctor. It is pointed out that the doctor should take into account the patient's religious beliefs in order to achieve the reintegration of the latter's psyche. This process of individuation is seen as the finding of self, a goal recognized in both Yoga and medieval, alchemical, philosophy. The European effort to replace the collectivity of the Church with the collectivity of the State is interpreted as a reflection of the European's deep seated longing for a patriarchal order, for authority. The domination of the individual by the state is rejected because it deprives the former of his rightful destiny. The aim of psychotherapy is stated: to educate people towards independence and moral freedom. To attempt to subject this aim to a particular political system is viewed as making psychotherapy the tool of totalitarianism. The need to integrate the individual into society is recognized, hence extreme individualism is not advocated. However, it is concluded that the individuation process must give free play to nature and that psychotherapy must be dedicated to the goal of individual development. 2 references.

000578 General problems of psychotherapy. IX. Fundamental questions of psychotherapy. In: Jung, C., Collected Works of C. G. Jung, Vol. 16. 2nd ed., Princeton University Press, 1966. 384 p. (p. 111-125).

The history of man's exploration of the psyche from Paracelsus to Freud is reviewed and the subjective element in theories of psychotherapy is noted and illustrated by reference to Freud's rigid insistence on the pleasure principle and Adler's emphasis on the will to power. In order to avoid too much subjectivity in treating his patients, the doctor is urged to undergo analysis, himself, to gain a knowledge of his own attitudes before treating patients whose attitudes may vary greatly. The psychotherapeutic process is recognized as a dialectic process in which both patient and doctor will become deeply and often painfully involved. Since many factors, social and external as well as internal and unconscious, influence every man and must be taken into account by the doctor, collective traditional values as well as the patient's own individuality are considered major elements in the reconstruction of his personality. Within each man, there is a superego which may come into conflict with his own psychic system, thereby creating a neurosis. Various types of neuroses are described, and the belief that the patient can be cured, when shown where his conflicts lie, is expressed. To accomplish this cure, each individual's philosophy of life and the compensatory relationship between the conscious and the unconscious must be considered. This implies that the main task of the psychotherapist is to unveil the unconscious without preconceived ideas. Since the unconscious is a collective phenomenon whose existence is indicated by the reappearance of certain archetypes and mythologems throughout the history of man, it is concluded that a true understanding of the unconscious will necessitate a consideration of the unity of the collective unconscious. 2 references.

000579 Specific problems of psychotherapy. I. The therapeutic value of abreaction. In: Jung, C., Collected Works of C. G. Jung, Vol. 16. 2nd ed., Princeton University Press, 1966. 384 p. (p. 129-138).

Abreaction is defined, its therapeutic effect evaluated, and the transference relationship between doctor and patient is discussed. The value of abreaction, i.e. the reenactment of a traumatic experience in achieving the reintegration of the patient's individuality is questioned. Instead, it is proposed that the relationship between doctor and patient has the greatest therapeutic effect: it provides the patient with the support needed to overcome the effects of his neuroses; it requires the doctor to enter into the psyche of his patient probing deeply into the origins of the neuroses in order to lay the groundwork for the patient's return to reality. The strictly sexual interpretation of the patient's neurosis is regarded as limited in its value. Transference, the dependence of the patient on the doctor, is seen as a stage that will lead to the patient's attaining a position of equality with the doctor. It is considered important that the patient see not only the nature and cause of his neuroses but also envisage his own psychological goal, his own growth toward a whole psyche.

000580 Specific problems of psychotherapy. II. The practical use of dream-analysis. In: Jung, C., Collected Works of C. G. Jung, Vol. 16. 2nd ed., Princeton University Press, 1966. 384 p. (p. 139-161).

The rejection of dream analysis by many as a valid method to penetrate the unconscious is acknowledged, but its practical usefulness is upheld. Several cases are cited to support the conclusion that dreams must be taken as diagnostically valid facts. Dreams are often anticipatory and provide valuable information for understanding the patient and planning his treatment. Although the doctor himself may regard his patient's dreams as confused, he must realize that his confusion lies in his own lack of understanding, and that a true understanding will be attained when both doctor and patient reach agreement on the dream content as the result of joint reflection. Suggestion is considered to have serious limitations as a therapeutic technique, since it can hamper the patient's willingness to face his own problems and to make his own judgments and decisions. The analysis of dreams is preferred because the nocturnal unconscious psychic activity, covers a wide gamut of conditions and developments. They require careful interpretation by the doctor; however, nothing in them is certain but uncertainty. For an adequate understanding, a series of dreams must be analyzed rather than a single dream taken out of context. The idea of sublimation proposed by Freud to save man from the imaginary claws of the unconscious is rejected since the unconscious is not considered to be any more demoniacal than the conscious. Compensation -- the balancing of elements in both the conscious and the unconscious -- is considered to be a basic law of psychic behavior. Unconscious compensation is only effective when it cooperates with an integral consciousness; however, the values of the conscious personality must remain intact. The belief that the patient's philosophical, religious and moral convictions must be taken into account is reiterated. The conclusion is drawn that dreams reveal more clearly the evolutionary stratification of the psyche than does the conscious mind and that assimilation of unconscious contents can lead the conscious mind back to the natural state of the patient's own being. 1 reference.

000581 Specific problems of psychotherapy. III. The psychology of the transference. In: Jung, C., Collected Works of C. G. Jung, Vol. 16. 2nd ed., Princeton University Press, 1966. 384 p. (p. 163-201).

The problem of transference is reviewed and discussed in terms of alchemical symbolism in order to provide some orientation in the study of the unconscious. Mystic marriage, coniunctio, which played an important part in alchemy and was concerned both with chemistry and a kind of mystic philosophy, is discussed, since it sheds light on the mystery of chemical combination and is related to transference in psychology. The history of this symbolism is outlined because of its usefulness in the exploration of the unconscious. The complexity of transference, a partly instinctive process difficult to weigh, is analyzed, and the danger inherent in taking over the patient's psychic sufferings is mentioned. The incestuous aspect in transference is recognized and is described as a flurry of unleashed opposites within the awakened unconscious that must be reconciled. These assaults of the unconscious are symbolized in alchemy by Mercurius who is both friend and panacea, good and evil. Religions, particularly Christianity, are considered to be great psychotherapeutic systems. Modern man's hostility to religion is considered as increasing the danger of dissociation between the ego conscious and the unconscious. The many analogies that exist between alchemical symbols and the study of the unconscious show that the study of this medieval speculative philosophy and science can shed great light on the process of individuation and the analysis of the unconscious. 18 references.

000582 Specific problems of psychotherapy. III. The psychology of the transference: an account of the transference phenomena based on the illustrations to the "Rosarium Philosophorum." 1. The mercurial fountain. In: Jung, C., Collected Works of C. G. Jung, Vol. 16. 2nd ed., Princeton University Press, 1966. 384 p. (p. 203-210).

The symbols used in the first illustration of the "Rosarium Philosophorum," an illustration of the mercurial fountain, are described and analyzed in terms of the psychology of the unconscious. The illustration contains the alchemical symbols of quaternity -- the four elements which merge into a fifth entity, the quinta essentia, the circular basin, and the seven planets. This last symbol evokes the image of Mercurius, the mother of all seven, since he is also his own mother and father. The three essences of Mercurius are represented by the serpent. The sun and moon appear above the triad as the indispensable parents of the mystic transformation. The progression from 4 to 3 to 2 to 1, the alchemical axiom of Maria, represents four mutually antagonistic tendencies that must be reduced to a final unity. The quaternity, one of the most widespread archetypes, represents the arrangement functions by which the conscious mind takes its bearings; the circle expresses the primordial image of man and the soul, and the number four stands for the pluralistic state of a man who has not yet attained inner unity. The triad, the agent of upwelling, appears as masculine; the dyad, as feminine. Psychologically the triad represents desire, instinct and determination, while the dyad corresponds to the psyche's reaction to the conscious mind's decision. The water signifying the unconscious, represents the ebbing and flowing of the circle of life. These symbolic forms of universal archetypes are considered to be unconscious projections of the alchemists. 3 references.

000583 Specific problems of psychotherapy. III. The psychology of the transference: an account of the transference phenomena based on the illustrations to the "Rosarium Philosophorum." 2. King and queen. In: Jung, C., Collected Works of C. G. Jung, Vol. 16. 2nd ed., Princeton University Press, 1966. 384 p. (p. 211-235).

The alchemic king and queen figures, symbolizing both the marital and the incestuous brother/sister relationship, are discussed and interpreted in the light of the psychological processes of projection and transference. The gesture of the clasped left hands, pointing to a secret path, is seen as a reference to man's dark, unconscious side and to the dubious nature of the affective relationship: heavenly and earthly as well as incestuous. The right hands, holding flowers, appear compensatory. The 4/5 arrangement of the flowers represent fire and air as the active, masculine element, water and earth as the passive, feminine element with the fifth flower as the quinta essentia. Although the symbols in this illustration all emphasize nature, a hidden, spiritual meaning is also suggested as is the triple nature of Mercurius -- masculine, feminine and divine - who was seen as the earth-bound partner of the Holy Ghost, who wards against the ominous darkness of nature's secrets. Mercurius is beyond sex, in a state reached only when male and female come together into one. The concept of Anthropos is viewed as an eternal idea, present in various cultures. The love factor in the illustration, a love with a sinister touch of incest, is analyzed, and the conclusion is drawn that incest symbolizes union with one's own being -- individuation or becoming a self. By means of several diagrams the complex nature of projection and transference that occur in the doctor/patient psychotherapeutic relationship is analyzed. The doctor's task is to make the patient conscious of the meaning of the transference in order to enable him to arrive at the ultimate reintegration of his personality. The counter crossing of the sexes symbolized in the Rosarium and in fairy tales is illustrated and analyzed. This counter crossing occurs in various and complex forms in life. On the psychological level, the tangle of cross-cousin marriage is seen in transference. In a world of mass mindedness, it is deemed necessary that the individual consciously attempt to integrate his personality in order to counter the psychic dissociation of modern man. 17 references.

000584 Specific problems of psychotherapy. III. The psychology of the transference: an account of the transference phenomena based on the illustrations to the "Rosarium Philosophorum." 3. The naked truth. In: Jung, C., Collected Works of C. G. Jung, Vol. 16. 2nd ed., Princeton University Press, 1966. 384 p. (p. 236-240).

The illustration of the nude couple, symbolic of Sol and Luna, is analyzed as a symbol of the union between the conscious mind and the shadow. The accompanying text indicates that the alchemists recognized the moral and psychological implications of their opus. The presence of the dove above the nude figures indicates that this union is spiritual as well as erotic. The illustration is analyzed psychologically: instinct and the primitive psyche have emerged into consciousness; ego and shadow are no longer divided; a precarious unity has been attained. 1 reference.

000585 Specific problems of psychotherapy. III. The psychology of the transference: an account of the transference phenomena based on the illustrations to the "Rosarium Philosophorum." 4. Immersion in the bath. In: Jung, C., Collected Works of C. G. Jung, Vol. 16. 2nd ed., Princeton University Press. 1966. 384 p. (p. 241-246).

Several versions of the descent into the bath motif are presented and this theme is discussed in terms of its religious and psychological implications. According to the alchemists, this "solutio," or dissolution of the king and queen, represents a return to the dark initial stage in the mother's womb; within the lustral water, a new birth is being prepared. The king stands for the spirit; the queen represents the body. The two can only be united in the soul, a hermaphroditic being symbolized by the mixture of oil and water. A connection is made between this alchemical representation and the Mass, wherein the two substances are mixed in the chalice. The immersion in the bath is interpreted psychologically as a descent into the unconscious, the dove represents the union of the opposites from above and the bath represents the union from below: opposition and identity. When interpreted in the light of transference, it represents the stage at which the sexual fantasies coloring the transference are recognized while the longing for transcendental wholeness remains. 9 references.

000586 Specific problems of psychotherapy. III. The psychology of the transference: an account of the transference phenomena based on the illustrations to the "Rosarium Philosophorum." 5. The conjunction. In: Jung, C., Collected Works of C. G. Jung, Vol. 16. 2nd ed., Princeton University Press, 1966. 384 p. (p. 247-256).

The illustration of the king and queen immersed in water and joined in a passionate embrace is analyzed as a biological symbol for the union of opposites. The coniunctio brings to birth something that is one and united. The water is seen as the boiling solution in which the two opposing substances unite. In psychology, the transference, as symbolized by the coniunctio, comes about unintentionally. In trying to resolve the transference, the doctor is cautioned to avoid doing violence to the patient's unconscious. 2 references.

000587 Specific problems of psychotherapy. III. The psychology of the transference: an account of the transference phenomena based on the illustrations to the "Rosarium Philosophorum." 6. Death. In: Jung, C., Collected Works of C. G. Jung, Vol. 16. 2nd ed., Princeton University Press, 1966. 384 p. (p. 257-266).

The alchemical illustration of the king and queen, lying dead in the sea that has become a sarcophagus, is interpreted as an archetypal image of a stage in the individuation process. The king and queen have melted into a single being with two heads. Once the opposites unite, all energy ceases. The picture represents putrefactio -- the decay of a once living person from which new life will arise, hermaphroditus. There is a hint of incest which must be punished. The coniunctio is seen as the union of lucid consciousness and nocturnal light, the unconscious, of the active, masculine side of woman -- animus -- and the passive, feminine side of man -- anima. Animus and anima represent semicollective and impersonal quantities, and their conflict must be considered in this light. Man's unconscious, conscious and superego are often at cross purposes. It is concluded that the union of the conscious and the unconscious results in a combination of the two, the self which is both ego and nonego, subjective and objective, individual and collective. 4 references.

000588 Specific problems of psychotherapy. III. The psychology of the transference: an account of the transference phenomena based on the illustrations to the "Rosarium Philosophorum." 7. The ascent of the soul. In: Jung, C., Collected Works of C. G. Jung, Vol. 16. 2nd ed., Princeton University Press. 1966. 384 p. (p. 267-272).

The alchemical illustration in the Rosarium of the soul rising to heaven is analyzed and compared with psychological disorientation. Ego consciousness has collapsed with the patient's recognition of the collective unconscious and the psychic nonego. Both doctor and patient must strive to overcome this soulless state. Faced with disorientation of the patient, the doctor must use views and ideas capable of grasping unconscious symbolism and eschew abstract intellectualism. His aim should be to rouse the patient to mental activity in order to integrate the conscious with the unconscious. In describing other aspects of the picture, it is noted that their psychological interpretation leads to the mystery of inner experience which defies scientific description. 9 references.

000589 Specific problems of psychotherapy. III. The psychology of the transference: an account of the transference pheonmena based on the illustrations to the "Rosarium Philosophorum." 8. Purification. In: Jung, C., Collected Works of C. G. Jung, Vol. 16. 2nd ed., Princeton University Press. 1966. 384 p. (p. 273-282).

The purification process illustrated in the fall of dew on the two headed figure in the tomb is explained by means of quotations from the Rosarium. Water symbolizes wisdom and spirit as seen in Christ's parable of the Samaritian woman at the well. In the illustration under discussion the dew is the moisture heralding the return of the soul which occurs through divine intervention, not knowledge. This interpretation emphasizes the belief that a patient must go beyond intellectual understanding and develop a feeling relationship with the contents of the unconscious. When that has been accomplished, he should proceed toward the imaginative activity of intuition which gives outlook and insight into wholeness, the union of opposites having brought light out of the darkness of night to reveal the real meaning of that union. 6 references.

000590 Specific problems of psychotherapy. III. The psychology of transference: an account of the transference phenomena based on the illustrations to the "Rosarium Philosophorum." 9. The return of the soul. In: Jung, C., Collected Works of C. G. Jung, Vol. 16. 2nd ed., Princeton University Press. 1966. 384 p. (p. 283-305).

The return of the soul depicted in the ninth picture of the Rosarium is interpreted as a representation of a transcendental process equivalent to developments in the psychic nonego. The rational man must make a distinction between himself and eternal man, but the ego must not be overwhelmed by archetypal truths of the unconscious. The alchemist's endeavor to unite the purified body with the soul corresponds to the psychologist's efforts to free the ego consciousness from the contamination of the unconscious. Both alchemist and analyst must engage in rigorous self-examination and self-education to accomplish this task. A distinction is made between masculine and feminine psychology, and the function of animus and anima in man and woman. A lengthy quotation from the work of a 17th century theologian and alchemist is interpreted as a myth of love and woman that sprang from the masculine unconscious, the anima. Though no texts from the women alchemists exist, it is held that the feminine unconscious produces a symbolism generally compensatory to the masculine. The "soul" which accrues to ego consciousness in the opus has a feminine character in the man and a masculine character in the woman. The alchemists are viewed as having grasped the paradoxical darkness of human life and the emergence of new birth out of opposition. 11 references.

000591 Specific problems of psychotherapy. III. The psychology of the transference: an account of the transference phenomena based on the illustrations to the "Rosarium Philosophorum." 10. The new birth. In: Jung, C.,Collected Works of C. G. Jung, Vol. 16. 2nd ed., Princeton University Press, 1966. 384 p. (306-320).

The tenth picture in the Rosarium, the new birth, is commented on in relation to the theory of perfect numbers: ten is a perfect number representing unity on a higher level, whereas one is the "res simplex" of God's creation. The denarius, the culminating point, the higher unit, can be viewed as a symbol for the Son of God philosophically connected with the platonic conception of the bisexual first man to envisage. The alchemists seemed to envisage anything unknowable as best described in terms of opposites. In a long poem on birth and rebirth, quoted in the text, an essentially Christian pardox of virginity and fecundation is discovered: "everything is already dead and yet unborn." It is proposed that there is a timelessness in the unconscious to which the alchemists' paradoxical concept of man and his immortality coincides. The history of the sexual element in the unconscious is traced and it is concluded that, contrary to Freud's belief, it is only one element among many. The alchemist with his squaring of the circle and modern man with his circles and quaternities are viewed as reaching for a wholeness which resolves all opposition. 8 references.

000592 Specific problems of psychotherapy. III. The psychology of the transference: epilogue. In: Jung, C., Collected Works of C. G. Jung, Vol. 16. 2nd ed., Princeton University Press. 1966. 384 p. (321-323).

The reasons for choosing alchemical projections of unconscious contents to explain the process of transference are given. Alchemy projects unconscious contents in archetypal forms just as do mythological tales and dreams, visions and delusional fantasies. The mystical marriage (coniunctio) corresponds to transference both in psychotherapy and in normal human relationships. Because of these parallels, it is considered valid to use a symbolic historical document to support the arguments and experiences relating to transference. The examination of the series of pictures served to illustrate the process of transference in a different light, a process believed to be one of the most important syndromes in the process of individuation. Because of its collective contents and symbols, it also transcends the individual personality.

000593 Appendix: the realities of practical psychotherapy. In: Jung, C., Collected Works of C. G. Jung, Vol. 16. 2nd ed., Princeton University Press. 1966. 384 p. (327-338).

The atypical and individual character of psychogenic disturbances is examined and used to warn psychotherapists against strong attachments to certain methods in their attempts to treat their patients. Since even the terms of diagnosis, such as hysteria, obsessional neurosis or schizophrenia, admit of numerous definitions and variations, it is not surprising that fixed therapeutic methods cannot be applied to individual patients. Therapists are also warned about the dangers of counter-transference wherein an analyst with his own neurosis -- or through lack of knowledge -- may too closely identify with his patient. A case study of a young woman, whose dreams and physiological symptoms could not be understood by the analyst is presented. Only after the discovery that her condition coincided with the symbolism of Tantric Yoga, to which she may have been exposed as a child during her stay in Java, was any progress made. With the aid of an understanding of Tantric philosophy, the patient was able to achieve an

ordinary life as a wife and mother. This case illustrates the psychotherapeutic procedure and underscores the real task of the analyst: to discover and encourage the individuality of the patient, and to enable him to synthesize childhood experience and adult life.

17 THE DEVELOPMENT OF PERSONALITY

000594 Psychic conflicts in a child. In: Jung, C., Collected Works of C. G. Jung, Vol. 17. Princeton University Press, 1970. 235 p. (p. 1-35).

Observations of a 4-year-old child's curiosity about and eventual discovery of the facts of life are the basis for a discussion of the development of sexuality in children. Although a scientific explanation of the mechanics of birth was presented to the child, she preferred her own fantasies which involved the use of sublimation, compensation, logical reasoning and myth making. In explaining this preference for fantasy, it is suggested that the scientific presentation restricted the development of the thinking function whereas the fantasies stimulated it. The Freudian interpretation of infantile sexuality as "sexuality" pure and simple is presented and debated. As a replacement for the Freudian theory of "polymorphous perverse" a theory of a "polyvalent" disposition i proposed to explain the origin of the thinking function: according to the Freudian view, the thinking function develops out of sexual curiosity; according to the theory of polyvalent disposition the development of the thinking function coincedes with sexual curiosity. Reducing the origins of thought to mere sexuality is considered to be antithetical to the basic facts of human psychology. 3 references.

000595 /Introduction to Wickes's "The Inner World of Childhood."/ Introduction to Wickes's "Analyse der Kinderseele." In: Jung, C., Collected Works of C. G. Jung, Vol. 17. Princeton University Press, 1970. 235 p. (p. 37-46).

The study of Mrs. Wickes' "Inner World of Childhood" is recommended as an aid to understanding the effects of the parental unconscious in the psychic development of children. The difficulties in child-rearing, outlined in the introduction, are examined in the light of the thesis that the unexamined portions of the unconscious psyches of parents can cause psychic disorders in their children. To cope with this problem, parents are urged to develop a profound self-knowledge. The collective unconscious is also seen as an important factor in the child psyche prior to the development of ego consciousness; the dreams of very young children contain a high incidence of mythological symbolism, evidence the perennial content existing in the human soul and passed from generation to generation. After the development of ego consciousness a small portion of this collective unconscious survives and is considered as the mysterious spiritus rector of our weightiest deeds and our individual destiny.

000596 Child development and education. In: Jung, C., Collected Works of C. G. Jung, Vol. 17. Princeton University Press, 1970. 235 p. (p. 47-62).

A brief history of analytic psychology is provided as a basis for examining the role of the school in the development of the psyche. An analysis of the difference between Freudian psychoanalysis and analytic psychology reveals that the former recognizes only the sexual instinct as a cause of nervous disorders, whereas the latter maintains that other factors, including the parental unconscious, play important roles in the development of both the normal and abnormal personality. In applying the biogenetic law that ontogeny recapitulates phylogeny to the development of the psyche, four stages are noted: animal unconsciousness, identification with the family, primitive intelligence, and finally civilized individual awareness. The individual psyche that develops between the ages of three and five when the child first grasps the significance of "I," does not gain a significant degree of independence from instinct and environment until after puberty. Consequently the influence of the parental unconscious on the child's unconscious and the child's identification with the family lasts well into the early school years. Schools, therefore, serve an important psychological function in that they assist the the child in freeing himself from unconscious identification with the family, thereby allowing him to become properly conscious of himself. Since this type of education is basically psychological, it is transmitted, in large part, through the example of the teacher who must present a model of healthy behavior to the child. Because teachers are so influential in developing the child's psyche, they are urged to gain a deeper self-understanding by making use of methods of dream analysis. 1 reference.

000597 Analytical psychology and education. Lecture one. In: Jung, C., Collected Works of C. G. Jung, Vol. 17. Princeton University Press, 1970. 235 p. (p. 63-80).

A brief outline of the development of psychology is provided and its major accomplishments -- dream analysis, the discovery of the unconscious, and the role of the unconscious in mental disorders -- are listed. A knowledge of analytic psychology and dream analysis is recommended to educators who wish to understand their pupils. Since the findings of abnormal psychology illuminate normal behavior, five case studies of disturbed children are used to illustrate the five main groups of psychic disturbances: backward children, psychopathic children, epileptic children and the various forms of psychotic and neurotic children. In addition, because the analysis of children is difficult, educators are urged to view such constructs as the Oedipus complex figuratively, not literally, and to reject Freud's theory that the relationship between parent and child is primarily sexual. Instead of regarding the child's sexual longings for its parents as a primary causal factor of neurosis, it is suggested that the repressed material in the parents' unconscious causes neurosis in the parent which, in turn, radiates out to the child's unconscious. Neurotic states are thus passed from generation to generation via contagion. It is proposed that this situation be remedied by having parents willingly face the repressed material in their own unconscious. 4 references.

000598 Analytical psychology and education. Lecture two. In: Jung, C., Collected Works of C. G. Jung, Vol. 17. Princeton University Press, 1970. 235 p. (p. 81-107).

The psychological hypotheses of Freud and Adler are analyzed and contrasted with the methods, aims, and purposes of analytic psychology. Freud's theory based on the ramifications of the sexual instinct in the human psyche, and Adler's concept of self-preservation, are both rejected as explanations of the ultimate causes of human behavior because such single broad hypotheses ignore complexities. The differences between the Jungian and Freudian concepts of psychic development are illustrated by reference to religion and to parent-child relationships. Scientific psychology is then examined and judged to be both a human and a natural science by virtue of its subject matter and methodology. Its role among the sciences is to investigate the investigative tool itself. In response to those critics who maintain that, due to the arbitrary nature of the ego, the subject matter of psychology is

beyond scientific study, it is argued that the psyche, in relation to consciousness, is pre-existent and transcendent. Attention is given to the aim of analytic psychology, namely to understand life as it appears in the human soul in order to help the individual to adapt his behavior to the demands of external life and to those of his own being. To accomplish this goal, the investigative methods of association, symptom analysis, anamnestic analysis and the analysis of the unconscious are suggested as means of probing the unknown in the patient. The first two methods are only briefly described, while the second two are presented in detail and illustrated by several examples. 10 references.

000599 Analytical psychology and education. Lecture three. In: Jung, C., Collected Works of C. G. Jung, Vol. 17. Princeton University Press, 1970. 235 p. (p. 108-132).

Theories concerning the causes of neurosis are examined, with a distinction made between suppression and repression. The tendency to explain every neurosis in terms of repression of infantile sexuality is rejected, because it neglects the individual's willingness to repress discordant knowledge and experiences and interprets neurosis as having its causes in the distant past or in present cultural conditions. Consequently, instead of a doctrinaire Freudian approach to psychotherapy, it is suggested that each case be treated according to its own peculiarities. In order to justify this latter approach, four case histories, two of which are mirror opposites, are presented. Further enlightenment about the causes of neurosis is derived from an analysis of the composition of the unconscious. It is theorized that the unconscious has two parts: the personal and the collective: the contents of the personal unconscious consist of everything forgotten or repressed by the individual, consciously or unconsciously; those of the collective unconscious consist of the structural deposits of psychic activities that were repeated innumerable times in the lives of our ancestors. Although neither the conscious mind nor the personal unconscious is usually aware of the existence of the collective unconscious, material from the collective unconscious will occasionally break through into the personal unconscious by means of a dream with mythological content and meaning that is beyond the intellectual horizons of the individual. 3 references.

000600 The gifted child. In: Jung, C., Collected Works of C. G. Jung, Vol. 17. Princeton University Press, 1970. 235 p. (p. 133-145).

The education and the most beneficial means of developing the psyche of the gifted child are discussed. The fact that schools too often neglect the gifted child in their preoccupation with educating the slow, is not considered harmful to the former, since genius, unlike talent, can neither be hindered nor helped. However, grouping school children according to ability is considered detrimental to the gifted child. Insofar as the gift of genius in one intellectual area is often balanced by inferiority in another, such grouping would produce onesided products and would deprive the gifted child of the benefical moral effects of observing that average children are his betters in certain areas. The development of the child's psyche is influenced more by the warmth and personal example of the individual teacher than by the school curriculum. Within the curriculum, the humanities are recommended over the sciences in developing the child because it is believed that they inculcate the sense of cultural continuity and form the bridge between the past and the future.

000601 The significance of the unconscious in individual education. In: Jung, C., Collected Works of C. G. Jung, Vol. 17. Princeton University Press, 1970. 235 p. (p. 147-164).

Three types of education are presented, and dream analysis is discussed as an aid to individual education. The first of the three types, education through example, is considered the basis for all education, deriving its strength from the phenomenon of psychic identity. Collective education, the second type, is based on principles, methods and rules, and has as its aim the checking of the destructive, anti-social impulses in man. If students resist collective education because of attitudes acquired at home that render them unfit for collective education, the third type, individual education is required. It is here that dream analysis is recommended: since the child's consciousness develops from the unconscious state, it is understandable that early environmental influences often reside in the unconscious and remain unchanged by collective education. Since dreams are the product of unconscious psychic activity, dream analysis is seen as a vehicle for bringing to the light of consciousness the hidden contents of the unconscious that must be changed. As an example of the therapeutic benefits that can be derived from dream analysis, a case history, including the analysis of two dreams is provided.

000602 The development of personality. In: Jung, C., Collected Works of C. G. Jung, Vol. 17. Princeton University Press, 1970. 235 p. (p. 165-186).

The origin, development, purpose, and components of personality are examined and discussed. Personality, defined as the individualization of the objective psyche shared by all men, is developed by submitting to the personal law of one's own being. This personal law is likened to a vocation or an inner voice that calls one from the life of the herd to an individual life; only the man who can consciously assent to the power of this inner voice becomes a personality. Though the term "inner voice" is used figuratively, it is intended to represent a powerful psychic factor that has an objective existence. The call of this inner voice is not seen as completely pleasant: both great evil and great good are contained therein. The negative aspects of this force are illustrated by reference to the Gospel account of the temptation of Christ by the devil. Myths that present the threatening forces surrounding the birth of the hero and the heroic life are seen as expressions of an awareness of the dangers surrounding the attempt to become a personality. Failure to heed the inner law of one's being, however, is considered to result in condemning one to ignorance concerning the purpose of one's life. In classical Chinese philosophy this psychic law is expressed through the concept of "Tao," an interior way likened to the flow of water and considered as the source of fulfillment. It is concluded that, because of the resemblance between the Tao and the psychic state resulting from individuation, personality may be defined as Tao. 1 reference.

000603 Marriage as a psychological relationship. In: Jung, C., Collected Works of C. G. Jung, Vol. 17. Princeton University Press, 1970. 235 p. (p. 187-201).

The effect of the psychological development that occurs in marriage partners during middle-age is discussed, and the resultant change in the marital relationship is analyzed. Prior to middle-age, the marital relationship is governed by biological imperatives; at middle age the force of these imperatives diminishes and the partners are free to become themselves. This transformation influences the psychological relationship of marriage, since changes occur in the roles that the partners

have played. It is considered likely that marital friction will develop during this transformation process, since the confusion that accompanies growth breeds feelings of disunity and discontent. If the real cause of the difficulty is not recognized, each of the partners may hold the other responsible for the discontent. In addition, the different needs of each partner complicate this growth period. A detailed explanation of these changing needs is presented and it is observed that usually a woman feels wholly contained spiritually in her husband, and the man wholly contained emotionally in his wife. 2 references.

18 THE SYMBOLIC LIFE

000604 The Tavistock lectures: on the theory and practice of analytical psychology. Lecture I. In: Jung, C., Collected Works of C. G. Jung, Vol. 18. Princeton University Press, 1976. 904 p. (p. 5-35).

In a 1935 lecture at the Institute of Medical Psychology (Tavistock Clinic) in London, the nature of consciousness, its relationship to the unconscious psyche, and its functions are discussed. Psychology is said to be a science of consciousness and of the products of the unconscious psyche, which can be explored only in terms of its conscious manifestations. Consciousness itself is intermittent and narrow and is a product of perception and orientation to the external world depending on reference to an ego. Functions and components of consciousness are both ectopsychic, relating the contents of consciousness to facts and data from the environment (sensation, thinking, feeling, intuition), and endopsychic, relating the contents of consciousness to postulated processes in the unconscious (memory, subjective components of conscious functions, emotions and affects, and invasion of consciousness by unconscious elements). Differentiation of functions is examined in relation to personality types. In open disucssion following the lecture, definitions and implications are further explored.

000605 The Tavistock lectures: on the theory and practice of analytical psychology. Lecture II. In: Jung, C., Collected Works of C. G. Jung, Vol. 18. Princeton University Press, 1976. 904 p. (p. 36-69).

In a 1935 lecture at the Institute of Medical Psychology (Tavistock Clinic) in London, unconscious processes of the mind and means of access to them are discussed. It is emphasized that unconscious processes cannot be observed directly but only through their products that enter consciousness. Unconscious processes that cross the threshhold of consciousness are divided into the personal unconscious, comprised of material of an individual origin, and the collective unconscious, comprised of archetypes of mythological character that belong to all of mankind, reflect the history of the human brain, and can become active in social groups. A diagram of the structure of the psyche in terms of these and related concepts is provided. Three methods of approaching the unconscious -- word association tests, dream analysis, and active imagination -- are suggested, and the word association test, which depends on delays and errors in producing verbal associations to words, is described in detail with examples from case histories. In open discussion following the lecture, the unconscious is further defined and related to Freudian theory, and the word association test is further explained.

000606 The Tavistock lectures: on the theory and practice of analytical psychology. Lecture III. In: Jung, C., Collected Works of C. G. Jung, Vol. 18. Princeton University Press, 1976. 904 p. (p. 70-101).

In a 1935 lecture at the Institute of Medical Psychology (Tavistock Clinic) in London, dream analysis is discussed as a source of information in psychotherapeutic treatment with reference to a specific clinical case. After preliminary words on complexes (defined as agglomerations of associations that are like fragmentary personalities) and on the use of word association tests in family research, the clinical case is presented. In contrast with Freudian dream analysis, dreams are seen not as distorted representations of censored incompatible wishes but as manifestations of what the unconscious is doing with the complexes. In contrast with Freud's technique of free association, the process of amplification is employed to discover the context of the dream content. Special explanation is offered of the hero motif, dragon motif, and the wand as mythological symbols appearing in dreams. Open discussion of dreams following the lecture and a clinical case are included.

000607 The Tavistock lectures: on the theory and practice of analytical psychology. Lecture IV. In: Jung, C., Collected Works of C. G. Jung, Vol. 18. Princeton University Press, 1976. 904 p. (p. 102-134).

In a 1935 lecture at the Institute of Medical Psychology (Tavistock Clinic) in London, archetypal images in dreams are explored. Dreams containing such images indicate that the dreamer's psychological situation extends beyond the personal portion of the unconscious and relates to the universal problems of mankind. Examples of dreams with universal motifs from mythological and Biblical sources are examined, and it is asserted that those dreams, like all others, are indications that the individual is acting at variance with unconscious conditions. A specific dream with mythological content is presented and such symbols as the serpent, the cave, water, treasure, the dagger, and the city are analyzed. In open discussion following the lecture, the similarities and differences between the present approach and that of Freud are explained.

000608 The Tavistock lectures: on the theory and practice of analytical psychology. Lecture V. In: Jung, C., Collected Works of C. G. Jung, Vol. 18. Princeton University Press, 1976. 904 p. (p. 135-182).

In a 1935 lecture at the Institute of Medical Psychology (Tavistock Clinic) in London, the psychology and treatment of transference are examined. Transference is described as a specific form of projection in which subjective contents are unconsciously extended to another person. Types and etiology of transference, transference by therapists, and reasons for transference illustrated by cases. Treatment of transference has four stages: 1) the patient's realization of the subjective value of the images that trouble him; 2) discrimination between personal and impersonal contents; 3) differentiation of the personal relationship with the analyst from impersonal factors; and 4) objectification of impersonal images. The relationship of therapy to religion is incorporated. In open discussion following the lecture, a short account of the technique of active imagination is given.

000609 Symbols and the interpretation of dreams. 1. The significance of dreams. In: Jung, C., Collected Works of C. G. Jung, Vol. 18. Princeton University Press, 1976. 904 p. (p. 185-195).

In a portion of an essay written in 1961, the significance of dreams is said to be that symbols are unconsciously and spontaneously produced in dreams, allowing the investigation of the unconscious aspects of conscious psychic events. Dreams are the universally accessible and most common source for the investigation of man's symbolizing faculty and are the chief source of knowledge about symbolism. In analyzing dreams, only the material that is clearly and visibly indicated as belonging to the dream by the dream images themselves should be used; free association as practiced by Freud may not produce a correct interpretation. The beliefs of primitive tribe members regarding dreams are compared to those of moderns, and it is suggested that human consciousness, because it is relatively new historically, is discontinuous and resists the unknown parts of the psyche even in members of modern society.

000610 Symbols and the interpretation of dreams. 2. The functions of the unconscious. In: Jung, C., Collected Works of C. G. Jung, Vol. 18. Princeton University Press, 1976. 904 p. (p. 196-202).

In a portion of an essay written in 1961, various functions of the unconscious are described as an example of the subliminal material on which spontaneous production of dream symbols is based. The unconscious is a repository of temporarily eclipsed contents that continue to influence conscious processes. A barely audible sound will be perceived alternately as audible and inaudible depending on the attention being paid to it; for example, physical stimuli in an hysterical patient may produce the effect of anesthesia. Contents can also arise out of unconsciousness, as when subliminal sense perception affects behavior, or when an unconscious recollection enters a creative work due to cryptomnesia. It is hypothesized that material becomes unconscious because conscious contents must lose their energy (the attention given to them) or their specific emotional tone in order to make room for new contents. A distinction is made between intentional contents derived from the ego/personality and unintentional contents from a source not identical with the ego.

000611 Symbols and the interpretation of dreams. 3. The language of dreams. In: Jung, C., Collected Works of C. G. Jung, Vol. 18. Princeton University Press, 1976. 904 p. (p. 203-215).

In a portion of an essay written in 1961, the analysis of dreams is examined in terms of the images and symbols that appear in them. Many dreams present images and associations that are analogous to primitive ideas, myths, and rites (Freud's "archaic remnants"), yet these elements are functional and serve as a bridge between conscious means of expression and more primitive, pictorial means. Dreams are attempts to reestablish psychic equilibrium by restoring images and emotions that express the state of the unconscious. Typical dream motifs are mentioned, and several dreams are recounted and analyzed. One of Jung's dreams is analyzed by Freud and Jung himself; the two psychoanalysts disagree in the dream analysis.

000612 Symbols and the interpretation of dreams. 4. The problem of types in dream interpretation. In: Jung, C., Collected Works of C. G. Jung, Vol. 18. Princeton University Press, 1976. 904 p. (p. 216-226).

In a portion of an essay written in 1961, describing the method of and approach to understanding dreams as the main source of natural symbols, the importance of personality types -- introverted and extraverted -- is explained. The difference between the extravert, who is concerned with externals, and the introvert, who is concerned mainly with the way he takes a situation, plays a great role in the analysis of dreams. No therapeutic technique is uniformly applicable to all patients, since every case is an individual in a specific condition. Examples are given to illustrate that the interpretation of dreams and symbols depends largely on the disposition of the dreamer, for symbols may have several meanings, even opposite ones for different patients.

000613 Symbols and the interpretation of dreams. 5. The archetype in dream symbolism. In: Jung, C., Collected Works of C. G. Jung, Vol. 18. Princeton University Press, 1976. 904 p. (p. 227-243).

In a portion of an essay written in 1961, the archetype -- an inherited tendency of the human mind to form representations of mythological motifs -- is examined in terms of its primary importance in dream interpretation. The symbolism in dreams and other phenomena that occur in dreams are not of individual origin but derive from innate patterns of the human mind. Examples of dreams with religious and mythological symbolism are given, and a contrast is developed between primitives who live their symbols and the moderns who reflect on them. Because the modern mind is said to be dissociated and confused, it is concluded that the past as well as the present must be understood in order to gain perspective on the powers that operate outside the realm of free will. An understanding of myths and symbols is essential in this regard.

000614 Symbols and the interpretation of dreams. 6. The function of religious symbols. In: Jung, C., Collected Works of C. G. Jung, Vol. 18. Princeton University Press, 1976. 904 p. (p. 244-252).

In the context of a discussion on symbols and the interpretation of dreams, written in essay form in 1961, it is pointed out that religious symbols, although they represent beliefs that cannot be proved, give meaning to man's life and help him find his place in the universe. It is pointed out that many persons have lost faith in religion and ask psychiatrists questions that were once reserved for theologians. Such symbols as the golden age, God/man, the cross, and the Hindu lingam are discussed, and the importance of imagination and intuition in the interpretation of dreams and symbols is emphasized.

000615 Symbols and the interpretation of dreams. 7. Healing the split. In: Jung, C., Collected Works of C. G. Jung, Vol. 18. Princeton University Press, 1976. 904 p. (p. 253-264).

In a portion of an essay written in 1961, the loss of moral and spiritual values in the modern world and the function of dreams in bringing numinous or spiritual symbols into consciousness from the unconscious are discussed. The emotional energy that is attached to numinous phenomena does not cease to exist when it disappears from consciousness but reappears in unconscious manifestations, in symbolic happenings that compensate for disturbances of the conscious psyche. Although man finds that neither his religions nor his philosophies provide powerful ideas to give him security, he forgets that God speaks chiefly through dreams and visions. The importance of assimilating and integrating the conscious and unconscious is emphasized.

000616 The symbolic life. In: Jung, C., Collected Works of C. G. Jung, Vol. 18. Princeton University Press, 1976. 904 p. (p. 267-290).

A seminar talk to the Guild of Pastoral Psychology, London, 1939, is presented which answers two questions on why believing Roman Catholics are seldom subject to neurosis. It is suggested that Catholics do become neurotic but seek the help of priests instead of doctors. It is also suggested, however, that the small number of complex manifestations in Catholics may be due to the church's attention to the symbolic life that all men need. The confession, the father/confessor, the mass, and other sacraments embody the mystery that reaches back into the history of the human mind. In answer to a second question, the need and place of God in the psyche are demonstrated from clinical cases, and uncertainty is expressed regarding the historical future of religion. Discussion follows concerning ritual, symbolism, neuroses among Protestants, and other topics relating to religion and mental health.

000617 On occultism. On spiritualistic phenomena. In: Jung, C., Collected Works of C. G. Jung, Vol. 18. Princeton University Press, 1976. 904 p. (p. 293-308).

In a 1905 lecture, an historical overview of spiritualistic phenomena -- animal magnetism, clairvoyance, prophecy, visions -- is presented and personal experiences with mediums are discussed. Spiritualism has a dual nature: 1) a theoretical, scientific side; and 2) a religious side, thus touching on two different areas of human experience. Personal experiences with mediums produced demonstrations of table turning, automatic writing, and speaking in a trance, and the resemblance of some phenomena to symptoms of emotional disturbances is noted. It is concluded that spiritualistic phenomena are difficult to understand and that their reality is in question although by no means disproven.

000618 /On occultism. Foreword to Jung: "Occult phenomena."/ On occultism. Foreword to Jung: "Phenomenes occultes." In: Jung, C., Collected Works of C. G. Jung, Vol. 18. Princeton University Press, 1976. 904 p. (p. 309-311).

In the foreword to "Phenomenes Occultes" by C. G. Jung (1939), occult phenomena, particularly the question of the soul's existence after death, are examined. The essays in the book are described as dealing with the idea of immortality and its functional value, not with the metaphysical question of immortality. The idea of immortality exists worldwide and is therefore real -- a characteristic of psychic life. It is argued that for reasons of psychic hygiene it is best not to forget such universal ideas, and if they have disappeared, from neglect or intellectual disfavor, they should be reconstructed as quickly as possible regardless of alleged philosophical "proofs" for or against their existence.

000619 On occultism. Psychology and spiritualism. In: Jung, C., Collected Works of C. G. Jung, Vol. 18. Princeton University Press, 1976. 904 p. (p. 312-316).

In a foreword to "the Unobstructed Universe" by Stewart Edward White (1948), spiritualism and spirits are discussed in terms of their relationship to the unconscious mind, and parallels with psychology are suggested. Spirits, it is argued, appear to be psychic phenomena whose origins lie in the unconscious. They are shadowy personifications of unconscious contents, conforming to the rule that activated portions of the unconscious assume the character of personalities when perceived by the conscious mind. In spiritualism, therefore, communications of spirits are statements about the unconscious. Spiritualism as described in White's book is compared with aspects of modern psychology, and it is concluded that one aim of both is to compensate the narrowness of the conscious mind by deepening its knowledge of the unconscious.

000620 /On occultism. Foreword to Moser: "Ghost: false belief or true?"/ On occultism. Foreword to Moser: "Spuk: Irrglaube oder Wahrglaube?" In: Jung, C., Collected Works of C. G. Jung, Vol. 18. Princeton University Press, 1976. 904 p. (p. 317-326).

In the foreword to a book on parapsychological experiences, "Spuk: Irrglaube oder Wahrglaube?" (Ghost: false belief or true?) by Fanny Moser (1950), prejudice against belief in parapsychology is said to be grounded in an archaic unconscious fear of ghosts, and a personal experience of ghost like phenomena is recounted. It is argued that rationalism and superstition are complementary and that the more rationalistic one becomes in his conscious mind, the more alive becomes the world of the unconscious. Parapsychological phenomena are of interest to the psychologist because they provide information about the exteriorization of unconscious processes, their content, and the possible sources of such phenomena. The personal experience is analyzed in terms of possible perceptions and reconstructions of the unconscious.

000621 On occultism. Foreword to Jaffe: "Apparitions and precognition." In: Jung, C., Collected Works of C. G. Jung, Vol. 18. Princeton University Press, 1976. 904 p. (p. 327-329).

In a foreword to "Apparitions and Precognition" by Aniela Jaffe (1958), it is pointed out that "wonder tales," warning visions, and other strange happenings are frequently reported in the form of ghost stories, and other superstitious happenings. The book regards such experiences as psychic facts and asks such psychological questions as who sees ghosts, under what conditions, and what a specific ghost symbolizes. It is concluded that the psychology of the unconscious has shed light on many parapsychological questions and it can be expected to do likewise in the area of wonder tales.

000622 The psychogenesis of mental disease. The present status of applied psychology. In: Jung, C., Collected Works of C. G. Jung, Vol. 18. Princeton University Press, 1976. 904 p. (p. 333-334).

In a 1907/1908 statement, the current status of applied psychology in German Switzerland is summarized. A psychological institute existed in Bern; courses and programs were available in Zurich; and several associations and societies were in existence.

000623 The psychogenesis of mental disease. On dementia praecox. In: Jung, C., Collected Works of C. G. Jung, Vol. 18. Princeton University Press, 1976. 904 p. (p. 335).

In an abstract contributed to the First International Psychoanalytic Congress (1908), it is hypothesized that depotentiation of the association process, which consequently has a dream like quality, seems to indicate that a pathogenic agent which is absent in other disorders contributes to dementia praecox (schizophrenia).

000624 /The pathogenesis of mental disease. Review of Sadger: "Konrad Ferdinand Meyer. A pathographic-psychological study."/ The psychogenesis of mental disease. Review of Sadger: "Konrad Ferdinand Meyer. Eine pathographisch-psychologische Studie." In: Jung, C., Collected Works of C. G. Jung, Vol. 18. Princeton University Press, 1976. 904 p. (p. 336-338).

"Konrad Ferdinand Meyer: Eine pathographisch-psychologische Studie" (A pathographic/psychological study) by Isidor Sadger (1908) is praised for illustrating the development of the poet's whole personality as a psychological process rather than simply proposing a diagnosis or forcing his pathology into a clinical frame of reference. It is suggested that the task of the "pathographer" is to describe in intelligible language what is actually happening in areas of the psyche that the biographer ignores, and that previous psychographic works failed to do.

000625 /The psychogenesis of mental disease. Review of Waldstein: "The subconscious self."/ The psychogenesis of mental disease. Review of Waldstein: "Das unbewusste Ich." In: Jung, C., Collected Works of C. G. Jung, Vol. 18. Princeton University Press, 1976. 904 p. (p. 339-342).

In a review of "Das unbewusste Ich und sein Verhaltnis zur Gesundheit und Erziehung" (The subconscious self and its relationship to education and health) by Louis Waldstein (1908), the history of German scientific knowledge is outlined in terms of the rejection of Mesmerism and suggestion therapy and subsequent recognition of the existence of the subconscious. The book is praised for shedding light on the regions of the psyche from which all human achievements, creative works, and nervous disorders spring, and for rejecting the dogmatism that viewed neuroses as organic brain diseases.

000626 The psychogenesis of mental disease. Crime and the soul. In: Jung, C., Collected Works of C. G. Jung, Vol. 18. Princeton University Press, 1976. 904 p. (p. 343-346).

Reflections are offered on the dual personality of the criminal, who is torn between respectability and crime, and on the fact that crime seems to appear to the criminal as something foreign that gains a hold on him so that eventually he has no knowledge of what he is about to do. Cases are presented to illustrate the personification of the criminal instinct and the transfer of evil instincts from one person to a second, who then unconsciously commits a crime that he would otherwise not have committed. In the case of the transmission of evil instincts it is pointed out that the more evil a person is, the more he tries to force on others the wickedness he does not want to show in himself.

000627 The psychogenesis of mental disease. The question of medical intervention. In: Jung, C., Collected Works of C. G. Jung, Vol. 18. Princeton University Press, 1976. 904 p. (p. 347-348).

In answer to a questionnaire asking doctors' opinions on the permissibility of a sex change operation in the case of a transvestite, the ethicality of the operation is upheld on grounds that it was not illegal, that the patient wanted it, and that the doctor felt no injury was done. It is suggested, however, that the transsexual operation, which involved castration, may violate collective emotions about a collective taboo and may be hazardous to the medical profession for that reason.

000628 The psychogenesis of mental disease. Forword to Custance: "Wisdon, madness and folly." In: Jung, C., Collected Works of C. G. Jung, Vol. 18. Princeton University Press, 1976. 904 p. (p. 349-352).

In a foreword to "Wisdom, Madness and Folly" by John Custance (1952), which describes manic-depressive insanity, the intellectual insistence by most investigators that psychoses have purely physical causes is lamented. On the contrary, investigation of schizophrenia made possible the deciphering of the products of insanity and a consequent unlocking of fundamental psychic processes in the unconscious. The book likewise shows how the delirious flight of ideas and uninhibitedness of the manic state lower the threshold of consciousness to such an extent that the unconscious is exposed and made intelligible. When the inhibitions of the conscious mind are removed, collective, archetypal symbols of a religious and mythological nature are revealed. The book is praised as a contribution to knowledge of the psychic contents that underlie pathological states.

000629 The psychogenesis of mental disease. Foreword to Perry: "The self in psychotic process." In: Jung, C., Collected Works of C. G. Jung, Vol. 18. Princeton University Press, 1976. 904 p. (p. 353-356).

In a foreword to a book on schizophrenia, "The Self in psychotic process" by John Weir Perry (1953), the importance of examining the psyche, rather than the physical brain, of the disturbed patient is emphasized. In schizophrenics, the unconscious mind is autonomous, unsystematic, and disordered, and attempts to understand its contents are reviewed. The book is welcomed as recognizing the importance of studying the mental patient's psyche, and the need to understand the historical origins of the psyche is emphasized.

000630 /The psychogenesis of mental disease. Foreword to Schmaltz: "Complex psychology and somatic symptom."/ The psychogenesis of mental disease. Foreword to Schmaltz: "Komplexe Psychologie und korperliches Symptom.' In: Jung, C., Collected Works of C. G. Jung, Vol. 18. Princeton University Press, 1976. 904 p. (p. 357-358).

In the foreword to a book on the treatment of a case of psychosomatic illness, "Komplexe Psychologie und korperliches Symptom" (Complex psychology and somatic symptom) by Gustav Schmaltz (1955), it is pointed out that a neurosis is an expression of the whole person and cannot be treated solely within a medical and/or scientific framework. Important in the etiology and therapy of neuroses is the individual's attitude, which rests on personal and collective premises that can be both pathogenic and curative. It is reemphasized that the psychology of neurosis goes beyond medical confines and must take into account these pathogenic factors.

000631 Freud and psychoanalysis. Sigmund Freud: "On dreams," 25 January 1901. In: Jung, C., Collected Works of C. G. Jung, Vol. 18. Princeton University Press, 1976. 904 p. (p. 361-368).

Freud's "On Dreams" (1901) is described and explained. Topics include manifest and latent dream content, classifications of dreams, children's dreams, dream feeling and affect, self-analysis of dream content, dream work effects and dream function purposiveness, and reasons for the obscurity and confusion of dreams. An outline of topics follows.

000632 /Freud and psychoanalysis. Review of Hellpach: "Basics of a psychology of hysteria."/ Freud and psychoanalysis. Review of Hellpach: "Grundlinien einer Psychologie der Hysterie." In: Jung, C., Collected Works of C. G. Jung, Vol. 18. Princeton University Press, 1976. 904 p. (p. 369-373).

"Grundlinien einer Psychologie der Hysterie" (Basics of a psychology of hysteria) by Willy Hellpach (1904) is reviewed, criticized, and related to Freud's work on the same subject. Singled out for attention are suggestibility, symptoms, and a chapter elaborating the principles covered earlier. Certain biases and exaggerations of the Freudian school are refuted, yet no new insight into the genesis of hysteria is offered. Despite criticisms of focus, style, intelligibility, and omissions of case material, Hellpach's treatment of sociological and historical aspects of hysteria is commended.

000633 Freud and psychoanalysis. Reviews of psychiatric literature. In: Jung, C., Collected Works of C. G. Jung, Vol. 18. Princeton University Press, 1976. 904 p. (p. 374-387).

Reviews of the psychiatric literature from 1906 to 1910 are compiled. Authors reviewed are: 1906: L. Bruns, E. Bleuler, and Carl Wernicke; 1907: Albert Moll, Albert Knapp, and M.

Reichhardt; 1908: Franz C. R. Eschle, P. Dubois, Georg Lomer, E. Meyer, and Sigmund Freud; 1909: L. Lowenfeld, Karl Kleist, Oswald Bumke, and Christian von Ehrenfels; 1910: Christian von Ehrenfels, Max Dost, Alexander Pilcz, W. von Bechterew, M. Urstein, Albert Reibmayer, P. Nacke, Th. Becker, A. Cramer, and August Forel.

000634 Freud and psychoanalysis. The significance of Freud's theory for neurology and psychiatry. In: Jung, C., Collected Works of C. G. Jung, Vol. 18. Princeton University Press, 1976. 904 p. (p. 388-389).

In a discussion of Freud's contributions to the understanding of hysteria and obsessional neurosis, Freud's method of psychoanalysis bridges a gap in the theory of psychogenesis by demonstrating that a determining individual psychological factor can be found for every symptom. Freud has become important for psychiatry particularly in elucidating the symptoms of dementia praecox (schizophrenia), analysis of which uncovers the same psychological mechanisms that are at work in the neuroses, thus making intelligible the individual forms of illusionary ideas, hallucinations, paraesthesias, and bizarre hebephrenic fantasies.

000635 /Freud and psychoanalysis. Review of Stekel: "Conditions of nervous anxiety and their treatment."/ Freud and psychoanalysis. Review of Stekel: "Nervose Angstzustande und ihre Behandlung." In: Jung, C., Collected Works of C. G. Jung, Vol. 18. Princeton University Press, 1976. 904 p. (p. 390-391).

In a review of "Nervose Angstzustande und ihre Behandlung" (Conditions of nervous anxiety and their treatment) by Wilhelm Stekel (1908), a book containing case material on states of nervous anxiety, Stekel, a pupil of Freud, is commended for providing the medical public with an insight into the psychological structure of the neuroses. The individual reactions of the patient are recorded for each case presented, the psychogenesis of each disorder is discussed, and the progress during psychotherapy is described. On the premise that in each individual, states of nervous anxiety are determined by psychosexual conflicts, Freud's assertion that neurotic anxiety is in essence a converted sexual desire is supported.

000636 /Freud and psychoanalysis. Editorial preface to the "Yearbook."/ Freud and psychoanalysis. Editorial preface to the "Jahrbuch." In: Jung, C., Collected Works of C. G. Jung, Vol. 18. Princeton University Press, 1976. 904 p. (p. 392).

The preface to the first volume of the "Jahrbuch fur psychoanalytische und psychopathologische Forschungen" (Yearbook of psychoanalytic and psychopathologic studies), explains how in 1908 a group of followers of Freud's psychology decided that a periodical was needed to gather and publish studies applying this psychology to nervous and mental diseases. The "Jahrbuch" resulted.

000637 /Freud and psychoanalysis. Marginal notes on Wittels: "Sexual privation."/ Freud and psychoanalysis. Marginal notes on Wittels: "Die sexuelle Not." In: Jung, C., Collected Works of C. G. Jung, Vol. 18. Princeton University Press, 1976. 904 p. (p. 393-396).

In notes regarding "Die sexuelle Not" (Sexual privation) by Fritz Wittels (1909), a book advocating that humans must live out their sexuality, the relationship of sexual morality to Freudian psychology is discussed. It is argued that psychoanalysis, like every proper science, is beyond morality. Because it is rational, it is neither moral nor antimoral, offering no prescriptions but only knowledge. It is recognized, however, that persons other than psychoanalysts will interpret Freud in their own ways and ascribe morality or licentiousness on the basis of their own interpretations.

000638 /Freud and psychoanalysis. Review of Wulffen: "The sexual offender."/ Freud and psychoanalysis. Review of Wulffen: "Der Sexualverbrecher." In: Jung, C., Collected Works of C. G. Jung, Vol. 18. Princeton University Press, 1976. 904 p. (p. 397).

"Der Sexualverbrecher" (The sexual offender) by Erich Wulffen (1910), a book dealing with sex crimes and sexual misdemeanors, is reviewed. The book is commended for attention to criminal case histories, the psychological and social foundations of sexual offenses, sexual psychology, sexual characterology, and sexual pathology, but the absence of psychoanalytic viewpoints is noted.

000639 Freud and psychoanalysis. Abstracts of the psychological works of Swiss authors (to the end of 1909). In: Jung, C., Collected Works of C. G. Jung, Vol. 18. Princeton University Press, 1976. 904 p. (p. 398-421).

Abstracts of the works of Swiss authors concerning psychoanalysis are compiled for 1900 through 1909, and related works of some German authors are noted. Critical comments are included for most selections. Authors represented are: Bezzola, Binswanger, E. Bleuler, Bolte, Chalewsky, Claparede, Eberschweiler, Flournoy, Frank, Furst, Hermann, Isserlin, Jung, Riklin, Stein, Ladame, Maeder, Muller, Pfister, Pototsky, Schnyder, Schwarzwald, and Wehrlin.

000640 /Freud and psychoanalysis. Review of Hitschmann: "Freud's theory of neurosis."/ Freud and psychoanalysis. Review of Hitschmann: "Freud's Neurosenlehre." In: Jung, C., Collected Works of C. G. Jung, Vol. 18. Princeton University Press, 1976. 904 p. (p. 422).

"Freud's Neurosenlehre" (Freud's theory of neurosis) by Eduard Hitschmann (1911) is reviewed as a clear and simple introduction to the problems of psychoanalysis for the beginner. It is said to present an excellent picture of the present state of psychoanalysis addressed to the theory of neurosis, and it is hoped that it will reach a large public in order to help dispel prejudices and mistaken opinions held by medical men because of inadequate knowledge of the psychoanalytic literature.

000641 Freud and psychoanalysis. Annual report (1910/11) by the president of the International Psychoanalytic Association. In: Jung, C., Collected Works of C. G. Jung, Vol. 18. Princeton University Press, 1976. 904 p. (p. 423-426).

In the annual report of the International Psychoanalytic Association for 1910/11, growth in the organization is reported and goals for the future outlined. Branches of the organization are encouraged to educate their members, to plan and execute scientific research, to husband the store of knowledge provided by Freud and transmit it, and to adhere to the principles of psychoanalysis until they are fully confirmed or refuted. The beginning of the journal "Zentralblatt fur Psychoanalyse" is noted, and a future journal ("Images") is announced.

000642 Freud and psychoanalysis. Two letters on psychoanalysis. In: Jung, C., Collected Works of C. G. Jung, Vol. 18. Princeton University Press, 1976. 904 p. (p. 427-429).

Two letters (1912) defending psychoanalysis against oral and published attacks are presented. In the first, a speaker to the Keplerbund is accused of lack of objectivity and serious distortion of Freud's work. In the second, the Freudian concept of sexuality is clarified as being broader than the usual usage of the word implies, including all instinctual forces beyond the instinct of self-preservation. Psychoanalysts disclaim responsibility for inferred misconceptions and errors that arise from others' interpretations of their work.

000643 Freud and psychoanalysis. On the psychoanalytic treatment of nervous disorders. In: Jung, C., Collected Works of C. G. Jung, Vol. 18. Princeton University Press, 1976. 904 p. (p. 430-432).

The application of the psychoanalytic method to psychoneurotics is discussed in the context of a case history involving a childhood sexual conflict, reported in 1912. Using parapraxes, fantasies, and dreams as data, psychoanalysis seeks to uncover conflicts, which are often between sexual wishes and opposing moral and esthetic tendencies, and free the psyche of such conflicts. The necessity of dealing with sexual matters in psychotherapy is emphasized; childhood impressions persist, although repressed, throughout one's life and survive in the unconscious until uncovered by psychoanalysis.

000644 Freud and psychoanalysis. A comment on Tausk's criticism of Nelken. In: Jung, C., Collected Works of C. G. Jung, Vol. 18. Princeton University Press, 1976. 904 p. (p. 433-437).

A review by Victor Tausk of an article by Jan Nelken (1913) is criticized for misinterpreting the significance of symbols in schizophrenic fantasy. The symbols, rats and mice (cloacal animals) gnawing at the genitals (castration) are said by Tausk to represent the infantile defecation (anal) complex. The response is that reduction of fantasies to infantile mechanisms is not enough. The therapist must ask why certain infantile channels of interest are being reactivated in the present and find out what they mean to the patient. Even if infantile or primitive symbols are approached analytically, the Zurich school is not content with reduction and with establishing their self-evident existence. Rather, by comparing them through similar material, this school tries to reconstruct the actual problems that led to the employment of these primitive patterns and seeks expression through them. In the case at issue, it is argued that the teleological significance of the castration motif in the fantasy must be clarified.

000645 Freud and psychoanalysis. Answers to questions on Freud. In: Jung, C., Collected Works of C. G. Jung, Vol. 18. Princeton University Press, 1976. 904 p. (p. 438-440).

In 1953, replies are given to questions regarding Freud: 1) the part of Freud's work that Jung accepts; 2) the role of Freud's work and views in the development of Jung's analytical psychology; 3) the role of Freudian sexuality in the etiology of neurosis; 4) the extent of Freud's contribution to knowledge of the psyche; and 5) the value of Freud's therapeutic procedure. Freud is criticized for overemphasis of sex, yet his contribution to knowledge of the psyche is praised. The character and attitude of the therapist are regarded as more important than the method of therapy, and Freud's "prejudice" in the therapeutic approach is criticized. In sum, however, it is said that the present purpose is not to criticize Freud but to build on his work by further investigating the unconscious that Freud's own school has neglected.

000646 On symbolism. The concept of ambivalence. In: Jung, C., Collected Works of C. G. Jung, Vol. 18. Princeton University Press, 1976. 904 p. (p. 443-445).

In discussion of a paper by Eugen Bleuler, ambivalence is defined and regarded as a valuable addition to terminology. Rather than being a driving force, however, ambivalence is hypothesized to be a formal aspect found everywhere. Examples are given from the history of language, from dreams of opposites, from mythology and religion, and from erotic jokes. Also included are brief comments on displacement of affect (von Speyr) and on sacrifice (Franz Riklin).

000647 On symbolism. Contributions to symbolism. In: Jung, C., Collected Works of C. G. Jung, Vol. 18. Princeton University Press, 1976. 904 p. (p. 446).

A contrast between hysterical fantasies and those of dementia praecox (schizophrenia) is described, and a case of a neurotic female is presented as an illustration. In order to understand schizophrenic fantasies, historical parallels must be adduced, because the patient suffers from the reminiscences of mankind and his language uses ancient images of universal validity. The case presented illustrates the documentation and elucidation of a recent fantasy by historical material, ethnological traditions, and mythological parallels.

000648 Two essays on analytical psychology. Adaptation, individuation, collectivity. In: Jung, C., Collected Works of C. G. Jung, Vol. 18. Princeton University Press, 1976. 904 p. (p. 449-454).

Adaptation, individuation, collectivity, and their interrelationships are explained in papers written in 1916. Psychological adaptation is said to involve adaptation to inner and outer conditions, and its energetics are described. In analysis, a resistance often arises from the demand for individuation, which is against all adaptation to others. Since breaking the patient's previous personal conformity would mean the destruction of an esthetic and moral ideal, however, the first step in individuation is guilt, which requires that expiation be offered to a new collective function -- namely humanity. In return for individuation, a person must bring forth values that are an equivalent substitute for his absence in the collective personal sphere. Individuation and collectivity are further discussed in relation to society, the unconscious, the God concept, the soul, and love.

000649 Two essays on analytical psychology. Foreword to the Hungarian edition of Jung: "On the psychology of the unconscious." In: Jung, C., Collected Works of C. G. Jung, Vol. 18. Princeton University Press, 1976. 904 p. (p. 455-456).

In the foreword to the Hungarian edition of C. G. Jung's "On the Psychology of the Unconscious" (1948), pleasure is expressed at the appearance of the book in Hungary, and a brief introduction is provided. The aim of the book is to acquaint the reader with the main problems of the psychology of the unconscious, but only within the limits prescribed by direct medical experience. Because it is only an introduction, relations with the history of human thought, mythology, religion, philosophy, the psychology of primitives, and so on are only suggested.

000650 /The structure and dynamics of the psyche. Forewords to Jung: "On psychic energetics and the nature of dreams."/ The structure and dynamics of the psyche. Forewords to Jung: "Uber psychische Energetik und das Wesen der Traume." In: Jung, C., Collected Works of C. G. Jung, Vol. 18. Princeton University Press, 1976. 904 p. (p. 459-460).

Forewords to two editions of Jung's "Uber psychische Energetik und das Wesen der Traume" (On psychic energetics and the nature of dreams) are presented. The first edition (1928) is said to deal with the unsolved problem of dream interpretation and the important question of the fundamental psychic factors -- the dynamic images that express the nature of psychic energy. The second edition (1948), to which two papers were added, attempts to clarify psychic phenomena by means of concepts from fields of research other than psychology. It is emphasized that medical psychologists must probe more deeply into the important compensatory relationship between the conscious and the unconscious.

000651 The structure and dynamics of the psyche. On hallucination. In: Jung, C., Collected Works of C. G. Jung, Vol. 18. Princeton University Press, 1976. 904 p. (p. 461).

An interpretation of hallucinations is offered in which hallucination is said to be not only a pathological occurrence but a normal one as well, for psychic contents often come to consciousness in hallucinatory form. It is suggested that such hallucinations derive from a still subliminal, maturer personality that is not yet capable of direct consciousness. In the case of primitives, they come from a subliminal thinking or intuiting at a level that is not yet capable of becoming conscious.

000652 /The structure and dynamics of the psyche. Foreword to Schleich: "The miracles of the soul."/ The structure and dynamics of the psyche. Foreword to Schleich: "Die Wunder der Seele." In: Jung, C., Collected Works of C. G. Jung, Vol. 18. Princeton University Press, 1976. 904 p. (p. 462-466).

In a foreword to "Die Wunder der Seele" (The miracles of the soul) (1934), a collection of essays by Carl Ludwig Schleich, the discoverer of local anesthesia, Schleich (1859-1922) is compared to Paracelsus as a representative of a period of transition in medicine and as a revolutionary in his time. Schleich is credited with aiming at the unitary view of psychic and physical processes that later gave strong impetus to medical and biological research. Despite the lack of psychological knowledge at the time, Schleich was able to break through to a recognition of the psyche and the fact that it was related to the body, thus questioning the assumptions of biological causality and materialism.

000653 The structure and dynamics of the psyche. Foreword to Jacobi: "The psychology of C. G. Jung." In: Jung, C., Collected Works of C. G. Jung, Vol. 18. Princeton University Press, 1976. 904 p. (p. 467-468).

In a foreword, Jolande Jacobi's "The Psychology of C. G. Jung" (1940) is described as a concise presentation of the elements of Jung's psychological theories, a presentation that Jung himself had not had time to prepare. The belief is expressed that the time has not yet arrived for an all inclusive theory covering the contents, processes, and phenomena of the psyche, and Jung's concepts are regarded as tentative attempts to formulate a general scientific psychology based on immediate experience with human beings. A brief foreword to the Spanish edition (1947) follows.

000654 The structure and dynamics of the psyche. Foreword to Harding: "Psychic energy." In: Jung, C., Collected Works of C. G. Jung, Vol. 18. Princeton University Press, 1976. 904 p. (p. 469-470).

In a foreword to "Psychic Energy" by M. Esther Harding (1947), the author is congratulated for successfully providing a general orientation to the problems of modern medical psychotherapy, based on personal practical experience. The book is said to clarify often misunderstood concepts regarding psychic facts, and it is recommended to patients as well as doctors.

000655 The structure and dynamics of the psyche. Address on the occasion of the founding of the C. G. Jung Institute, Zurich, 24 April 1948. In: Jung, C., Collected Works of C. G. Jung, Vol. 18. Princeton University Press, 1976. 904 p. (p. 471-476).

In an address on the founding of the C. G. Jung Institute (1948), past achievements in psychology are summarized and directions for the future suggested. In the previous 50 years, Freud and Janet had laid foundations in methodology and clinical observation; Jung had studied the associative reaction, distinguished the attitude types and function types, and discovered the collective unconscious; and a connection had been forged between complex psychology and physics. Possibilities for the future are continuation of the association experiment; the elaboration of case histories (particularly in the areas of paranoia, symbolism, and dreams); research into the processes of compensation in psychotics and criminals; and study of the psychic structure of the family in relation to heredity, the compensatory character of marriage, mass behavior, and the psychology of religion.

000656 The structure and dynamics of the psyche. Depth psychology. In: Jung, C., Collected Works of C. G. Jung, Vol. 18. Princeton University Press, 1976. 904 p. (p. 477-486).

Depth psychology is defined as the branch of psychological science that is concerned with the unconscious, and its history is summarized. The empirical approach to the unconscious is said to be recent, dating from about the turn of the 20th century. Pioneers in experimental research in this area were Janet and Freud, and Freud's investigations and theories are described and contrasted with those of Adler and Jung. Jung's contributions after his parting with Freud are outlined: the modes of compensation by the unconscious in extraverted and introverted attitude types, the roles of the orienting functions of consciousness, the formulation of archetypes, and the definitions of the personal unconscious vs. the collective unconscious.

000657 The structure and dynamics of the psyche. Foreword to the first volume of studies from the C. G. Jung Institute. In: Jung, C., Collected Works of C. G. Jung, Vol. 18. Princeton University Press, 1976. 904 p. (p. 487-488).

In a foreword to the first volume of studies from the C. G. Jung Institute (1949), it is pointed out that the publications in the series will represent many sciences, since psychology is the intermediary between the disciplines. These publications are expected to show the great diversity of psychological interests and needs, particularly those of the psychology of the collective unconscious, a young science which draws heavily on studies of mythology and comparative religion.

000658 The structure and dynamics of the psyche. Foreword to Frieda Fordham: "Introduction to Jung's psychology." In: Jung, C., Collected Works of C. G. Jung, Vol. 18. Princeton University Press, 1976. 904 p. (p. 489-490).

In the foreword to Frieda Fordham's "Introduction to Jung's Psychology" (1953), she is commended for producing a readable summary of Jung's attempts at a more comprehensive understanding of the human psyche. Because Jung has no formulated theory, it is difficult to give a concise account of his ideas, particularly because of his digressions into the field of general psychology. These digressions are defended, however, as necessary to the formation of a base for the evaluation of pathological phenomena.

000659 The structure and dynamics of the psyche. Foreword to Michael Fordham: "New developments in analytical psychology." In: Jung, C., Collected Works of C. G. Jung, Vol. 18. Princeton University Press, 1976. 904 p. (p. 491-493).

In a foreword to "New Developments in Analytical Psychology" by Michael Fordhan (1957), a paper on transference is singled out for discussion. The problem of transference is said to occupy a central position in the dialectical process of analytical psychology, making great demands on the doctor's skill and moral responsibility. Transference forcibly brings about a dialogue that requires both patient and analyst to acknowledge their partnership in a common process of approximation and differentiation. As the patient frees himself of his infantile state of unconsciousness or from unbounded egocentricity, the analyst must allow himself to display a degree of humanity that the patient needs in order to assure himself of his right to exist as an individual.

000660 The structure and dynamics of the psyche. An astrological experiment. In: Jung, C., Collected Works of C. G. Jung, Vol. 18. Princeton University Press, 1976. 904 p. (p. 494-501).

In an experiment to demonstrate synchronicity (the chance creation of meaningful arrangements that appear as if a causal intention had been at work), nearly 1000 horoscopes of married persons were examined in terms of oppositions and conjunctions of the sun, moon, Mars, Venus, ascendant, and descendant. In the first of three batches, the conjunction of sun and moon was the most frequent of the 50 aspects; in the second, moon and moon; in the third, ascendant and moon. Although figures were not mathematically significant in any one batch, it is pointed out that the recurrence of the moon conjunction appears highly improbable on a random basis. Results are discussed in terms of implications for causality and probability theory, and it is suggested that numbers themselves may possess an autonomy like that of archetypes and may condition consciousness instead of being conditioned by it. Astrology is described as a remnant of the gods whose numinosity can still be felt even in a scientific age.

000661 The structure and dynamics of the psyche. Letters on synchronicity: to Markus Fierz. In: Jung, C., Collected Works of C. G. Jung, Vol. 18. Princeton University Press, 1976. 904 p. (p. 502-507).

Synchronicity is discussed in letters to Markus Fierz (1950 and 1954). Fierz is questioned about his mathematical evaluation of the results of Jung's comparison of the horoscopes of 400 married pairs. The statistics confirmed the traditional view that sun/moon aspects are marriage characteristics, yet their conjunction is attributed to synchronicity rather than causality. It is denied that the study was undertaken to prove the truth of astrology; rather, it was to demonstrate a case of "meaningful coincidence."

000662 The structure and dynamics of the psyche. Letters on synchronicity: to Michael Fordham. In: Jung, C., Collected Works of C. G. Jung, Vol. 18. Princeton University Press, 1976. 904 p. (p. 508-509).

In a letter to Michael Fordham (1955), synchronicity is said to tell something about the psychoid factor (the unconscious archetype), which tends to gather suitable forms of expression around itself. As an archetype is amplified, it is difficult to prove that the amplificatory associations are not causal, yet they may represent cases of synchronicity instead. It is possible that the psyche, analogous to the natural course of events, is based on synchronicity, as contrasted with scientific reconstructions of reality based on statistical averages. Doubt is expressed, however, that the psyche is based exclusively on the synchronistic principle.

000663 The structure and dynamics of the psyche. The future of parapsychology. In: Jung, C., Collected Works of C. G. Jung, Vol. 18. Princeton University Press, 1976. 904 p. (p. 510-511).

In answer to a questionnaire (1960), parapsychology is defined as the science dealing with biological or psychological events showing that the categories of matter, space, and time (and thus causality) are not axiomatic, and other answers regarding parapsychology are given. Research in the psychology of the unconscious is necessary, but repeatable experiments and statistical verification may not be possible in this field. The most important part of parapsychological research will be the careful exploration and qualitative description of spontaneous events. Parapsychological phenomena are said to be favored by the presence of an active archetype, a situation in which the deep, instinctual layers of the psyche are activated.

000664 The archetypes and the collective unconscious. The hypothesis of the collective unconscious. In: Jung, C., Collected Works of C. G. Jung, Vol. 18. Princeton University Press, 1976. 904 p. (p. 515-516).

A lecture on the hypothesis of the collective unconscious (1932) is presented in abstract form. Whereas for Freud the unconscious is essentially a function of consciousness, Jung holds the unconscious to be an independent psychic function prior to consciousness and opposed to it. The unconscious may be divided into a personal and a collective unconscious, the latter being a psychic propensity to a regular functioning, independent of time and race and having products comparable to mythological motifs. Examples of the symbolism of the circle (mandala symbolism) are presented.

000665 /The archetypes and the collective unconscious. Foreword to Adler: "Discovery of the soul."/ The archetypes and the collective unconscious. Foreword to Adler: "Entdeckung der Seele." In: Jung, C., Collected Works of C. G. Jung, Vol. 18. Princeton University Press, 1976. 904 p. (p. 517).

In a foreword to "Entdeckung der Seele" (Discovery of the soul) by Gerhard Adler (1934), the author is commended for presenting a complete and rigorously objective account of the psychotherapeutic approaches of Freud, Alfred Adler, and Jung. Because psychological theories have broken out of the domain of medical psychotherapy and have become known to scientists in other areas and to laymen, informed public opinion suffers the same confusion as the science of medical psychology itself. It is implied that Gerhard Adler's book should help allay some of the misunderstandings.

000666 The archetypes and the collective unconscious. Foreword to Harding: "Woman's mysteries." In: Jung, C., Collected Works of C. G. Jung, Vol. 18. Princeton University Press, 1976. 904 p. (p. 518-520).

In a foreword to M. Esther Harding's "Woman's Mysteries: Ancient and Modern" (German translation, 1949), the importance of the historical aspects of the human psyche, as manifest in the psychology of primitives, folklore, mythology, and comparative religion, is emphasized. The book is considered an attempt to describe some of the archetypal foundations of feminine psychology, specifically a systematic survey of the archetypal material of feminine compensation, which is an attempt by the unconscious to balance a disequilibrium in

the conscious mind. The relationship of the unconscious and the instincts in neurosis is examined, and the roles of historical knowledge and therapeutic myths are explained.

000667 The archetypes and the collective unconscious. Foreword to Neumann: "The origins and history of consciousness." In: Jung, C., Collected Works of C. G. Jung, Vol. 18. Princeton University Press, 1976. 904 p. (p. 521-522).

In a foreword to "The Origins and History of Consciousness" by Erich Neumann (American edition, 1954), the author is commended for presenting facts in a pattern and creating a unified whole in a way no pioneer of Jung's generation could have done. The book opens in the realm of matriarchal symbolism, based on the uroboros, and on this foundation is built a unique history of the evolution of consciousness and a representation of myths as the phenomenology of consciousness. The work is praised as valuable for its contribution to the psychology of the unconscious; the author has placed analytical psychology concepts on a firm evolutionary basis and erected a comprehensive structure in which the empirical forms of thought find their rightful place. The importance of the personal temperament and assumptions of the author in the area of psychology are also noted.

000668 The archetypes and the collective unconscious. Foreword to Adler: "Studies in analytical psychology." In: Jung, C., Collected Works of C. G. Jung, Vol. 18. Princeton University Press, 1976. 904 p. (p. 523-524).

In the foreword to "Studies in Analytical Psychology" by Gerhard Adler (German edition, 1952), several problems covered in the book are summarized. Singled out for discussion is the peculiarity of analytical psychology as compared with the materialistic and rationalistic tendencies of the Freudian school. The author is praised for his handling of the psychology of dreams, the role of the ego, the question of whether and how the raising to consciousness of unconscious contents is therapeutically effective, and the religious aspect of psychic phenomena. The book is said to fill a gap in psychological literature because of its clarity and its numerous illustrative case histories.

000669 /The archetypes and the collective unconscious. Foreword to Jung: "Configurations of the unconscious" (1950)./ The archetypes and the collective unconscious. Foreword to Jung: "Gestaltungen des Unbewussten" (1950). In: Jung, C., Collected Works of C. G. Jung, Vol. 18. Princeton University Press, 1976. 904 p. (p. 525-526).

In a foreword to "Gestaltungen des Unbewussten" (Configurations of the unconscious) by C. G. Jung (1950), the topics discussed in the book are summarized: 1) the work of the poet as manifestations of the contents of the unconscious; 2) the rebirth motif, as expressed in drama, the principal theme of poetic art; 3) a case history of a transformation process illustrated by pictures; 4) a survey of mandala symbolism drawn from case material; and 5) a psychological study of E. T. A. Hoffmann's "The Golden Pot" by Aniela Jaffe.

000670 /The archetypes and the collective unconscious. Foreword to Wickes: "The inner world of man."/ The archetypes and the collective unconscious. Foreword to Wickes: "Von der inneren Welt des Menschen." In: Jung, C., Collected Works of C. G. Jung, Vol. 18. Princeton University Press, 1976. 904 p. (p. 527-528).

In a foreword to "Von der inneren Welt des Menschen" (The inner world of man) by Frances G. Wickes (1953), fantasy is discussed as a natural expression of life rather than a sickness. Fantasies have a positive aspect as creative compensations of the conscious attitude, which is always in danger of onesidedness. Fantasy is the natural life of the psyche, a vital activity that nourishes the seeds of psychic development and is important for the cure of psychogenic neuroses and mild psychotic disturbances. The book is said to illustrate the value of fantasy by describing typical figures and phases that are encountered in involuntary fantasy processes.

000671 /The archetypes and the collective unconscious. Foreword to Jung: "From the roots of consciousness."/ The archetypes and the collective unconscious. Foreword to Jung: "Von den Wurzeln des Bewusstseins" (1954). In: Jung, C., Collected Works of C. G. Jung, Vol. 18. Princeton University Press, 1976. 904 p. (p. 529).

In the foreword to "Von den Wurzeln des Bewusstseins" (From the roots of consciousness) by C. G. Jung (1954), the ninth volume of the "Psychologische Abhandlungen," it is explained that the central theme of the book is the archetype. The book consists mostly of works that grew from Eranos lectures and approaches archetypes from the viewpoints of history, practical and theoretical psychology, and case material. Although the existence and efficacy of archetypes are easily demonstrated, their phenomenology presents difficult problems, as the book shows. It is concluded that no simplification of the concept is possible at this stage.

000672 /The archetypes and the collective unconscious. Foreword to van Helsdingen: "Pictures from the unconscious."/ The archetypes and the collective unconscious. Foreword to van Helsdingen: "Beelden uit het Onbewuste." In: Jung, C., Collected Works of C. G. Jung, Vol. 18. Princeton University Press, 1976. 904 p. (p. 530-531).

"Beelden uit het Onbewuste" (Pictures from the unconscious) by R. J. van Helsdingen (1957) is described as a discussion of a case treated by Jung himself with the use of drawings by the patient. The patient had lived in both the Orient and Europe as a child and adolescent, and these environments combined with her inner disposition to produce a series of pictures expressing an infantile archaic fear. The pictures not only illustrated the phase of treatment that brought the contents of the patient's neurosis to consciousness but were also an instrument of treatment, reducing the half conscious or unconscious images in her mind to a common denominator and fixating them. It is explained that the therapeutic effect consists of inducing the conscious and unconscious minds to collaborate, thus integrating the unconscious and remedying the neurotic dissociation.

000673 The archetypes and the collective unconscious. Forword to Jacobi: "Complex/archetype/symbol." In: Jung, C., Collected Works of C. G. Jung, Vol. 18. Princeton University Press, 1976. 904 p. (p. 532-533).

"Complex/Archetype/Symbol" by Jolande Jacobi (1957) is described in a foreword as explaining the important connection between the individual complex and the universal, instinctual archetype and between the archetype and the symbol. Complexes are described as autonomous, forcing themselves on consciousness or resisting conscious efforts to reproduce them. They give rise to such actions as slips of the tongue and falsifications of memory and judgment. Complexes rest on emotional aptitudes or instincts, and the formal aspect of the instinct is defined as the archetype. It is hoped that Jacobi's book will help clarify some misunderstandings of Jung's work.

000674 The archetypes and the collective unconscious. Foreword to Bertine: "Human relationships." In: Jung, C., Collected Works of C. G. Jung, Vol. 18. Princeton University Press, 1976. 904 p. (p. 534-536).

In a foreword to "Human Relationships" by Eleanor Bertine (Swiss edition, 1957), it is noted that Freud and Adler drew conclusions on the basis of neurotic patients and tried to apply them to society, whereas analytical psychology has pointed out more general human facts, such as attitude and function types, that play a role in neurosis but are also a normal part of the human constitution. Although Freud put the Oedipus complex in a central place in his theory, it is argued that other typical patterns (archetypes) also exist and regulate the relationships among human beings. Examples abound in mythology, folklore, dreams, and psychoses and exert a decisive effect on human relationships.

000675 The archetypes and the collective unconscious. Preface to de Laszlo: "Psyche and symbol." In: Jung, C., Collected Works of C. G. Jung, Vol. 18. Princeton University Press, 1976. 904 p. (p. 537-542).

In a foreword to "Psyche and Symbol" by Violet S. de Laszlo (1958), the historical basis of psychic processes is discussed. Like other sciences, psychology must take account of the past, specifically the history of the psyche. Dreams or fantasies that appear psychotic may be well within the range of normal human experience as validated by historical comparison. The mind, like the body, has predetermined individual aptitudes or patterns of behavior, and man will to a certain extent function psychologically according to his original patterns. Archetypes represent these inherited patterns of psychic behavior, and their significance is summarized.

000676 /The archetypes and the collective unconscious. Foreword to Brunner: "The anima as a problem in the man's fate."/ The archetypes and the collective unconscious. Foreword to Brunner: "Die Anima als Schicksalsproblem des Mannes." In: Jung, C., Collected Works of C. G. Jung, Vol. 18. Princeton University Press, 1976. 904 p. (p. 543-547).

"Die Anima als Schicksalsproblem des Mannes" (The anima as a problem in the man's fate) by Cornelia Brunner (1963) is described in a foreword as a record of an eight-year dialogue in which the partners recorded both their conscious and unconscious reactions. Although the technique appears unscientific, it is defended as a guarantee of psychological objectivity because it represents what happens in reality. The main subject of the dialogue was the question of the anima, the feminine element in the male personality. Rider Haggard is cited as the classic exponent of the anima, and his creative writing is recommended as a good introduction to Brunner's book. It is concluded that the dialectical process is always a creative adventure out of which transformation may develop.

000677 Civilization in transition. Report on America. In: Jung, C., Collected Works of C. G. Jung, Vol. 18. Princeton University Press, 1976. 904 p. (p. 551).

In a paper abstracted by Otto Rank (1910), impressions of North America are described. The psychological peculiarities of Americans, which indicate intense sexual repression, would be accessible to psychoanalysis. Reasons for the repression are in the specifically American complex -- living with lower races, mainly Negroes. Living with barbarous races has a suggestive effect on the instincts of the White race and lowers it. Strong defense mechanisms are therefore necessary and are manifest in aspects of the American culture.

000678 Civilization in transition. On the psychology of the Negro. In: Jung, C., Collected Works of C. G. Jung, Vol. 18. Princeton University Press, 1976. 904 p. (p. 552).

In an abstract of a lecture (1912), the psychology of the Negro is explained. The psychoses of Negroes are the same as those of White men, but diagnosis is difficult because the Negro is superstitious, does not understand what one wants of him, and cannot look into his own thoughts or retell hallucinations or dreams. The Negro is religious and pictures the white man as an ideal. In dream examples, the wish or task to adapt to the White man appears frequently, and many sacrificial symbols appear. The latter fact is cited as evidence that such symbols are not only Christian but have their origin in a biological necessity.

000679 Civilization in transition. A radio talk in Munich. In: Jung, C., Collected Works of C. G. Jung, Vol. 18. Princeton University Press, 1976. 904 p. (p. 553-557).

In a radio talk in Munich (1930), observations on thought processes of the Chinese and of Africans are offered. The unconscious psyche of Europeans shows a tendency to produce contents analogous to those in older Chinese and later Tantric philosophy. It is suggested as a working hypothesis that such parallels indicate that European psychic processes are being influenced by an eruption of the Oriental spirit. In Africa the psychic life of primitives was studied to unearth the elements primitives have in common with Europeans. Processes that are in the unconscious of Europeans are conscious to primitives. For example, the European thinks in dreams what the primitive thinks consciously; for the primitive, dreams may not even be distinguished from reality. Comparisons are illustrated with examples of primitive responses to a request and of primitive dreams.

000680 /Civilization in transition. Forewords to Jung: "Contemporary Psychic Problems."/ Civilization in transition. Forewords to Jung: "Seelenprobleme der Gegenwart." In: Jung, C., Collected Works of C. G. Jung, Vol. 18. Princeton University Press, 1976. 904 p. (p. 558-560).

Three forewords to "Seelenprobleme der Gegenwart" (Contemporary Psychic Problems) by C. G. Jung are presented: first edition (1931), second edition (1933), and Italian new edition (1959). The volume is described as dealing with contemporary problems, not solutions. Psychic endeavors are problematical and questions are still being formulated. Of particular concern is the problem of the soul, which is said to torment modern man even more than it did his ancestors. In the Italian edition, the volume is described as evidence of the attempt by doctors to build up a medical psychology of living human beings to answer questions that could not be answered by academic means alone.

000681 Civilization in transition. Foreword to Aldrich: "The primitive mind and modern civilization." In: Jung, C., Collected Works of C. G. Jung, Vol. 18. Princeton University Press, 1976. 904 p. (p. 561-563).

In a foreword to "The Primitive Mind and Modern Civilization" by Charles Roberts Aldrich (1931), historical attempts to understand primitive psychology are summarized. Contributions of the fields of mythology, folklore, history, and comparative religion are mentioned, and it is pointed out that a psychology that would be helpful to the task did not exist before. Freud's "Totem and Taboo" is cited as an early contribution of new psychology to this investigation, but Freud applied an existing theory, while Jung used a comparative

method. It is concluded that the new psychology is not yet advanced enough to present a theory of the mind that would have universal application, yet movements are being made in that direction.

000682 Civilization in transition. Press communique on visiting the United States. In: Jung, C., Collected Works of C. G. Jung, Vol. 18. Princeton University Press, 1976. 904 p. (p. 564-565).

In a press communique on visiting the United States in 1936, interest in observing the changes over the previous decade is expressed. A disclaimer of political leanings is made in an attempt to prevent attempts to link Jung's name with any political party. It is pointed out that Jung is interested in the undeniable differences in national and racial psychology, which account for serious misunderstandings and mistakes in international dealings and in domestic social frictions. The change in America from a pioneering to a rooted society is noted.

000683 Civilization in transition. Psychology and national problems. In: Jung, C., Collected Works of C. G. Jung, Vol. 18. Princeton University Press, 1976. 904 p. (p. 566-581).

In a lecture at the Institute of Medical Psychology (Tavistock Clinic), London (1936) the question of psychology and national problems is discussed in the context of World War I and subsequent events. It is suggested that some aspects of the world situation are amenable to psychological evaluation. Certain individual symptoms arise from misery and disorder, including positive ones such as greater effort and organization and negative ones such as emotional formation of groups with infantile and archaic psychology. When formed, groups such as nations exhibit traits common to all the people but none of their individual achievements; they react like a primitive group being. The implications of this psychological formulation are elaborated as they relate to democracy and other forms of government, the state, ruling groups, money, individual leaders, and state symbols. The role of the collective unconscious in political processes is described, and it is suggested that political events occur in cycles, with another era of dictators, Caesars, and incarnated states about to begin.

000684 Civilization in transition. Return to the simple life. In: Jung, C., Collected Works of C. G. Jung, Vol. 18. Princeton University Press, 1976. 904 p. (p. 582-588).

In answer to a questionnaire on the effects of wartime conditions on the Swiss people (1941), observations on the quality of Swiss life and the nature of the Swiss character are offered. The return to the simple life is welcomed even though it demands considerable sacrifice and is not voluntary. Recent social conditions are compared to negative examples from America, and the propensity of people to live for and in the future is deplored. A minimum degree of austerity is pronounced beneficial, as it enforces simplicity, which is true happiness; but to live simply without bitterness is a difficult moral task for many people. Instead of relying on team spirit, it is suggested that priority be given to developing the individual personality, and the Swiss characteristics of mistrustfulness and obstinacy are suggested as virtues that have protected the Swiss in the past. It is concluded that more good for Switzerland will come from sober skepticism and sure instinct than from propaganda talk and artificial stimulation of team spirit and rational regeneration.

000685 /Civilization in transition. Epilogue to Jung: "Modern man in search of a soul."/ Civilization in transition. Epilogue to Jung: "L'Homme a la decouverte de son ame." In: Jung, C., Collected Works of C. G. Jung, Vol. 18. Princeton University Press, 1976. 904 p. (p. 589-590).

In the epilogue to "L'Homme a la Decouverte de son Ame" (Modern man in search of a soul) by C. G. Jung (1944), it is pointed out that Jung's psychology rests on experiences with human beings, not with academic postulates; therefore it is concerned with the unconscious mind rather than just the contents and functions of consciousness. It is predicted that investigation of the psyche is the science of the future, for the greatest danger to man is a psychic danger, particularly from the masses, in whom the effects of the unconscious accumulate and stifle the reasonableness of the conscious mind. To protect himself from war, it is concluded that man must not arm himself but must discover the psychic conditions under which the unconscious mind overwhelms the conscious mind.

000686 Civilization in transition. Marginalia on contemporary events. In: Jung, C., Collected Works of C. G. Jung, Vol. 18. Princeton University Press, 1976. 904 p. (p. 591-603).

The belief that science has depsychized or dedeified the natural world, removing the gods and demons and driving them back into men's unconscious minds, from which they arose originally, is discussed in terms of contemporary events in Germany in 1945. Although many scientific achievements are admirable, returning these gods and demons to man's psyche is compared with giving him an intoxicating poison. The fact that Hitler was able to rise to power is attributed to this state of affairs. In contrast to the Germans, the Swiss resisted, possibly because of their smallness as a nation, their consequent distrust, defiance, and obstinacy, and their tradition. Religion and psychology are discussed as possible remedies, and it is concluded that only the individual can effect change, and he must change himself.

000687 Civilization in transition. Answers to "Mishmar" on Adolph Hitler. In: Jung, C., Collected Works of C. G. Jung, Vol. 18. Princeton University Press, 1976. 904 p. (p. 604-605).

In answer to questions by Eugen Kolb of Mishmar (The Daily Guardian) in 1945, Adolph Hitler is characterized as an hysteric, specifically a pathological liar who believed his own lies. Because of his personal conviction, he was able to persuade the masses, especially since the German people were discontent at the time and harbored a national inferiority complex. Hitler's associates are characterized as social misfits, psychopaths, and criminals, while Hitler himself controlled public attitude by influencing the unconscious of normal people through the application of mass psychology and the herd phenomenon.

000688 Civilization in transition. Techniques of attitude change conducive to world peace: memorandum to Unesco. In: Jung, C., Collected Works of C. G. Jung, Vol. 18. Princeton University Press, 1976. 904 p. (p. 606-613).

In a 1948 response to a request by the United Nations Educational, Scientific and Cultural Organization (Unesco), the use of psychotherapy to change attitudes in a way conducive to world peace is suggested. Psychotherapy as practiced by Jung and his school is described as a technique for changing mental attitudes by integrating unconscious contents into consciousness, and the method is outlined. It is emphasized that the method is applicable only to individuals with relatively high intelligence and a sound sense of morality, and only a small number of such persons, after undergoing treatment, could form a leading minority that might become a nucleus for a larger body of people. The need for teachers and the difficulty of finding suitable ones is mentioned. A nation is considered as the sum of its individuals, and its character corresponds to the moral average of its citizens. Thoughts for im-

plementing this method include: 1) publicizing the foregoing ideas among the appropriate persons; 2) providing treatment for those who feel their own attitude needs revision; 3) allocating money to favor the serious candidates.

000689 Civilization in transition. The effect of technology on the human psyche. In: Jung, C., Collected Works of C. G. Jung, Vol. 18. Princeton University Press, 1976. 904 p. (p. 614-615).

Observations regarding the effect of technology on the human psyche are offered. Considering that technology consists of procedures invented by man, it is not entirely outside the human sphere; certain modes of human adaptation to it are possible. The repetitious procedures of technology are compared to the patterns of primitive labor, yet it is suggested that modern man does not have the same tolerance for them. In modern man, technology is an imbalance that leads to dissatisfactinon, preventing man from exercising his natural versatility. On its own merits, technology is neither good nor bad but depends on the individual's attitude toward it. To prevent his other mental capacities from atrophying, for example, an engineer may study philosophy. The final question is whether man has sufficient reason to resist the temptation to use his technology for destructive purposes.

000690 Civilization in transition. Foreword to Neumann: "Depth psychology and a new ethic." In: Jung, C., Collected Works of C. G. Jung, Vol. 18. Princeton University Press, 1976. 904 p. (p. 616-622).

In a foreword to "Depth Psychology and a New Ethic" by Erich Neumann (1949), the problem of formulating ethical principles in light of the study of unconscious processes is discussed. Moral principles that seem clear from the standpoint of ego consciousness become inapplicable when the compensatory significance of the shadow (the unconscious) is considered in the light of ethical responsibility. The role of the medical psychologist in dealing with evils as manifest in neuroses is described as a moral problem, yet ethical problems are intensely individual for the patient, and it is suggested that absolute ethical rules are incapable of formulation. The collective morality or "old ethic" is contrasted with the "new ethic," defined as differentiation within the old ethic, confined to individuals who, driven by unavoidable conflicts of duty, are trying to integrate the unconscious into consciousness. Neumann is commended for attempting to formulate the ethical problems raised by the discovery of the unconscious.

000691 Civilization in transition. Foreword to Baynes: "Analytical psychology and the English mind." In: Jung, C., Collected Works of C. G. Jung, Vol. 18. Princeton University Press, 1976. 904 p. (p. 623-624).

In a foreword to "Analytical Psychology and the English Mind" by Helton Godwin Baynes (1950), previous books by Baynes are briefly discussed and the present volume is described as writings on the complex psychic conditions characteristic of medical psychology. It is noted that psychology requires the medical psychologist to deal with such complex factors because the psychotherapeutic process can only take place on that level. Baynes is praised for not oversimplifying the field but rather drawing from a great variety of theoretical and practical points of view and opening possibilities and connections worthy of further discussion.

000692 Civilization in transition. The rules of life. In: Jung, C., Collected Works of C. G. Jung, Vol. 18. Princeton University Press, 1976. 904 p. (p. 625).

In response to a question regarding rules of life, a personal endeavor to live by no rules is revealed and the dangers of living by rules are suggested. It is said that no rules can cope with the paradoxes of life. Moral law, like natural law, represents only one aspect of reality. Rules are usually made in order to suppress the tendency to disobey them. Although people can follow certain regular habits unconsciously and learn about them by questioning others, most people prefer instead to establish rules that are the exact opposite of what they are doing in reality.

000693 Civilization in transition. On flying saucers. In: Jung, C., Collected Works of C. G. Jung, Vol. 18. Princeton University Press, 1976. 904 p. (p. 626-631).

In anwser to questions (1954), the nature of flying saucers is discussed. The position is taken that the empirical basis is insufficient to allow any conclusions as to the nature of flying saucers, yet something is definitely seen (it is not known what). The phenomenon may be a subjective or collective vision produced by the unconscious as compensation for the apparently insoluble political problems of the modern world. Possible natural or physical causes are suggested, and reports of flying saucer landings are described as having mystical components. If flying saucers prove to be extraterrestrial, the impact on mankind would be devastating, as our entire technology would be rendered obsolete. The possibility that saucer sightings are associated with certain psychic states is further elaborated.

000694 Civilization in transition. On flying saucers: statement to the United Press International. In: Jung, C., Collected Works of C. G. Jung, Vol. 18. Princeton University Press, 1976. 904 p. (p. 631-632).

In a statement to United Press International (1958), a report that Jung believes in the physical reality of flying saucers is denied and his opinion that insufficient empirical evidence exists to support or disprove their material existence is restated. Jung concerns himself only with the psychological aspect of the phenomenon and believes that something is seen, but it isn't known what. The thing seen could be material or psychic, and each has its own kind of reality. Relations with the Aerial Phenomena Research Organization are summarized.

000695 Civilization in transition. On flying saucers: letter to Keyhoe. In: Jung, C., Collected Works of C. G. Jung, Vol. 18. Princeton University Press, 1976. 904 p. (p. 632-633).

In a letter to Major Donald E. Keyhoe of the National Investigation Committee on Aerial Phenomena (1958), the opinion that inadequate information is available to allow conclusions regarding the physical reality of flying saucers is elaborated, and the position that something is seen but one does not know what is restated. The fantasy material accompanying saucer observations is noted, and it is pointed out that any new experience has two aspects: 1) the fact itself; and 2) the way one conceives of it. The possibility that the American Air Force or the government is withholding facts about flying saucers is suggested and condemned as unwise, as rumors spread in an atmosphere of ignorance.

000696 Civilization in transition. Human nature does not yield easily to idealistic advice. In: Jung, C., Collected Works of C. G. Jung, Vol. 18. Princeton University Press, 1976. 904 p. (p. 634-635).

In a comment on an article, "Analysis and Faith" by William H. Roberts (1955), the difficulty of giving men moral direction is discussed. Although Roberts gives proper value to man's mental and moral attitude, it is argued that, due to inertia and prejudice, human nature does not respond to idealistic advice. Liberation from inhibitions and prejudices is suggested, yet the value of such liberation depends on the goal toward which it will be used. Finally, Roberts is criticized for ignoring relevant literature from the previous 40 years on the dialogue between religion and psychology.

000697 Civilization in transition. On the Hungarian uprising. In: Jung, C., Collected Works of C. G. Jung, Vol. 18. Princeton University Press, 1976. 904 p. (p. 636).

In contributions to a symposium (1956), the suppression of the Hungarian people by the Russian army is condemned as an abominable crime, and the people of Western Europe are criticized for attributing the blame to someone else, ignoring their own consciences. The political events in Hungary would not have been possible without previous European deeds of shortsightedness and stupidity. It is concluded that the focus of the deadly disease lies in Europe.

000698 Civilization in transition. On psychodiagnostics. In: Jung, C., Collected Works of C. G. Jung, Vol. 18. Princeton University Press, 1976. 904 p. (p. 637).

Use of psychodiagnostics to determine the suitability of a candidate for a job is defended as being more accurate than most employers' evaluations of job seekers, which may be based on illusion and projection. Opposition to psychodiagnostics is pronounced stupid, and hope for future improvement in methods is expressed. Psychodiagnostics is welcomed as promoting understanding of others.

000699 Civilization in transition. If Christ walked the Earth today. In: Jung, C., Collected Works of C. G. Jung, Vol. 18. Princeton University Press, 1976. 904 p. (p. 638).

In a symposium published in "Cosmopolitan" (1958) it is hypothesized that if Christ reappeared today he would be interviewed and photographed by the press and would not live longer than a month. He would die being fed up with himself, as he would see himself banalized beyond endurance. He would be killed by his success, morally and physically.

000700 Civilization in transition. Foreword to "Hugh Crichton-Miller, 1877-1959." In: Jung, C., Collected Works of C. G. Jung, Vol. 18. Princeton University Press, 1976. 904 p. (p. 639-641).

In a foreword to "Hugh Crichton-Miller, 1877-1959" (1961), highlights of 30 years of friendship with Crichton-Miller are remembered. Selected for discussion are the first meeting in England, when Crichton-Miller invited Jung to address his clinic staff; a crisis in the Society for Psychotherapy, when Crichton-Miller supported Jung in thwarting German attempts to increase the international representation of the society by admitting unqualified members; and a personal conversation about religion during Crichton-Miller's terminal illness.

000701 Psychology and religion. Why I am not a Catholic. In: Jung, C., Collected Works of C. G. Jung, Vol. 18. Princeton University Press, 1976. 904 p. (p. 645-647).

Reasons for his not being a Catholic are summarized by Jung: 1) he is a practical Christian to whom love and justice mean more than dogmatic speculations that are unprovable; 2) he is a doctor who could not help his patients if he believed he possessed ultimate truth; 3) he is a man of science who does not believe that what he himself believes or understands is the only and final truth. This unwillingness to commit himself is explained by the necessity to understand persons with differing religious beliefs. The schism that besets Christianity also exists in Jung, and one cannot come to terms with this conflict by imputing wrong to someone else but by solving it within oneself.

000702 Psychology and religion. The definition of demonism. In: Jung, C., Collected Works of C. G. Jung, Vol. 18. Princeton University Press, 1976. 904 p. (p. 648).

Demonism (possession) is defined as a peculiar state of mind in which certain psychic contents, the complexes, assume control of the personality in place of the ego, at least temporarily, so that the free will of the ego is suspended. Ego consciousness may be present or eclipsed. Demonism occurs frequently under primitive conditions and may be deliberately induced or epidemic. Medically, it belongs partly to the psychogenic neuroses and partly to schizophrenia.

000703 /Psychology and religion. Foreword to Jung: "Symbolism of the spirit."/ Psychology and religion. Foreword to Jung: "Symbolik des Geistes" (1948). In: Jung, C., Collected Works of C. G. Jung, Vol. 18. Princeton University Press, 1976. 904 p. (p. 649-650).

In a foreword to "Symbolik des Geistes" (Symbolism of the spirit) by C. G. Jung (1948), the five essays in the book are described: 1) an account of the spirit archetype; 2) a description of the development of the primitive nature spirit into the "Spirit Mercurius;" 3) a description of the historical development of the ungodly spirit Satan (by Riwkah Scharf); 4) a sketch of the historical development of the Trinitarian concept; and 5) a description of an Eastern text describing meditation for the attainment of Buddhahood. It is pointed out that in discussions such as those of the Trinity, metaphysical views cannot be considered, for a belief such as the Trinity is subject to scientific observation only to the extent that it is a human concept falling within the sphere of psychology. Such observation does not affect the object of the belief in any way.

000704 Psychology and religion. Foreword to Quispel: "Tragic Christianity." In: Jung, C., Collected Works of C. G. Jung, Vol. 18. Princeton University Press, 1976. 904 p. (p. 651-653).

In a foreword (1949) to "Tragic Christianity" by Gilles Quispel (unpublished), Gnosticism and psychotherapy are discussed. The mental products of Gnosticism demand the same psychological understanding as do psychotic delusional formations. But the philologist or theologian concerned with Gnosticism usually has no psychiatric knowledge. Explaining Gnostic ideas in terms of themselves is said to be futile, for such explanation does not reveal their actual significance for the development of Western consciousness. It is suggested that the archetypal motifs of the unconscious are the psychic source of Gnostic ideas, of delusional ideas, of symbol formation in dreams, and of active imagination in the course of analytical treatment of neurosis.

000705 /Psychology and religion. Foreword to Abegg: "East Asia thinks otherwise."/ Psychology and religion. Foreword to Abegg: "Ostasien denkt anders." In: Jung, C., Collected Works of C. G. Jung, Vol. 18. Princeton University Press, 1976. 904 p. (p. 654-655).

In a foreword to "Ostasien denkt Anders" (East Asia thinks otherwise) by Lily Abegg (1950), differences between Eastern and Western psychology are discussed. Knowledge of Eastern psychology is said to be a helpful basis for criticizing Western psychology and understanding Occidental prejudices. A parallel is noted between the Western unconscious psyche and the manifest psyche of the East. Our Western unconscious has a demonstrable tendency toward wholeness. In the East it is consciousness that is characterized by an apperception of totality, whereas in the West a differentiated and onsided awareness has developed. With it goes the Western concept of causality, as contrasted with the Eastern one of synchronicity, which is said to be the key to understanding the Eastern apperception.

000706 Psychology and religion. Foreword to Allenby: "A psychological study of the origins of monotheism." In: Jung, C., Collected Works of C. G. Jung, Vol. 18. Princeton University Press, 1976. 904 p. (p. 656-659).

In a foreword (1950) to "A Psychological Study of the Origins of Monotheism" by Amy I. Allenby (unpublished), the existence of an archetypal God image is confirmed in the context of a discussion of inherited unconscious contents. Analysis of dreams has shown that some dream elements are of unconscious origin, as they are not known to the dreamer and may also appear in myths and fairy tales. One such element is the God image, which is of prime importance in determining human behavior. The image is that of wholeness, the symbol of the self, manifest in mandala symbols. Modern psychology is defended against criticism that it destroys religious ideas by psychologizing them; rather, psychology tries to renew the connection with the realities of the psyche to provide roots for consciousness.

000707 Psychology and religion. The miraculous fast of Brother Klaus. In: Jung, C., Collected Works of C. G. Jung, Vol. 18. Princeton University Press, 1976. 904 p. (p. 660-661).

A possible parapsychological explanation for the claim that Brother Klaus lived without material sustenance for twenty years is offered. Mediums have been shown to manifest measurable ionization during a parapsychological phenomenon, and an emission of ectoplasm capable of acting at a distance has been demonstrated. It is suggested that nourishment could occur similarly by the passage of living molecules of albumen from one body to another.

000708 Psychology and religion. Concerning "Answer to Job." In: Jung, C., Collected Works of C. G. Jung, Vol. 18. Princeton University Press, 1976. 904 p. (p. 662).

"Answer to Job" by C. G. Jung (1952) is described as a personal confrontation with the traditional Christian world view, occasioned by the impact of the new dogma of the Assumption. It reflects the struggles of a physician and theological layman with religious questions. The questions raised were motivated by contemporary events, and the central question of the book is what a benevolent God has to say of falsehood, injustice, slavery, and mass murder in Europe and much of the world.

000709 Psychology and religion. Religion and psychology: a reply to Martin Buber. In: Jung, C., Collected Works of C. G. Jung, Vol. 18. Princeton University Press, 1976. 904 p. (p. 663-670).

In response to an article (1952), a defense is raised to a charge of Gnosticism by Martin Buber. Jung replies that he is neither Gnostic or agnostic but a psychiatrist whose prime concern is to record and interpret empirical material. Because views and opinions about metaphysical or religious subjects play a great role in empirical psychology, it is necessary to work with concepts corresponding to them. The reality of the psyche includes archetypal images that are not identical with the corresponding intellectual concepts yet have great effect on the conscious mind. It is stated that every assertion about God, for example, is a human statement, a psychological one, and must be distinguished from God as a metaphysical being. Yet this is neither to deny God nor to put man in God's place. The particular problems of the doctor in dealing with religious matters are offered in conclusion.

000710 Psychology and religion. Address at the presentation of the Jung Codex. In: Jung, C., Collected Works of C. G. Jung, Vol. 18. Princeton University Press, 1976. 904 p. (p. 671-672).

In an address at the presentation of the Jung Codex, a Gnostic papyrus acquired for the C. G. Jung Institute (1953), the psychological significance of the texts is summarized. The Codex gives some insight into the mentality of the second century A.D. and early concepts of Christ and helps explain why the Christian message was taken up by the unconscious of that age. The therapeutic necessity of confronting the patient with his dark side is a continuation of the Christian development of consciousness and leads to phenomena of assimilation similar to those found in Gnosticism, the Kabbala, and Hermetic philosophy. Since historical comparison with earlier stages is important in interpreting modern phenomena, the discovery of the Gnostic texts is of great practical value to research.

000711 Psychology and religion. Letter to Pere Bruno. In: Jung, C., Collected Works of C. G. Jung, Vol. 18. Princeton University Press, 1976. 904 p. (p. 673-678).

In a letter to Pere Bruno de Jesus-Marie, O.C.D. (1953), the means of establishing the existence of an archetype is demonstrated by the example of the prophet Elijah. Because the biography of Elijah contains mythical motifs and parallels, and because posterity has added elements that are clearly mythological, it is concluded that Elijah does indeed represent an archetype. The phenomena of assimilation, or mythical attributes, of Elijah are described from early history to contemporary times, establishing the figure as a living, or constellated, archetype. An archetype becomes active when a lack in the conscious psyche calls for a compensation by the unconscious. What is lacking is the immediate relation with God, and Elijah represents the ideal compensation for Christians, Moslems, and Jews. Further comments on the appearance of archetypes are offered in conclusion.

000712 Psychology and religion. Letter to Pere Lachat. In: Jung, C., Collected Works of C. G. Jung, Vol. 18. Princeton University Press, 1976. 904 p. (p. 679-691).

In a letter to Pere William Lachat, questions and thoughts provoked by Lachat's booklet on the reception and action of the Holy Spirit are offered. Definitions of God, Christ, and the Trinity are discussed, and specific points in the booklet are questioned. All theology is said to be a series of archetypal images intended to describe an unimaginable transcendence; together they comprise the collective unconscious. Because the unconscious is ambivalent, producing both good and bad effects, the image of God is also twofold. The dangers and fears of surrendering oneself to the Holy Spirit are said to be so great in view of this ambivalence that no one today would suggest that he is possessed by it. The task of the Holy Spirit is to reconcile and unite the opposites in the individual through a special development of the soul, which, like God, is paradoxical. The Holy Spirit will manifest himself in the psychic sphere of man and will be presented as a psychic ex-

perience. He then becomes the object of empirical psychology, through which he can translate his symbolism into the possibilities of the world. The Holy Spirit becomes of extreme importance, for it is thanks to him that the man of good will is drawn towards the divine drama and mingled in it, and the Spirit is one.

000713 Psychology and religion. On Resurrection. In: Jung, C., Collected Works of C. G. Jung, Vol. 18. Princeton University Press, 1976. 904 p. (p. 692-696).

The Resurrection of Christ is discussed as an historical fact in the biography of Jesus and as a psychological event. As an historical fact, the Resurrection is doubtful and might be attributed to an individual and/or collective vision. At the time, however, spiritual reality could not be demonstrated to the uneducated except through tangible miracle stories. Psychologically, the Resurrection represents the ancient myth of the hero who conquers death and restores life; it represents the projection of an indirect realization of the self that had appeared in the figure of Jesus of Nazareth. The image of the God/man lives in everyone and is incarnated (projected) in Jesus so that people can realize him as their own self and confirm the fact that their psychic reality is not bound by time and space. The Christian church is criticized for understanding spiritual existence only as a body and a physical event, and it is suggested that this anachronism cannot long survive.

000714 Psychology and religion. On the discourses of the Buddha. In: Jung, C., Collected Works of C. G. Jung, Vol. 18. Princeton University Press, 1976. 904 p. (p. 697-699).

The usefulness of the discourses of the Buddha as a source of understanding in therapeutic treatment is explained. In response to arguments that the Christian religion offers ample consolations, it is pointed out that faith is often absent and that an unfamiliar doctrine can promote understandings that have been lost in one's familiarity with his own belief system. The discourses offer Western man new ways of disciplining his inner psychic life, which Christianity often does not. In response to criticism for regarding religion as "mental hygiene," it is argued that the doctor uses whatever views of the world are helpful or therapeutic to ease suffering, including religious ideas. Buddhism is singled out because its essence is deliverance from suffering through maximum development of consciousness.

000715 /Psychology and religion. Foreword to Froboese-Thiele: "Dreams -- a source of religious experience?"/ Psychology and religion. Foreword to Froboese-Thiele: "Traume -- eine Quelle religioser Erfahrung?" In: Jung, C., Collected Works of C. G. Jung, Vol. 18. Princeton University Press, 1976. 904 p. (p. 700-701).

In a foreword to "Traume -- eine Quelle religioser Erfahrung?" (Dreams -- a source of religious experience?) by Felicia Froboese-Thiele (1957), the book, which draws on dream material, is described as the first to investigate how the unconscious of Protestants behaves when it has to compensate an intensely religious attitude. The dreams in question are shown to have religious meaning, an unconscious expression that compensates the extremism of the conscious religious attitude and reestablishes the approximate wholeness of the personality through individuation. The author is commended for her case material, and the book is recommended to both doctors and theologians.

000716 Psychology and religion. Jung and religious belief. In: Jung, C., Collected Works of C. G. Jung, Vol. 18. Princeton University Press, 1976. 904 p. (p. 702-744).

Questions and answers regarding Jung and religious belief are presented. Answers cover the nature of religious truth and the psychic consequences of the search for it; the relative importance of consciousness and unconsciousness and the role of the unconscious in religious experience; the existence of images of God despite God's inaccessibility and the impossibility of proving his physical existence; the importance of other disciplines for the psyche; the force and implications of evil (Satan), the principle of opposites, and the quaternity as a symbol; conceptions of Christ and Job; the concept of Tao as a union of opposites and the question of whether a similar concept exists in Christianity; faith as a belief in projected contents of the unconscious; objections to the view of God as the Summum Bonum; a defense against charges of Gnosticism; Christ as an archetypal image identified with the self and the relationship of this image to good and evil, God, and the Holy Ghost; and the relationship of religious experience to mythology and the psyche.

000717 Alchemical studies. Foreword to a catalogue on alchemy. In: Jung, C., Collected Works of C. G. Jung, Vol. 18. Princeton University Press, 1976. 904 p. (p. 747).

In a foreword to a catalogue on alchemy (1946), the language of alchemy is said to reveal little of a chemical nature but something that is purely symbolic or psychological. Alchemical language does not disguise a known content but suggests an unknown one, or, rather, suggests itself. It is concluded that the archetypal contents of the collective unconscious are being projected and that alchemy is a projected psychology of the collective unconscious on a par with mythology and folklore. Its symbolism is similar to that of dreams and religion.

000718 Alchemical studies. Faust and alchemy. In: Jung, C., Collected Works of C. G. Jung, Vol. 18. Princeton University Press, 1976. 904 p. (p. 748-750).

The drama of Faust is described in terms of its primary sources in alchemy, which are on the one hand dreams, visions, and parables, and on the other, personal and biographical notes regarding Goethe's dramatic poem. In alchemy, transformation applies not only to chemical materials but to man as well, and the central figure is Mercurius, who enters the Faust story as Mephistopheles. The story is further explicated in alchemical terms.

000719 Alchemical studies. Alchemy and psychology. In: Jung, C., Collected Works of C. G. Jung, Vol. 18. Princeton University Press, 1976. 904 p. (p. 751-753).

The relationship of alchemy and psychology is explained in terms of the symbolism of the two disciplines. Because the alchemists did not understand the nature and behavior of chemical substances, they drew conscious parallels between the unknown processes and mythological motifs and thus explained the former. These unknown processes were then amplified by the projection of unconscious contents. Comparative research has confirmed that alchemical symbols are partly conscious variations of these mythological motifs and partly spontaneous products of the unconscious, parallel with the content of modern dreams. The principal symbol of the transformed substance in alchemy is Mercurius, and the ways in which this symbol is consistent with characteristics of the unconscious are outlined. It is shown how the alchemical opus portrays the process of individuation, but in a projected form, because the alchemists were unconscious of this psychic process.

000720 /The spirit in man, art, and literature. Memorial to Jerome Schloss./ The spirit in man, art, and literature. Memorial to J. S. In: Jung, C., Collected Works of C. G. Jung, Vol. 18. Princeton University Press, 1976. 904 p. (p. 757-758).

In a memorial to Jerome Schloss (1955), the nature of death and Schloss's preparation for it are described. Rather than a meaningless end, death is viewed as an accomplishment for which one prepares during the later half of his life. Schloss is eulogized as a person of rare clarity and purity of character who taught Jung a good deal. He freed himself from earthly bonds and saw visions of his death and his rising soul in the last weeks before he died.

000721 /The spirit in man, art, and literature. Foreword to Schmid-Guisan: "Day and night."/ The spirit in man, art, and literature. Foreword to Schmid-Guisan: "Tag und Nacht." In: Jung, C., Collected Works of C. G. Jung, Vol. 18. Princeton University Press, 1976. 904 p. (p. 759-761).

A foreword to "Tag und Nacht" (Day and night) by Hans Schmid-Guisan (1931) is presented, and a memorial to the author is offered. The book, which relates the adventures of an allegorical hero, is said to open up a world of experience that has long been locked away -- the sensuous world of Eros. It is compared with "Hypnerotomachia," written 500 years earlier, and a passage from the latter is quoted to demonstrate the similarity. In memoriam, Schmid-Guisan's association with Jung in the study of analytical psychology and as a friend is remembered. Both were interested in the influence of temperament on the formation of psychological concepts. In conclusion, Schmid-Guisan's humanity and sensitivity are praised as the results of unending work on his own soul.

000722 The spirit in man, art, and literature. On the Tale of the Otter. In: Jung, C., Collected Works of C. G. Jung, Vol. 18. Princeton University Press, 1976. 904 p. (p. 762-764).

"The Tale of the Otter" by Oskar A. H. Schmitz (1932) is described as a product of the author's psychology, a literary form for a content that could have been expressed in other ways. The fairytale form was used because it provides simple and direct communication regarding the nature of the psyche from the heart of Schmitz to that of the reader without the mediation of rationality and intellect. The tale describes an experience of the unconscious and the resulting transformation of both the personality and the figures in the psyche. It explains the transformations of Schmitz's soul that he underwent in preparation for death.

000723 The spirit in man, art, and literature. Is there a Freudian type of poetry? In: Jung, C., Collected Works of C. G. Jung, Vol. 18. Princeton University Press, 1976. 904 p. (p. 765-766).

The pathological interpretation of great poetry in terms of Freudian or Adlerian theory is opposed on grounds that it adds nothing to understanding and distracts from the deeper vision offered by the poet. If a work of art can be explained in the same way as a neurotic symptom, then it is not art, or the explainer has misinterpreted its meaning. Although some artistic efforts can be reduced like hysterical symptoms to the facts of neurotic psychology, great art is a creation of something superhuman and should not be subject to such analysis.

000724 The spirit in man, art, and literature. Foreword to Gilbert: "The curse of intellect." In: Jung, C., Collected Works of C. G. Jung, Vol. 18. Princeton University Press, 1976. 904 p. (p. 767).

In a foreword (1934) to J. Allen Gilbert's "The Curse of Intellect" (unpublished), the author's criticism of the intellect is welcomed. The main trouble with the intellect, which has done great damage to Western civilization, is that it escaped man's control and became his obsession, ceasing to be a tool and beginning to shape man's world.

000725 /The spirit in man, art, and literature. Foreword to Jung: "Reality of the soul."/ The spirit in man, art, and literature. Foreword to Jung: "Wirklichkeit der Seele" (1934). In: Jung, C., Collected Works of C. G. Jung, Vol. 18. Princeton University Press, 1976. 904 p. (p. 768-769).

In the foreword to "Wirklichkeit der Seele" (Reality of the soul), the fourth volume of C. G. Jung's "Psychologische Abhandlungen" (1934), contents of the book are explained and recent advances in theory are described. The book contains essays reflecting various aspects of current psychology. Only recently have such persons as W. M. Kranefeldt, Hugo Rosenthal, and Emma Jung begun to clarify the confusion surrounding psychological theory. Jung's own contributions concern the philosophical problems of modern psychology and its applications, and the essays suggest answers to questions asked by persons of varying backgrounds and interests. The diverse facets of complex psychology are said to be a simplified reflection of the great diversity of the psyche itself, and it is emphasized that a foremost task of the human mind is to search for a greater knowledge of man's psyche.

000726 The spirit in man, art, and literature. Foreword to Mehlich: "J. H. Fichte's psychology and its relation to the present."/ The spirit in man, art, and literature. Foreword to Mehlich: "J. H. Fichtes Seelenlehre und ihre Beziehung zur Gegenwart." In: Jung, C., Collected Works of C. G. Jung, Vol. 18. Princeton University Press, 1976. 904 p. (p. 770-772).

In a foreword to "J. H. Fichtes Seelenlehre und ihre Beziehung zur Gegenwart" (J. H. Fichte's Psychology and its relation to the present) by Rose Mehlich (1935), the points of view of philosophy and empiricism are contrasted, and the characterization of Jung as "romantic" is questioned. As an empiricist, Jung grounded his views in experience rather than reducing them to an ordered system as a philosopher would. The book on Fichte's psychology shows an analogy between Jung's point of view and that of Fichte, which was based on systematic, nonempirical formulations. In terms of romanticism, the subjective component of experience is emphasized. It is concluded that the book is a welcome contribution to the study of a specific attitude that has recurred many times historically.

000727 /The spirit in man, art, and literature. Foreword to von Koenig-Fachsenfeld: "Transformations of dream problems from Romanticism to the present."/ The spirit in man, art, and literature. Foreword to von Koenig-Fachsenfeld: "Wandlungen des Traumproblems von der Romantik bis zur Gegenwart." In: Jung, C., Collected Works of C. G. Jung, Vol. 18. Princeton University Press, 1976. 904 p. (p. 773-775).

In a foreword to "Wandlungen des Traumproblems von der Romantik bis zur Gegenwart" (Transformations of dream problems from Romanticism to the present) by Olga von Koenig-Fachsenfeld (1935), the book is welcomed as filling a gap in the philosophical side of complex psychology, and the rapprochement between empirical psychology and philosophy is explained. Although experimental and medical psychologists originally used purely scientific methods, it became obvious that their principles had to be subject to philosophical criticism because the object of their judgment was the psyche itself. No judgment about the psyche can be totally empirical but is reduced to phenomenology, or pure experience. The resemblance of this concern with experience to that of the Romantics is suggested in a brief history of Romantic thought. It is conceded that Jung's psychological conceptions can be regarded as "Romantic," but they are also scientific and rationalistic. The underlying premise is the reality of everything psychic, a concept based on an appreciation that the psyche can also be pure experience.

000728 /The spirit in man, art, and literature. Foreword to Gilli: "The dark brother."/ The spirit in man, art, and literature. Foreword to Gilli: "Der dunkle Bruder." In: Jung, C., Collected Works of C. G. Jung, Vol. 18. Princeton University Press, 1976. 904 p. (p. 776-778).

In a foreword to "Der dunkle Bruder" (The dark brother) by Gertrud Gilli (1938), the play is described as modern insofar as the central process of Christianity -- the drama through which man seeks to experience the innermost source of life in the form of God -- is reflected in human motivations. The redemption mystery is discussed in terms of the Judas figure, which embodies the darker side of the redeemer, and the universality of the redeemer figure. True redemption is not social or political liberation but a return to God. It is suggested that man lives in constant conflict between the truth of the external world and that of the psyche, and the drama described in the play occurs within each person as he seeks the deeper truth.

000729 The spirit in man, art, and literature. Gerard de Nerval. In: Jung, C., Collected Works of C. G. Jung, Vol. 18. Princeton University Press, 1976. 904 p. (p. 779).

The psyche of Gerard de Nerval (pseudonym of Gerard Labrunie, 1808-1853) is discussed in terms of his posthumously published novel "Aurelia." The book, which relates his anima and psychosis, shows how the collective unconscious broke into Nerval's experience and explains why he was unable to connect the unconscious with reality and assimilate its archetypal contents before his suicide.

000730 The spirit in man, art, and literature. Foreword to Fierz-David: "The dream of Poliphilo." In: Jung, C., Collected Works of C. G. Jung, Vol. 18. Princeton University Press, 1976. 904 p. (p. 780-781).

In a foreword to "The Dream of Poliphilo" by Linda Fierz-David (1947), based on Francesco Colonna's "Hypnerotomachia Poliphili," the book is described as the first serious attempt to unlock Poliphilo's secret and unravel its dream symbolism with the help of modern psychology. The success of the author's interpretation is attributed to the sensitiveness of the feminine mind. The tortuous ways of the masculine mind, setting traps for itself with its own vanities, are exposed and illuminated, and it is concluded that modern man can learn from this example.

000731 /The spirit of man, art, and literature. Foreword to Crottet: "Moon-forest."/ The spirit in man, art, and literature. Foreword to Crottet: "Mondwald." In: Jung, C., Collected Works of C. G. Jung, Vol. 18. Princeton University Press, 1976. 904 p. (p. 782-783).

In a foreword to "Mondwald" (Moon-forest) by Robert Crottet (1949), the author's account of the primitive Lappish Skolts in northern Finland is praised as sensitive and evocative of the wholeness of prehistoric nature and preconscious humanity, which to the civilized man is unfathomable. Crottet's emotional narrative brings back echoes of a nearly forgotten knowledge, as he describes the clash of two cultures and pleads for the preservation of the life of the primitives.

000732 The spirit in man, art, and literature. Foreword to Jacobi: "Paracelsus: selected writings." In: Jung, C., Collected Works of C. G. Jung, Vol. 18. Princeton University Press, 1976. 904 p. (p. 784-785).

In a foreword to "Paracelsus: Selected Writings" edited by Jolande Jacobi (1951), the influence of Paracelsus on succeeding generations is noted, and the book is commended. Paracelsus, in whom Jung became interested when trying to understand alchemy, was a paradox and a true mirror of his century. The book emphasizes his moral aspect and draws heavily on original texts. A particularly helpful feature is a glossary of Paracelsus' concepts, which are difficult for persons unfamiliar with alchemy.

000733 /The spirit of man, art, and literature. Foreword to Kankeleit: "The unconscious as the seedbed of the creative."/ The spirit in man, art, and literature. Foreword to Kankeleit: "Das Unbewusste als Keimstatte des Schopferischen." In: Jung, C., Collected Works of C. G. Jung, Vol. 18. Princeton University Press, 1976. 904 p. (p. 786-787).

In a foreword to "Das Unbewusste als Keimstatte des Schopferischen" (The unconscious as seedbed of the creative) by Otto Kankeleit (1959), the book is called a descriptive survey of the phenomena and problems facing the practicing psychotherapist in his daily work, and Jung's contribution regarding the creative process is presented. The book goes beyond pathology to the realm of psychic life in general and to a concern with guiding the patient back to a balanced life by giving him a balanced picture of the psyche to offset his own limited experience of it. In regard to creativity, it is said to spring from the unconscious and to be manifest in dreams.

000734 The spirit in man, art, and literature. Foreword to Serrano: "The visits of the Queen of Sheba." In: Jung, C., Collected Works of C. G. Jung, Vol. 18. Princeton University Press, 1976. 904 p. (p. 788).

In a foreword to "The Visits of the Queen of Sheba" by Miguel Serrano (1960), the content of the book is described as comprising spontaneous products of the unconscious with no significant cognitive element. The unconscious presents itself to the author in its poetic aspect, while Jung sees it mainly within its scientific and philosophical, or religious, aspect. The unconscious is said to be the matrix, background, and foundation of all the differentiated phenomena called psychic -- religion, science, philosophy, art. The experience of the unconscious in any form is an approach to wholeness, the one experience lacking in modern civilization.

000735 The spirit in man, art, and literature. Is there a true bilingualism? In: Jung, C., Collected Works of C. G. Jung, Vol. 18. Princeton University Press, 1976. 904 p. (p. 789).

In answer to the question of whether there is a true bilingualism, the issue of definition is raised. Some people living abroad begin to think and dream in the second language, and a second language can be implanted even at the expense of the original language. It is concluded, however, that because of the limits of memory, a bilingual or trilingual state ends by damaging the scope of one's vocabulary as well as the greatest potential use of each language.

000736 /The practice of psychotherapy. Reviews of books by Heyer: "The organism of the mind."/ The practice of psychotherapy. Reviews of books by Heyer: "Der Organismus der seele." In: Jung, C., Collected Works of C. G. Jung, Vol. 18. Princeton University Press, 1976. 904 p. (p. 793-794).

In a review of "Der Organismus der Seele" (The organism of the mind) by Gustav Richard Heyer (1932), the book is praised as an unprejudiced view of the essential problems of modern psychotherapy and its conflicting views and as a step toward an objective psychology. The psychologist is warned against the unscientific delusion and his own subjective prejudice represents a universal and fundamental psychological truth. Contradictory views are necessary in the evolution of any science, but they should seek an early synthesis rather than be set up in opposition to one another. It is concluded that an objective psychology will not be the work of one individual therapist but the result of many psychotherapists' work.

000737 /The practice of psychotherapy. Reviews of books by Heyer: "Practical psychotherapy."/ The practice of psychotherapy. Reviews of books by Heyer: "Praktische Seelenheilkunde." In: Jung, C., Collected Works of C. G. Jung, Vol. 18. Princeton University Press, 1976. 904 p. (p. 794-796).

In a review of "Praktische Seelenheilkunde" (Practical psychotherapy) by Gustav Richard Heyer (1935), the diversity of neurotic manifestations and their treatments are described. Modern medicine has tended to regard neurosis as a single quantity or category of illness, yet it is suggested that neurosis is an amalgam of several diseases that require an equal number of remedies. It is inferred from the diversity of psychotherapeutic techniques applied to neurosis that there is a corresponding diversity of psychopathological states. Through the differential success of treatment the psychotherapist will learn the various kinds of psychic pathology, psychic biology, and psychic structure.

000738 The practice of psychotherapy. On the "Rosarium philosophorum." In: Jung, C., Collected Works of C. G. Jung, Vol. 18. Princeton University Press, 1976. 904 p. (p. 797-800).

The contents of the "Rosarium Philosophorum," an early, if not the first, text covering the field of alchemy, are described. The "art" of alchemy, whose practitioner must be of a sound mental disposition, must operate within nature and consists of uniting the opposites, which are represented as male and female, form and matter. The four roots or elements, the prima materia or initial material, and the alchemical process are explained. The process of creation is performed outwardly through a chemical operation and inwardly through active imagination, as matter itself is believed to be passive. The "Rosarium" further discusses the secret of the aqua nostra in alchemy and develops the idea of the coniunctio, the reunion of the imperfect body with its soul or anima, of which it had been deprived. The coniunctio symbolism is described as a common motif in alchemy, concerning the problem of opposites projected into matter and uniting to produce a third thing.

000739 The practice of psychotherapy. Preface to an Indian journal of psychotherapy. In: Jung, C., Collected Works of C. G. Jung, Vol. 18. Princeton University Press, 1976. 904 p. (p. 801).

In the preface to a special issue devoted to Jung's work in an Indian journal of psychotherapy (Psychotherapy, April

1956), a contrast is made between India's orientation toward introspection, fostered by a highly differentiated spiritual culture, and Europe's historical tendency to depend on the sensory aspects of the external world. A collaboration between the two outlooks is proposed, as the mystery of the psyche can only be understood when approached from opposite sides.

000740 The practice of psychotherapy. On pictures in psychiatric diagnosis. In: Jung, C., Collected Works of C. G. Jung, Vol. 18. Princeton University Press, 1976. 904 p. (p. 802).

A diagnosis of latent schizophrenia is proposed on the basis of pictures drawn by a patient. The pictures show a tendency to translate living reality into abstractions to cut off emotional rapport with the object and a tendency to emphasize the ego at the expense of the self, which represents the unwanted whole.

000741 The development of personality. Foreword to Evans: "The problem of the nervous child." In: Jung, C., Collected Works of C. G. Jung, Vol. 18. Princeton University Press, 1976. 904 p. (p. 805-806).

In a foreword to "The Problem of the Nervous Child" by Elida Evans (1920), the importance of parental attitudes in the creation and alleviation of childhood neuroses is explained and the infantile origin of adult neuroses is pointed out. Most neuroses originate from a faulty psychological attitude that begins with incompatible familial influences and hinders adjustment. Parents' mental attitudes are crucial, for children imitate their parents' states of mind, and family therapy is often indicated in cases of childhood neurosis or as a preventive psychiatric measure. Of particular importance are manifestations of the child's sexual instinct, for sexual activity may be a symptom of abnormal development and may block the normal outlets for energy and channel it toward premature or perverted sexual interests. It is concluded that the child's attitude, and hence neurosis, is determined by both inherited and environmental factors, and that the latter may be changed by suitable methods.

000742 The development of personality. Foreword to Harding: "The way of all women." In: Jung, C., Collected Works of C. G. Jung, Vol. 18. Princeton University Press, 1976. 904 p. (p. 807-810).

In a foreword to "The Way of All Women" by Esther Harding (1933), differences in masculine and feminine psychology are recognized and a means for resolving the conflict between them is suggested. Neither men nor women understand much of women's psychology, which includes a peculiar spirituality, but this is hardly surprising, because people know almost nothing of the unconscious psyche and such knowledge is necessary to understanding. Between the sexes, a conflict exists between man as a biological, instinctual creature and as a spiritual and cultural being. A compromise between the two can be achieved only in relation to the other sex. Psychology is therefore needed as a method of relationship, providing real knowledge of the other sex instead of arbitrary opinions, which are the source of misunderstandings. Harding's book is welcomed as a contribution to knowledge of human nature and a clarification of the confusion in relations between the sexes.

000743 The development of personality. Depth psychology and self-knowledge. In: Jung, C., Collected Works of C. G. Jung, Vol. 18. Princeton University Press, 1976. 904 p. (p. 811-819).

In answer to questions from Jolande Jacobi about depth psychology (1943), the importance of the unconscious in an understanding of the psyche is emphasized and the following points are made: 1) disregard for the unconscious makes one unaware of his own unconscious conflicts, producing injurious effects on marriage and on children; 2) whereas the old psychology viewed only the contents of consciousness, depth psychology recognizes that an unconscious process underlies every conscious one; 3) because the unconscious is complex, the various schools of depth psychology that approach it from biological, physiological, mythological, and religious points of view all have validity; 4) care must be taken to avoid preconceptions in the analysis of data in depth psychology; 5) analytical psychology uses interpretation of dreams and drawings and the analytical relationship to reveal the patient's total psychological situation and help him restore the original wholeness of the personality; 6) analytical psychology does not regard itself as a substitute for religious confession, but often functions in a similar way; 7) knowledge of the unconscious can bring an increase in tension, followed by release; 8) preoccupation with oneself is not "egocentric" in the usual sense but is necessary for growth; 9) greater self-knowledge gives one a more realistic view of one's abilities and opens the door to greater communication with others; 10) because individuals differ, integration of the unconscious takes place in many different ways.

000744 The development of personality. Foreword to Spier: "The hands of children." In: Jung, C., Collected Works of C. G. Jung, Vol. 18. Princeton University Press, 1976. 904 p. (p. 820-821).

In a foreword to "The Hands of Children" by Julius Spier (1944), it is suggested that such discredited arts as palmistry can be resurrected and tested in the light of modern scientific knowledge. The view of modern biology that man is a totality does not exclude the possibility that the hands, which are intimately connected with the psyche, may by their shape and functioning reveal psychic peculiarities of the individual and provide clues to his character. Spier's work is described as intuitive, although based on wide practical experience, and as a valuable contribution to the study of human character in its widest sense.

000745 The development of personality. Foreword to the Hebrew edition of Jung: "Psychology and education." In: Jung, C., Collected Works of C. G. Jung, Vol. 18. Princeton University Press, 1976. 904 p. (p. 822).

In a foreword to the Hebrew edition of "Psychology and Education" by C. G. Jung (1958), it is pointed out that analytical psychology has contributed to knowledge of: 1) adults who still have disturbing infantilism; 2) the complex relations between parents and children; and 3) children themselves. Psychic disorders of children are usually connected with the psychology and attitudes of parents and educators, and it is suggested that the most important question after the education of the child is the education of the educator.

000746 /Addenda. Foreword to: "Psychological papers," Volume I. Addenda. Foreword to "Psychologische Abhandlungen," Volume I. In: Jung, C., Collected Works of C. G. Jung, Vol. 18. Princeton University Press, 1976. 904 p. (p. 825).

In a foreword to the first volume of "Psychologische Abhandlungen" (1914), these "Psychological Papers" are described as comprising the work of Jung and his pupils and colleagues in the areas of psychopathology and general psychology. The compilation is said to result from a desire to publish all similar works stemming from one school in a central place.

000747 Addenda. Address at the presentation of the Jung Codex. In: Jung, C., Collected Works of C. G. Jung, Vol. 18. Princeton University Press, 1976. 904 p. (p. 826-829).

In an augmented version of an address at the presentation of the Jung Codex, a Gnostic papyrus acquired for the C. G. Jung Institute (1953), the psychological significance of the texts is summarized. The Codex gives insight into the mentality of the second century A.D. and early concepts of Christ and helps explain why the Christian message was taken up by the unconscious mind of that age. The text is described particularly as a phenomenon of assimilation, representing the specifically psychic reactions (originating in the unconscious) aroused by the impact of the figure and message of Christ on the pagan world. The therapeutic necessity of confronting the patient with his own dark side (the unconscious) is a secular continuation of the Christian development of consciousness and leads to phenomena of assimilation similar to those found in Gnosticism, the Kabbala, and Hermetic philosophy. Since real understanding of the human psyche requires knowledge of man's spiritual history, the Codex will be of great practical as well as theoretical value at the Institute.